PENGUIN  CLASS

THE MEMORIAL FEAST FOR KÖKÖTÖY KHAN

The bard Saghïmbay Orozbaq uulu, renowned for his Soviet-era *Manas* epic, was born in about 1867, near lake Issyk Kul, in the Semirech'e region of Turkestan (then newly annexed by Russia), the youngest son of a poor former retainer of a Kirghiz nomadic chieftain; he lived under Tsarist and, after 1917, Bolshevik rule in the region that became northern Kyrgyzstan. In his teens, inspired by dream callings, Saghïmbay began learning to sing traditional epic poetry from leading bards of the day. He also learned to read. A master of oral genres such as folktales, extempore songs, and poetic sparring contests with other bards, he gave celebrated performances at gatherings, including memorial feasts. In 1916 Saghïmbay and his family fled indiscriminate Russian reprisals after the Central Asian Rebellion. During a hard year in Chinese Turkestan, he was among the bards who sang epics for fellow Kirghiz refugees. Back at home in the central Tien Shan range, he met the folklorists Qayum Miftaqov and Ïbïrayïm Abdïraqmanov, and from 1922 to 1926 composed for them in oral performance his epic narrative of the life of the hero Manas, comprising more than six times the number of poetic lines in the *Iliad* and the *Odyssey* combined; one episode of this classic text is translated here. Dogged by poverty and denied support by Soviet officialdom, Saghïmbay grew ill, stopped performing, and died in the Qochqor valley in 1930, visited to the end by visions of Kökötöy's memorial feast. No records survive of the epic he sang to highest acclaim, *Semetey*, about Manas's son. Saghïmbay's three wives bore him eight children who survived, including Amanqul, who learned to sing epics from his father, but did not return from the Second World War.

Daniel Prior was born in Michigan in 1963. He studied linguistics at Yale University, worked in China, Kyrgyzstan (during and after the breakup of the Soviet Union), and Japan, and received a doctorate in Central Eurasian studies from Indiana University. His other publications include *The Semetey of Kenje Kara: A Kirghiz Epic Performance on Phonograph* and *The Šabdan Baatïr Codex: Epic and the Writing of Northern Kirghiz History.* He is Professor of History at Miami University.

Saghïmbay Orozbaq uulu

The Memorial Feast for Kökötöy Khan

A Kirghiz Epic Poem
in the Manas Tradition

Composed in oral performance by
SAGHÏMBAY OROZBAQ UULU

Translated from the complete text by
DANIEL PRIOR

PENGUIN BOOKS

PENGUIN CLASSICS

UK | USA | Canada | Ireland | Australia
India | New Zealand | South Africa

Penguin Books is part of the Penguin Random House group of companies
whose addresses can be found at global.penguinrandomhouse.com

First published in Great Britain in Penguin Classics 2022
001

Translation, front matter and back matter copyright © Daniel Prior, 2022

The moral right of the translator has been asserted

Set in 10.25/12.25pt Sabon LT Std
Typeset by Jouve (UK), Milton Keynes
Printed and bound in Great Britain by Clays Ltd, Elcograf S.p.A.

The authorized representative in the EEA is Penguin Random House Ireland,
Morrison Chambers, 32 Nassau Street, Dublin D02 YH68

A CIP catalogue record for this book is available from the British Library

ISBN: 978-0-241-54421-1

www.greenpenguin.co.uk

Contents

THE MEMORIAL FEAST FOR KÖKÖTÖY KHAN

Preface

In early 1992, the two librarians of the foreign language reading room in the old national library building in Bishkek, Kyrgyzstan, invited me into their office. My borrower's card had mown through most of the interesting books in their collection that I could read, but they knew my curiosity about the Kirghiz epic *Manas*. Did I know that an Englishman had written about *Manas*? I did not. A key was produced from a desk drawer, and the glass front of a large wooden *shkaf* full of books was unlocked and opened. From off the shelves a green cloth-bound book was placed in my hands: *The Memorial Feast for Kökötöy-Khan*, by A. T. Hatto.[1] The rules of the *redkii fond* (rare and valuable book collection) forbade the lending of items stored in the locked cabinet. The librarians glanced at each other to confirm their agreed plan: if I promised to be careful and to return the book on time, I could take it home to read, never mind the rules.

No librarian has ever done me a greater favor. Communion with Arthur T. Hatto's dual-language edition of a version of *The Memorial Feast for Kökötöy Khan* from the mid-nineteenth century marked the clear point of my life passage from the ramblings of an increasingly aimless traveler to the explorations of a suddenly inspired scholar. I enacted the metamorphosis by purchasing horses and equipment, hiring a Kirghiz animal doctor as an assistant, and riding through the Tien Shan mountains and the

1. *The Memorial Feast for Kökötöy-Khan (Kökötöydün ašı): A Kirghiz Epic Poem*, edited for the first time from a photocopy of the unique manuscript, with translation and commentary by A. T. Hatto (Oxford: Oxford University Press, 1977); hereafter *MKNB*.

grasslands of Jeti-suu on the itinerary of the epic poem's hero, Boqmurun, along the way interviewing herders about old place names that connected their localities with the world of the epic. My initial field report of that expedition, once I managed to get it to Professor Hatto, led to apprenticeship in his comparative study of heroic and epic poetry, and a three decades long, on-going study of the Kirghiz epic tradition.

From the mid-nineteenth-century epic texts opened up to scholars by Arthur Hatto (1910–2010), I did not venture into close study of the twentieth-century *Manas* material until Saghïmbay Orozbaq uulu's massive *Manas*, created in the 1920s, appeared in an edition in Kyrgyzstan that permitted the reading of the bard's complete utterance. It had not occurred to me to do a translation of Saghïmbay's *Manas*, but the charm of his creativity and the staggering scale of his ambition shone through in the new edition, more vividly than in the abridgments that were the only versions permitted to be published in the Soviet era. Here, it seemed, was a door to introduce a wide readership to the outstanding Kirghiz *Manas* tradition, and a key to understanding its unparalleled status as a cultural landmark in Central Asia. Getting to know Saghïmbay better as a poet and as a human being was not my primary motivation in doing this translation, but it was one of the richest rewards. I am happy to bring English readers to the door of his tent, and hope that others will take the challenge to open up more of his works to English audiences.

Paths to producing a translation of this kind are narrow and difficult, both inside and outside the academy. All of the people who sustained me with their help and advice amount to a catalogue of heroes and heroines truly Kökötöyan in proportions. The bardic gifts to grace them all with stylish epithets elude me; I can only record my sincere thanks:

For many favors, courtesies, and examples set, to teachers, colleagues, and friends: Gulnara Jamasheva, Laili Ükübaeva, Ishen Obolbekov, Karl Reichl, Umut Korkut, Asel Isaeva, and Chris Atwood.

To colleagues, students, sponsors, and librarians in the National Academy of Sciences of the Kyrgyz Republic, Indiana University, and Miami University. In the Slavic–Eurasian Research Center at

Hokkaido University, to Tomohiko Uyama and the Foreign Visitor Fellowship Program. On a fellowship there in 2015, under working conditions that any Inner Asia scholar would have to call perfect, this book took shape.

Among surviving fellow members of the *comitatus* of the late Professor Arthur Hatto: to John D. Smith and Marion Gibbs, who like Hatto are translators of Penguin Classics in their fields. John Smith read the entire *Kökötöy* translation and gave it the benefit of his wise criticism.

Formerly of the National Library of the Kyrgyz Republic: to Gulnara Mederova and Liudmila Timofeeva, who changed a life as only librarians can, and to Jyldyz Bakashova, who first presented me with a copy of the published text upon which this translation is based, not an easy book to find.

To Simon Winder for opening the pages of Penguin Classics to one of the most oral works in the series to date, with imagination and curiosity that recall another translator's stories of working with the series' first editor, Dr. E. V. Rieu; and to the skillful and patient team at Penguin Books.

Close by in the inner clan: to Laurie, Henry, and Georgia Prior, who know best from life with and without the worker what the work really was.

Many years in the making, this book has to be a sort of memorial feast for the *arbaq*, departed spirits, of my comrade and wrangler Rasul Sopiev "who picked out for me a yearling from among the amblers," mentor and friend Arthur Hatto "who fed me on the best fruits from all over," supporters Sadybakas Umurzakov, Vladimir Galitskii, Vladimir Ploskikh, and Samar Musaev, collaborator Theodor Herzen, first preceptor in epic studies Fred C. Robinson, first patron Ilse Laude-Cirtautas, and sage teacher György Kara.

No one who deserves as much recognition as those named above must stand between me and any blame for faults in what follows. Saghïmbay and earlier bards of the Kirghiz epic tradition are due an altogether different order of homage. The book is dedicted to them.

D. P., April 2022

A Guide to Pronunciation

Only one frequently appearing name in the translation is given a household spelling: Kirghiz. A suitable English pronunciation of the name rhymes with the two vowels in *Burmese* and may be accented on either syllable. The word's native spelling is *Qïrghïz* according to the system used in this book, pronounced as explained below.

The following letters have particular sounds in the Kirghiz names and terms found in the translation.

a   as in *father*
ay   as y in *why*
e   as in *bet*
ey   as in *they*
g   as in *give*
gh   a gliding voiced consonant with the tongue in q position, like Parisian French r
i   as in *liter* when accented, as in *lit* when unaccented
ï   as the vowel in the second syllable of *roses*, but may be accented in Kirghiz
k   as in *keep*
ng   as in *sing*
ngg   the sequence ng–g
ngh   the sequence ng–gh
ngk   the sequence ng–k
o   as in *toss*
ö   like German ö in *können* or French eu in *jeune*
q   similar to k, but with the tongue further back, giving a guttural sound

r   like Spanish or Italian r
u   as in *lute*
ü   like German ü in *über* or French u in *tu*

The doubled vowels aa, oo, uu are lengthened verions of a, o, u. The doubled vowel ee is pronounced as in *matinee*.

The accent in Kirghiz words and names can be approximated in most cases by placing stress on the last syllable.

An apostrophe written within a name signifies the location of a dropped sound in a contracted word, and can be ignored for pronunciation purposes. Hyphens divide root elements of analyzable compound names of steeds, weapons, places, and ethnic groups (e.g. Kök-ala, Kök-art); such hyphens are omitted from names of people (e.g. Kökqoyon).

List of Abbreviations

MK   *The Memorial Feast for Kökötöy Khan*, any version of the epic or all versions together.

MKNB   [Nazar Bolot,] *The Memorial Feast for Kökötöy-Khan (Kökötöydün ašı): A Kirghiz Epic Poem*, edited for the first time from a photocopy of the unique manuscript, with translation and commentary by A. T. Hatto (Oxford: Oxford University Press, 1977). [At the time of publication, the attribution of the text to the bard Nazar Bolot was uncertain.]

MKSO   [Saghïmbay Orozbaq uulu,] *The Memorial Feast for Kökötöy Khan*, in *Mso a*, vol. 8/9 (2014), pp. 10–194; also that text's translation in this book as cross referenced hereafter.

MKWR   [Anonymous,] "Bok-murun," in *MWR*, pp. 159–225.

Mso a   [Saghïmbay Orozbaq uulu,] *Manas: Heroic Epic of the Kirghiz People*, academic edition according to the variant of Sagymbai Orozbakov, 9 volumes in 8, ed. Samar Musaev et al. (Bishkek, 1995–2014), in Kirghiz.

Mso b   [Saghïmbay Orozbaq uulu,] *Manas: Heroic Epic of the Kirghiz People*, according to the variant of Sagymbai Orozbakov, ed. Samar Musaev and Abdyldazhan Akmataliev (Bishkek: Khan-Tengir, 2010), in Kirghiz.

MWR   *The Manas of Wilhelm Radloff*, ed. and trans. A. T. Hatto (Wiesbaden: Otto Harrassowitz, 1990).

Foreword

Oral stories differ from written ones not only in the way they are conveyed. They feel different; they occupy a different reality. For adults who read, penetrating the peculiar essence of a substantial oral narrative may be as great a challenge as the one faced by children learning to use letters. It requires practice, and texts as transparently close to their oral sources as possible. This translated oral poem is unusually close to its source.

The many lives of the Kirghiz *Manas*, a Central Asian Turkic epic, have the distinction of being one of the best-documented traditions of oral heroic epic poetry in the world. (A more often-repeated claim to fame, that it is the "longest" epic, says less about its value.) There are good written and audiovisual records of Kirghiz epic performances spanning the mid-nineteenth to the twenty-first century. This makes *Manas* an important historical monument of oral literatures worldwide. The most influential single telling of *Manas* is the classic version recorded in the 1920s from unique oral performances by the bard Saghïmbay Orozbaq uulu. The life Saghïmbay breathed into the old heroic stories has helped to secure the preeminence of *Manas* among the epic traditions of the horse-riding nomadic peoples of Inner Asia, although its popularity has never spread westward. Other bards have produced different versions; Saghïmbay's enormous *Manas*, however, occupies a seminal position in modern Kirghiz culture and a crucial node in the long history of the epic tradition. What Saghïmbay achieved in his sung composition in collaboration with folklorists and scribes was in essence the creation of a written classic out of oral lore.

The second quarter of the twentieth century was not a good

time to begin to classicize epics about "national" heroes in the young Soviet Union. In 1952 *Manas* came close to being banned and suppressed. Kirghiz scholars refused to repudiate their intellectual patrimony in the face of Stalinist pressure, but the success of their defense came at a cost. The texts for public consumption were drastically abridged and purged of incidents and allusions that ran afoul of Soviet socialist thought. After the Kyrgyz Republic gained independence in 1991, the state embraced *Manas* as its ideological foundation, a perhaps unique status for an epic poem anywhere in the modern world, and a uniquely rapid turnabout in an epic's fortunes from official disapproval to its opposite. Communist China has made its own uses of the branch of the tradition known to its Kirghiz minority. Throughout good times and bad over the last century, Kirghiz have looked to Saghïmbay's *Manas* as an iconic embodiment of their heritage.

The icon has not been easy to get to know "in person," as text. Access to Saghïmbay's original utterance via western languages is especially difficult. The complete poem translated here, *The Memorial Feast for Kökötöy Khan*, is one of the major episodes of Saghïmbay's telling of *Manas*. The term "episode," however, is rather misleading, as Saghïmbay's version of the poem consists of approximately 13,500 poetic lines, more than the *Odyssey*.[1] It is an engaging story, by turns rambling, earthy, stirring, strange, shocking, bombastic, and funny, which kaleidoscopically illuminates the culture, history, lore, and society of Central Asia's nomadic peoples – and the mind of the poet who captured it all. For the Kirghiz, the feast is a byword for a large to-do where no expense is spared, and they have a proverb which means, "Kökötöy's memorial feast – that was the start of many conflicts." But *Manas* is not merely a function of Kirghizness; it is also a work of art that speaks of and to humanity. Kirghiz epic heroism should appear familiar to readers of other oral epics, while adding original angles to the picture.

1. Kirghiz epic verses are shorter than Homeric Greek ones; in terms of word counts in English, Saghïmbay's *Kökötöy* is about 70 percent the length of the *Odyssey*.

The basic situation of *The Memorial Feast for Kökötöy Khan* can be put quite simply: getting together with people one doesn't necessarily want to see. What should happen, what can happen, and what does happen in such a situation are different things. To deal with the possible dissonances, cultures use manners; they may work out the imaginable extremes via genres such as comedy or tragedy. The genre here is less familiar now: epic. The heroes know their etiquette, but their social wherewithal ranges further and disconcertingly deeper, and includes pugnacity, arm-twisting, and mass violence.

The story plays out on a vast geopolitical stage with ethnic and religious overtones, but on the human level it appears at first to be about a young hero's efforts to stand out. The Muslim khan Kökötöy's death occasions the grand memorial feast, to which his heir, young Boqmurun, invites other heroes from all over the world, both Muslims and infidels.[1] The two opposing sides are unable to stay at peace during the feast and games, and the young hero cannot stop the strife. The Muslims, dominated by their supreme hero Manas, restore order with enormous force. In other words, it is the Muslims' massive reprisal upon the infidels that brings the epic to a close. Kökötöy left a vast fortune, but the epic that bears his name is not about the defense or loss of that fortune; he left a vacant throne, but the epic only skirts the question of succession of rule. The touchy self-assertiveness of these heroes locks them in unending recursions of violence and vengeance. Singling out a protagonist is a matter of historical analysis of the tradition.

The feast and games in *The Memorial Feast for Kökötöy Khan* mirror those themes in the famous twenty-third book of the *Iliad*, where the Achaeans suspend their war on Troy to mourn the fallen Patroclus. But the narrative realizations of the feasts in these two epics are near opposites. The treatment in the *Iliad* is the minor one, its smaller scale conforming to its simpler structure: heroes on one side of a convulsed geopolitical fault line pause their all-out war, and use feasting and sports to bring closure to their grief for a crucial comrade killed in battle; quarrels

1.   In the translation, Infidel is capitalized, like an ethnic name.

over questions of fairness ensue, which are controlled by the giving of largesse. In *The Memorial Feast for Kökötöy Khan*, heroes from both sides of a tense geopolitical fault line come together and quarrel – uncontrollably, over the fair allocation of largesse – amid feasting and sports in honor of an aged hero who died in his bed and whose entire narrative significance hinges on the problems his death imposes on the living; all-out war convulses the close of the feast.

Kirghiz epic bards and audiences imagined the location of the momentous border between the tradition's Muslim and infidel nomads, between "us and them," more or less where it lay in real life after the mid-eighteenth century (where the borders between the Central Asian republics and China remain today). The historical era from the mid-eighteenth to the mid-nineteenth century is one answer to the question of "when" the action of the epic takes place, though in fact the question has both a multiplicity of answers and no answer at all. Kirghiz epic time is quasi-historical. Faded memories of events and names of people as early as the fifteenth century are sensible in the background; onstage, the heroes shoulder muskets. The bards' use of framing genealogies and references to "then" and "now" show that they and their audiences viewed their epics as prologue to the present. Our bard, Saghïmbay, asserts through occasional asides that the memorial feast for Kökötöy Khan was the origin of a number of important Kirghiz customs; at other points he allows his epic time to slip subtly and fleetingly into the recent past or his own present times.

Given its epic scope and its status today as an ethno-national foundation story, *Manas* stands at the threshold of numerous pathways into Eurasian cultures, literatures, and history. One path leads back to the Kirghiz author and the resources of tradition and individual creativity with which he worked. Saghïmbay Orozbaq uulu (1867–1930) was a member of a generation of bards who inherited the fully oral, heroic epic tradition while coming of age under the newly established Tsarist colonial regime in Central Asia. In this new reality, the two worlds of the old heroic epics, the stories and their frame in lived experience, no longer transparently related to each other. Bards, their chiefly patrons, and their audiences could no longer tie art and life together with epic. The pacified Kirghiz tribes developed diverse cultural expressions to meet their times, some of them in the increasingly common form of written literature. Nostalgia set in. Saghïmbay, a renowned poet and storyteller in many oral genres, also knew how to read; with access to both oral and written streams of knowledge, he used his curiosity to absorb vast amounts of information. In his *Manas* he seems intent upon presenting as much of it as possible. Saghïmbay's nature as an innovator in his storytelling tradition is one of his most engaging and at the same time challenging qualities as a poet. One of his epic innovations was a humanistic attitude, sometimes almost lyrical and inward. This makes parts of his epics easier to fathom than the nineteenth-century texts with their stringent, archaic tenor.

Fated to reach the height of his creative maturity at a turning point in history, Saghïmbay represented a source of traditional input to the new Soviet culture machine. His *Manas* came into being because he met a folklore collector who had heard he could sing the entire story, and who proposed to record it in writing. The manuscripts, written in Kirghiz in a version of Arabic script, are preserved and are the basis of the text translated here. The written text of Saghïmbay's *Manas* barely received any recognition during his lifetime, and he did not live to see his legacy become complicated by ideological disapproval as Stalinism spread its poisons throughout Soviet society. Nevertheless, his legacy continued and is becoming more widely understood. Meeting Saghïmbay on his own terms can be an astonishing and humbling experience. He is worth getting to know.

The varied wholeness of Saghïmbay's *Kökötöy*, like the nature of any long epic, unfolds as it goes on. Heroes may be folksy and touchy, cruel and generous, stiff-necked and nonchalant. There are no interested gods in this world, above or below; there is little magic, and there are no monsters to fight close by, only men; the heroes breathe freely, and we with them. In his stewardship of the grand old epic, Saghïmbay was first and always a poet. He had a rare talent for dramatizing dialogue between heroes. His love of people and of nature, his deep spiritual side, his senses of comedy and crudity brought out the vitality of his Kirghiz language and refreshed at times the more sinewy, stylized expressions of these sentiments, vigorous in their own way, that were favored in the nineteenth century.

Although there are no sound recordings of Saghïmbay's performances, we can guess what the songs sounded like by analogies with the known work of other bards. Kirghiz epic poetry is sung poetry, without instrumental accompaniment. Verses consist of seven or eight syllables in a meter often approximated by 6/8 musical time, two bars to a verse. The normal rhythms have a striding character that evokes riding on horseback. The Kirghiz even name some of their verse forms after the gaits of their horses, like "pacing" and "jog-trot." The poetic stride is complemented verbally by what Viktor Zhirmunskii called rhythmico-syntactic parallelism, a Turkic pattern of lining up grammatically similar words in successive verses to create a kind of natural rhyme reinforced by rules of vowel harmony within words. There are no set rhyme patterns; the poet deploys his parallelistic effects ad lib, verse by verse. Similarly, melodies progress not in stanzas but verse by verse. Some bards are highly skilled melodists, and the best are masters at combining musical, poetic, and narrative form into a unified whole.

Once recorded in writing, an epic text acquires the ability to travel far beyond the confines of its original oral performance milieu. This is how we are able to know great epics with oral origins like the Greek *Iliad* and *Odyssey*, the Sanskrit *Mahābhārata*, the German *Nibelungenlied*, the French *Chanson de Roland*, and the Spanish *Poema de Mio Cid*. These epic touchstones have the status of classics, and in each case the journey from oral epic performances to literary manuscripts – the textualization of oral composition in performance – was a process about which too little is known. The Kirghiz *Manas* belongs to this rank of epics, yet unlike them it brings along with it a richly documented context, which reveals how individual bards' contributions to the oral epic tradition were put down in writing. Analysis shows that the texts are not perfect; scribes erred, and sometimes bards did as well. Such flaws in the fabric help to reveal the wondrous art of its weaving.

The need for translations of Saghïmbay's *Manas* has been felt for a long time. The full text was frustratingly difficult of access for many years, despite the fact that the manuscripts, housed in the National Academy of Sciences of the Kyrgyz Republic in Bishkek, have been the subject of study and partial dissemination in one form or another since their creation in the 1920s. All publications of *Manas* from the Soviet Union suffer heavy deletions and alterations of religious, ethno-national, and class content deemed incompatible with socialist doctrine. The first ostensibly complete, unaltered publication of Saghïmbay's *Manas* appeared only in 2010, in a single huge volume of 1,829 pages.[1] Although not a scholarly edition, at the time of its publication it constituted the best, most complete witness to Saghïmbay's *Manas* text. Subsequently the stalled publication of the full scholarly edition of Saghïmbay's *Manas* was brought to completion, the last volume (which contains *Kökötöy*) appearing in 2014.[2]

Given the possibility for the first time to examine any part of Saghïmbay's *Manas* epic as it was created by him at its full length, an explorer of the tradition is drawn first of all to the bard's *Kökötöydün ashï* 'Kökötöy's Memorial Feast' (or 'The Memorial Feast for Kökötöy Khan'). This epic alone was recorded earlier on, in two separate versions, both of which, from the mid-nineteenth century, have been published with English translations direct from the Kirghiz originals by Arthur Hatto.[3] There are compelling prospects for comparing Saghïmbay's *Kökötöy* with the two nineteenth-century versions. Even as Saghïmbay strove to leave his mark on the tradition, he was embedded in it, and the older texts help to resolve the shape of his enormous creation.

1. *Manas: Heroic Epic of the Kirghiz People*, according to the variant of Sagymbai Orozbakov, ed. Samar Musaev and Abdyldazhan Akmataliev (Bishkek: Khan-Tengir, 2010), in Kirghiz; hereafter *Mso b*.
2. *Manas: Heroic Epic of the Kirghiz People*, academic edition according to the variant of Sagymbai Orozbakov, 9 volumes in 8, ed. Samar Musaev et al. (Bishkek, 1995–2014), in Kirghiz; hereafter *Mso a*. The *Kökötöy* poem is the first part of vol. 8/9.
3. *MKNB*; "Bok-murun," in *The Manas of Wilhelm Radloff*, ed. and trans. A. T. Hatto (Wiesbaden: Otto Harrassowitz, 1990), pp. 159–225. Hereafter, the volume *The Manas of Wilhelm Radloff* will be referred to as *Mwr*, and the "Bok-murun" poem as *MKwr*.

We cannot be sure how many written copies came between the original field records of the recording sessions and the surviving manuscripts of Saghïmbay's *Manas* that the archivists have labeled "original." A number of leaves of these unique manuscripts, including in the *Kökötöy* codex (shelf no. 209, dated 3 October 1925, Archives of the National Academy of Sciences of the Kyrgyz Republic), look like field records in the hand of the person who is known to have been Saghïmbay's main scribe, Ïbïrayïm Abdïraqmanov. The academic edition of Saghïmbay's *Manas* points out a number of places where the manuscripts have undergone alterations, mostly erasure and replacement of words. In most of these cases it is not possible to establish the original reading. The manuscripts' chief editor, Samar Musaev, theorized that these alterations date to the late 1930s, when Saghïmbay's *Manas* was being prepared for publication and certain passages dealing with Islam and Turkic ethnic identity were changed to avoid political criticism.[1]

The 2010 Kirghiz edition of *The Memorial Feast for Kökötöy Khan* (Mso *b*, pp. 1444–595), consisting of 13,482 verses, formed the original basis of my translation. This was supplemented by restored verses and improved readings from the 2014 academic edition (*MKso*, in Mso *a*), the last verse of which is 13,595. My digital photographic copy of manuscript 209 also supplied some supplementary and corrected readings. Minor variations in the spellings of names and terms have been normalized for the sake of readability.

Saghïmbay's poetry, like that of many Kirghiz epic bards, can be translated literally more readily than it can be translated intelligibly. It is often necessary to supply words in the translation that are only implicit in the text. An extreme example of this is an image of battle-frenzy overtaking Manas's frame: "the hair on his body [stood up bushy enough to spin yarn] for five pairs of stockings," where the bracketed words had to be added to Saghïmbay's impetuous narration. The translator's task becomes truly difficult when the implicit words are ambiguous or simply not apparent. At times even the literal meaning is

1.   Mso *a*, vol. 8/9, p. 7.

elusive. Saghïmbay's bold verses frequently chafe at the stric-
tures of syntax, and sometimes gambol freely outside it. The
Kirghiz language has a tendency to de-emphasize finite verbs in
favor of runs of gerunds and participles; these build up in the
oral poet's verses like icons of action, perfect for his urgent
drive onward but, like the rocks and clods thrown up by the
hoof-beats of one of the poem's many galloping horses, difficult
to gather up and arrange in a line of grammatical time. Some
uncertainty of this kind is apparent already in the punctuation
the scribes used in the manuscripts, which later editors often
ignored and emended in their publications of the text, and
which I in turn had to parse in my own ways.

The prose rendering offered here attempts to present Saghïm-
bay's poetry to English readers accurately and intelligibly
without belying its nature. That the needle on the tuning meter
of the translation should incline more toward the reader than
the poem is an inevitable result of my choice to render verse
into prose, and of my exertions, perhaps at times a little hard-
handedness, with the reins of the spirited, noble beast of the
epic. I mean Saghïmbay no disrespect by having tidied up some
of his living constructions, and on balance can at least offer
him the compliment, which I admit I am proud to do for his
sake, of having translated one of his epic poems directly from
Kirghiz into another language entire for the first time.

To readers primarily interested in enjoying the text, to those
seeking an introduction to new subjects, or to those versed in
other epics who are looking for a novel vantage point on the
genre, this book's structure will present different pathways. It
would be a daring venture for any sort of reader to bypass the
section before the translation, How to Read the Epic. It pre-
views important characteristics of the text and of the translation,
and points to a few areas of initial concern to new readers of
this epic. The richness of meaning in Saghïmbay's poetic cre-
ation begins to come into focus in the translation, and in
endnotes there, signaled by asterisks. These analyze and explain
points a native audience would have understood implicitly, or
provide additional illumination from history, culture, and epic
tradition. Some of the endnotes point ahead to fuller analyses

in the Introduction to a Reading of the Tradition. Positioned after the translation, this "introduction" consists of a number of sections that open up in-depth background and offer textual comparisons with the older versions of the narrative. Readers have the choice to explore the Introduction to a Reading of the Tradition as they wish. It may suit the curiosity of some to read parts of it at the outset, or to refer to it while reading the translation. Others may turn to it once their acquaintance with the epic is complete (Arthur Hatto, whose idea for this part of the book I borrowed from his Penguin Classics translations, used the heading "An Introduction to a Second Reading."[1]) In any case, readers of all interest levels should consider bookmarking the Notes at the end of the translation, the Index containing explanations of personal, geographic, and ethnic names in the back of the book, and the maps in the front.

A hardy or epicurean few who finish most of that may find in the Kirghiz epic tradition an entrée into diverse Inner and Northern Asian oral cultures with epics: the Qaraqalpaq *Edige*, the Özbek *Alpamish*, the Qazaq *Qoblandï Batïr*, the Khanty *Song of the Golden Hero-Prince*, the Qalmaq *Jangghar*, the Ainu *Woman of Poi-Soya*, and more.

Discussions on the history of the Kirghiz epic tradition are often shaped, directly or indirectly, by Eurasian views on folk culture that tend to accept as primordial things that I am inclined to analyze as historical, and to place greater emphasis on ethno-national identity than on authorial individuality. This book is not a place to engage in or cite specialist argumentation, but from time to time my own ways of saying things – in the background and interpretations, not in the translation proper – may place appreciable distance between me and some other exponents of the tradition. Instead of pointing out (or hiding) every instance of what may be unusual views of mine, here all at once is what I think a responsible critic might say about my overall perspective: that it sometimes misses the reverence of the Kirghiz in accounting for what their epic poetry

1.   *The Nibelungenlied* (Harmondsworth: Penguin Books, 1965) and Wolfram von Eschenbach, *Parzival* (Harmondsworth: Penguin Books, 1980).

may mean to humanity; that it traces historical processes in the Kirghiz oral heroic epic tradition that call into question its continuity in certain generations; that it sometimes magnifies the value of the mid-nineteenth-century epics at the expense of the longer twentieth-century texts; that my notions of value arise from comparative assessments of the quality of epic poets' heroic plots and characterizations; that in framing those comparisons I seek balance between local Kirghiz cultural knowledge and global characteristics of oral heroic epic poetry. By the end I hope to have implicated myself fully in all such charges.

How to Read the Epic

Here, via translation, is a record of a sung poem that was written down at the very moment of its oral composition in performance. Behind that singular creative act lay an intricate landscape of ongoing oral tradition that the bard Saghïmbay and his audience negotiated on the emergent pathways of his song. Every line, so far as we know, was written down as the bard's words rang in the air. In other words, the text translated here originated as a stenographic transcription. Unlike, for instance, *Beowulf*, another unique manuscript of an epic, which was "composed to be projected in public performance – to be sung or spoken aloud,"[1] our text harbors no vision of a return to life through the human voice. The manuscript was meant for the archive shelf and the scholar's desk. It cannot give us the sense we get from *Beowulf*, or the *Iliad*, or the *Nibelungenlied*, that the written text as such has a new audience in mind. What we gain in compensation is a vista on the original singer and audience whose moment of interaction the text fossilizes – a view that extends far closer to the hearth fire of oral tradition itself than any ancient or medieval epic can bring us, but also presents problems of its own nature. "You had to be there," the text sometimes seems to whisper.

What did the people who were there know that we don't know? What did they relish that we wouldn't notice? What do we balk at that they took in stride? Some of the present age's restlessness with reading epics for entertainment may arise from their frequent fusion of an ostensibly single-stranded story with

1. *Beowulf*, trans. Michael Alexander (Harmondsworth: Penguin Books, 1973), p. 9.

stylistic techniques that are anything but simple. Set descriptions, epithets, catalogues, allusions, and other compositional formulas of oral epic constantly remind readers that the poem's primary audience had ways of knowing that were fundamentally different from the written knowledge more familiar to us. The reader's job is first to accept that there are different, oral ways of knowing, and next to trust that the oral ways can be better understood by reading the epic. Equipped with an approximation of oral knowledge, one can begin to join in the equally special oral ways of *enjoying* the epic. In the epic world, it is not enough that a hero's gun is formidable; it is given its own name and résumé: "Aq-kelte, unerring at close range or long, equalizer of near and far, its barrel and muzzle of finest steel, prodigious smoker, its lock of Ïspan make, fearsome of sight and true of shot" (p. 145). A hero's horse isn't just large, beautiful, well cared for, and spirited, he is a set piece of these traits:

> That praiseworthy racer, the enormous Qula – his coat like the feathers of the eagle-owl, his back piled with richly ornamented saddle-cloths; let out to his ease on ground strewn with sand and set to drink on lands strewn with wells, distinguished by his mane erect as the onager's, rump round and full like a drum – good fortune rested upon him; with ears pricked up like candle-flames and upon his left flank a mark Ayqojo had left where he stroked him with his hand, this was a well-favored creature excelling all other beasts in form! (p. 98)

And this only in passing as the steed, Manas's, makes an entrance. Even bits of genealogical information could become familiar refrains for the seasoned audience. The repeatable, expandable, collapsible nature of the content was what enabled the oral poet to create, and what kept the epics ever-new; the paradox of oral poetry is its "formulaic" and at the same time perennially original nature. The alert audience was encouraged to revel in their connoisseurship as they listened (Will he mention the mark on Qula's flank? It must be coming up ...).

  Horses are a whole world unto themselves for the epic heroes. Their forms, colors, sizes, markings, breeding, conditioning, gaits;

their stamina, speed, intelligence, spirit, tempers, humors, foibles; their capacity to enlarge the self-concept of humanity in racing and war; their torments of extreme exertion and endurance; the miraculous ability of a few choice beasts, known as *tulpar*, to spread wings and fly: these are, we are led to infer, the most cherished of all the freely held interests of the nomad heroes of Inner Asia, to which few facets of human existence could hold up more than a reflection. Nomad heroes' passion for the horse is seen perhaps nowhere better than in *The Memorial Feast for Kökötöy Khan*, which hinges on the running and results of the great horse race, and which comes to a head in a dispute over the herd of horses posted as the prize for the winning racer. Because the heroes appreciate them so, in summarizing heroes' attributes in the Index I have listed their steeds before their wives, "plus-ones" at the feast if mentioned at all. It must be added that these same heroes relished eating horse meat, and that neither horses nor women were safe from heroes' lashes.

The heroes and heroines in Saghïmbay's *Kökötöy* are legion; a few major figures should be watched for. Kökötöy, the wealthy khan of Tashken, utters his last testament as the epic opens, and is dead before the real action begins.[1] Kökötöy's teen-aged orphan son, Boqmurun, steps resolutely into adulthood and organizes the solemnities and festivities that follow. In his bold actions he is hindered by Baymïrza, the miserly advisor of his late father, and helped by Jash Aydar, his youthful herald and envoy. But despite his determination and daring, it is not the heroism of Boqmurun that is fully realized in this epic. Manas, a Kirghiz khan from nearby Talas who had long been an ally of Kökötöy, and whose imposing power and truculence are a thing apart even among heroes, gradually overshadows Boqmurun's intentions. Manas is joined in co-presidency over Kökötöy's great memorial feast by the elder statesman Qoshoy, khan of the Qataghan tribe, the most likable character in the epic. Other heroes come to their minor roles in this epic with side business of

1. Kökötöy's whole presence in the known Kirghiz epic tradition began and ended with his deathbed, until Saghïmbay gave him a bit of a back story in an earlier episode, which is summarized in this poem's prologue.

their own, which traditional audiences could delight in recollecting through the bard's allusions: Ürbü, the eloquent orator (though in Saghïmbay's *Kökötöy* he comes up ironically tongue-tied for a key speech); Er Töshtük, whose marvelous adventures in the underworld are only touched on here but are the subject of an independent epic; Er Kökchö, the formidable Qazaq (Kazakh) warrior, to whom Saghïmbay, teasing the Kirghiz' wealthier, more powerful neighbors the Qazaqs, gives an air of style and luxury greater than his valor; Almambet, converted prince from the enemy side who is Manas's sworn brother and closest companion, appearing in this poem mainly as a weather-conjurer. Manas has a trusted old kinsman, Baqay, a trusted old companion, Qïrghïl Chal, and a *comitatus* of heroes, the Forty Companions, most of whom appear only in catalogues. Manas's wife Qanïkey, the most praiseworthy figure in the entire epic tradition, is a formidable heroine of action in other epics, though here she has but one scene and no spoken lines. These home heroes are all horse-mounted nomads of the Kirghiz and related Turkic peoples, whose heroic deeds partly reflect their drive to defend and promote their religion, Islam, in the face of grim, powerful infidel foes. Saghïmbay sometimes uses an older name, Noghoy, as the ethnic label of the best of the home heroes, reflecting the historical Noghay Horde.

The enemy side is led by the khan Qongurbay of Qïtay, son of Alooke. Qïtay is in one sense a realm identifiable with China (Qïtay being one of that country's historical names), though Saghïmbay, in keeping with the older Kirghiz epic tradition, dramatizes it as a tribe of mounted nomad warriors of the east. The Qïtay nominally dominate but essentially act in league with the Qalmaq, Mongols whose homeland abuts that of the epic Kirghiz and Qazaqs. The Qalmaq are led by their khan Joloy, a strong-man and warrior equal in mettle to Qongurbay, but roguish and grotesque. Joloy's fellow Qalmaqs include the heroes Ushang and Boroonchu, and the battle-maiden Sayqal. Joloy's wife Ayghanïsh, wiser than her husband, appears at a critical moment to upbraid the obtuseness of his actions. The infidel woman warrior Oronghu plays one half of a rank sex scene, surely one of the most unerotic in all literature, and then defends her sex in a magisterial reproach of the male onlookers. These are only a handful of the crowds of characters named in the epic. Many more have little or nothing to do in the story, though they are listed as heroes and heroines in the Index.

The essential action of the plot is simple, and was known to all traditional audiences: Kökötöy Khan's death occasions a series of funeral observances that culminate in the grand memorial feast, to which his heir Boqmurun invites all the world's heroes, both friends and enemies. Spectacles ensue, egos are bruised, rough games get out of hand, and scores are settled with enormous violence; Manas emerges as the one supreme hero who dominates everyone. Saghïmbay's version of this plot can be divided into three "acts," each with a different hero as its focus: Kökötöy's testament, in Part 1; Boqmurun's initiating and putting on the burial, the fortieth-day memorial feast, and the grand memorial feast, comprising Parts 2–8; and the events during and after the grand memorial feast, where Manas and Qoshoy officially preside and where Manas is effectively paramount, comprising Parts 9–17. The plot was basically traditional, though Saghïmbay made it very much his own.

The Memorial Feast for Kökötöy Khan plays out on one of the widest geographical stages of the traditional Kirghiz epics, and the inquisitive Saghïmbay outdoes the range of his bardic forerunners in bringing the world to the feast. If we equate identifiable place names with their face value in current geographical knowledge (not necessarily an accurate exercise, since the poet's imaginings may have differed from today's maps) the lands mentioned in the epic stretch from France to Japan and from India to Siberia. Closer in to the familiar country shared by Saghïmbay and his home heroes, we are in the hands of a well-traveled, expert nomad guide within the environs of the Tien Shan range, as far as three days' ride from its flanks – space bounded approximately by lake Balkhash in Kazakhstan, the cities of Yining (called Qulja in our text) and Kashgar (Qashqar) in China, the Hisar (Ïsar) valley in Tajikistan, and the city of Turkistan (Türküstön) in Kazakhstan. The story is centered at the feasting ground, in the high, broad valley of Qarqïra in Kazakhstan, east of lake Issyk Kul (Ïsïq-köl), at a mid-point between Boqmurun's realm of Tashkent (Tashken) and Beejin, the Qïtay realm to the east. Beejin should not be equated too readily with the city of Peking. In the mid-nineteenth-century Kirghiz epics Beejin was an imprecisely imagined place and even a tribe, somewhere in northwest China, close enough to inflame the Muslim nomads' zeal for struggle against the infidel. Saghïmbay's wider world-view (in part, sadly, due to his displacement in China following the 1916 Turkestan Rebellion) gave him a more accurate under-standing of the location of China's capital, but many of the traditional epic verses he sang reflect older conceptions of the not-too-distant Beejin.

Readers who start with an awareness of certain challenging aspects of Saghïmbay's *Kökötöy* text may be better able to meet the epic on its own terms. Part 1, "Kökötöy's Deathbed Testa-ment," is a long, digressive, shilly-shally preamble that may seem like an obstacle to the beginning of the action. It may be skipped if it brings on an allergic reaction; inoculation to the problems it presents may come from reading other parts of the epic. Those who read Part 1 will gain, at least, a generous taste of Saghïm-bay's discursive style; a panoramic view of real and fantastic lands, peoples, and other creatures of the world from the point of view of a Central Asian poet who does not take himself or the subject too seriously; and first acquaintance with musings on right living and God's plan by an intelligent man of Muslim faith. One will also find a bit of set-up on why Boqmurun feels motivated to hold such a massive and expensive memorial feast.

In Part 12, "Qoshoy and Joloy Wrestle; Qoshoy Beats Joloy," Saghïmbay narrates a traditional episode mostly brilliantly, but for one scene, the finding of a pair of wrestling breeches for Qoshoy to wear. Saghïmbay tried to adapt this traditional pas-sage to do something narratively that it had never before been required to do. The new task was to foreshadow the birth of Manas's son Semetey, whose own epic was to follow. The way Saghïmbay got to the moment of foreshadowing was over an unusually rough path of narration, and readers of this transla-tion cannot be spared every trouble in negotiating it. To simplify: there is a superb pair of ibex-leather breeches made by Manas's wife Qanïkey, which are found to suit Qoshoy. This detail was traditional. Outside this narrow thread of logic, however, Saghïmbay strews the path with enigmatic new rants, threats, recollections just in time, premonitions, death-faints, walk-on parts, backtracks, flashbacks, flash-forwards, and insults. The perspectives offered in the comparative note, "The wrestling breeches" (pp. 302–4) can help those who wish to fathom, if not fully clarify, the passage's mysteries. Here, as throughout the text, the sympathetic reader must try to approximate the oral ways of knowing.

The affair of the wrestling breeches is also one of many places in the story where a peculiar feature of Kirghiz epic heroism looms into view. The heroes have a penchant for harsh and impetuous insults, taunts, and threats. Even one accustomed to the hardness of heroes in other epics may be jarred by Kirghiz heroic scorn. There are plenty of instances of a fairly usual sort of taunts and insults between heroes from opposing sides, as when Boqmurun tells Joloy, "you're a dog digging in the ground," or when Qongurbay calls Boqmurun, "stinking yogurt, moldy curd, good-for-nothing coward!" But what are we to make of the seemingly unwarranted abuse heroes heap on their own? Upon meeting Boqmurun for the first time, Manas tells this openly grieving son of his deceased ally, "You're a nobody!" He calls a lesser hero a "piece of carrion" simply in getting his attention. Qoshoy calls Kökchö, a friendly hero as eminent as himself, a "fancy milksop" as he asks him for a favor.

Such cruel posturing was usual in the Kirghiz epic tradition, though Saghïmbay dialed it up a few notches. Boqmurun's dire threats to his fellow chiefs to attend the feast and bring their racing horses, or else, are one place where the nineteenth-century *Kökötöy* epics match Saghïmbay's spleen. The threats of harm for non-attendance that accompany each one of the series of invitations are long, detailed, and ingeniously varied oral formulaic set pieces. When Saghïmbay has Boqmurun say, with incredibly ruthless, deliberate rage, "I'll shatter the door-frame of your yurt, make your young lads weep, and set your mares kicking away off the mountainsides; shatter the trellis-frames of your yurt and set your virgin mares kicking away off the high, grassy slopes; make your young ladies and maidens weep," he is only getting started – and it is an invitation to an ally. There were good political reasons for a hero to add threats for non-attendance when inviting peers to an important feast; these are discussed in the Introduction to a Reading of the Tradition.

It is possible to spy familiar names and terms behind the veils of their Kirghiz pronunciations. Close to Saghïmbay's stomping-ground, we can safely think of Tashken as Tashkent, Samarqan as Samarkand, Ïsïq-köl as lake Issyk Kul, and so on. But can we be sure that Saghïmbay, from his lifelong home in Central Asia, had an understanding of Orol that would jibe with Ural on our maps? Can we distinguish for sure whether Saghïmbay meant the river, the mountain range, or some other sense of the place? Are we really helped in understanding Saghïmbay's utterance and the Kirghiz epic tradition by "translating" Qïtay as "Cathay" or "China," or Orus as "Russia," simply because these equivalencies can be found in the writings of scholars? Rather than attempting to resolve myriad such questions, this translation leaves most names in the forms Saghïmbay used. One exception is a pair of place names that read alike in the original but are spelled differently in the translation for clarity, Türküstön the city near the Syr Darya (usually spelled Turkistan in western usage), and Türkestan the land of the Turks, or Central Asia (Turkestan). A number of entries in the Index identify or suggest equivalencies with more familiar forms of the names.

The titles of the epic's seventeen parts are translated as they appear in the original text, some in slightly shortened form. The flow of the narrative sometimes washes right over one of these boundaries without pausing, as at the start of Part 9, where the title arises in mid-conversation between Boqmurun and Manas. This is because these headings were not a traditional part of the oral epic narrative. It is often not clear whether a heading was uttered by Saghïmbay or devised by the scribes. In any case, the latter almost certainly contributed to the decision to include them – a useful addition, if one does not mind an occasional spoiler.

A Note on the Illustrations

The years of Saghïmbay Orozbaq uulu's life were the first in which peoples of Inner Asia were extensively photographed. The Russian, Finnish, and French expeditions responsible for the photographs accompanying this translation focused on documenting everyday life, "types" of ethnic physiognomy and dress, and rituals and games of colonized native peoples in Russian and Chinese Turkestan. Many of these scenes, recorded to bring the exotic Orient closer to a European public, were familiar ones for Saghïmbay and his audiences. In 1912 Saghïmbay was a featured lamenter at the grand memorial feast pictured in the frontispiece illustrations to Parts 1 and 4, though there is no known photograph of him at that event. Only two photographs, the frontispiece illustrations to Parts 12 and 13, date to after Saghïmbay's lifetime.

The Russian scientist Sergei Mikhailovich Prokudin-Gorskii, a pioneer of color photography, composed the image on the cover, of a crowded sporting event at Samarkand, Russian Turkestan, from a series of three separate negatives shot through different colored filters. The time intervals between the separate exposures created colorful anomalies in the resulting composite where figures were in motion.

The Kirghiz scribes who wrote down the oral epic text *The Memorial Feast for Kökötöy Khan* also faced challenges in making a static record of a fleeting moment, the bard's performance.

List of Illustrations

Frontispiece: Painted portrait of Saghïmbay Orozbaq uulu, reproduced with permission of the Chingiz Aitmatov Institute of Language and Literature, National Academy of Sciences of the Kyrgyz Republic.

Part 1: Women mourners in the late Shabdan Dzhantaev's yurt beside his funerary effigy, 1912. Sergei Evgen'evich Dmitriev, *Izviestiia Imperatorskago Russkago geograficheskago obshchestva* 48 (1912), no. 6–10, pp. 529–44, plate 1.

Part 2: Kirghiz man (24 years old) near Uch Turfan, *c.*1906–8. C. G. E. Mannerheim, general ethnographic image collection of the Finno-Ugrian Society; reproduced with permission of the Finnish Heritage Agency.

Part 3: Mounted sport at Afrasiab, Samarkand. Hugues Krafft, *À travers le Turkestan Russe* (Paris: Hachette, 1902), plate following p. 184.

Part 4: Crowd attending the memorial feast for Shabdan Dzhantaev, 1912. Sergei Evgen'evich Dmitriev, *Izviestiia Imperatorskago Russkago geograficheskago obshchestva* 48 (1912), no. 6–10, pp. 529–44, plate 1.

Part 5: Kirghiz migration, *c.*1878–92. Courtesy of the Central State Cinematic, Photographic and Phonographic Archives of the Kyrgyz Republic.

Part 6: Horse rider, Central Asia, mid- to late nineteenth century. Turkestan Album. From the collection of the Peter the Great Museum of Anthropology and Ethnography (Kunstkamera), Russian Academy of Sciences, MAĖ I 1718-70.

A Note on the Maps

The maps identify places to reflect Saghïmbay's mental geography ca. 1925. Places are named only if mentioned in the poem, so some usual landmarks, like the Caspian and Aral seas and lake Balkhash (the large body of water in the north of Map 2) are not labeled. Forms of names follow Saghïmbay's Kirghiz usage, as in the translation. For example, the cities of Tashkent and Kashgar are labeled Tashken and Qashqar; the mountains commonly known as Tien Shan are labeled Ala-too. The Index lists some important names in their common forms as cross references, but country names in the poem cannot be matched exactly with modern states.

Map 1 shows post-1991 borders of the following countries: Afghanistan, China, Kazakhstan, Kyrgyzstan, Mongolia, Russia, Tajikistan, Turkmenistan, and Uzbekistan.

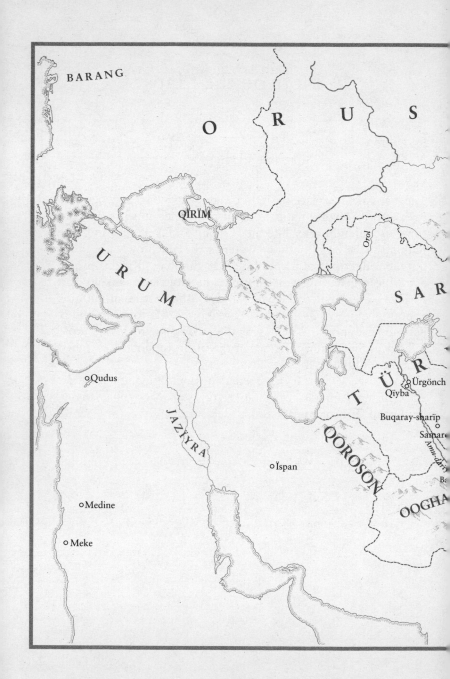

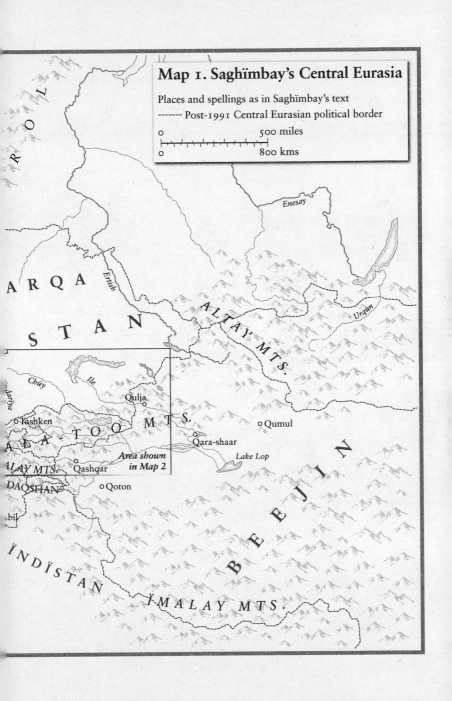

Map 1. Saghïmbay's Central Eurasia

Places and spellings as in Saghïmbay's text

------ Post-1991 Central Eurasian political border

0   500 miles

0   800 kms

R O L

A R Q A

S T A N

Enesay

Ertish

ALTAY MTS.

Urqun

Chüy

Ile

Qulja

Tashken

A-TOO MTS.

Qumul

Qara-shaar

Area shown
in Map 2

Lake Lop

B E E J I N

LAY MTS.

Qashqar

DAOSHAN

Qoton

bil

ÏNDÏSTAN

ÏMALAY MTS.

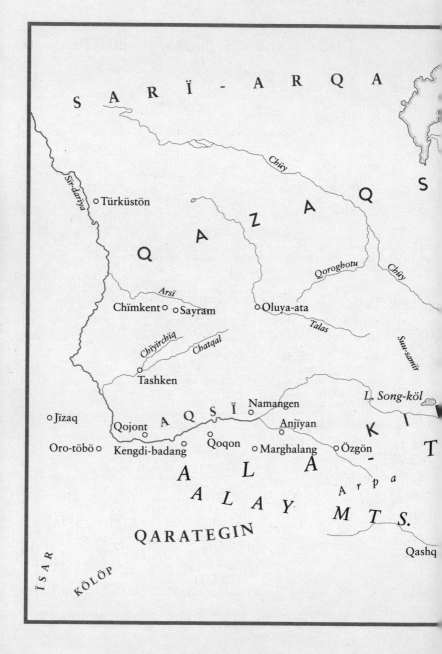

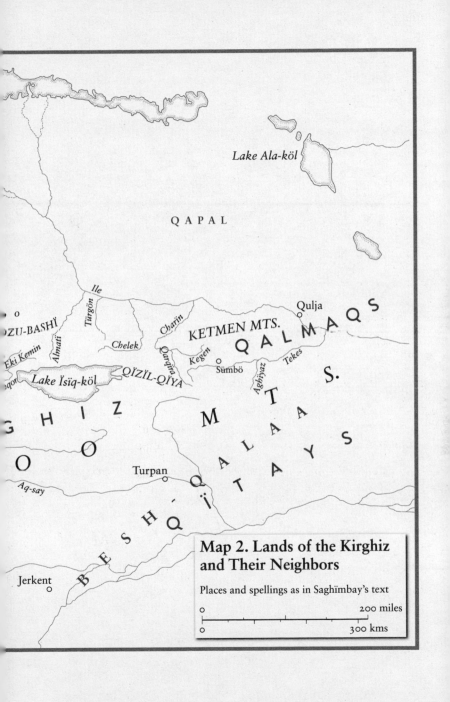

Lake Ala-köl

QAPAL

Ile

Türgön

ZU-BASHÏ

Eki Kemin

Almatï

Chelek

Charïn

KETMEN MTS.

Qulja

QALMAQS

agon

Lake Ïsïq-köl

QÏZÏL-QIYA

Qarqïra

Kegen

Sümbö

Aghïyaz

Tekes

G H I Z

O

Z

M

T

A

O

O

A L A

Aq-say

Turpan

B E S H - Q Ï - Q A L A

T A Y S

Jerkent

Map 2. Lands of the Kirghiz and Their Neighbors

Places and spellings as in Saghïmbay's text

0   200 miles

0   300 kms

THE MEMORIAL FEAST
FOR KÖKÖTÖY KHAN

I

Kökötöy's Deathbed Testament

In the land of Sïyamun and Altay, in the country of the Kirghiz of the forty tribes, lived Babur Khan, then Buura Khan, then Töböy Khan, then Kögöy Khan. Kögöy had three sons: the name of the eldest was Noghoy, the middle one was Shïghay, and the youngest one's name was Chïyïr. These were the kinsmen of the Qara Kirghiz that had split off from Ughuz Khan. The numerous Kirghiz lived everywhere in their country, the land of the Altay, where the descendants of their forefather Qara Khan had spread out and later come under the sway of Qarach Khan. The son of Noghoy was Jaqïp; those others had died off from the face of this false world; Jaqïp's son was Manas,* and in those days the Kirghiz were part of the league of Alach. Shïghay's son was Japaq, and Japaq named his son Chïnqojo. Manas's only son, planning to take Chïnqojo's wife, got into a sore fight with him;* the place where they fought was the city of Ürgönch. In those days Er Manas[1] made all kinds of lightning raids on his enemies. He bloodied the Qalmaq and raided the Qanghay; a morning's ride for him was as far as the Ïmalay, so he crushed many a nation, and a great many of his enemies went over the mountains to the south, to Ïndïstan.

The lands under Kirghiz rule, with the Qara-qum desert on the right-hand side, were these: down as far as Baghdat, they say, and up as high as Balïq and Badaqshan was all Kirghiz; also Oluya-Ata, great Tashken, peerless Qoqon, Marghalang,

---

*   Asterisks in the translation, starting with those on this page, refer to the Notes that begin on p. 239.

1.   "Er Manas": Er is a title of respect for warriors.

the city of Özgön at the confluence, lake Ïsïq-köl in the Ala-too mountains, with steppes encircling its banks – from up in the Altay and on the Amur, the Enesay river and Qosh-mürü, the two rivers Ertish and Urqun – all these lands were occupied by the Kirghiz; further on there was the desert of Qumul, and lake Ala-köl by It-ichpes, and Bar-köl, Tur-köl, and Ker-köl: in former times the numerous Kirghiz could barely fit inside that whole territory.

When Manas left the Altay and toppled the standards of the enemies he fought in different lands, he would let the obedient ones convert to Islam, but the defiant Infidels he would decapitate, and stuff their heads into the filth of their own stomachs. He conquered the Qalmaqs: Tekes, and Orgho whom he destroyed, and Tulus from whom he took the river,* and Alooke of Anjïyan, who could not bear Manas's fury or even give battle, and fled.

There was another Qara Kirghiz, Kökötöy son of Janadil, who had his encampment right at Tashken, but he and another who resided in that same place, Panus, the governor, who had his being in the very center of twelve-gated Tashken, were under Qïtay suzerainty. For five years running, reports had gone up from Panus to Beejin, and surely were being read at the court of Esen Khan, but five years turned to six and hardly a word came in return.

It was just then, as things were going on thus and Panus Khan had seated himself on the throne, that Manas emerged from the Altay, yearning for his people the teeming Kirghiz and for Türkestan his homeland, and came charging down the Chüy valley,* felling every foe that fought him. Er Kökötöy said, "My kinsman is coming!" and took two hundred thousand of his men – no settled folk under town rule but nomadic tribesmen all – and went out to meet Manas, for he had heard of his greatness before.

Kökötöy's potentate Panus, who had made himself khan, was vexed and amazed that Kökötöy should show him no deference, but instead go out to meet Manas. "He wields his own authority, going off at the head of an army – he is his own *bek*![1] Or he has made himself into one, and he won't leave me unmolested, but will prove the undoing of my rule!" said Panus the

---

1.　"*bek*" means "chief."

padishah (and, customarily, all the clans of the Kirghiz have given Kökötöy the name Özübek).[1] Leading Manas in his revolt against his khan, Kökötöy took control of Tashken. Panus, the khan whom the Qïtay had established there, became a Muslim, but those who did not submit were beheaded.

Manas was pleased that Kökötöy had recognized him as a kinsman and had come out to meet him. Here the Alach multitude had arrived only to find Kökötöy, one of their elders! Manas was well pleased, and every one of the innumerable Kirghiz felt great happiness. Feeling so gladdened, out of the satisfaction of his heart Manas began to think about giving some cattle to his uncle, his aged grandfather, Kökötöy.* But as he looked around and sized up the man's property, here was wealth beyond human reckoning – a fortune that surely would never decrease! – in cattle, coin, and seven hundred and thirty-five slaves bought in cash. Vast were his lands; his people teemed. Still, in his heart's satisfaction and joy at Kökötöy's attentions in coming out to meet him, gray-maned* Manas thought about picking out and giving to him the choicest virgin the world over; but at the age of eighty-four Kökötöy wouldn't have the strength to perform, Manas Baatïr thought. He was at a loss for what to do. Then he thought of something: "Property is necessary in this life, but in the next life one needs religion. Kökötöy is getting on in years, in fact he is quite old, and when he dies it will throw the Kirghiz tribes into confusion. If his end comes before mine, while there is life left in me I will requite the service he's done me: I'll make an announcement to the whole world, give abundant alms, and show gratitude far in excess of anything seen before in this country. I'll spare no expense in organizing all the know-how it will take, and it shall become an example for the rest: everyone shall talk about Kökötöy's memorial feast! I'll get the Kirghiz to slaughter all their cattle and serve the meat to all comers, Muslim and Infidel – let them gather together once and for all! I'll put some ingenuity into this, so that the marvels of it live on by word of mouth until Judgment Day! That way I can ease my heart," thought Manas

1. "Özübek" means literally, "himself a *bek*," "a *bek* in his own right." Saghïmbay is imagining the origin of the ethnic name Özbek, i.e. Uzbek.

to himself – and so we have come to the epic of Kökötöy's memorial feast.

The Qazaq and the Kirghiz give memorial feasts – they even say that a person who isn't given one is not human. To give a feast for his father a man may expend his herds and his strength and hand over all of his cattle for the sake of his good name; there are those too who just stick with their nearest relations, for whatever reason. Kökötöy had recognized that Manas was a relative and paid him the compliment of going out to greet him, and for that reason Manas made every effort in giving his memorial feast. All the people of the Qazaq and Kirghiz observe the custom of giving memorial feasts, and the Özübek too, in their way; as it says in the sharia, have respect for the dead. Kökötöy's close relations were in Tashken but he was little known to his more distant kin, so when Manas became Manas, sired by Jaqïp, and his wealth grew vast and he had chased the swarming Qïtay back to Qaqan, in the days when his belt was buckled tightly round his waist, – but one could chatter on, given time! –

Kökötöy was ailing, death was catching up to him. He had the croup. It was clear his last hours were upon him; his mind was failing, fever had reached his brain, strength was leaving him, and his death was at hand. As he was about to die, preparing to depart this fleeting world for the true world beyond – there was a kinsman of his, Bay, with whom he had lived as a close neighbor, whose son was named Baymïrza, sensible in his speech and of well-known intelligence – this Baymïrza, son of Bay, summoned all the people of the city of Tashken and brought them before Kökötöy, who lay with his head on a pillow. There he uttered his last testament:

"It looks as if the end is near; death is about to pluck my soul away! I leave a son who is young and riches unguarded. I leave a storehouse full of gold, even my wife Ayïmkül,* and all my people, the Kirghiz. There is that one known as Boqmurun[1] – I neglected to bestow a name on him, and now what? Here I am in my death-throes, and snot dangles from his nose. The lad can't

---

1. "Boqmurun" means "Snot-Nose."

stop sniveling! But the people have always doted on him. Not only the people, I have also! What a scandal for his father, that I haven't given him his proper name!

"Now, you needn't make a big deal of my death or wipe out my herds for a feast.[1] Bury me with a banquet such as you would give to a new daughter-in-law, like something where the children play around; like a memorial feast for an old woman or a respectable poor person. No need for anyone to know I'm alive or dead; it would not do for my people to be thrown into confusion. Slaughter two or three head of cattle, give out forty or fifty robes as gifts, and be done with it – that should settle things. A death requires cattle just as sure as poplars grow on a riverbank, but what's the point of squandering them? The living need cattle just as sure as a poplar grows where you plant it, just as a horse needs fat under the mane to be truly plump; and when his father dies a boy needs cattle to do everything that needs to be done.

"I have nine thousand and ninety horses and ninety thousand five hundred sheep, but my only son Boqmurun could still squander that many in a mishap, I fear. I have two thousand three hundred camels; I have given away daughters as brides in eleven lands, so my eleven sons-in-law are all over the world; I have six thousand and eighty cows, for our forefathers kept cattle and set us, the sons of men, on that path. Of asses I have two thousand – it looks like the end is near, I can feel death closing in on my borrowed soul! – and of yaks nine thousand. My greatness is known throughout the land; I have gold piled up in a storehouse, and for a people I have the Kirghiz of the six fathers;* my fame has traveled throughout the world – 'Kökötöy', they say, 'is a very rich man!' I have two rooms full of silver and sixty barns packed full of polished white rice. A thousand precious gems: ninety emeralds – see for yourself, all of it! – rubies, sapphires, pearls, two rooms of those – of such wonders as eyes can see and ears can hear I have much! There's *buulum* and *buta*, eighty

---

1.   In the last testament that follows, Kökötöy frequently alternates between prohibiting and enjoining lavish expenditures on his funeral obsequies. See the comparative note, "Kökötöy's testament" (pp. 290–91).

thousand robes made of *deyilde*, masses of brocaded red cloth and *zerisabar*.

"But my only son, Boqmurun! I know he's been a mischief-maker his whole life; he's got no sense. Fifteen years old this year and without consulting anyone he hears talk of Aqun and Tülkü in Ooghan, hears talk of their great wealth, of Qanïshay daughter of Tülkü. Love and desire are nothing but fun and games for him! Off he's gone, my son, to fetch her, and before he returns evil death will take me! I depart without seeing my son! He's gone on a long journey and filled my heart with troubles. Almighty God, hold back death from a man consumed with sorrow! The willows I've planted remain; the cattle I've pastured remain; the money I've amassed remains; the wives I married remain, grieving widows; the slaves remain that I have acquired in the course of managing my vast holdings. God gave me property, but a small family. My only son Boqmurun has no direction in life, he's drunk on wealth. Don't let him slaughter the lamb and leave the mother bleating! Don't let him slaughter the mother and leave the lamb an orphan! Don't let him scatter my wealth and goods and abandon my cattle and leave them lowing, don't let him slaughter the yaks and leave my soul in the torments of hell! Don't let him set my camels free, or slaughter my yearling fillies and make the mares neigh – not one whinny!

"Think deeply on this, for I have wealth and property of every kind: don't let it be strewn all over the earth! My racer, Maaniker, my six storerooms full of goods – don't let the doors of my treasury be opened! Don't allow my abundance of gold to be scattered among all the peoples, Infidel and Muslim alike! My herds of horses fill six river valleys, and I have huge amounts of property and goods; don't let the mullahs and *khojas* steal them! Don't even let them look! Don't open the doors of my treasury and let my abundant gold, cows, and camels be distributed among the peoples, Infidel and Muslim! Don't squander my possessions, don't break up my herds as if you were clothing a bride so generously in *kete*-silk that the hem of her gown drags on the ground as she moves liltingly along, as if you were clothing girls so generously in red brocade that the hems of their red brocade garments drag on the ground as they walk winsomely along! For the solemnities on the day of my death don't let them dig a fancy grave with the niche hollowed out and present to the mullah who performs the *dooron* three hundred camels with curling tusks, dangling lower lips, towering humps and necks as slender as a duck's, and nine hundred virgin mares, and three thousand cows; and drive six hundred oxen with massive horns in among the cows; and, to please the people near and far, don't slaughter large numbers of sheep, don't go to all that trouble! My abundant wealth sits unclaimed; my son is under age, fifteen years old. Don't count out a thousand silver ingots and spread the word that Bay Kökötöy has died; don't count out ten thousand gold coins and make a fanfare all over the world that Bay Kökötöy has died! Don't gather all the people from the seven climes, tread the earth to dust, have split firewood set alight, and invite every single Infidel and Muslim, and thus exhaust all my wealth! Don't lay me on a golden bier or have me wrapped in white muslin with a border, or do anything fancy for the laying-out of my corpse! For my departure to the next world don't spend a lot of money; don't have me shaved with a saber or washed with kumiss,* or have me tied up head to toe in red brocade; don't get a leading prince to wash my body, or have it tied up in cloth of gold, or washed with water of Zamzam or clad in a corselet, or wrapped in *shayinggi*; don't let the bards sing my praises; don't entomb me in any sacred place or lay my bones to rest with a distribution of my great riches! Do not try to bear my body to its final rest in any way that violates this legitimate testament!

"Don't have a messenger mounted on Maani-ker, clad in a mail-shirt and sent out to tell all the people on the face of this illusory world, 'Bay Kökötöy has died, he has seen the ultimate worthlessness of his earthly riches and has gone to the true life beyond; Kökötöy's daughters have reached adolescence and his wealth has grown thick as grass in springtime, so come and cast earth on his grave!' Don't let countless multitudes of people come, or let tramping armies descend; make sure that my only son Boqmurun doesn't go to all that trouble, make sure he follows my instructions! Don't let anyone go off under the sun and bring the news to Küböy, for that would set a precedent for one and all! Don't let anyone go off under the moon and bring the news to Abay, or let everyone gather and come together at my memorial feast! Don't let my son bring such affliction upon the entire Kirghiz population; see that he looks to his own strengths!

"To the end of the earth – to him who has his residence beyond that limit – who has his stronghold in the deserts of Jazïyra, to Choyun Alp son of Donghoq of immense size, of the race of giants; to scissor-eared Qaman Alp, to the evil folk on the frontiers of Jajuj and Majuj – do not send the news! Nor to the iron-naveled Kiten who swarm in masses, who are descended not from *divs* but from *peris*; nor to the *jinns* and demons this side of Köyqap mountain – they have a throne of gold that they grew out of the ground, for they are versed in magic; there is a stream there called Saghïra, the abode of no one but *peris* – don't set a messenger atop Maani-ker to announce over the whole face of the earth what has befallen me; don't have anyone bring news of my death to the black bastard *divs* and then turn back home; don't let anyone survey the city of Qaqan, go in among the Qaz-moyul people, and set a bearing north by Ursa Major.

"There is a people, the Jetim-muruq, who resemble ogres, with one big ear for a covering inside which they take defensive measures if they hear of an enemy, and the other ear they use as a bedroll; their eyes are on their foreheads, and they are like roaming animals with less sense than a simpleton; listening to them one cannot fathom their muttering speech; you would say they are animal rather than human, and each one has a horn longer than a lance – God Almighty has created all kinds! – their chief is called Küshön, of mixed descent from both *divs* and *peris*, whose abode is hard by Köyqap; an ordinary mortal who ran across him would perish at the sight – let no one tell them the news! May no such destruction befall any man of our people!

"In the west there are red-haired giants who ride no animals but go on foot, with legs like minarets and arms like poplars; each step they take is a hundred fathoms; they eat the dirt off the ground and sink trenches just by walking or standing. Let no one send the news to such as them, let it not result in a loss for all the sons of the Kirghiz!

"There is that one that ranges through the western lands, that roams the southern reaches, with six wings and four legs, whose hoof-beats strike the ground alight in blazing red flames; who flies at a gallop beneath the cloudy sky and over the billowing grass such as no man has ever known; the rocks that shoot up from his pounding hooves land at a distance of a morning's ride, farther than the eye can see; my horse – my *tulpar* – Maani-ker! Baymïrza son of Bay, I have a bone to pick with my son: after I have suddenly died and my only son Boqmurun has appeared home out of nowhere, don't let him tell the news and say 'My father has died – come!' to that thorough intimate of heroes begotten of Bay Jaqïp, the tiger, Baatïr Manas, a lion among men, who in his ferocity has conquered countries; don't let the sons of the Kirghiz of the forty tribes arrive with an outcry!

"My son must not say to those arriving in tears, 'Let this order of mine go out to the world; they shall know of my brotherliness! I will clothe my guests in robes of honor, and if they lament my dear father, if they halt, submerged in sobbing, if they wish to honor my dear father and their loudly wailing voices fill the skies to bursting, I will honor such men, I'll give them whatever I can and say, "Be wealthy!" for a blessing.'

"Do not let the excitable little rascal receive the people of Qumul! Do not let him assemble the many peoples from far-off lands, from Oluya-Ata, Tashken, populous Qoqon, or Marghalang; from the city in the valley, Samarqan, or Oro-töbö, or Qojont; from the city in the ravine, Qoton – or sow discord among those peoples! Or go to Jerkent of the seventy cities, or the country around Baghdat, or range along by Badaqshan or Balïq, Qïrïm or Balïq – he mustn't tell the Qïtay or Orus! Make sure he does not spread the news to the ignorant and enlightened alike that he intends to pay last respects to his father's remains!

"There is a land, they say, at the edge of the world where seventy tribes live, while the Arabs make their homes in the desert, and the Ayat make their homes by lakes; dwarves, and the Itaalï, the women of whom are human, but the men dogs* – I have heard of those, don't let him send the news to them! Or to Mïsïr or Qudus – don't let him bring great affliction on the sons of the Qara Kirghiz!

"The Qazaq, Kirghiz, and Qataghan, the Jediger, Noyghut, and Dumara – all of us are descended from one father. Together with the Qalmaq, who are so populous, we descend from Man-ghul. The Manghul are related to the Tatar – death follows life for one and all, and every living soul has its time! – There are Qaraqalpaq, Üyshün, Qanglï, Teyit, Baghïsh, and so many countries where talk of the Qara Kirghiz has spread.

"Among the Qalmaq there are the Tïrghoot and Shibe, who eat frogs, snakes, and serpents; don't let them swoop down on the Kirghiz, don't invite the swarming Qïtay to the memorial feast! Notwithstanding, Ïndïstan and the cities of Qoroson have much to be fearful of the Kirghiz, from the sword of him who invites and entertains by command!

"The seas of Lop and Shor – there are all kinds of folk in those places: the beings called Quturuq, with backsides of fish and heads of men, who live a thousand years and suck thirty-fathom sheatfish into their mouths for food; and those called the Bayandas, with legs divided like people and heads that look like fish; and another aquatic race are the *jinns* called Jetelek. In that sea are forty-winged birds, astounding creatures, each one with eighty heads, that eat emeralds and live, each of them, five or six thousand years.

"And there is a bear called Ketechek with hair like ropes sev-eral fathoms long. So many creatures walk on dry land, and those parts have some besides! Panthers, tigers, lions, and even such beings as the aquatic Ayïs and the Suruq, who capture water-tigers; some of them have two heads and some seven, with swords for fingernails and stones for eyes, navels of iron and teeth of fine steel; none of those beings takes shelter in a lair, be it winter or summer. Seas there are, and many lakes, and under the waters of the seas, deserts where not a soul lives. Under the seas there are many mountains as well, abounding in various foes who would swallow each other on sight. Do not send the news to such as them! Let it not result in a loss for all the Qara Kirghiz!

"After I have died and trekked on from this world, after the candle of my soul has burned out, seven river valleys full of herds will remain; seventy kinds of trees planted on seven *tash* of land will remain; seven tents full of gold and silver, seven thousand five hundred *nar* camels, and three thousand two-humped camels remain; my neighbor, that giant Qoshoy, remains.

Baymïrza must take careful note of all the fruit trees in my orchards, for there is no lack there: apples, walnuts, grapes – the people know and are apprised that I have filled six *tash* of land with every sort of grapevine; yet let the Kirghiz not take it as an example, for all their works and achievements shall not remain come Judgment Day!

"Don't let Boqmurun get a great many tawny-headed sheep and have them counted out and make a big clamor before the people, 'I will give my father's memorial feast!' and divide off eleven thousand head from the herds of horses, and spread the news to the masses, and have four thousand camels readied and such a great quantity of cattle driven on and moved in for the first prize in the horse race, with cameleers tending the herds of camels – four hundred persons in all to go along – horse-herds accompanying the horses with the mares tied up, and out of those four hundred people twelve to manage things; and of cows, large cattle as they're called, driving two thousand; – pay close attention to my words, they are worthy of respect! – and having them elect fifty out of those four hundred people, thirty women and twenty men – don't allow those to be the overseers!

"Do not gather and flaunt the riches I have at my court for the common people to see! My emeralds, precious gems, *zerisabar*, rubies, sapphires – don't let them be set and displayed on my mourning-effigy! I have a son who's impetuous, see that he doesn't use up my prodigious wealth! See that my pearls, my coral, my necklaces of coral are not advertised and put on exhibition to the commoners; that no sort of precious luxuries of mine are gracelessly shown off before my mourning-effigy. Let none of these many fine things of mine come under the gaze of the common people; let my dear spouse Külqanïsh not sit beside my mourning-effigy! *Buulum*, *buta*, *dürüyö*-silks – all part of this transient world! Let not the women of my people raise their voices from morning till night day after day in weeping. Let not the young brides and maidens of my household sing laments, 'My padishah–father is no more!' or dwell upon my praises, or enumerate my riches, for those who do not know first-hand will think it empty boasting, and shake their heads and criticize. Let them not lament me from morning till night, harping on till the meat's cooked through; let them not lament me at any time, harping on till the food's cooked through; they may do right by my earthly remains but still leave openings for criticism.

"Alongside Tashken is a broad island where our herds fill the steppe; alongside the dusty tracks is a broad island where our herds fill the mountains! Do not let Boqmurun slaughter a mare for the evening meal, or a yearling foal for the midday meal, or a sheep for refreshment during the day, or dissipate the khanly prestige I have achieved among the Kirghiz by squandering my herds or misjudging my greatness; may he not figure out how to open my ninety-foot-wide iron chest with its nine keys and its hundred bolts and scatter all my red gold coin and pale silver ingots over the whole world!

"For the banquet on the day of my burial have a Ninety* slaughtered[1] – make it a hundred, for there will be guests to feed, and those who arrive should be honored, and respect shown for their hunger, so let them eat their fill – and have the pitiless grave dug and my body placed in the niche, and give the grave diggers their gratuity, the opening of the niche having been set in on the right-hand side, and turn my face toward the *qibla*;* give these sound instructions to my orphaned son Boqmurun! Have me wound in brocade and washed with water of Zamzam by ninety mendicants; have my earthly form wound in red brocade, all the windings having been washed in kumiss; have me dressed in a corselet and wrapped in *shayinggi*; have me entombed in a sacred place, and singers sing my praises; have me entombed by men of good repute, and poets sing my praises; have mullahs come from Badaqshan and Baliq, from the Arab people, chief and first among Muslims, from Misïr and Qabïl, from countries that excel in learning – mullahs from all kinds of lands full-of-mullahs who never let their Qur'ans out of their hands – and have a Ninety of white camels presented when you go out to meet the arriving esteemed ones, and fit out as funeral offerings a roan stallion and a bay stallion; and have

---

1.   From this point Kökötöy begins to speak of his wishes in positive terms, which contradict his earlier instructions for frugality. See the comparative note, "Kökötöy's testament" (pp. 290–91).

the learned men of this world read the Qur'an for three months, having welcomed all those mullahs who come and having supplied anything they may lack; and have water from the well of Zamzam sprinkled on my shroud; have nine thousand blue-black horses, all of them fat and sleek, presented to the performer of the *dooron*! Say, 'Kökötöy has died!' and comfort anyone who arrives to see and is down-hearted.

"Let my riches be used up; let the people know I have died! I have amassed great wealth, but I have felt regret for the poor; there are people that have felt my generosity – from olden days we have our customs with the dead! – there are quarters that have felt my benefactions. And there is a young lad who has lost his papa! Allow room to everyone who comes mourning my passing, out to the distance of half a *tash*, to raise their lamentations; let them pay respects to my departed spirit, and let my wives,* their heads wrapped in white scarves, recount my obituaries and cry 'Our father!', and let it be an example to the rest. My only son Boqmurun is in love with a girl, it seems. Do not bury me until my son marries his beloved, until he can cast earth on my grave! As soon as he left I could foresee the handfuls of earth he would cast, as I have known from the beginning the truth about this awful world: the illusory world is *without* truth! Let no one be buried without a covering of earth!

"God alone made everything; without Him the wife bears no children, once born a person cannot live on without dying, and the estate one amasses on the steppe cannot exceed what is humanly possible. Holy God made Adam; man encounters all kinds of animals. There are panthers, and tigers – consider, my brethren, and understand, is there any four-footed creature that cannot be man's captive? Lions and lionesses, the noblest of all beasts, the most courageous of animals, have their native haunts, but even they cannot escape a man. By the will of Allah, the Forty Chilten cannot be caught! There is also the *ketelik*, another animal, and the *qutulas*; the elk,* the elephant – all of them, know well, sons of men, at our disposal for sacrifice, within our ability to restrain! The ounce, the bear, the wolf all fear men; their wish is never to see a man, for man is greater than they!

"The Almighty One has given us greed, and once that greed

entered us it became our misfortune, inseparable from us. Unavoidable death has become an iron perch, and today I have come to roost upon it! I lose all hope for this false, perishable world! If there were no mountains or heights, we would not appreciate the steppe; if man were free of evil, we would not value the good! Animals make their homes on slopes of mountains mottled white with snow. You of black hair and bent legs, consider this well!

"If you wish to understand it all, you who are descended from Adam our ancestor, then know that ultimately not one man shall remain in this false world; never has one of our ancestors said, 'I will remain' and done so, never has anyone built a defense against death! The Lord of earth and sky walks with you, unseen by your eyes. He, after all, is power, He is strength; He inhabits you from top to toe. It is He who gives to you according to your attitude. If you do bad things and pray that good things be given unto you, He is always suffused within you, observing when you do ill, walking right beside, suffused in you. Many a soul has eyes and the ability to see, yet knows not what to do; 'God has punished me!' are the words of the damned. There is no relief from Him on any side; your God is aware and hears each and every thing you say. Both within you and without you, He is there. You do not heed your Master as long as you are free, but do wrong to someone and get your deserts, and suddenly you are praying for the Creator's mercy on your soul! There is something called Greed, an undisputed enemy – know it well! There is another enemy who never dies, alive inside you, called Wrath, and this Wrath has the tongue of the devil. Greed and Wrath originate in hell; Haughtiness, another one of your enemies – where does it come from? – from the devil! Know this, all of you, great and small: The devil is your greatest enemy! Your closest kinsmen, always there to help you, are your Intelligence and Honesty and Self-restraint; if you make friends with these, then in the final reckoning you shall not suffer the onslaughts of Judgment Day! May your souls be at peace, may the worst of all your enemies be a lazybones! If you do all your work lazily, you shall find yourself quite alone!

"These are the words of Kökötöy son of Janadil to Baymïrza!

You have been a person near to my heart – I say, don't rush me, my boy – Having reached the age of eighty-four I meet my death, yet without Boqmurun standing beside me and hearing my last testament! Don't let my dear Qanïshay* and Külayïm sit for a full year, for twelve full months wearing black, covering themselves with black silks adorned with pure gold, throwing a black shawl over their heads, putting money into the treasury and constructing my mourning-effigy out of all kinds of finery in a large white tent![1] Let them not sit forever paying their respects to me and weeping and wailing without stopping; let them not spread the news to the whole world! What's the use of going to all the trouble to have the fattest animals slaughtered, to have the racing-prizes set aside, to mount a messenger on Maani-ker, to clothe him in a corselet, and to send the news across this whole transient world – to bring the news to the Qïtay with their evil intentions, separated from men since the time of Adam, who marry their own sisters and hate their fathers, and for this reason were separated from us?

"The teeming Öyrot with their red topknots* and the faithless Qïtay have a great many formidable leaders! 'Muradïl son of Qïrmuz, train up your horse Qïl-jeyren! The first prize is beyond reckoning, and if your horse wins, it shall be yours! Nowhere else in the world is there such wealth!' – don't say that! To that great chief of the Qïtay, red-topknotted Nezqara: 'Train up your horse Chabdar, get ready for racing! Where else are there such prizes? One of the Qara Kirghiz, Kökötöy, has passed away; put Too-toru in reserve as a driver-in-at-the-finish!' – don't let Jash Aydar, who knows seventy languages and shows great zeal at the very mention of the Religion, who grew up an orphan, whom God sends a share of food and drink from the lands and waters of the earth, visit that Nezqara!

"Don't bring the news to black-maned Boroonchu, saying, 'Nowhere else in the world is there entertainment such as this! Train up your horse Qïl-küröng and choose a boy to race him!' – don't be in a hurry to visit that one!

1. Here Kökötöy switches back to prohibitions. See the comparative note, "Kökötöy's testament" (pp. 290–91).

"Do not let him reach Oronghu, who lives by the banks of the Oyuq, whom no man has ever beaten – that one called Oronghu is a woman, a soreheaded grouch of an unbeliever, the fat on her face twelve fingers thick, her flesh like a scabby epiglottis, the fat on her backside four fingers thick! – and say, 'Train up your Qula-bee, nowhere on earth have such arrangements ever been made! The wealthy man named Kökötöy has passed away in the wide land of Türkestan!'

"There is a people called the Sïyqïn who have a *div* named Suqal, who never in their lives see a horse, so the greater part of them go on foot – a nation of rogues, with all kinds of giants five hundred fathoms tall whose manners are not those of men; whose custom is to eat the sheatfish from the sea; don't let Jash Aydar say to Suqal, 'Train up your horse Sal-qashqa, get ready for racing!'

"Do not let him turn southward and say to Alooke of the Soloon, 'Train up your horse Aq-böyröq and choose a boy to race him!' Don't let the news be spread to that Qalmaq named Ushang; by no means let him hear of it, saying, 'Train up your Sal-qula, such a memorial feast is surely out of the ordinary!'

"Don't let everyone know about all the herds of animals being set up for the racing-prizes, or about Bay Kökötöy's level of prosperity! Do not let him pass on from there and reach him whose father entered into no betrothal – there is no mistake in saying it! – Alp Joloy, whose mother entered into no marriage; our people have no fighter as tough as he! Don't say, 'Train up your horse Ach-buudan and choose a smart jockey!'

"There is a tribe called the Toqshuker who reside in Choyunchang; do not let Jash Aydar go to Bozkertik there! 'Broad of girth and long of neck, his croup towering like a gray hill,* Boz-changhïl – if you have such a racer, train him up! The rich man known as Kökötöy has died in the place known as Türkestan, so find a boy to race Changhïl-boz and enter him in the race!' – do not pass by that way spreading the news!

"Soorondük son of Solobo is the foremost hero of the Chong Beejin; that's a powerful tribe who leave no one who goes to war with them in good health! 'Train up your Tel-küröng; there's a skill known as horse-racing, so prepare yourself!' – don't let Jash Aydar pass by Soorondük!

"Now, at Emil there are two rivers, a notable feature of that country – the saying has become proverbial – and at the present time there is a white-beard who made off toward Qïtay along paths untrodden by the Kirghiz, who, unable to turn back once ejected by the Qara Kirghiz, sought a place among the Qalmaq – old Khan Alooke; but he who rules a multitude of men, who forsook the land of Anjïyan, who keeps his cool when the enemy engages, Alooke's formidable son Qongurbay – go and tell *him*![1] Go without fear and say that he should train up his horse Al'-ghara, that the man whose horse comes in first in the race shall gain some profit on Bay Kökötöy's account!

"To everyone Jash Aydar visits, without exception – young and old, even *nar* camels bearing their loads – let him make his eloquent speech and tell the men who vie for glory not to drag their heels but to get moving and come, for their honor's sake! Of heroes who grasp iron-tipped lances and make them flash in single combat fearlessly as the blows land, let him omit no one! Of those wrestlers with massive forearms skilled at grappling opponents by the pant-legs and trouncing them, who can beat a thousand single-handed – let none of those wrestlers sit this out! To those who say, 'Who was this Bay Kökötöy? I'll just stay quietly at home, never mind showing up for this child of the teeming Kirghiz who says, "Come to my father's memorial feast!"' – it will be their death! I'll show them this is no lie, but the honest truth! I command it!

"When he departs from those of Qïtay lineage, let him not deliver the news to the dwarves or the Itaali![2] He mustn't make the dwarves' eyes start from their heads saying Khan Kökötöy has died! Their women are human but their men are dogs, that was the will of Almighty God, and if one of their dogs puts his tail in water, it rains. There's no flowing water there, only lakes, but the fires they kindle are hot like ours; desert everywhere and not a puff of wind, but the cattle bring forth offspring

1. Kökötöy reverts to do's . . .
2. . . . Then back to don'ts.

there – don't let Jash Aydar mix with them and then pass by, or bring the news to the tribe known as Küsayïsh! There are deer on their mountains and an island called Türmö-qarïsh; on the near side of that place is the sea of Lop. There are all kinds of places!

"There are *peris* to the south, and a vast lake that's a five months' journey to cross, and the desert of Qubayïs; there is a giant called Choyun Qulaq and his people, called Chong Tarang, who grow up making the sign of the cross according to their custom: do not let Jash Aydar bring the news to the Tarang, saying, 'Train up your horse Chong-ala, choose a boy to race him! The riches you seek are in our land, Türkestan!' Don't let that be the cause of an uncontrollable uproar that brings disaster upon all the sons of the Kirghiz!

"Do not let Jash Aydar turn to the west and spur his horse on, letting Maani-ker get worked up to his full strength, and go flying and thundering along! Those to the west will scorn you for mentioning the Prophet, for they know no tale besides that of their 'Lord', which they'll tell you from start to finish, and say, 'Our Lord is the creator, and no one else made us.'* The worst of all the Heathens, should Jash Aydar get so far in carrying the news, is a big man named Qashalaq, who himself alone has seven hundred thousand slaves. If you say, 'There are such beings as angels and devils', he will kill you in an instant for saying such a thing. That people's khan, named Qashalaq, is the biggest villain there is among the Heathens. He has a horse called Shalqï-ker; he himself is a being different from human; do not let Jash Aydar travel west, to the ends of the earth, and say, 'Train up your Shalqï-ker!' There's a howling wind there, a danger to men's borrowed souls. A man sent flying by that wind doesn't stand a chance; let his head be made of stone, it's still the end of the world for him. There's no remedy but death; once borne away on that wind your parentage avails you naught.

"Do not let my herald go downstream from there on the right hand; let him go no further! *Peris* there are none, but *divs* there are with soot five inches thick on their faces and no belts about their waists; though they live a thousand years, not one day do they ever wash their faces! Their nails grow unclipped, and never in their lives do their bodies enter the water! Barefooted,

bareheaded, covered with hair, they go about naked, with heads
the size of feasting-cauldrons, the brows above their eyes like
black he-wolves lying prone, each single strand of their hair like
a long black lead-rope; their mouths so large a horse's head
would fit inside, teeth like rocky cliffs, ears flopping loosely
about like a herdsman's fur hat with the flaps down, snot flowing
from their noses like the torrent that rushes out from under a
glacier! If you wish to know their lineage, it's Köshönggür:
descended not from *peris* or *jinns*, not quite resembling humans
either; if you wish to know what to call them, it's *div*, and they
eat the grass like animals, and use one ear for a covering and the
other ear for a bedroll. So wild are they that they live even in the
rocks, even in the water. Their appearance is like an animal, but
with ears for covers and bedding. They make their home in
Jazïyra and Qap – I should mention they are descended from
Töshölük the *div*. They teem in numbers beyond reckoning, a
people known for their fiendishness, yet they differ somewhat
from *divs* and *peris*. One of them is named Aqdöö, their wise
chief; one is named Kökdöö, and they live at Qap and Jazïyra,
quite near to humans. Animals unused to Köyqap that wander
there live on and on and never die, every single one! They have
women there too, who provide the food, though no one erects
any tents, and they go around naked like the men, I suppose. If
one of us were to stray away from our country and see one, if we
strayed away from our land and saw one of their ravishingly
beautiful girls – just imagine a son of the Kirghiz happening
upon her and seeing her walking around – it would nearly make
his heart leap from his breast and kill him! Do not let Jash Aydar
carry the news to Kökdöö! Let it not result in a loss for the teem-
ing sons of the Kirghiz!

"Don't let him go to Medine and Meke, to the Arabs of the
five tribes! One of those tribes is Qurayïsh, whose works are
those of the Almighty – don't let him go to that prince, the
Prophet's descendant, the old man, Mazabïl by name, and bring
the news that the rich man named Kökötöy has passed away,
and tell him to come and pay respects; and don't let Jash Aydar
pass on from there!

"There are camping-grounds in the valley of the Orol where

the twelve tribes of the Orus are found. All their affairs are well
managed by their heroes and strong-men, and enemies who
approach them looking for a fight are torn to pieces. Don't let
Jash Aydar tell them the news, let it not result in a loss for all
the sons of the Kirghiz!

"Let him not pass on from there, to Badaqshan and Balïq, to
the Tajik, those people with a different forefather. Their khan is
Abdïlqadïr, who has an army of a hundred thousand men. Don't
let Jash Aydar tell them the news and say, 'Train up Qachïr-ker!
Khan Kökötöy has died all of a sudden, so ready yourselves
without fail, and if your horse should surprise us and win the
race, the amount of your takings will be the likes of which there
is none other on earth!' Don't let that suffering befall our land!

"If your Aydar should spring onto his horse and proceed on
from there – for in my mind's eye I can see him delivering every
single one of his invitations between Buqaray-sharïp and the
ruins of Chambïl! – do not let him go to him who lives, ungov-
erned by anyone, on the middle Chatqal, and wears a tunic
impenetrable by bullets – Muzburchaq son of Buudayïq, and
say, 'Train up your Muz-qara! None other than Kökötöy Bay
has died, so buck up and set your mind to it!'

"Don't let him pass on from there, don't let him turn to the
south, where food is dear and salt is cheap, where the summers
are awful and the winters not bad; there's a stalwart man of the
Qïpchaq whose people never stray from his borders, named
Eleman, the rich: his permanent quarters are at Qoton, and his
wife's clothes are of *torghun*, *tubar*, and *shayï* silks.

"Do not let him go to Er Töshtük who keeps his horse Chal-
quyruq and summers on Kerme-too, and rush in with the news,
saying, 'Bay Kökötöy has died, and beasts have been allocated
for the first prize in the race! He whose horse overtakes the
others gets it, and all those with no racers will be left burning
with regret!' Don't let him deliver that news and move on!

"In Samarqan there is Sanchï – don't let Jash Aydar bring
him the news and move on!

"Now, there is one who makes his home on the broad Talas,
fierce in his fury, whom no opponent can beat in a fight: do not
let Jash Aydar go to that one whose home and kin are in Talas,

that paramount hero, Manas, and give him the news, saying, 'Khan Kökötöy has died; he has succumbed to the will of Almighty God, Allah! They have buried him with dignity, now you preside over his memorial feast!' By bringing him here thus you would cause unspeakable woes for my tiny handful of people! Don't go to Er Manas and say, 'Any man with some learning must know that as long as there are sons of Adam, cruelty abounds; one hears the angry words of all sorts of enemies and afflicts them in turn; one's eyes close, never to open again, and then let him fear for his borrowed soul! If he has amassed great wealth and his animals have multiplied until they no longer fit upon the face of the earth, but his wives never gave birth before they reached old age, so that he leaves no child;* and if his herds remain on the hoof, his paternal relations can then say, "Since the herds remain in place and haven't been passed down to a son, split them up, divide everything up as spoils," for that is the cruel way things are done! The herds of a man who dies without issue are constantly beset by enemy armies, and his relations contend with one another! A man who dies unblessed by sons may as well have five kopecks to his name, it's all for naught!' Don't go to Er Manas and say, 'God Who made everything is my only help in the afterlife!' Don't go say those things to that lion, don't have Maani-ker ridden to exhaustion and make that hero weep at the news, and then pass on! He's a sympathetic hero, don't make his chest heave in sorrow.

"Don't let Jash Aydar pass on from there to that world-famous master of nimble oratory, Ürbü of the Qïpchaq, son of Taz, and say, 'Train up your twin black horses and find a summering-place for your people on the upland pastures! Kökötöy's memorial feast is going to be a wonder to behold and an occasion of entertainment for all the Infidels and Muslims who assemble for the righteous proceedings!' Don't have him tell everybody, 'Come see heroes in heated contention, wrestlers struggling for holds, wise orators winning debates, skillful riders wrestling on horseback, and marksmen shooting muskets; – and, since we're calling it a feast, people dining on every sort of dish! – wise men doing business, engaged in give-and-take; race-horses taking the prizes, everybody getting something out of it – wrestling, the untether-the-camel game, roughnecks playing cross-the-lake, judging elephants by piling loads on them, the tug of war to test men's strength, swimmers diving bravely into the rapids and racing to victory – and so that you will know well that this man has died, that the solemnities for Kökötöy are well carried out, the president of the feast will be none other than that child of the Kirghiz, Manas son of Bay Jaqïp' – don't have your herald say that to them and pass onward, don't let him depart from there with long-suffering Maani-ker on an endless errand!

"There is one who summers in the Sarï-arqa, who lords it over the numerous Qazaq, who never shrinks from a foe in battle, who keeps his horse Kök-ala – his copper boot-heels capped in gold – Er Kökchö son of Aydar Khan: these descendants of Ughuz, rich and poor alike, will have a frightful time! Those swarming enemies, the Qalmaq and Qïtay with their topknots red as blazing fire – those sons of the Qalmaq and Qïtay, at the very mention of Khan Kökötöy's memorial feast will all come on a-hungering – if we invite them and tell them to come, then Kökchö the Qazaqs' grandee will give them the command, and then will woe befall my people! Letting him know the location of the feast would make me like the victim of a bird of prey! The teeming Kirghiz would be sunk in poverty.

"Baymïrza, here beside me, have you heeded what I have said? Though I prepare to leave this world, while my soul has not fled I wish to speak unhurriedly, in behalf of him who is still living this transient life, so that the admonitions I leave behind may serve as guidance for my posterity: tell everything I have said to my son, Boqmurun! See that he doesn't try to breed his young ewes;* let the sheep grow fat! See that he castrates his rams and makes wethers of them! See that he castrates his stallions and makes geldings of them! But I would also say to my son: learn by heart every one of the thousand and one names of Allah, omitting none, for by learning the names of God and respectfully caring for the people you will not upset their harmony. All the children of Adam must know the ways of death, both for the present and for times to come! Our forefathers said, 'One man's daily bread is no good for another'; our forebears said, 'One man's fortune is no fortune for another'. Gold and silver I leave behind; unthinkingly I have devoted myself to this illusory world! *Nar* and two-humped camels I leave behind; cattle beyond reckoning I leave behind; my dear Ayghanïsh and Küljar I leave behind!* Islam, one learns, is the true religion; its summit is in heaven. Learned men know this: that the true sharia is our support, and both the living and the dead require cattle, come what may. I worked hard in my youth and the Almighty Creator gave me wealth. I adopted the son of a spirit;* will my words of paternal greeting reach my son? Those of Kirghiz lineage are a great nation who teem in their multitudes in Oluya-Ata, great Tashken, Oro-töbö, Samarqan, populous Qoqon and Marghalang. Numerous as they are those people have lived in submission and practiced the Qalmaq religion, though being Kirghiz by nature they must not remain as Qalmaqs.* Make sure that my son delivers this appeal to my kinsman, the lion Manas!"

Having spoken these words Kökötöy let out a puff of bluish smoke, and his soul escaped his breast.

The many people standing before him raised a great cry. One is filled with regret for the dead; one is left with nothing but bitter tears. "He's died!" they cried in their sorrow as they bent over his corpse and wept. This transitory world is a false one! Every one of the sons of the Kirghiz was reduced to sobbing.

His son Er Boqmurun arrived home just as they were laying out the body, and Qanïshay the daughter of Tülkü gave out a polite cry of grief upon the death of her father-in-law, which built to an anguished groan. As they say, "from the bride's legs and the shepherd's staff"* – that's what we've been taught. Boqmurun came on weeping and wailing in his sorrow that he had gone away and would never see his father alive again.

"Father, who had me swaddled and laid on a bed of down, who had me housed on well-trodden ground, who consoled me when I cried and had me clothed in white *qadek*, who fed me the choicest honey of all the sweets, the choicest mane-fat of all such delicacies, who picked out for me a yearling from among the amblers, who picked out the finest *shayï* from among the *torqo*-silks, who felt joy at my laughter and distress at my tears, who sacrificed tawny-headed sheep for me, who called for me when I went out of sight, who fed me on the best fruits from all over and made me sole owner of a fortune to compare with any other on earth – have you really gone to your grave?! Have you really passed on with your wish unfulfilled to see and bless me once more? I ignored your august advice, and now death's poison has found you out before I could return home from my long journey! Death has arrested you before you could give your last testament! Dear father, I could not look in your eyes one last time while you lived!" Having uttered these words with a great cry Boqmurun gave himself over to intense sobbing and shuddering fits of tears; his body, quivering like a branch submerged in a stream, was racked with sobs.

The populace of spacious Tashken was thrown into confusion, young and old alike. Not a soul among the sons of the Kirghiz was without grief; they said, "He was a horse to those on foot, a man apart from cruel oppressors, food to the hungry; to us, who loved him dearly, he was the outright leader of the Kirghiz! Our tears of grief fall down – our Kirghiz leader, have you really left us?! Taxing the people was the way of our previous rulers, but Kökötöy was as a coat to the frozen; in this false world his wealth was enormous! If you were a falconer, he was your bird of prey; if the sons of the Kirghiz experienced discomfiture, he was their black hawk of good omen and inescapable, gnashing talons! Such was our prince. God has delivered death to our iron-taloned one, to our gyrfalcon with talons of watered steel; he who was our corselet has crumpled – died! In stature like a spruce tree running generously with fresh sap, he was good in so many ways to the sons of the teeming Kirghiz!"

When they saw that Kökötöy had died, the people of the wide realm of Ughuz grieved, and bent over his corpse weeping and wailing in their distress at his passing; not one of them was unmoved as the tears flowed and they spoke those words, as the many sorts of common people gave themselves over to bitter sobbing.

There was no one to speak a word to quieten them, so it was not until the middle of the night with stars shining all around that the people managed to take a breath and stop their crying. Looking about at the crowds and seeing that calm had prevailed, Baymïrza of the black beard quieted his own bawling voice and went outside, leading the boy Boqmurun, whose tears no one as yet could keep from flowing. Having looked right and left to see that no one was around and having checked the yurt-covering for listening-holes, he sat the boy down and gave him the speech he had prepared:

"Give a feast for your father like the banquet for a new daughter-in-law; put on games as for an old woman. What your own dear father said to me, his last testament, was 'Do not let my people, the Qïr Ughuz, ravage my wealth with feasting. You can ravage away but you can't make a dead man rise again! Have them quietly bury me without all the mischief, have them bury my worthless remains. Then keep my tin-faced gate between the people and my shining gold and silver; do not let them open it with a key and scatter my wealth!'

"In making his last testament your father had us invite great numbers of people from all over this transient world. I had never heard of some of the names he gave; he omitted no one of human parentage, not one of the descendants of Adam! As death came on he thought of all sorts of advice. His body was in so much pain that I wondered if he was delirious – I heard him mention so many different peoples that I kept asking myself, What is the origin of that tribe? One could see that death was at hand, and I wasn't sure whether he still had control of his mind. He lay for two or three days; I couldn't see why he wasn't getting exhausted, but he left out not a single place on the face of this illusory world! Your father thought out a massive piece of counsel once he had laid himself down! I wondered, were his thoughts under the influence of a black spirit as malevolent death made ready its final approach? Or was he perhaps playing around and making empty jokes? 'Once I have passed on all of a sudden, once I have suddenly died, ride my horse Maani-ker hard and bring everyone together, from east and west! My wealth is so great that I shan't be a burden on anyone in the world: deliver the news to every land that everyone on the face of the earth is assembling!' he said, and then: 'Impose no levies on my Qara Kirghiz people! However much the expenses come to, I have plenty of wealth to cover them; clearly no one will be saddled with the cost!'* He named all sorts of peoples that no one has ever heard of, and certainly no one has ever met in person: 'Omit none of the descendants of Adam!' he said; he wanted the news sent not only to the people on this side of the earth but also to the *divs* and *peris* on the other side. Deliver the news, he said, and give food to all the people, even the fish-men of the sea! The last testament your father gave was a speech unlike any I have ever heard before – it seems there are even more beings under the sea than on dry land! 'My wealth is extraordinary, so invite everyone to the feast!' he said.

"He ordered that no one should move from this spot for an entire year – twelve months – but when the full twelve months of the year are completed, guards should be posted in the stronghold at Tashken, and his encampment should migrate away from Tashken pretty-as-a-maiden's-skullcap, taking no one else along from other tribes – 'Make sure everyone hears that there will be pious feasting!' he said – masses of foals should be tethered on the hilly ground at Chïmïgent, and all the people, excluding only paupers, should be led onward; his vanguard encampment should move out for the summer into the Sarï-arqa. The sheep should get their spring pasturing at Qozu-bashï and Qopo;* the herds won't fatten on the grass at Boroldoy by Almatï, where they return both summer and winter. He said to have the horses fattened up on the hilly spring pastures of Altïbay, then to move on, rollicking along as you migrate, mounting brown amblers and keeping to the grassy mountainsides, the young brides donning *kete*-silks and riding gray amblers through the scrubland, the maidens wearing red garments, the young fellows shooting off guns of Urum make – 'May my people attract great admiration!' he said – the boys with their loaded guns of Barang make; 'Let all the Kirghiz sing laments, saying, "Our good grandfather has died!"' he said. The camels should have no rings put in their noses;* the people should not be allowed to wander. The cows should get lead-ropes and be milked, and the calves tied up; don't tire out the herds of cattle. Give orders to the shepherds: 'Don't tie hobbles on the rams or drive them hard on the march, and don't stop twice in the same place!' Have the shepherds drive the herds steadily on and fatten up all the cattle – so said your father as he lay there, though his throat was parched. 'Have them make their summer encampment at Üch Qarqïra and train up my horse, Maani-ker; when three years have come and gone, have my people prepare the memorial feast! On the banks of Üch Qarqïra, in the valley of the Üch-bulaq, have my people set up their yurts and send out the dreadful news of my death!'

"That was what your dear father said. Of course, I always considered him an intelligent man, but won't the spirits of departed ancestors punish us all the same? Telling us to spare no expense to put on a memorial feast such as no man has ever wished for – it's all very seductive talk – judge the horses and set them a-racing, plant and unfurl the blue standard with its blue banner – even as he died your father brought such excitement to our hearts! He wanted people all over to hear of Kökötöy's memorial feast, he wanted the multitudes of people he left behind to have it as his legacy. He said, 'Tell the sons of Ughuz to be on their guard at all times, for those damned uncircumcised pricks the Qïtays are going to steal the first prize of the thoroughbred that comes in first place in the race! Make sure the Qïtays see what that will get them!'* Whatever we're supposed to make of that, he also told us to put on jousts, and to let the prize go to whoever beat his opponent, Infidel or Muslim. He said to put on matches for the powerful wrestlers and let whoever's strength was greater throw his opponent, and to have skillful riders wrestle on horseback. He wanted every one of the world's best masters to come, and he wanted your people to eat their fill. He said, 'Invite those seeking vengeance, let them attack my people!' Your father Kökötöy said some wild and strange things! 'Turn aside,' he said, 'and put on every sort of game in the world! Have them ford the Qaynar, and let women and men compete together at untying the tethered camel!' I don't know whether it was serious or in jest, but Khan Kökötöy said, 'Let this be a guide to my survivors' –"

Baymïrza was just getting started, but Boqmurun, his eyes streaming with tears, countered him with a question: "He has gone from this false, alluring world to the next, and he's told us what to do! Baymïrza, you were his friend; I am his wretched son. Shall we do as he says, or not? You are his friend-unto-Resurrection-Day. You, please, answer me! Reward or punishment, the Creator alone knows what we'll receive!"

Baymïrza stood there shaking his head, and said, "We shouldn't do it. We'll get together some old worn-out mares with dried-out, puckered brains, some runty yearlings, a few animals like that, invite the well-off folk near the camp, and put something on like the memorial feast for an old woman, like the banquet for a new daughter-in-law. Let's do as your dear father said: bury him."

The young lad sat there looking at him, trying to fathom what he had just heard. "You should be someone I can trust, and I should be the one to act!" said Boqmurun, clapping his hands.

Baymïrza stood there open-mouthed. "And what of it?" he said.

"Baymïrza, aren't you getting on? Am I not one of the youngest lads? Won't I be even less of a person if I fail to put on the memorial feast my father requested in his last testament? He made his pronouncement, it seems, 'Don't do this,' but then he departed for the next world. Don't you see, he was about to pass on to the next world; 'Do it' is what he was saying! Don't you see, he was about to depart to the hereafter; what he was saying to his survivors was 'Give my memorial feast'! We owe my father a memorial feast. It was apparently just what he was requesting. As a descendant of Ughuz he was at pains to have a memorial feast put on that would stand out as a lasting example. Papa was a lord of the Alach!

"But his speech was full of strange, outlandish things. Let me go to Manas. When Manas left the Altay and my father heard about it in due course, it seems he ignored Panus Khan and went out to meet Manas. How can I sit at home and not inform that hero? To him for whom the whole world has become fodder, him whose deeds are as balm to the people, who if his affairs but sag is succored by those helping spirits the Forty Chilten – that friend of Allah the Creator, his every deed swift and effective, his troops numbering sixty thousand, that protector of the people of Alach known as the Noble Khan, his words widely acclaimed, his troops numbering ninety thousand, whose preceptor is Aziret Aali, whose wife is a delicate houri, whose land is the abundant Talas all abloom and burgeoning with fruit, that man who has come into his prime – if he is not a hero, who is?! – sorrow to the hearts of warlike foes, the lion, Manas Baatïr – I'll go to Er Manas the wise, and tell him what my father said; I will inform him of what has happened without delay! I'll find out what he makes of it, whether it's the way you said or something else – I'll see if he's got an ax to grind. If he understands how to render service to my father, he will think of just what to do. He and my father both are sons of the Kirghiz, with Qïzïr for a protector; I will see what Manas says!"

The morning was long past; it was getting late and the sun was low. What a fine hero, this Boqmurun, all of fifteen years old, to think of mounting himself on Maani-ker – Maani-ker, that enormous beast – and setting off for Manas! It was already evening as he got under way. God will know how much of this story is truth and how much is falsehood: for the horses we have today it would be a journey of several days, but he arrived at the time of evening prayers. It was not a gait so much as flight; Maani-ker broke the bonds of earth and went like an arrow-shot, skipping from ridge to ridge as his mighty hooves etched the earth; he flew on and on like a bow-shot, skipping from crest to crest, his ears pricking up like candle-flames, his tail brushing the earth, water streaming from the pits of his forelegs, steam pouring from his nostrils, dripping sweat and taking sharp breaths, grinding the stones under his hooves to dust. Er Boqmurun, his waist cinched tight, eyes sparkling like fire, biting his own lip nearly off – for that is what heroes do – rode on, long past morning, as evening fell and the stars came out. Boqmurun, cutting a gallant figure in his corselet, arrived with Maani-ker worked up to full strength. The meeting on Manas's council-mound was just breaking up, and Prince Manas was turning toward home.

2

Boqmurun Journeys to Consult Manas after Kökötöy's Death*

Boqmurun gave his greeting to the hero, and Manas cast his eye over the wretched, bereaved boy. "Say your name, boy, who are you? By your sad eyes it looks as if you have something painful to say; by your foul mood you seem ready to weep." Casting a searching gaze in the gathering dusk, Manas asked the boy what was on his mind.

As soon as the gray-maned hero asked this question, Boqmurun let the tears well up in his eyes and he softly wept, facing Manas: "I am one of those called Kirghiz; having lost my father I am beset with cares! I am Kirghiz by descent; having lost my father I come before you! Kökötöy son of Janadil has migrated on from this world; my shining candle has been put out! My name is Boqmurun. When my father died I was not in my home encampment. I had been on a three-month journey to the Ürgönch, and just as I was reaching home with my new bride the mournful day arrived. I had tarried in Ooghan, and arrived at the very moment my father departed for the next world. As I was arriving my father was passing away! He migrated away to a place from which no one returns; my burning candle has been put out! He has migrated onward to a sorrowful place; he has gone to the land Barsa-kelbes![1] From our forefather Ughuz we have taken the name Kirghiz. Ruling over us had been the vile Qïtay; when you yourself, hero, came to us, my father threw off his lord and went out to meet you. Just as I was returning from my in-laws he departed on the road of no return! He told

1. "Barsa-kelbes" means "If-One-Goes-One-Does-Not-Come-Back."

everything to his friend named Baymïrza, who sent me to you to explain what he said.

"We are in a strait! As my dear father departed for the here-after, apparently he gave word for me to look for you, Er Manas. If I've talked too long it's my fault, my father has not even been buried yet! Let me, a grieving youngster, listen to your advice and return home. The purebred *tulpar* still has its mane; the vast riches and cattle are still there; the thick stands of birch and willow that he planted and tended are still there. Everyone knows that his apples and walnuts rival the best there are. You, great leader of the Kirghiz, grant us permission to mourn! Our cries for consolation must go to you; the women are drained of tears from all their weeping! His abundant cattle will hardly be enough for the feast he ordered, and as for me and the Kirghiz, we have no desire at all to wait on the Qïtays! If I obey his orders there will hardly be enough for the Man-ghuls! Apparently he said, 'Tell everyone! Deliver the news all over – to the *divs* and the *peris* – to the people under the sea!' He mentioned everyone from the west to the east, people we've heard of and people we haven't. 'Do as I say, for my honor,' he said. 'My cattle fill six river valleys; don't skimp when you give my memorial feast!' he said. 'Let no one's wish go unfulfilled; my enormous wealth and well-tended cattle must not be a cause of torment for me. When you bury me in the ground have ninety thousand animals sacrificed for my sins! My cattle of four kinds,* my mounds and mounds of gold, my emeralds, my gems – let the young see a spectacle! Make it surpass all the world's memorial feasts!'* Having ordered me thus to give a solemn feast greater than any other before, and having spoken of things the people had never done, of things no one had ever imagined in their dreams, my father departed for the next world. I thought you would be able to make sense of it, for I am but a young boy. Bewildered and confused I have sought you out."

The weeping lad fell silent. Er Manas let out a groan, and his affection for Kökötöy glowed within him. "If I were to be bur-ied all of a sudden, if I were to pass on from this world, if my death suddenly arrived, I had thought you would be a source of strength for the masses of common people of the Qara Kirghiz tribes. I often used to think that, if an assembly were to be called, you would be a man, speaking audaciously and at length. You're a nobody! You have not lived up to my expectations. Please! Act as though you rule from the Urqun river to Tashken; send out a stalwart to deliver the news to the different peoples who live so far away: 'My father Kökötöy has passed away, lurking death has got him; take careful heed of this message of mine!' Please, without revealing any secrets to anyone, utter your decree! This matter is surely ours to handle; when I think back on the service he rendered to me, Kökötöy blessed-by-Qïzïr was someone closer to me than my father. The way of the prophets has become distorted. One person has the religion of Musa, another the religion of Ïysa;* one prefers the long bones for sacrifice and the other the spine. It has been only a short time since we entered the religion of Islam at the prompting of Ayqojo of the grizzled beard. Precedents for customs – bride wealth and marriage – have not taken root among the teeming Kirghiz. The Qalmaq people became separate, and, as we know, are on the path of unbelief; the Qazaq, Kirghiz, and Dumara are facing difficulties, unsure of which customs to follow. Taking wives and giving away maidens has become a great amusement for them, and customs surrounding death simply haven't arisen yet.* The people haven't yet been taught the skills!

"Fix our old Kökötöy's banner to its standard, and until a full forty days have passed leave him at home unburied! Then inform the people that your dear father the khan has died, in strongest possible language – inform and invite me as well! – saying, 'Those who don't come, I'll cut off their heads! I'll end their years in a trice!' Have your heralds speak menacingly – no polite words! – have them speak thus and wipe the smiles off the faces of one and all! Delaying the burial of the remains and having all the married women sing laments, crying 'Dear father!' – let these things become customary when people die in the future; let it become proverbial for those who see it that you, Boqmurun, have done everything to bury your father properly! Many will rise on Judgment Day; let your deeds stand as an example! Let your words spread quickly over the

world! Work at it, sparing no industry; I am at your service!
Now go, don't wait another moment! Return home this very
night! Think of yourself as a giant, humiliating those that bear
grudges against you; think of yourself as a great man of sur-
passing mastery, bestowing gifts! Be that, boy! As long as I have
life left in me, I will be a helper to you. Means can be found for
covering the expenses of this false world; dear old Khan
Kökötöy gave me support when he came out to meet me and
placed himself at my service!"

Manas thus eased the worry in the boy's heart, cheered him
up, gave him a drink, and sent him back home with these words
of encouragement: "There are *ulama* and mullahs; please give
to them from the wealth you have in hand to provide for your
father's life in the hereafter. There are pilgrims on the roads
making the haj, dervishes, *ishans*, eloquent orators – there are
no few of the poor and homeless. Give to them, as much as you
can afford, and if your wealth does not suffice, send the charges
to me alone!" His beloved elder kinsman having departed to
the next world, Manas thus explained the need to discern who
was rich and who poor.

Boqmurun set off for the spacious city of Tashken; the hero
had made his touching entreaty and received his answer. Maani-
ker, like a bird in flight, arrived that very night; Boqmurun
riding thus could scarcely fathom the speed. He had gone away
seeking wisdom; now he spoke and informed the people. They
did not even know that he had been away on that errand.
"Obey my commands! Take note of my mastery!" he said.
Ordering Jash Aydar to mount a racer – an enormous animal,
Tor'-ayghïr with flesh under his mane thick as a maul – and
clothing him in a gold-adorned corselet and sending him on his
way on a journey of six months, –

words in the box . . . even then some mean
anyone then knows, and was himself here with range of by
weeks or moments. There are some individuals presence,
to the final statement we can in each a single
might . . . and the sentences even as

3
Boqmurun Sends Out
the Announcement *

– having Jash Aydar inform the people that his feast to bury
Kökötöy would take place at the tribal boundary. From Ïsar and
Kölöp at one end to Qazïq and Jölök on the other he sent the
news to everyone, except for the Infidels. Badaqshan and Balïq,
the commoners at Baghdat, Oluya-Ata, Tashken – for the burial
he did not invite anyone who wasn't a Muslim. Boqmurun sent
word to Qashqar, and those who assembled with their leader old
Qoshoy were without number. "He who makes his home on the
Talas shall attend my father's last rites – let Manas come without
delay!" he said. He prepared a lavish, unparalleled reception for
Kökchö son of Aydar Khan; nothing in the world could top the
luxuries he laid in. He spread the news; he didn't stop at Kökchö:
Kerkökül son of Kökmök, Janay son of Köchpös Bay – he invited
many people to Kökötöy's burial. To make a splendid display he
had the side niche in the tomb lined with gold.

"They're going to express condolences for my father," he
thought. "How can people who deliver their condolences go
home empty-handed? The scholars will take their gratuities but
the governors will go empty-handed; the *ulama* will take their
gratuities but the chiefs will go empty-handed; those with skills
will take their fees but those in power will go empty-handed."
And Boqmurun, son of the khan, cared about the multitudes. He
assembled black *nar* camels hung with bells, their throats pendu-
lous as leather pails; the silver ingots alone that he heaped up
reached the height of the assembly-mound; his gold filled a yurt;
his herds of cattle at pasture filled Anjïyan and the Chüy. For the
sake of him whose wealth was so prodigious; for the sake of all
those who would come under Baatïr Manas's leadership; so that

a righteous path would remain in memory of the deceased, he allotted gold ungrudgingly, and more cattle than the eyes could take in.

"Whatever their pretexts, let them take away riches! Let them enter their horses – and race their horses! – let each owner of a winning horse get a huge haul! Let the scholars recite the Qur'an! Let no man who arrives go home with an unfulfilled wish! Let my skillful planning be recounted to the great honor of the Qara Kirghiz, till the very end – until Resurrection Day! Let it be a tradition henceforward, an ornament for our tribe, something unforgettable that people shall speak of till the end of time! Qarïnbay was rich, they say, and he died; but he was so stingy he drew water with a spoon. His wealth ended up scattered everywhere! He was miserly to a fault, until all his wealth availed him nothing. It disappeared; his coin turned to stone and his riches were swallowed up by the earth – that's the inconstancy of this false world for you! So many people have died and left their cattle ownerless! We aren't dead, we're alive – but one of our number has died," thus Boqmurun was thinking as he summoned all the people and with great numbers of excellent horses held the race in honor of the burial.

Departed souls cannot be revived; a burnt tree cannot be planted; no one who arrived was not weeping bitter tears! He let everyone who came weep with grief and regret; he let everyone present weep and mourn this cruel world. Then he said, "Far be it from me to make you wail for want of pure silver coin!" and he had his treasury opened and so much wealth distributed to the sons of the Qara Kirghiz that the poor, the homeless and the needy were thrown into confusion by his munificence.

He had unbroken horses rounded up and given out; he gave his solemn oath and promise that he would not take back any of the wealth he distributed. Several of those who couldn't find halters or bridles took it badly; they threw their belts around the horses' necks, but some couldn't keep them from slipping out of their hands and were left with nothing at all. "This stupid animal!" they said, "This is what I get for a rich man's funeral gift! No bridle for his head so I put my belt around his neck, and that only made him snap my belt in two! I've ended up completely empty-handed!" Others who were on foot managed to chase down a few horses and catch them and bring them back. Someone would say, "I'm going to mount that one," and he would throw his bowed legs over and get his seat, and say "This is a good horse!" while the others stood around, and then he would spur it while checking the reins and it would rear up, and he would hit the ground! Others simply fell off the horses they'd received; others were all in a hubbub trying to run them down and overtake them from behind; and some were even going around asking, "Why did he give us these?" Also present were those who knew how to handle horses well, who got bridles over their heads and restrained them, fitted them out with saddle and tack, and mounted up, yelling and exulting their warrior hearts. More than those, however, were the ones who bad-mouthed poor so-and-so for not showing up: "He's so poor he can't lift his head out of bed, and he missed getting this rich man's funeral gift! How can he lie at home without even lifting his head?!" But greater still was the number of those cutting capers and shouting, "Good! This horse will do!" One could also see a few taking away camel-geldings with tusks awry, lower lips dangling, humps towering, necks slender as a duck's gently bobbing as they walked uphill, the fleece on their knees and throats waving. As they led their camels along on lead-ropes those men were saying, "Now I'm somebody! What a gift I've received after Bay Kökötöy's death!" Also to be found were those fussing about saying, "Poor so-and-so hasn't shown up? Go fetch him right now!" and those sending a gift horse speeding off on a lead-rope to some poor fellow who'd stayed home in a nearby encampment, crying havoc and rousting him, "Oh no you don't! Quit your lolling about and get over here now! The devil take you, you've missed out on all the loot!" or galloping along two-up, shouting, "Grab that one for me!" and making up each other's lacks; there were even some stupid louts who pulled down old parts of Kökötöy's walls and searched about, hoping to take away whatever they could find.

Those who set the new calves and yearlings to lowing and milked their mothers produced lakes of milk – they no longer belonged with the poor! Tying up cows for themselves, the poor became rich. Those who took five or ten sheep from Kökötöy's endowment were saying, "I'll tend this little flock just so," but their thoughts turned to the worries of owning sheep; while those left out in the cold as far as the sheep were concerned said, "Goats! Now there's a smart choice, I'll get some of those," and drove off five or ten of them without a care in the world.* "Khan Kökötöy has died!" – "They've parceled out all his cattle!" they said; but there remained string after string of *nar* camels – such exceeding wealth in cattle! – and there remained the gold in the treasure-house. The Kirghiz and Özübeks thought, "What a job!" and wandered about, unsure of what they should do. If a poplar sprouts by the river but doesn't grow, surely it will wither: both the living and the dead need cattle.

A Friday evening came; thirty-six days had passed since Bay Kökötöy's death. Just try and imagine: who that has ever died could be likened to him? Everyone there, young and old, had had mares slaughtered for their dinner, had had foals slaughtered for their evening meal; legions of serving-boys had set tea and every sort of dish all around; they whipped sultanas in milk and served that; they served gratuitous amounts of meat. They carefully searched for all the poor people and brought them there, leaving out no one. This one old man who had died was richer than anyone else on earth!

Cattle abounded everywhere. Boqmurun had a hundred thousand head of sheep in the Alay; his idea, however, was to leave not a single head. Qara-qulja is a narrow place,* as they say, but there he had another hundred thousand head that had been amassed by Bay Kökötöy, who was rich, as they say, in all four kinds of cattle in the finest condition. Above Tashken there are mountains with vultures around their summits, sheer cliffs where nothing can be built; between Namangen and Tashken there is the yellow steppe of Ayqïm, where he had another hundred thousand head – Er Boqmurun was a lad who could pay respects to his father! Try to comprehend his wealth: he had ninety thousand camel-geldings, a glory for which he was famous! Who could be likened to him – who ever has made such an outlay in cattle for the deceased?! In Oluya-Ata and Chïmkent, Orol and Sayram, and back as far as Aqsï he had those beasts known as camels – surely the mark of a prince! Ranged along

the Sïr-darïya he had those beasts known as bovines – a tally of
his cows would reveal two hundred thousand head; his yaks
were off in the mountains. Profuse wealth reveals itself! Horses
numbering seven hundred thousand, the stallions separate from
the rest, and seven hundred horse-herds making regular rounds
to count off the tallies: two hundred thousand in the Alay – such
wealth brought him fame, and his glory spread far and wide –
two hundred thousand stayed at Aq-say above Qashqar; three
hundred thousand lodged in Arpa and Song-köl – for all that
Kökötöy was much talked about! – his small and skinny ani-
mals filled the banks of the Ketmen-töbö.

So far the Kirghiz had simply reveled in Kökötöy's feast;
Boqmurun's intention was to use up every single animal. Eighty
thousand garments of *deyilde*-cloth, their surfaces covered with
floral designs in gold, their value a cause of bewilderment to no
few – though the next day they had them in the bazaar shouting,
"Two thousand gold pieces! Three thousand gold pieces!" – for a
long time the elder statesman Kökötöy had quietly amassed this
wealth. Everyone has some wealth, but who ever left anything
like that behind when he died?! Of lengths of red brocade there
was no counting; there was no fortune in the world like this. Six
strong buildings were filled with his cloths of *atlas, tubar,* and
torghun; there was *doolon* and fine white cambric as well, and
great quantities of *buulum* and *buta*; he had five rooms full of
beyqasam – it was not humanly possible to survey a fortune like
that! – *baashayï*, brocade – and standing guard over them were
ninety-six Qalchas. Besides all this there was so much else that
hasn't been mentioned! His silver ingots were piled high as a
mountain; his gold filled a yurt ten paces across. Kökötöy was his
name, of the line of Kirghiz khans, paragon of the Kirghiz, son of
Janadil, grandson of Baqatil – son of the stalwart Kirghiz.

Those that had seen Kökötöy pass on to the next world told
others, and people learned of it thus from each other. Those
who are knowledgeable maintain that the descendants of
Ughuz Khan are all close by, not at all spread out; and so we
have the custom when someone has died to distribute cattle
among the Qazaq and Kirghiz.

On the thirty-sixth day noble Manas made his departure,

having liberally sent dispatches all around to announce it. The host of heroes let out a dull roar and sent columns of dust wheeling upward, their drumbeats rolling like distant thunder; banner-poles clattering, the ear-piercing shrill of the shawms – playing the instrument called the shawm is a formidable skill; those who hear and see it done can imagine just what an impression it made on Boqmurun! – the growling tones of trumpets, the lively chirruping from the copper-flute players, the rat-a-tat beat of the tambours, the flags falling loosely, the crescent-finials of the banners all a-glitter, the bawling of the call to prayer –

Now let's try and list those forty outstanding wolves the companions of Manas,* for every one of those heroes was there. There was your good father Baqay, and Er Almambet Baatïr coming serenely on; Chalïbay son of Küldür and Ajïbay all full of fun; that gyrfalcon of the Kirghiz, Qutunay, Majik son of Qaratoqo, Chalik son of Qambarbek, Satay son of Charghïl Biy, Atayï son of Ardalïq, Ümöt of the Üyshün, and Ümöt's son Jaysang; Qaraqojo of the Arghïn whose close companion was wisdom; Boobek, Shaabek, Shükürü of sound opinions, Altay of the Arban, Törtay of the Dörbön, sullen Tölök the fortune-teller whose divinations were out of the ordinary, Aghïday the scapulimancer whose pronouncements came true, squad leader Toqotoy, Qïrghïl Chal head of the Forty, Eleman who oversaw the people, Qalqaman who inspected the commoners and held authority over the encampment to see that none strayed; that golden-leaved poplar, magnificently handsome Serek who could utter sixty wise words in the time it takes a fallen horse to get up – had he not such skill he would scarce deserve the name Serek!* – and he who never fumbled a leveled lance or retreated from an enemy, Khan Sïrghaq at Manas's side – behold these heroes! – Serek and Sïrghaq tough in close combat, Qosh Abïsh son of rich Qonghurooluu, Er Ïbïsh who led the troops, Alaken son of Alïmbek, one versed in magic, they say; there was that lion, Majik; and those who, when the Kirghiz army went campaigning and made a march in darkness could follow a wolf's tracks unerringly: Qadïr, Jaynaq, and Shuutu, those friends of the khan who, when the teeming Kirghiz army went campaigning and made a march in the middle of the night could follow a fox's tracks unerringly, who neither lost their way nor complained: Tümön, Jaynaq, and Shuutu well-known to the teeming host; and from the Qazaq, Joorunchu, Qayghïl, Bögöl, Toorulchu, Kerben son of Shïnghï, Dörbön distinguished by his eloquence; that wolf, lucky Bögölü who spied enemies from afar; the tactful İrchï Uul, and most formidable of all Er Tazbaymat, who rode in front holding the standard wherever the troops marched.

At that time Tashken was independent; Manas had defeated Panus after sovereign rule had devolved to Kökötöy. Just like their forefathers who left the Altay, these were churners of kumiss; they spent the winters in built houses, and the summers – as was the Kirghiz custom – in fancy white yurts with smoke-hole frames of bent birch-wood, the doors and the beams of the door-frames decorated with all manner of carved designs, dome-poles covered with knurling, the doors and lattice-frames painted in variegated colors, the reeds of their screens wound with silk. It was fancy white yurts, splendid in every way, that Boqmurun had had set up some distance from the town walls;* and he had the arriving mourners led in past the tents pitched here and there to the place where Kökötöy's red standard was raised, its crescent-moon finial glinting under the blue sky, the silken banner fluttering on its wooden pole at the touch of a breeze – thirty fathoms high – picture it!

When the lion Manas saw this signal from afar he let out a moan like thunder, and approached to the distance of a horse-race course. "The hero is coming! Your brave one is coming!" – the messenger named Alaman came on ahead with the news.

Boqmurun gathered at his side no fewer than six thousand youths of the Kirghiz of the forty tribes and the dependents living among them, and had them all wrap red turbans around their heads. With turbans on their heads and wands of fig-wood in their hands,* he gave the order, "Raise your lamentations! Say 'Dear father'! He who departs for the next world has done so by Allah's will!"

Boqmurun, son of the rich man, placed himself at the head of the mourners, his head bent with wretched sobbing so that the front of his coat was wet with tears: "When I was yet a small kid and had not mounted a horse, I valued not my country!

When I swaggered about but had not yet mounted a horse, I valued not my people! All unwashed and dirty I valued not my land! I was young and lived a spoiled life, drunken and utterly reckless! I had but taken a few steps on my own when my father passed on from this world, unbeknownst to me! I am left mourning my loss; my words have become bitter plaints! Let not this child, who has scarcely begun to learn anything about life, be bereft in his youth! You, my father, lie dead; I am parted from you at a young age! Such, it seems, is the fate meted out to me by God. Poorer I have become than my friends and comrades! Just as I reach fifteen years of age my noble father has departed for the next world; how can I, Boqmurun, in the face of such torment, do otherwise than weep bitter tears?! My father, you have disappeared before you could teach me about life and set me on a horse, before you could show me how to respect the people! This burden of solitude has plunged me into a dark night! I look around but there is no company for me on life's path; such is my sorrow!" Thus stooped with mournful sobbing as he contemplated his father's death, Boqmurun let the tears pour out, crying like a camel-calf for its mother.

Manas of the Qara Kirghiz arrived, weeping loudly. He had with him his sworn retinue of forty men – the Forty Heroes who attended him – and his baggage borne by *nar* camels; in the lead were Baqay and Qïrghïl Chal, their white beards fluttering as they rocked along on their amblers. Take a look at those heroes! Eighty thousand men came on with a rumble and an earth-shaking roar, howling and tramping as the dust rose in clouds. Manas arrived then, and everyone let out a loud cry – the Qazaq and Kirghiz have their customs of mourning handed down from their forebears. There were about a hundred thousand people there, and forty thousand to see to their needs. The grooms held their horses while Boqmurun, that boy of fifteen, directed their reception. He had the horses tied up to the tethering-lines and the arriving people graciously led to accommodations and entertained.

No sooner had he given out the command to see to the guests' needs and they were resting in their accommodations than Er Kökchö son of Aydar Khan arrived on their heels as well – that tiger, noble Kökchö, with thirty thousand men in his retinue.

His men had scarcely been conducted to their various places when Eleman came on with about two thousand troops, making a dull moan in sympathy with the others.

Seeing all these lamentations and thinking, "Just as Boqmurun has asked, everyone is paying his respects! As they approach the encampment they raise their voices loudly in cries and lamentations!" – he of deep, pure wisdom, the leader of the Eshtek, Jamghïrchï, came on sobbing bitterly and saying, "What a custom they have! What a people are these! Let us not stand by and watch, let us raise a din as they do! An elder of theirs has passed on, and all the Kirghiz are bent over with cries and sobbing!" and his men letting out loud, whooping cries, saying, "What a custom the Kirghiz have!" Grooms took the horses of those just arrived and spread before them rugs of red silk.

They had barely quieted down and seen to this and that task when Ürbü came on with three thousand troops, who saw those that had arrived before and gave themselves over to bitter lamentations.

He who made his home along the Amu-darïya, he who fought with unyielding honor against foes who marched against him – from Kömök above Balïq, one exceedingly fortunate and a son of the Kirghiz to boot – Baghïsh, leader of the Jediger – yes, Baghïsh of the Jediger was descended from that line as well – he too arrived, having taken the road across Sar'-qol pass leading two and a half thousand troops; these men who had accompanied him to the burial he allowed to be divided up and taken here and there for accommodation.

He who summers at Uluu-chat and lovingly trains his race-horses, old Shïghay, came on with an earth-shaking din, and the teeming mass of assembled people absorbed his company as well and gave them accommodation.

Late the following day, long past noon as evening was coming on, those two of the silken pavilions and costly shoes of governors, from teeming Qoqon, Marghalang, Oro-töbö and Samarqan, from the lands down the Syr Darya as far as Arsï and Jölök, from the lands that spread up as far as Ïsar and Kölöp – Saalay Datqa and Sïnchïbek came on with ninety thousand Sarts. Let one of

their richest men die and see who takes note of it, let the summons
to his funeral go out and see who obeys it!

Those arriving for the burial filled the broad plain of Tashken.
There was no room indoors or out; many went into the city.
What, in the end, was there to tell to the boy Boqmurun about
lavishing riches past counting to his father's memory? He slaugh-
tered mares for their evening meal, yearlings for their dinner, and
sheep for daytime refreshment; he slaughtered a feast's worth of
animals for the deceased. He served breads of different sorts, and
honey in yellow cups; he minced rib-fat of horses and served
it with mane-fat. He slaughtered a hundred thousand bulls;
those arriving tired and hungry feasted freely till they were full.

Mustapa the True Prophet made the pronouncement of the
sharia whence it has spread to us here; so Boqmurun took none
other than Ayqojo of the grizzled beard and placed him in charge.
Ayqojo assembled the learned men, and the lofty and the lowly
observed the rites according to the sharia. Then Boqmurun
awarded his *keperet* by driving in two hundred thousand sheep
and tethering ninety thousand cows, and had fully forty-one mul-
lahs recite the *janaza*, and had the *buraq at* fitted out. A crowd of
friends took hold and carried the *tabït*; then he made the *bidiya*.
For the *salootu namaz* and the *janaza* the people stood shoulder
to shoulder in row after row until you could not see the other
end; a shout from one side of the crowd would not be heard on
the other. They recited the *namaz* and the *tekbir* without *sajide*,
and fitted out the racer named Chong-toru as the *buraq at*.*

In that wise they buried your forefather, Bay Kökötöy; the
earth cast on his grave as they uttered their invocations rose
like a hill until it became a mountain – much time has passed
since then, but to this day the tomb of your forefather Kökötöy
still stands! The mullahs divided up their garner, contending and
fighting to the death with one another there and then. First one
encounters the sharia; higher than that is Truth, and higher still
is the Way; crowning them all is Knowledge. Those who know,
know that much!

Then an announcement was heard: "Any one with a passion
for the horses! The dead are dead! Drive along your hearts'
desires and enter them in the race!" For the prize they tied up

nine thousand horned cattle many-colored as a carpet of flowers; fifteen thousand camels, those giants among beasts; twenty-five thousand horses, the most prized of all property among the sons of the Kirghiz, so they say; thirty thousand cows; and among the bovines five thousand yaks had been earmarked and driven in. That was the first prize. The prizes after the first went down by halves, and for the horse in last place the prize was nine cows and ninety sheep – still something worth taking away.

That wealthy man named Kökötöy had died and the people were getting a real feasting! Prizes posted for thirty horses – where could you do better than that? "Let no man's wish go unfulfilled!" – "Let the horses take the prizes!" – On that day every one of the Kirghiz saw some sort of gain from your good father. "Drive the horses down here!" – "Drive them over from Qoqon!" – "Those racers in fine fettle – set them galloping like hares!" Boqmurun had the horses driven up.

Everyone, we'll see, turns up in this part of the story. When gray-maned Manas arrived, Ïrchï Uul son of Ïraman, of the forty-knot tassel on the drawstring of his drawers, that fellow of the topknotted skullcap and effortless speech, had composed a lament for Kökötöy, nothing very long-winded: "God made him a happy wealthy man, a man rich in untold herds of cattle, with a layer of fat a span deep over his ribs! The Qara Kirghiz had a quite seemly respect for him; his maidens wore red silks and his lads rode yearling amblers!" Having spoken thus he withdrew with six flag-bearers trailing him and raising a loud cry; Er Boqmurun was gladdened by his words. He had them bring Ïrchï Uul a string of nine amblers and select for him ninety gowns of *torqo*; he also covered him with nine gowns, one after the other, of *deyilde*-silk each worth a thousand gold pieces; he made that gabbling singer extremely happy! Then he had him conducted, surrounded by this bounty, across the horse-racing ground through parting crowds of onlookers. In him the Qazaqs had the fulfillment of their desires. Look all over this inconstant world: singers performing in memory of the dead is a legacy that has come down from him!*

They had started the horses at night. The people were relaxing and enjoying themselves, but no few, those who had trained their racers to get them into top condition, were standing around filled with desire for victory, and peering into the west. The call was heard, "The horses are coming!" and everyone present joined the row of onlookers.

Those people back then did not know about dragging horses to the finish; they were people who refrained, it is said, from any fumbling antics on the course when they raced their horses. It was at that feast, in fact, that sending out riders to pull racehorses to the finish was first done. Pressing Aq-qula from behind and beginning to overtake him was Ach-buudan: there's your reason that Manas gave a loud cry of alarm and said, "My Forty Companions! Have you gone missing?! Pull Aq-qula along!" Talk of pulling race-horses to the finish began right then and there; today, there is not even one person who can ride who would refuse to pull a race-horse to the finish.

Along one of the low ridges there was a prominent elevation where the assembled princes had climbed up; a few of them, were you to look, had gone right up to the brow of the ridge and fixed their eyes on the huge, dark plain in hopes of seeing the horses. The start had been on the previous day in the evening; on this day, past noon, a thick cloud of dust could be discerned in the direction up from Qoqon.

The horses were first spotted when they came to Kengdi-badang; on the mountains north of Anjïyan* the leader could be distinguished: it was Baghïsh's horse, Sur-kiyik! His hooves seemed only seldom to touch the ground and the dust billowed out behind him; those of the Jediger tribe let out a mighty, earth-shattering yell. The jockey barely clung to the reins as the sword-steel bit dangled low; the ground beneath the horse's hoof-beats was rent into pits deep as hearths. At that the sons of the Kirghiz – all of them now – let out a great shout. Sur-kiyik, it seemed, was a *tulpar*.

After him, on came Eleman's beast called Tel-toru. Third came one of the name-bearing horses among Er Kökchö's many herds, Kök-ala's younger sibling, Jar-mangday the black with-a-blaze, black and built like a hound. Fourth among them was your prince's horse, Tel-toru; fifth was Meenet-kök, Sïnchïbek's beast; sixth was Arghïmaq that belonged to Muzburchaq;

seventh was Jel-qayïp owned by Aqbay–Mambet – what a racer he was! Eighth came Baqay's horse Mal'-toru; ninth, it could be seen by the dust rising up high as a mountain, was Seyit's horse Jel-qara; tenth in order, it turned out, was Jügörü's beast Or-qïzïl. – At that time everyone's best racers were there; shall we really mention more of the horses in the minor race? There were prizes for the top thirty; naming ten or so was enough of a feat, no? Yammering on about racing horses is for bumpkins from the hills! Those who won prizes took them; the men whose horses were racers saw some profit.

"Soldiers have come crowding in and paid their last respects to my father. Let no one's wish go unfulfilled! The brave men who raced the horses should take no part in what's next. May Allah bless my father!" said Boqmurun. He continued: "You, countless guests! After my father died many troubles have befallen me. From his youth my father was obsessed with amassing worldly riches. I could ignore that but it would do no good! The heaviest toll comes in the next world, I've heard; perhaps this will do some good?" Then spurring his horse he hurried home, where he had six storerooms full of silver dirhams. He flung two of them open, leaving the rest, and from those two rooms he brought out every last coin. Boqmurun then gave a commandment regarding all those dirham coins. He instructed men to load the silver onto six carts, and to haul them out to the gates, which he had them open that very day, and distributed the money to the common people.

As when farmers pour out wheat by placing it in the gathered-up hems of their coats, it was too much to dole out with their hands. No one could believe it, but no one went away empty-handed! They told them, "Take what you can off the ground!" "Those of you saying, 'Why should I take it?' stand aside and watch!" "Young and old, take it!" "Those of you saying 'It's too hard for me', stand aside over here!" Then they flung the bright coins right out at them, and all the coins were scattered like peas falling from the sky.

Some people fell to the ground, sweeping spread-eagle in the black dirt, but the coins got covered and disappeared like hail fallen from the sky. Other people were grubbing in the soil grabbing handful after handful, or were saying, "You got what

I was going to take!" and slugging it out, or picking over the
coin-strewn ground and laying hold of them one by one, or say-
ing, "You took that before I could get it!" and wrestling each
other, or rooting around saying, "It got covered in dirt!" Others
were working things out with their fists in groups of three or
four; some were even tying others up with camel-hobbles.

On the fortieth day exactly[1] the people who had wandered off
here and there came back. The ninety men who had washed the
body of the deceased had, to the amazement of the people, been
clothed in ninety robes of honor made of nine-layered *torqo* for
their work during those days; that rich man's son Boqmurun had
shown off how prosperous he was. He had said, "Have them
bring in mullahs!" and "Spirits of my father's departed ances-
tors! Bless him if you are able!" He had had forty thousand
mullahs stay on, had had forty thoroughbreds outfitted and set
a-running and a-galloping; had had the Qur'an read for forty
days. Now he set about putting on the fortieth-day feast.

He called in the leaders of the mountain Kirghiz tribes and
had them assemble: old Qoshoy, head of the Qataghan; Baghïsh
of the Jediger; Aghïsh son of old Jetkir – the leaders of the people
came. Word of Kökötöy's glory passed down for these many
years, to Alïmseyit and Aydar Khan and all the people of the
Alach – this one man became widely renowned – whose original
homeland was Badaqshan, ruled over by Chegish Khan. – The
call came, "They're racing horses again!" "It's time for galloping
powerful racers!" they were saying, and "The brave man whose
horse comes in first will find happiness!" and "Holding races at
memorial feasts is a cherished custom of the Kirghiz!"

Down in the valleys, along the banks, are the Tarsa; closer in
are the Parsï; Parsï is the Tajik language – try to pay attention
and remember the word, you mullahs who are recording
Manas!* – on the mountain slopes are the Qalcha; so many sons
of the Kirghiz have fallen to them as war booty! The heroes
Ketelik and Dögüsh came; all kinds of people came. Qazaqs and
Kirghiz in great numbers, who swirled on every side like a black-
haired torrent. From Ooghan came Aqun Khan with a host of

---

1.   Forty days after Kökötöy's death.

commoners hunched over with their belts cinched tight, their
hare-like ears standing straight up out of their heads, jaunty but-
tocks sticking out showy as a mountain sheep's, necks like drawn
wire – more or less like devils! People eyeing their form were
saying, "Even beasts don't bear young like that!"

All over, as summoned, race-horses were coming in from every
direction, their stance in the rear wide as a notch in the moun-
tains, the space between their legs wide enough to fit a yearling
heifer; hooves like pure iron, thigh muscles like mountain crests –
if one could not speak of their gait as such, it was because they
moved as fast as black ravens in flight! – flight as swift as ravens,
yet the blows of their hard hooves able to break solid rocks!

The race-horses were being assembled; the people were all
gathering. This Boqmurun – what a man! As a great crowd of
people were beginning to wail and lament the late Köküm[1]
Khan, horses arrived from down below, from Jööt and Tarsa,
from Qarategin and the Qalcha. As before, the hero Manas
Khan got word and came as well. Khan Qoshoy of the Qata-
ghan; Kökchö of the Qazaq; Eleman came from the Qïpchaq;
Jamghïrchï of the Eshtek, khan in his own small nation; elo-
quent Er Ürbü; the khan's maternal nephew Jügörü; Kerkökül
son of Kögüsh; Janay son of Köchpös Bay – almost everyone
on earth was gathering for the fortieth-day feast! Sïnchïbek in
Anjïyan; Muzburchaq of the gray-flecked beard; they all came
and gathered then, saying, "A feast!"

Khan Kökötöy was lamented in song for three days while the
people rested – no one from the Oyrot of the red topknots or
from the Qïtay turned out for the fortieth-day feast, where the
people stopped for three days. Boqmurun had open hearths
dug into the ground and seven hundred mares slaughtered, and
all his neighbors and relations feasted on butter of whitest
white; in an unprecedented display of luxury he had the plat-
ters passed around for six days.

Then Boqmurun had the first prize for the race brought out.
He was making sure that the value of the outlay was greater
than the last each time they raced. He had them make ready and

1.   "Köküm" is a nickname for Kökötöy.

post a hundred head of every kind of livestock; he had a hun-
dred ingots carried out, all of them gold ingots known as
shangshuur, and he laid them out neatly; then he counted out
ten thousand gold pieces. Thirty of his menial bond-women
mounted up on horses, fifteen men and fifteen women. (Is that
how we speak of the total, then? A woman, a man – in former
times you would buy them like livestock – what were they
called? The women were slave-women; the men were slaves,[1]
those were the words your forebears used. Kökötöy's wives had
become widows; all the sons of the Kirghiz used to do it when
someone had died; that is what your people in the past used to
say.) That was the first prize; the prize for the second-place
horse was about half the livestock posted for the winner.
Boqmurun saw that everyone got something; he posted prizes
for forty horses. Those fifteen men and fifteen women, since
they had been purchased previously – mind you, not for giving
as prizes – were apportioned out for the next nine horses, with
the tenth-place horse getting one woman and one man, just the
two people – He posted prizes for forty horses, but that thing he
did caused a scandal for the Kirghiz!*

As president he selected the prizes; the heroes were enjoying
themselves, and the racers arriving from every direction were
being driven in, seven hundred horses. They sent them down
the steep slope downstream from Tashken, where the dry,
thirsty steppe stretched farther than the eye could see. A hun-
dred men drove the horses, and three marshals went with them,
of khan-like bravery and faultless honesty. They started the
race towards nightfall; those jockeys who were careless with
their outfitting were sunk in despair for their lapses! When they
had reached lake Qara-köl – if you don't believe me go and
look yourself – the jockeys stopped their horses and let them
graze while they slept upright in the saddle. When dawn broke
those wayfarers awoke and got moving, still hungry and tired,

---

1.   "bond-women" is *chor*. "The women were slave-women": here, "women"
      is *qatïn* and "slave-women" is *küng*. "the men were slaves": here "men" is
      er and "slaves" is *qul*. Fifteen women plus fifteen men does not add up to
      thirty women: an interpretation is given in the Notes.

but every creature born of a mare they had allowed to drop its bit and search here and there unbridled, and take a drink from the stream there. It was in a place abounding in reeds, a stagnant marsh you would call it, where the reeds grew big around as a yurt, they say; that's where they had the turn-around point.

When the sun had nosed up over the horizon and risen again at last, Boqmurun stationed lads in even rows, taking charge over those who guided the horses in. Then he and Baymïrza went out together to manage the horses. "*Allahu akbar!* Go!" they cried one after the other; the jockeys were on their way, so far still that each one, peered at, would be lost to view. The horses went rushing on like the wind, flying like arrows from a bow, like arrows drawn from a quiver and loosed; if you looked at each one, he sped like the ball from a falconet-gun! Their four legs met the ground squarely, and the ground was cracked all around their hoof-prints. These were extraordinary racers, *tulpars*, that sank up to their pasterns when standing tethered; their chests jutting like a stag's; most of their jockeys were straining forward shouting, "God! Help me, please!" When you saw them on hilly ground they were hunched like hungry polecats; when you saw them on the broad steppe they dashed along like hungry wild sheep. The dust billowed up to the sky, the racing jockeys whooped, the galloping race-horses flew along; from the jockeys came a steady, shrill scream.

It was no longer early; it was getting late. During the cool of the afternoon, the majority of onlookers had said, "They ought to be coming," and were standing up to look, when, up from the course of the Qosh-aral rose a thick cloud of dust, and the horses came dropping down into view off the black hill at Zaqïm. On the elevation called Aq-döbö the excellent princes said, "What is Allah bringing us?", trying to guess the outcome. If you looked at the horse in front, it belonged to that exemplary hero from olden times, eloquent Ürbü of the Qïpchaq adorned-with-embroidery: Egiz-qara was its name, and it was coming on, well out in the lead. Coming up behind was Kerqashqa, a beast with an extraordinary stride, Kerkökül's horse, of a breed apart, that beast; he had run flat-out in that fortieth-day race and still had a day's hard running in him, but, with victory out of reach, he was coming in behind the winner. Qart-küröng, Ajï's horse, came in third; galloping in fourth was Seyit's horse Tar-qïzïl; Aq-borchuq, Qïrghïl's horse, came in fifth; sixth, its jockey bellowing and shouting his war-cry, came Qalcha's horse; galloping in eighth was Jel-qïzïl, Teyish's horse. If you looked at ninth place it was Toqotoy's Too-toru; tenth was Or-qïzïl, an animal purchased from the Sarts, Sïnchïbek's,* apparently. The rest came in one at a time, the jockeys on their backs hollering, while the majority of the crowd were unaware of who they were and had to ask each other. They let the finishers through up to the count of forty, then closed down the finish line to those that straggled behind. The death of your forefather Köküm gave rise to a lot of entertainment!

Your hero Manas presided in giving out the prizes in order, with your grandpa Qoshoy beside him, saying "Such-and-such horse's prize goes to so-and-so." Wherever you looked, wherever they could find space there was an abundance of wealth; the horses in the very last places were getting nines of livestock. That is how they put on the fortieth-day feast. Those proceedings were witnessed by all. Then the crowd broke up and went their separate ways home.

The strangers had gone and Boqmurun's own people were left; such stories about the past have made the rounds. The enterprising lad Boqmurun addressed his people: "The sharia of the true religion is correct: kinsmen, let us be in no hurry now! Let the cows' milk abound in lakes, let all the livestock multiply! When two years have passed from this year – in the third year – let us give the grand memorial feast! Kinsmen, my people, your effort is required: look after the rams and see that they fatten, look after the lambs and see that they grow into wethers, look after the camel-calves and see that they grow into adults! Those that don't look after any horses will have to walk! See that the herdsmen tend their cattle so that my home ranges grow rich – see that the herdsmen tend their cows! See that the tents fill up with wares; may God leave the trinkets uncorroded! May everyone win something at the grand memorial feast, may it be a marvelous spectacle, talked about until Resurrection Day! Castrate the stallions, make them geldings! Send letters all around to the ends of the earth! Have six thousand Sart householders come and sow different sorts of rice! Until the time is fulfilled – listen, commoners, one and all, young and old!

"The man known as Kökötöy was rich, they say; his fortune is very large. Even more than his cattle at pasture – greater than any in this illusory world – is the amount of his goods. The issue now is how to spend all this in his behalf and put on his memorial feast. No one survives past his appointed time; a khan does not die upon his throne; and a seed does not die if it lies in the ground. My God who brings happiness! All you Ughuz: pray for perfect harmony from your One Creator! If we glorify the deceased, it will put our jealous enemies to shame! Let it remain as an example for whoever lives in this illusory world! Kinsmen, witnesses! I have so many rooms full of riches, don't try to economize and hide the treasure-sacks! All you sons of Ughuz: nearby you have the splendid cities of Anjïyan and Tashken, but don't sell even one kid! There's *buulum* and *buta* – so much abundance of wealth for those who wish to hear about it: *qadek* and cotton stuffs, *shayï*-silks embroidered with the lute-neck pattern, everything one can lay hands on – *torghun* and *tubar* silks – so much of all those that we can speak of a glut; there are *soolan* and *dürdün* cloths as well. But don't up and sell even one of your animals! *Alchïn bayïr* and *atlas*: all of that you can have; the fabric called *azat* too.

"If your shirt wears out take a shirt, just make sure the cattle grow up and thrive! If your coat wears out take one of those, just keep fattening up the cattle you're tending! If you want to wear a sleeveless jacket, take one, enjoy it! There's every kind of marvelous thing. If you're down at the heels, there's all the yuft you need in my treasury to make boots; you wretched Qara Kirghiz tribe, just don't sell a single animal! There are hats for you to put on in summertime; if you want bedding there are skins for that; there's padded wear to put on in wintertime; there are black *nar* camels to load it all onto. The property Kökötöy has left fills several palaces – there are furs of marten and fox for your hats – just keep accurate counts of your cattle and refrain from selling them! You all, in your hundred fifty thousand tents, please stay together!

"This is what I have to say to you, my people: have a care for the giving of the feast! If you remain and prepare to give your feast, everyone will come to you for company. The earth itself is a round block; people will slither in from all over it. I have figures and totals for all who tread the ground, women and men, to the last iota. Then there are men under the earth, so many different kinds, *divs* and *peris* – Shïba and Cheri, Alatqaq and Chïngïroo, and creatures called Adamnoo big around as elephants, and creatures called Sayasa, and the Ubara-charköö, who are giants; the dwarves, the Itaalï, all kinds of creatures. Muslims and Infidels there are as well. In this world there are the numerous Köyök; many there are, and their food is tough grass. If we invite everyone to the memorial feast and skimp on the outlay, the Kirghiz will lose face!"

When he had finished his speech the masses of people attending him said, "He has spoken wisely," and accepted his commands. So they lived, selling not even a single kid or a single trencher of grain from the vast riches accumulated by Kökötöy. They got their shirts from Boqmurun. If anyone's clothes wore out he went right to the palace, where the chief treasurer sat with the appraiser beside him, giving out yuft to be made into boots; they supervised everything. The people preserved the herds, neither slaughtering nor selling, and survived for three years. No evil spirits visited them; the large cattle grew and multiplied. No misfortunes befell them; the sheep and goats grew and multiplied.

The people all lived in plenty and doted on their children, and Boqmurun now acted as head of all their banners – my One Lord Himself knows! The horses grew fat and full, and the people became impatient and asked, "When will he give the feast?" The warriors grew fat and bored, and said "Bring on the toughs!" The ladies and maidens grew excited. In winter the camel-bulls roared and the Kirghiz grumbled; in spring the bulls bellowed and the inhabitants of the world complained, "Isn't he going to give the feast?" The stallions neighed loudly, the goats bleated tremulously, the rams butted each other, the lambs grew up into big, fat, choice sheep; the cattle could not rise up from lying down; the bulls could not turn their necks; yaks filled the ravines. News of Khan Kökötöy's death had reached all peoples.

Boqmurun had six war-elephants maintained at royal expense, thickest-skinned of all animals and a delight to all who saw their strength; he had two rhinoceroses as well, for Er Kökötöy had been collecting widely for a long time. He kept three tigers, reddish lions with stripes, the strength of each one matching forty men; and ounces, five of them, housed separately, which played about, friendly with one another; six trained bears; and two young weanlings of the beasts called panthers. He had beasts called *qatïlet* with one leg and three arms, giants who were enemies of mankind. He had apes known as *tïqshï* that could do all kinds of dances; he had nine kinds of parrots that could talk in human language. I know of no one anywhere else who had such possessions as those Bay Kökötöy had acquired from his youth in the city of Tashken. He had two thousand mules! Who was his like among the Qara Kirghiz?

Boqmurun had provided for the memorial feast; now he took counsel on holding the solemnities. Three years had gone by and riches lay everywhere, indoors and out. Their horses skittered like onagers; if you looked at their foals, they were as big as three-year-old colts; if you looked at their mares, they were built like five-course brick walls, and they flirted and frisked like young beauties choosing men. With their women clad in black sable the Qara Kirghiz are long practiced at giving gala affairs. The horses had put on mane-fat atop their necks, and the people possessed all kinds of livestock. Many were camped for the summer at Suu-samïr and on the Alay; more still were summered at Aq-say, Arpa, and Song-köl. The several excellent princes kept cows at Aq-döbö and sheep at Ïsar and Kölöp; horses they had pastured at Arsï and Jölök. They had situated camels along the Sïr-darïya – Chïmkent and Sayram* were the places where camels were ranged. Fully three years had passed and Boqmurun's promise had come up again. When the appointed day came he raised a banner and erected a yurt inside the royal stronghold. This drew a respectful response. He assembled Qoshoy of the Qataghan, Kökchö of the Qazaq, Aghïsh and Qojosh, Aqbay, Ümöt, Mambet, and Er Kökqoyon the sultan; he brought in Aqun from Ooghan, and well-wishers from many other countries.

4

Boqmurun Assembles the People and Takes Counsel on Holding Kökötöy's Memorial Feast

Er Boqmurun spoke: "O friends! At this moment I have much on my mind: the death of my father, and the falseness of this world in the end. I had gone off blindly to my in-laws and did not listen to my father's own words. Regrets are all I have to hold on to! When he was alive, I was always pampered and slept all day. Now, dear uncles, since you ask about giving my father's memorial feast, I have prepared all kinds of riches for it; but there are stupid people who are abusing the wealth I've offered them on surety. It is certainly no lie that the ultimate end that awaits them is Judgment Day!

"I want the whole world to proclaim that this affair is the Kirghiz' doing; I want it to be something told of us until Judgment Day! My people, I have decided to appoint as president of the feast that poor devil, Manas the brave, to put on both the solemnities and the feasting, to take the gold out of its hiding places and distribute my vast fortune. If I spend everything my father amassed until I have to shake out the sacks, let it become something to talk about – for the sake of my father himself and his own words that he spoke as a last testament! I have observed and honored his behest. I heard everything he said, from first to last, from Baymïrza. Hear how Baymïrza here gave the gist of my father's speech." Er Boqmurun related his words: "'O my people!' he said. 'You are without white-bearded elders; how can I leave you?' Let us spend all that we must to do my father honor: for the sake of his testament,

because it is the Qara Kirghiz' affair, and for the sake of my
dear departed old father!

"Now I have ten thousand things to think about – being lib-
eral enough with my father's property – the disturbances my
encampment will face – judging race-horses. I'm thinking, shall I
hold a horse race? Dear uncle Qoshoy, what do you say? After
all, you are a son of the Kirghiz. From long ago our opinions
have been as close as kinsmen on the father's side. I'm thinking,
if I could manage to put on games, like having two men joust,
one from the Muslims and one from the Heathens taking
iron-tipped lances in their hands and charging at each other
unafraid – if I could keep my father's memorial feast going and
going thus, then I would be content. I want to set two wrestlers
on their feet, *divs* stronger than giants, and let everyone watch
them fight, let them get a good look at some wrestling. I want to
set two fellows from two countries competing in the game of
wrestling on horseback, and let the real man win it. Let this feast
become a lasting example to everyone in the future who attends
a memorial feast! This is what's on my mind; I've got to keep all
the burdens of this wealth from sapping my energy. I want two
bald men from two different countries to charge each other and
knock their shiny heads together. Let the people decide if my
father's fortune is great or small! What if we dig a hole in the
ground about hip-deep, and pound a stake in there and tie a
camel to it, and have women strip completely naked and tell
them, 'Untie the camel and it's yours'? Then I want to fell a hun-
dred dead spruces and make a long pole by lashing them end to
end, and set it up, and have a golden ingot hung from it, and say,
'Marksmen, fire at will!' and let them try to shoot it down. Put-
ting on a game like that I could have the finest sharpshooter that
walks the earth knock down that ingot. That's the business I
have in mind. I have no intention to spare myself, dear uncle, in
holding my father's feast! I'm eager for everyone to get here; the
talk about how I shall put on these solemn obsequies is dying
down. You are the person who can advise me how things really
should be done," Boqmurun said to your dear uncle Qoshoy.

That giant Qoshoy burst out laughing. "That's a tall order,
I'd say! Your late father ought to have nothing to complain

about! Khans leave golden thrones, and Allah has given you abundant good fortune. Right now you are fulfilling the destiny of the sons of the line of Ughuz. Everything you've said that has occurred to you to do, my boy – well, do it! The ordure in a slaughtered animal's stomach stays where you pour it out, but who in this vain, illusory world ever lives on without dying? The dirt stays where the washing's done, but in this ultimately false world not one person avoids death and remains. And yet canvas is found where there's thread to weave it; if you manage to pull off such an affair, people will talk and marvel about it until the Day of Resurrection. When a person finally dies, they say, 'Death has caught up with him'. You get a fort where there's lots of shooting; if you want to do such things, I won't say no. Let people praise this feast until the end of time! 'Kökötöy's memorial feast' will become a household phrase. Our enemies will be despondent, and people will have something juicy to gossip about until the Day of Judgment! If it's what you want to do, then do it, my boy. Your old uncle Qoshoy is here to help you." So said Er Qoshoy.

All the brave warriors present made a great uproar, saying, "Let it be so! If that's the way it is, let it be so!"

This lifted Boqmurun's spirits; the gray-maned lad was truly relieved. "But I've been wondering these past few days: once you've gone tramping off to your home countries, how am I to put on this feast here in Tashken pretty-as-a-maiden's-skullcap? I've made plenty of preparations. We're absolutely flush with indoor accommodation, and there are all kinds of groves as well – walnut, apricot, willow, there's lots of space.* But hard on the heels of the Kirghiz will come the Ooghan, and to one side of them there are the numerous Tatar. Straight that way we have the Qalcha, and beyond them such a lot of enemy peoples. If they were to enter the city all of a sudden, they could attack the peasants. To the west are the Qïzïlbash and the Tarsa. If Er Manas were to get violent with the brave men the Qïzïlbash put forward, he could destroy them. If as many people as we're planning come to the feast, how can we speak of fitting them inside little Anjïyan? Speak, dear uncle Qoshoy, and tell us where the feast should be held!" So said Boqmurun.

You have your white-beards and you have your black-beards, but when the words passed down from the ancients are uttered, what you will get is a lot of proverbs. Grandpa Qoshoy sat there carefully turning over his thoughts, giving full consideration to what the boy had said. Then he shook his head. "In the western regions there are many lakes as well as many waterless deserts."

His hat decorated with embroidery, his trousers of yellow buff, the metal trinkets on his belt-pouch tinkling from his silken sash, his copper boot-heels capped in gold – Er Kökchö son of Aydar Khan spoke to the assembly: "Dear uncle Qoshoy," he said, "I have seen a land called Sarï-arqa, right in front of the Altay. I have seen favorable ground everywhere there, with broad, gentle slopes, immense space. Its one flaw is that water is scarce."

As soon as Kökchö had finished that statement, Aqun opened his mouth to speak: "Shall we migrate from this spot and go north, then? And everyone living in the west, could they reach there even if they migrated for seven months? Tiger Kökchö, were you saying how a man needs a companion? You won't have one if we go there!"

Er Aqbay son of Jaydar, his eyes bright as candle-flames, spoke: "There is a plain with lots of space: the famous summer-pastures of the Alay, at the head of Qarategin. The water is pure, there's grass, and there's all the room in the world."

Then Mambet spoke: "The Alay won't work," he said. "We're going to have huge crowds descending on us, and our main task will be to keep the fires kindled. We would run out of firewood and be in a terrible jam."

Now Boqmurun had a word. "You haven't come to any decision. That's the one commandment from Allah the Magnificent when people meet in council. There's Suu-samïr to the east – what if we gave the feast there, uncle Qoshoy of the white beard?" That is what Boqmurun said.

Qojosh the strong-man replied, "Never mind that place. The mountains are too high and the space is too tight, and the wooded areas along the riverbanks are too dense."

Everyone there talked at once, naming his pick for where to

hold the feast. "Stop!" said your uncle Qoshoy, and he began to speak to the crowd: "If you've got sense, any of you – if your ancestors had anything to say about such matters, consider this: to the east there's lake Ïsïq-köl. Moreover, from the Tekes and Ters-suu northward it's featureless desert everywhere you look. But if you follow the Ile down, there's a place with plenty of ground for racing horses and everything suitable for holding a memorial feast. Everywhere you roam there are lively springs. The name of the place is Qarqïra, the Broad. They boil salt there, free of the slightest sediment traces, from brine that comes out of a crack in the earth. The spruces, birches, poplars – however many fires you'll be needing to light, the wood is ready to hand. And there's lots of ground for horse-racing. It's a fitting place to hold a feast."

When your uncle had finished this speech all the chiefs in unison gave their blessing, saying, "That's the place! Let's be off." After they gave their blessing, they broke up, but each kept to the appointed place and time of the feast. When the hottest days of summer had passed and the cattle had fattened up – when autumn had arrived and the peasants were sowing their crops, and those in Samarqan and Qoqon were taking in the early harvest from the rain-watered fields – everyone made ready to descend on the feasting grounds, their old Qoshoy chief among them. You see now, this is what they had done: those great rascally fellows had come to the council and then gone off their separate ways; it was when the sweltering summer days had passed and autumn was coming on that the people gathered to hold the memorial feast on the plain at Qarqïra.

5

Boqmurun Sets His Entire People Migrating and Goes to Qarqïra to Hold Kökötöy's Memorial Feast

When the others had dispersed, Boqmurun had his people counted. At this time he made even those who had not a straw to their names into moderately wealthy men.* From Anjïyan, Jïzaq and the land of Aziret Ayïp through the mountain pass at Kök-art he brought the numerous tents of the people by the name of Kirghiz; from Sayram and Chïmkent he had the Qazaqs counted up; and the Özübeks as well. As they filed past him Boqmurun had them swear their utmost loyalty to him, all three hundred thousand tents of them. Such dealings of our illustrious forebears make a lasting example for us today.

And had he not kept them at the task of fattening up the cattle? The rams he had had castrated had grown into three-year-old wethers, and the young ewes he had left unbred* had grown big and fat; Boqmurun had done very well by the peoples under his command. He had filled their saddlebags with goods; he had castrated the colts and made good horseflesh of them. For serving-men he took on forty thousand or so bachelor Sarts. He had the baggage-trains of the poorest nomads covered in rugs of red silk; to every girl over ten he gave a pair of little bells to wear. The young brides he had decked out in kete-silks; he saw to everyone's needs. The maidens he had dressed in red fabrics; he put himself at the service of all. He made his great success known to the whole world; old women got tail-fat to chew, and poor men got a thousand sheep to drive. He had his Kirghiz from spacious Tashken turn back from where they had been summering. The ladies he had decked out in Chinese satin; the commoners he made very fortunate indeed. Every camel in the line was a strong, swift racer, and every damned indigent pauper was leading a string of ten or fifteen mares.

All the cows began lowing – this is how it was as he got everyone under way – the sheep all started to bleat; those from other countries who witnessed it were astonished at the sight. The horses all started neighing; outsiders who had not followed the planning thought, "Every one of them is a rich man!" but those in the know saw the hand of Manas in the goings-on.* All the camels began bellowing; it looked as if the equipment was in good order. They had sharpened their lances; they had got the young men looking seemly; the baggage was all loaded on black *nar* camels hung with bells, their throats pendulous as leather pails. You couldn't tell the migrating households from the troops – Look what the descendants of the Kirghiz of the gray yurts do! Now we serve the head of the animal for the sake of honor and say, Well done, and we hold our memorial feasts close to home! – They made the camels kneel and put the baggage-saddles on them, and got their tackle all in order; the dangling tassels of their trappings drew traces in the dust, and the bells on their necks made a huge din.

They got Kökötöy's blue standard raised, and the flag streamed and rippled in the wind, its golden crescent-moon finial glinting as in moonlight. The fine young fellows, all decked out and caparisoned, bowled along casually beside the migrating host. There are simply no words to describe it all. You couldn't see from one end to the other. From the front to the rear it was three days' ride, but if you stretched everybody out single file it would have been a hundred days. They got the horses moving and drove them out; one could not help but smile at the racers tied on leads. They chewed rib-fat until it trickled down their chins as they rode, and then pitched their tents close together; they were having great fun.

This cavalcade of your dear elders, the Kirghiz, traveled for four days, the migrating host flowing on like a ceaseless stream and spreading out over Oluya-Ata, Chïmkent, and Sayram by the riverside, the enormous throngs of people driving along their thundering herds of horses.* They tied up the foals on their tethers and camped summer-fashion for seven days. Then they set off again on their route, talking and gamboling about on horseback, stopped on the way for one night, and came to Qozu-bashï and Qopo; there they made camp again. Then Boqmurun said, "Let's get the sheep so fat that our guests will be glutted with eating!" so they moved around a bit, shifting the flocks here and there to keep them on fresh grass. They spent twenty days there, and then went to Almatï, where Boqmurun gave everyone a rest for six days and let the horses get some air. Eshik and Türgön, it seems, is where he had had crops planted by sending men on ahead earlier.* Then they crossed Chabdar, and the cloud of dust they threw up announced to no few that Kökötöy's memorial feast was going to take place.

Along the banks of the Üch Qarqïra to the valley of the Üch-bulaq they came, all of the Kirghiz, in preparation for Kökötöy's feast; and the entire teeming throng settled down along the banks of the Qarqïra. Boqmurun had ninety thousand young stalwarts summoned and sent into the mountains to cut down firewood. Juniper, rowan, spruce – but not the green saplings – he had them chop stout, dry logs and pile them up on the broad plain. Then he affixed a red flag to the pole with its golden crescent-moon finial and set it aloft, and on that very day set about the feast.

Now he took orphan boys and widows, saying, "Whatever you do, keep your wits about you," and employed them to turn people away from the meat. He told them, "Don't let greedy people try to reach in to the meat while it's cooking for the feast. I don't care who it is – even somebody who comes off like a governor – don't even look him in the face, just grab that person, whoever he is, and poke him in the ass with a stake. Do not let idle hands reach for the meat at the memorial feast for Kökötöy! Do not let anybody sidle up to you, even if he's important-looking!" Thus he set up guards to keep away the poor, the starving, and the paupers from Özgön, Qoqon, and Marghalang who never had butter to eat.

Now the Qara Kirghiz tribe arrived, a hundred here, a

thousand there, each day more than the last, and set up a sea of
yurts on the plain at Qarqïra, where the grass stood higher than
a rider's stirrups. The feather-grass grew tall on the passes and
the roe-deer lolled about everywhere; in every thicket the red
deer and hinds were springing; the Özübeks who arrived then
were asking each other, "What do they call this place?"

"It's a very good place to hold a feast," said Boqmurun. "But
I have something else in mind. Maani-ker stands tethered, that
tulpar I have been training and grooming all these years, from
the very beginning, to deliver the announcement. Of all my
obligations, this is the most important. Come! Let's make good
on it once and for all." When he had spoken these words
Boqmurun called a general assembly. His aged companion by
the name of Qashïmbek, and Abdïqadïr, and Daghuluq – when
Boqmurun gave his summons his men crowded on in. Mïrza
Bayïz, and Nurqabïl – all those distinguished men joined the
assembly, for the announcement was going out – and Baymïrza
son of Qashïm – he gathered them all together.

6

Boqmurun Mounts Aydar on Maani-ker and Sends Him to Invite the People

"Many people have heard that Kökötöy's memorial feast is going to be held, and are following news from us. Matters are now well in hand. The horses have eaten their fill and fattened up; the men are all growing bored. This year rounds out the third since my father's death. How shall we make the announcement? How many people shall we bring to this gathering? Take charge of this feast, notables! Speak, wise men!" Thus Boqmurun made his request.

Baymïrza began the discussion. What he had to say was agreed to by all: "Let's certainly invite Anjïyan and Qoqon to the feast," he said, shifting from his earlier position. "The Qara Qalmaqs should get invitations, more or less. If we invite one man who knows how to preside over a feast, one man with the skills of a sovereign, let it be Manas alone. With the Qazaqs, Kirghiz and Qalmaqs we can pay due respects to the spirits of our departed elders. Let people come if they're generous types who bring gifts to a feast to offset the host's expenses. And we should let a few Sarts come. But let's not allow the holding of this memorial feast for your father to bring hardship upon the tribe of Özübek."

Baymïrza was just getting started, but Boqmurun caught his drift, and tears fell from his eyes. "Baymïrza, son of Bay, you rogue! Sir I-Have-Black-Tea-To-Drink, Sir I-Can't-Find-A-Yearling-To-Ride, Sir Anybody-Who-Agrees-With-Your-Opinion-Would-Have-To-Be-An-Idiot – you rogue! I gave you direct orders – or would you rather plan your own memorial feast? When Sarghïl broke up your encampment, I was the one who rounded up everything and brought it back to you. Just see that you put on the right kind of feast when your father Qashïm dies, you rogue! I'm planning to bottom out, more or less – to use up everything. I'm not going to leave a single soul on the face of the earth unfeasted. I'm going to bring together all the Muslims and all the Heathens, God willing.

"Who taught you to be so stingy, you rogue? I'm inviting all the men in that direction and the *div* people in that direction behind us – everyone over there, and everyone here. I'm going to bring the fish out of the sea! You eat, you drink, but you're never full. Never, ever, ever do you leave off with your wickedness! Since you have no idea of your own worth you think of nothing but greed. If you say what you just said a second time, you'll be sprawled dead on the ground in a twinkling! You and those five men who follow you around, ever since I can remember you are always thinking about depravity.

"I'll drape you in sable furs, just make this affair into something renowned until the end of time! Formerly we had no skills at this; the dead died and there was no feast. What I am trying to do here is open the feast with a sacrifice, distribute my wealth to the whole world, and spread the news to all the tribes, so that it becomes an example to the people for all time. And you're the person I thought would come up with all the ideas! My father Kökötöy amassed immense wealth. Notwithstanding, when his death came on, what good did it do him? A puff of blue smoke escaped from his breast and he lived no more.

"Think about it: some plants are cut down when they're little switches; others, God Almighty has decreed, grow into poplars. Some people have no father, but death comes suddenly, and surely never makes a mistake. Think about other people whose fathers are alive but they have no children; there is no one whose ancestors aren't buried in the bowels of the black earth. Think about other people who are motherless but their daughter still lives – what hasn't happened in this illusory world? Think about other people whose mothers are alive but they have no children – once my Lord has made His decree there's no medicine that will cure them. If you are going along single-mindedly on a long journey, don't gallop, just move along slowly. To each mortal comes his turn, so do what you have to do in the time you have. If a swarm of ants means to do you harm, wish them well, but kill them. One end awaits a man, so do what you're good at.

"The Heathens have a lot of malice in them, but all around you stand tough fighters, sons of many a father, like yours – old Qashïm. When I put out the call, you – Abdïqadïr, Daghuluq – you all came in a bunch – Mïrza Bayïz, Nurqabïl, this past year you have shown exceptional grit and hustle in putting on this feast. But if you start to think, 'Boqmurun has run out of something' – whatever you've got that's short, make it long! I am not going to scant my cattle. I'm inviting everybody on the face of the earth because it's a matter of honor, so don't start things off by getting upset with someone who's come to the feast. The wealth my father accumulated – if I checked and included everything – is increasing daily. None of you is poor anymore; you've become rich. The horses your boys ride are yearling amblers of all sorts; your maidens and young ladies are clothed in variegated *shayï*-silks. I want the last people on earth to tell the tale of my father's fortune as their example. Only Almighty Allah knows how many guests are going to come. Who besides God knows what He will decree? My heart is filled with dreams. Who can conquer so many dreams? Let your words be brief, my fine men!

"There is that one who is passionate about any work he does, who knows sixty languages, part-interpreter and part-poet, intimate with all the better sort of men; whatever business we have, near or far, he's handy at it; a lad destined for greatness among the Kirghiz, who has a polite response to any word, kind or cutting; he's got bravery, yet put him with artisans and he'll show good taste, and there's his poetic side as well, for he can hold forth at great length; a man who says, 'Your other Kirghiz chiefs needn't get involved in your business; let me do it!' –"

"That suits us fine!" said Abdïqadïr and Daghuluq. "The power is in your hands; let it be as you choose, Prince!" So they sat there eagerly conferring among themselves.

But Boqmurun had been summoning Jash Aydar.

Jash Aydar came to him. Boqmurun speaks to him: "Jash Aydar, hear this!" he says. "Here is a golden coat of mail. Know this coat's value: bought at Babïl, so costly that the people of Balïq were ruined trying to come up with the price; if you wish to hear how much it was, a thousand four-year-old horses settled the bargain. Put on this corselet! Then mount my horse Maani-ker and set off!

"Ride the great *tulpar* Maani-ker and learn his abilities. Of *qarabayïr* and *qazanat* stock, with lungs like sieves* and wings of copper, ears like cut reeds and fetlocks of copper; he'll stand at pasture unhobbled yet not thirst if you gallop him for forty days through brain-boiling heat and deadly thick of battle, he'll not suffer if you gallop him for forty days through endless desert wastes till the dung in him boils into a stinking mire – though galloping in such a desert he wouldn't take even one mouthful of water! In appearance he's a shapely horse with hide all gathered in and stretched taut over his back, and no matter how many days you run him, it's not his wont to get wheezy; forty wings on his right side and forty wings on his left, and the black hairs of his tail flowing like a flag. Gallop him like mad for weeks on end, for it's only then that he gets into peak condition. That's just the way he is: born of a mountain-sheep-spirit of the winds, sired by a *tulpar*-spirit of the steppes. If he runs for eighty days and the clods and stones thrown by his hooves are tumbling off to the distance of eight *tash*, he is a beast that only adds to his strength. If you ride him round the world, he's a creature that won't lose muscle; his abilities are second to none! He's a creature that can jump over an ocean sixty days' journey wide, a beast that can step over mountains ninety days' journey across, and cliffs untrodden by the ibex! He's got every ability. If any foe should hatch some evil plan and you chance to get away, or if you fall into an ambush and you happen to avoid capture and you're making your getaway – even straight through their campfires and the coals won't touch him! If they shoot at you in close ranks you won't get hit; cannonballs won't touch you; if they line up and shoot at you the bullets won't touch you!

"Now mount that racer Maani-ker, and pay close attention to what I tell you. Head in the direction of the *qibla* as you get under way, and don't look around. The nearest country you'll reach – listen to how I'm listing them – is on yonder side of Buqaray-sharïp, on the hither side of the ruins at Chambïl, where you'll find him who lives on the middle Chatqal, ungoverned by anyone, armed with a fathom-long watered-steel sword, Muzburchaq son of Buudayïq. Stop but don't get off your horse, and speak. Exchange polite greetings but don't waste time. Say, 'It's time for the gala affair; Kökötöy's memorial feast is happening! The Qara Kirghiz have taken up residence at the edge of Chenggeldi, on the plain of Qarqïra. Their encampment stretches a month's journey from end to end, occupying all the ground in that locale. No one is shaking his head in refusal! The prizes for the long-distance horse race teem past counting; there's every art that the eye can see or the ear can hear!' tell him. If he asks you about the first prize in the horse race, tell him, 'Nine thousand tawny-red *nar* camels.' And say, 'Ninety thousand other cattle, cows and horses mixed together, and a hundred thousand sheep will also be posted. This is how they are putting on the feast for Kökötöy! The last prize in the race is nine head of large cattle and ninety sheep. This announcement is but a hint at what Boqmurun has in store!' tell him. Say, 'There are two people, a man and a woman, included in the last prize' – Say, 'As for the wrestling, it will be between enemies, men foreign to one another; as for the horses that will take home prizes, they will be sixty in number. There are prizes for sixty horses; those that win them will have some gain! Where in this illusory world will you find planning like that?' Tell him I said, 'Train up your Tel-küröng, lead in your armed host, and come to my feast! If you do not come to my feast I'm going to get nasty.* It is not to your detriment but to your advantage that we have come here with this invitation. If you do not come to my feast, get ready to be sacked!' – tell him that! Say, 'If Tel-küröng does not come to the race, I'm warning you: I will seize that nag and ride him myself, descend on your herds of horses resting in the cool air and drive them up a canyon and away, and strip you of your bullet-proof coat of mail and put it on! I'll

shatter the door-frame of your yurt,* make your young lads
weep, and set your mares kicking away off the mountainsides;
shatter the trellis-frames of your yurt and set your virgin mares
kicking away off the high, grassy slopes; make your young
ladies and maidens weep, smash your roofed stronghold, set fire
to your clay stronghold, trample your noblemen so-like-well-
manned-falcons underfoot like felting-wool,* turn your willowy
virgins into ungainly scullery slaves, have your bleating sheep
rounded up, and impoverish your people; and as for your prop-
erty, you'll get a shaving! I'll have your lowing cattle tied up and
your possessions apportioned out, make your camels bawl, and
set your racers that have lived the easy life plodding off in train!'
Tell him I'll do as I please with him. Tell him, 'Boqmurun shall
slaughter you! No one shall be left alive!'

"If you go onward from there you'll come to Badaqshan and
Balïq where there are numerous peoples, and the khan, Maamït
Sultan, with even more people under him; he can muster six
hundred thousand troops. Say, 'Khan Kökötöy has died. He has
entered a dark place, the afterlife, from which there is no return.
His son, Boqmurun by name, has gone and encamped as we
speak on the plain at Qarqïra, with the entire population of the
city of Tashken, to give Kökötöy's memorial feast. A memorial
feast is one of our sacred acts of charity. I am inviting you to
this charitable entertainment and earnestly wish for you to
attend.' Tell him, 'Train up your racer and set your troops in
order; there will be something in it for you.' Say, 'Come to my
feast! If you do not come to the feast, the consequences of your
scornful attitude shall be on your head! Keep out of my sight
and hide your bitterness, for I will throw you into a panic; even
if you were a mountain I would dig you up and put you on the
apple-pile; I'll gouge out the eyes of your young girls and make
them suffer!' Let him ponder my words. Tell him, 'Make no
mistake, I am not the easy-going type! I will crush your roofed
stronghold. No son of Adam shall be able to keep me off you if
that's how you want it; you'll have no defense. I will set fire to
your clay stronghold and bring a raging bloodbath down upon
you!' Say, 'I'll take your girls in their red silks for my menials.
I'll give you a sacking that people will really talk about; I'll take

your boisterous beauties and make them cowering slaves, use
your bolts of yuft like blocks of dung-fuel, and flatten whatev-
er's not level! I'll do as I please with you.' Tell him, 'Boqmurun
shall slaughter you! No one shall be left alive!'

"When you pass on from there you'll come to Mïsïr and
Köpö where countless roads converge. He who rules Mïsïr is
Kemel son of Seyit, second to none,* victor in hostile contests.
Say, 'Khan Kökötöy has died. He has realized the falseness of
this world and submitted to the will of Almighty Allah. Now,
come and see his memorial feast. Those that stay away from his
feast are surely as good as dead! This memorial feast is being
held for a son of the Qara Kirghiz, a humble slave of Almighty
Allah. The first prize in the horse race is ninety thousand large
cattle and a hundred thousand sheep – but that's not all that's
planned – also for the first prize go nine thousand red-tailed
nar camels. Forty herders manage all those animals. Of female
and male slaves the first prize also includes eighty-two souls.
He whose horse comes in first gets it all, but he whose horse
doesn't even show up gets none of the loot. And there's more
being planned to enrich those that win it: the top sixty horses
will get prizes. Nine cattle and ninety sheep make up the prize
for the last-place horse; even if you get that, it's something –
and everybody knows about this thing that the Kirghiz do:
included with the very last prize are a man and a woman, a
married couple' – tell him that. Tell him he must come to this
feast I am putting on, and if he does not come, I'll have no sym-
pathy for his tears; the consequences of his scorn shall be on his
head! I will set his mules kicking away up the canyons, make
his women and girls weep, smash his yurt-doors, reduce his
roofed house to rubble and slaughter anyone I find inside, and
chop down all his willows! Tell him I will pound his built house
down to sand, turn his wives into widows, and make any man
of his I can get my hands on into a loutish slave! People shall
hear and talk about it – I'll trample his noblemen in the full
flower of their youth underfoot like bits of felting-wool, enslave
his women, have his cloths worn away to tatters and lay waste
his encampment! Tell him I will show the sons of the Qara Kir-
ghiz the way to his treasury, sell off here and there any strong

young men he's got, annihilate his people and pile his lands with their bodies!

"Sitting on his khanly throne in the west, where he blocks the path of the Heathen, at the very center of the earth is one, not God our Creator, but one who, though he is not God, is nevertheless not far removed from God, friendly and intimate and on the best terms with Him, he who constantly adds auspiciousness to good fortune, seated upon a golden throne delivered from God by Jebireyil – he who has brought the sharia to all the lands of the earth, the imam of the Arabs after Mustapa the conqueror of the world – Ayqojo. Say to him, 'The people have migrated and come to rest, and Kökötöy's memorial feast is beginning. If the Prophet extends his patronage and God gives His help, the entire world is going to assemble at this greatest of feasts.' Say to him, 'You have been invited, if you would deign to consider us ordinary men.'

"From there you will pass on, heading west, where there is the desert of Qubayïs. On the far side, if you can make it out, is lake Shor, a sea. In the desert of Qubayïs are a different sort of people. One has hair three fathoms long, another a hundred fathoms; whoever's hair they find is the longest they make their chief for the time being and reverence him, it would seem on account of his hair. There is no breeze in that place; one could live to the age of seventy and not feel a puff of wind. Considering their hair, this is actually good for their well-being. They all go about with heads uncovered, naked. Speak directly to their leader, face-to-face with their chief; as when speaking with Ayqojo, make your words delicate.

"As you pass onward from there you will come to the sea and many different localities. There are the Tayïp, a tribe of *peris*, in their own land. The *bek* of the Tayïp is Könök, who never looks eastward, so the people of olden times used to say. If he's still holding body and soul together, inform him that we have invited him to the memorial feast for Kökötöy. You will reach there mounted on Maani-ker; he hardly needs a rider to make the journey!

"In Jelpinish the land juts up; don't stay long there. Of winged creatures there are *jinns* there, and of mighty beasts there are elephants; who else could inhabit that place? Ride to the left and then to the right, and there's the edge of a sea. Along the shore live the Danghït people with their chief, Choyun Alp, a marvelous and numerous nation. Their practice is to tend the fish in the sea like cattle. Choyun Alp thinks himself quite a formidable fellow, imagines there's none in the world such as he. He just doesn't see other people these days! You confront him and say, 'Go and see the honor in which Türks of noble lineage are held. See that your armed host comes, and lead in the Danghït people. Many will gather in attendance at the memorial feast for Kökötöy Khan, son of the Kirghiz tribe from the city of Tashken! The feast is being held at Qarqïra.' Tell him to take this invitation very seriously. Tell him, 'If you do not take it seriously your people shall come to grief. The missing shall be found, and you shall be sacked and annihilated. People will talk about the sacking you receive. Your slender, angelic beauties who flounce like rushes on the riverbank shall become my slaves; this is what you have in store for you! Your swaggering lords shall be sold as slaves for four head of cattle apiece and their wives shall be widows; that is the day you have in store for you!'

"Don't tarry there; pass onward. If you travel for two days you will reach the confines of Orus. Go to Kerke Khan, and speak to him – speak so that the heart in him splits. Tell him what you have seen – that the memorial feast for Kökötöy, the leader of the people, is a splendid thing to witness. Tell him, 'Come to this memorial feast I am putting on. If you do not come, you are wishing disaster upon your own head. No grave shall give you refuge; though you find a door to enter, there shall be no seat of honor for you; though you see your flesh, your bones shall be gone.' Give him a good scolding. Tell him, 'What I say is no lie. Your people and even your racers that have never felt the halter shall know misfortune on your account. I will crush your house of stone; you can pray all you want but no defender shall be able to repel me. I will slaughter your yearling heifers at pasture and carry your brown-haired children off on the back of my horse; smash and throw on the fire your carts and sledges, your willows planted in groves; even your mumbling old men! The story of your fate will live on in your tribe. Your women shall be reduced to slavery, your men shall be reduced to ashes; your wives shall become widows and your livestock shall be sold for cash; your spouses shall become widows, and your window-sashes shall be removed and stacked up. I will scatter your gold, drag you from the refuge of your yurt, and expose your head; I will scatter your silver and sell all your people into slavery!' You will say that to the Orus; you will return safely to me!

"When you have passed on from there you will arrive at Barang. Go to Baltamat and speak to him – speak so that the heart in him splits. Say, 'Khan Kökötöy has died. He has followed the road from which there is no return. They washed him with water of Zamzam, wound him in *sarbap*-silk and buried him with pomp. Now they are holding his memorial feast. Come!' Tell him, 'If you do not come to the feast, then know that your death is at hand.' Tell him I will massacre his kinsmen and hand out his maidens as presents. The whole world will hear the story of what happened to him; people at the very end of time will still be telling vivid accounts of it. Tell him I will steal his maned horses and his pastured cows and utterly destroy and cast to the winds his goods packed away in chests; he shall be parted from his property as from his fun and games. Not one of his horses with flowing tails shall be left peeping up; I'll make women out of his virgins and firewood out of of his women! I will slaughter everyone he sees and then gouge out his eyes!

"In Sulayman's times there was a people who were defeated and their cattle wrested from them. This populous nation fled, from Qïtay, and became completely wild. Their new land was good to them, and the name Japan stuck.[1] They have a hero named Kötörüsh, and an island called Sïymun. Go and speak to their leader, speak with all your cunning. Say, 'These are the words of the surpassingly skilled Boqmurun. Death never errs; Boqmurun's father Kökötöy Khan has passed on from this world.' Tell him he should train up his Qaz-qula and drive in

1.   "Japan": The Kirghiz word *japan* means "wild."

his ponderous troops. Say, 'I am inviting you to the memorial feast I am holding, so come. If you do not come to this feast, know in truth that you shall die.' I will dig up his orchards down to the charred stumps, smash his august golden throne to pieces, dig up his fruit trees and level the ground, turn his heart into a hard, black, malignant tumor, make his livestock market a stampede, and drive his borrowed soul mad with impending doom. I will leave him not one head of cattle to drive nor one grain in his barn; will leave him not one soul alive, nor any honor to his learned men; will leave him not a grain of dust to blow in the wind! Tell him, 'I'll leave your reception-palace a ruin and slaughter you; this is no lie! I'll destroy your painted palace without a trace and slaughter every last one of you!'

"After delivering that message you will pass onward to those giants of the Qara Qalmaq, who at present are lords of untold hundreds of thousands, Joloy and Ushang. Make your way to them and say, 'I am inviting you; come to the memorial feast! If you do not come to the feast you shall be sacked – you can be sure of it. I will leave not one beast on your pastures, not so much as a race-horse's mane; not a willow log to light nor a coat to put on; not a path to tread in safety nor a house to enter, anywhere. I will leave you not even the strength to move; yet see that you don't feel sorry for yourself!' I will utterly ruin him, leaving not even the foundations of his houses, not even a yearling among his horses, nor the room to build a house on, nor a groom to marry a wife. I will bring a raging bloodbath down upon him and hand out his maidens as presents; bring down a mighty affliction on him and hand out his young ladies as presents. Let them abandon all hope – the wooing men, all those fleeing the land of the Qara Qalmaq – commoners and khans, young and old. With a stroke of my hand I will knock his yurt with its door-frame down off the mountainside and make of it a bleak ruin; with a stroke of my hand I will knock his spacious trellis-framed yurt down off the grassy mountain slope, thus easing my troubles, and make of it a spacious ruin! Let Joloy train up Ach-buudan and choose a jockey.* If he does not end up coming to the feast I will see that there's no remedy for him!

"From there you will pass on and arrive at Anjïlïq where you will find Muradïl son of Qïrmuz, and red-topknotted Nezqara; go to those men who fancy themselves heroes and speak to them sternly, inform them and turn away from there. I will have their racers captured; I will shower torments on their people! If I have to come after them, I'll topple their black fortresses and their gilded court-pavilions; if they don't show up at the feast I am putting on, they shall find out in all sorts of ways that their health and safety are no more! The missing shall be found and cut down as they duck in the tall grass; those I care to find shall be found and thrown into torment as they are cut down! I will slaughter those warriors themselves and make the tears fall from their dark eyes; I will take their girls for menial servants; they must not fail to understand that their bodies shall feel the pain of it! I will torment every drop of his people's black blood and rob their souls of comfort; swords shall fall on their necks and red blood soak their breasts. I'm summoning them in order to see them at the games for Kökötöy. I have summoned; now let them come to my feast. If they do not heed this summons, soldiers shall pay them a visit and torment shall be their lot. I'll show not a shred of mercy to young or old; I'll clean the gems and precious stones out of their assholes! Let them train up their horses for the feast; let their soldiers come on teeming as grains of sand; let them choose jockeys. If they do not come to the feast there shall be no finding a way out for any of them!

"From there you will pass on and bring your news. In the city of Chïn at the foot of the Qanghar mountains speak to that old man Alooke, tell him I have invited him to my father's feast. Also go and speak to him who ranges on the Qara-too mountains at Qaspang and at Chong-tabïlghï, at the entrance to gated Beejin, him who keeps a huge black, Qongurbay; to him and to old man Alooke together, say this: 'Whether you've got no horse to ride and have to walk, or whether you're no ordinary strong-man, but a *div*, come to this memorial feast I am putting on! If you do not come to this memorial feast, know that you shall face destruction.' Tell them their gardens shall be mown and their orchards chopped down; by order of

Boqmurun son of wealthy Kökötöy non-attendance is forbidden. Tell them I will turn their spring into autumn and their fallow fields into salt flats. I will burn their fortresses and reduce them to dunghills, and shit on their holy shrines. I will thoroughly massacre their *tïytay*, inflict total annihilation upon them, turn Chïn topsy-turvy. Let Qongurbay train up Al'-ghara, muster his worthy young men, and select a jockey. If he does not come to the feast I will see that there is no remedy for him, and that the benefit goes to the Qara Kirghiz. I will leave not one of his lofty buildings standing, not one mole on his body un-pummeled, not so much as the mane on a horse un-rustled. I will make his old people cry, 'Ah, woe!'; everyone shall suffer. Tell that to him, then pass onward from there.

"To black-maned Boroonchu and Oronghu from the Qanghay do not fail to say, 'Come to this memorial feast!' Let them train Qïl-küröng and Qula-bee and get them into good condition; let them summer on the mountains at Qïzïl and choose jockeys. If they do not come to my feast the consequences of their scornful attitude shall be on their heads! I will set fire to the goods in their shops and completely massacre their slaves, steal their cattle from the pastures – that they may get a sense of my powers! – and sink their old people in grief. I will slaughter any people I meet, gorge myself on their blood, and gouge out their dark eyes. I will smash their stone fortresses, fire their clay fortresses, tear up their meadowsweet bushes. I will knock flat anyone I find, crush their stone fortresses and make their people moan, young and old. They shall see Kökötöy's blue standard appear suddenly above them. That would wipe the comeliness off their faces; but tell them they must not let it come to that! Let them train up their race-horses with coats gray as clouds and pick jockeys to race them! If they do not come to this feast of mine I will bear the grudge, and they had better keep out of my sight; if they appear before my eyes they mustn't blame me for what happens!

"Then you will pass on from there. In the east is the place Kübö, full of the Dughul, a mix of humans and *divs*; the inhabitants of Suya are *peris*. Next to that place are Jajuj and Majuj; let me give you some information about them and tell you about their horses. They have a giant named Kiyengkesh and an unmounted fighter named Kishidash. You ask about Kishidash: if you lance him you can't pierce him, if you slash him you can't cut him. No son of Adam relying on his weapons could face him. If a mortal man were to happen upon Kishidash of a sudden, there and then he must say, 'O Zul Jalal!' and as a result that Heathen would be rendered very timid, and that would spell his death. Bullets and swords are useless; nothing will work except the cry, 'O Zul Jalal!' His body is not flesh but red-hot coals; if he but hears this name of God they will be quenched as if soaked by rain and he will depart for the underworld. Let your mind ponder this insight, for that Heathen has a sword, a gun, every sort of weapon and ammunition.

"Next to that place are other beings, every one of them vile, men with half-bodies and various strange races all sprung from intermingling of men and *divs* and *peris*: vulture-tailed Joon Alp, scissor-tailed Qaman Alp, onager-tailed Qutan Alp, and iron-naveled Kiten Alp – descended not from people but from Jeztumshuq, they form the race called Chïngïroo. Say to them that I have invited them to the memorial feast, and they must come. Say, 'Your non-attendance shall spell your death; you'll learn the meaning of trouble!'

"From there you will go on downhill and reach the borders of the dwarves and the Itaalï. Tell them that Kökötöy's memorial feast is going to be a sight to see, and he that stays home shall not remain unharmed.

"Aqdöö, Kökdöö, and Qïzïldöö are giants who go on foot and have never seen a horse; pass them by and head for the island at the angle of the Shor, where the Barang of the nine tribes live with their khan, Chatangayïsh. Let him train up his horse Qach-ala, let him get some benefit for himself, let him choose a jockey! If he does not come to the feast, I will see that there is no remedy for him. Tell him, 'Your blood shall flow like water, your soul shall not be safe, your authority shall vanish. If you do not come to this memorial feast, your soul shall be an utter loss!

"From there you will make your way onward to Khan Dömül, chief of the Döböt. That beggar had better come to this memorial feast, for whoever dares not to come shall doom his borrowed soul to sore affliction. Let him train up his horse Too-qara, let him set his mind to racing! Say, 'But of course you are coming to the feast; if you don't show up, then you die!'

"There's one khan, Atala, and one khan, Ündüchaq: they must come to my feast without delay. If they do not come, if they do not pay me this visit, I will persecute their sorry heads. Their men shall be enslaved needlessly, their wives shall be widows, their women shall be sold, and anyone who puts on airs shall be shot – none shall live!'

"From there you will be turning toward home. Speak to Aqun Khan. Then there is your old uncle Qoshoy; from him all the way to here everyone is Muslim: Töshtük son of Eleman, Jamghïrchï of the Eshtek, eloquent Ürbü, Khan Jügörü, and Chegish.

"Then among the sons of the Kirghiz lineage there is the magnanimous ruler Manas. You should appear before him and meet him personally, for unless you want to die – unless you want to head straight to your grave – unless you have a burning desire to depart for the next world – unless you are intent on death – you must tell him that I summon him to the feast. Tell him, 'This swaggering behavior of yours! You have a different role to play.' Say this directly to him, not to anyone else, or you shall die needlessly.

"On the slopes of the Ala-too beyond Anjïyan, hard by the Mïrghap, in Jazïyra, which you reach by Jet-qayt pass, speak to him whose remote ancestor is Jediger and his latter-day ancestor Jadiger – to Baghïsh son of Uyuq. Tell him to train up his horse Sur-kiyik, and get his people interested by telling them, 'They say there's going to be a memorial feast, and I'm going!' Tell him he must come to the feast I am putting on; if he does not, my battle-ax shall land on his head. Everything he owns shall be carried off as plunder and his old people shall be left plaintively crying. Tell him he must submit to my command and come see my masterful planning; if he says he will not come see, then let him know that he is truly planning his own burial. He shall see soldiers on the march robbing him utterly; he shall know disaster! Say all that to him, make sure that he listens, then return from that place to me."

Maani-ker was the horse that Jash Aydar mounted; a coat of mail was what he donned. His mission had been conferred and his leave granted; now he set out on his long journey. Maani-ker, that racer of enormous stamina, was at once lathered all over. Above the tossing grass, beneath the cloudy sky, one would not so much say he galloped as flew – yes, flew, that devil! – he went thundering off, smashing rocks with his hoof-beats. It took nine months to reach all the places Boqmurun had named, all those strange and varied places across the whole face of the earth.

By the time nine months had gone by,* the livestock had grown fat. At the place where the memorial feast was to be held, when he had encamped to make the preparations, Boqmurun had had the blue standard with its variegated blue banner raised up high to make his enemies feel abashed at its appearance. Three hundred thousand yurts had been set up, and chiefs were present from Boqmurun's father's line out to the distance of second cousins.* The domes of all the yurts had been covered in white worsted wool. Their frame-poles had been sharpened, and each of the points had its wrapping of worsted for when the tents would be struck and packed up and loaded onto pack-horses; every little invisible detail had been seen to as they were being set up.

So then it was the time when everyone was busy making final preparations for Bay Kökötöy's memorial feast. People were saying, "Are the guests coming or not?" and putting up decorations, as watchers were posted on all the roads; saying, "When are they going to get here?" as the warriors grew bored and lazy. The people were extremely well provided for; they were now in their fourth year of living in abundance. As they watched and waited, Er Baghïsh was thinking, "Well, his father was a close relation of mine, and he's sent me this announcement. He's probably waiting impatiently."

7

The People Arrive at Kökötöy's Memorial Feast

Er Baghïsh's horse was named Sur-kiyik. He himself was of direct noble descent. "People of my city, Chïyrasha," he said, "I will take my son Toltoy, my comfort and support, to accompany me, and I will go to the memorial feast without delay. It would be rude not to go; this is a unique occasion. All the better sort of people will be there, so my son should go and have a look. Let him see people so long as his father is alive, let him get an eyeful and see the world so long as he's got a horse. If he doesn't see the world, what is he going to see?"

So, Baghïsh took Toltoy along with him for the pleasure of giving him a look at the different nations and peoples, and got under way. It was not a short journey. They were a long time traveling; after thirteen days on the road they reached the banks of the Üch-bulaq and the valley of Üch Qarqïra where the yurts had been pitched for Kökötöy's feast. It was not early; the sun was already declining past midday, when Prince Baghïsh descended on the scene riding at the head of a retinue of four thousand soldiers. Right away animals were slaughtered and dressed and the food presented to him.

On his heels, with a red flag on his standard and making a mighty whooping noise, came that big man of the Qïtay, Er Qongur, with his damned posture of toughness, firing off his musket of Urum make as if his son and daughter-in-law had been attacked, as if chasing a fugitive escaped that very day – as if those who saw his power would be impressed! – as if his wife had been molested – firing off his *almabash*-musket as if an enemy had raided his encampment; so what if his traveling-tents were packed onto rhinoceroses and his trumpets and shawms were playing! Striking steel to tinder in his bronze-stemmed pipe and giving it a great, gurgling suck, he spread discord everywhere. Qongurbay had arrived with a hundred thousand troops.

That whooping Qïtay Muradïl son of Qïrmuz also arrived with ten thousand men moving inexorably on. Red-topknotted Nezqara arrived with seven thousand; Ushang of the Qalmaq came rumbling on with two thousand; Alooke of the Soloon with fifty thousand; that giant Joloy bad-tempered as a boar brought thirty thousand; Bozkertik of the Toqshuker, thirty thousand also; Soorondük son of Solobo, thirty thousand as well; black-maned Boroonchu, thirty thousand more. From the Qanghay there was Oronghu who came slinking in with ninety thousand men; Sayqal daughter of Qatqalang arrived with thirty thousand picked fighters. Not to be outdone, the khan's maternal nephew Jügörü arrived also, by way of Jïyrantï, with twenty thousand warriors. Those were the ones who arrived that first day, and rested. When dawn was breaking the next morning, Kerkökül son of Kökmök now arrived with two thousand men; Er Janay son of Köchpös with seven thousand.

After him, that rich boy Boqmurun's longing was requited, for your dear uncle Qoshoy the giant came on, rocking on his gray ambler, his brilliant white beard dazzling as he bawled out the call to prayer, 'Come!' he honked like a goose. With him came a vast army of thirty thousand sending the dust wheeling up to heaven, deafening the ears with their shawms and clattering their standards; they trod over everything in their great numbers.

Next came that one who had spent fully seven years beneath the earth and had come back to the surface a mere seven days previous: saying, "Boqmurun has got a peculiar idea about good manners; it won't do to stay away from the feast!" Töshtük now came on with four thousand soldiers in his retinue.

Before Töshtük had taken his seat or done anything, that one who summers in the Sarï-arqa and leads the Qazaq without number, who trains and keeps Ker-töböl tethered by his tent, who plucks off the heads of advancing enemies and chews them up; his hat decorated with embroidery, his trousers of yellow buff, the metal trinkets on his belt-pouch tinkling from his silken sash, his copper boot-heels capped in gold: Er Kökchö son of Aydar Khan arrived via the road from Orol with an army of thirty thousand soldiers.

There was no let-up behind him. That one who, in exchanging fire with enemies, covered them with dust on all sides, who covered battlegrounds with their blood; whose fury alone could cause enemies to err – Jamghïrchï son of Eshtek arrived then with seven thousand.

After him, he who summers at Eki Kemin, who keeps a pair of blacks trained and never comes out the loser in a contest of words – Ürbü, champion of the Faith and well-known spiritual guide, speaker of eloquent words and well-known wise counselor, the strongest of the Qïpchaq – he too came on then, in unusual splendor, attended by twelve thousand.

After him, he who lives between Buqaray-sharïp and the ruins of Chambïl, on the middle Chatqal, ungoverned by anyone, impossible to overturn at wrestling, an armful of weapons at his belt – Muzburchaq son of Buudayïq arrived at the memorial feast via the road from Chabdar with a host fully nine thousand strong.

To everyone who witnessed it this memorial feast was a unique sight. When the first-arrived guests and their dependents had spent eleven full days at the feast and the twelfth day had begun, Sarï Döö of the Saqalat came with a throng of six thousand; magnificent Keyqubat arrived as well with seven thousand; Khan Dömül chief of the Döböt and his three thousand men poured in; swaggering Choyun Alp, vulture-tailed Joon Alp, scissor-eared Qaman Alp and iron-naveled Kiten Alp, of the lineage of Jeztumshuq, a race that lives quite apart – they came with their ruler, three thousand troops in his personal suite and a hundred thousand besides. Maamït Sultan came as well from a very long way away, one of the bravest of brave warriors, with his host approaching two thousand. Kemel came with a hundred men; Ayqojo with three men; Ïybanküp came with a force of barely a hundred from across Chabdar; Bakürüsh came with a thousand men, maneuvering them all without so much as one false step. Then Aqun Khan arrived from Ooghan by way of the Ala-too with an army of about six thousand. When one beheld how many people had come, the heart leapt at the mass of humanity.

A month has thirty days, and in that time we beheld much of the world's population. With these guests we spent the entire summer; yet even before all the guests had arrived and before a month had passed the Muslims were all at a loss, for Manas Baatïr had not come. Now let the story tell of Jash Aydar, who had traveled to Manas.

Brave Sïrghaq and Er Serek were there, distinguished warriors of Manas; that ruthless hero Chubaq son of Aqbalta Biy was there as well, and he was not happy. It was to them that Jash Aydar made the speech he had been bringing around, speaking in the person of Boqmurun and delivering his pronouncements. One disrespectful syllable of it was all Er Sïrghaq needed to hear before he grabbed Maani-ker by the lead-rope and stripped Jash Aydar naked, and he was truly on the point of executing the lad there and then.* "Cut off my head, but don't expose my nakedness!" the lad said; that day the young Aydar had to grow up.

As they were about to kill him, Er Manas, who had been out hunting, suddenly came upon them. Jash Aydar cried out beseechingly, his face ashen; the wretch wailed in submissive tones: "Boqmurun was saying, 'How can I hold the memorial feast at tiny Anjïyan?' He was saying, 'How can I gather the people on such rich cropland?' He was saying, 'How can I put on amusements at Tashken pretty-as-a-maiden's-skullcap? The land outside the gates is crowded with houses. There are plenty of provisions for sustenance, plenty of cattle at pasture, plenty of ripening grain, numerous four-cornered skins full of kumiss – but there are also numerous ruins of four-cornered fortifications; how can I race horses there?' He was saying, 'I will make you, Baatïr, the president of this memorial feast!' I was coming to invite you, but your Sïrghaq, Serek and Chubaq were about to kill me – then I saw you, Gray-maned One! Your generals are on the point of killing me right here." The herald Jash Aydar had so many details to relate that he was gasping and about to faint.

When Manas saw this, he understood that the lad was terrified, and he burst out laughing. Not a little, reserved laugh – everything Manas did was a world-topper – he laughed as if there was nothing in his soul but laughter, baring his brilliant white teeth – no ordinary man's, the incisors broad as yurt-doors. "Heroes, what are you doing here?" he roared. "I am the one who gives the orders. Do not be angry at this messenger; it is I who have the authority to speak." Having thus told them off he had the herald Aydar clothed in a garment of *buulum* and had him presented with a roan ambler. "There now," he said. "I'll come in a few days. My greetings to those who have already arrived!" With that he sent Aydar on his way.

Once Aydar had departed, Er Manas set to mustering his troops. From up as far as Arsï and Jölök and down as far as Ïsar and Kölöp he gathered none into his force who was not Kirghiz. "Forward!" roared Manas, and the drum-rolls thundered. Ranging along the Ala-too and roaming from spring to spring, he headed for cooler country and had a stop at Suu-samïr. Then taking the road through windy Qochqor, Manas and his innumerable host came to the lakeshore at Cholpon Ata, by the banks of the Chong-qoy stream, toward evening. They rested there and played at casting knucklebones.* They proceeded along the lake, camping as they went; the space between the lake and the mountains was filled by the large army. Then late one morning the soldiers donned their armor of blue steel, and going at an easy pace they crossed Qïzïl-qïya by midday without any difficulty.

As they went the lion Manas sent word ahead of their arrival. Jash Aydar carried the news, saying, "Manas the brave is arriving! One flash of rage by him, and this whole encamped multitude will surely be slaughtered!" Thus he was announced in advance by the herald.

Upon hearing this Boqmurun pressed his people into service. He erected ninety pavilion-tents at Qïzïl-qïya pass; nine hundred chiefs, give or take, waited there, while nine thousand men rode out on the road Manas was traveling to meet and greet him. Manas's greatness was so well known that the multitude assembled there was in a state of agitation that day. As soon as they grasped the sternness of his announcement, a teeming multitude mounted up and went out to see Khan Manas, while nine hundred chiefs awaited him in their nine hundred yurts.

8

Manas Arrives at Kökötöy's Memorial Feast

Boqmurun had ninety mares slaughtered at the place-for-slaughtering-nineties and placed people at the ready along the road, but other than that he took no notice of anything, nor did he act on anyone else's advice. Unable either to think of any more instructions or to catch sight of anyone coming, paying little heed to anything, the normally composed Boqmurun was on that day feeling quite beside himself. Thus did the glorious lineage of the Kirghiz make its greatness known! That was the way with brave Manas – if merely laying eyes on him was tormenting, crossing paths with him was even worse.

A company of twenty men marched in his vanguard, his deadly sharpshooters, intrepid, unerring marksmen; their gun-stocks curved like plow-handles, fuses lit, with the butts of their muskets shouldered in firing position, they were a marvel to those who knew shooting. Ranging his muskets thus in a row Manas arrived at the memorial feast with loud professions of the Faith. A company of twenty men followed him, his intrepid, unerring archers, their quivers big around as a yearling colt's girth, their iron arrow-heads sharpened to fearsome points and quenched in poison; their deadly bows were drawn, and astounding cries were on their lips. On his right a company of twenty intrepid warriors, world-crushers; they drew their sabers and set them swinging as they made their way steadily on. On his left a company of twenty intrepid warriors, battle-wolves, with gleaming gold mail-shirts strapped on their frames; their vehemence sent shock-waves through the crowd. These heroes on the left lifted their crescent-moon-bladed battle-axes broad as doors as if to start swinging. Behind the

archers came warriors deftly wielding fearsome polished lances
with a firm grip, now gliding along at one with the road, now
bursting ahead as if sighting an enemy, ready to punch their
way through battle-lines. Their gold-adorned mail-shirts were
fastened tight; their lances covered entirely in gold flashed in
their midst, and they held aloft sixty *jaysangs*.* Thus the hero
made his entrance. Bringing up the rear came his sure-shot
artillery and ninety thousand fierce soldiers.

Trumpets roared, shawms blared, copper-flutes twittered; the
constant beat of drums thundered as if mountains were on the
move. When Manas came in among the feast-goers and
approached with that exceedingly forbidding air about him, no
one could stand up to his look of fury even to greet him. This
wasn't a man who bothered with greetings as you and I. Abïke
Datqa, his world-conquering tiger, led in the host with shawms
sounding in the rear, a banner fixed to his crescent-moon-
topped standard, and thirty stalwart companions.

In the front six pages led the way in, and in their midst that
enormous horse Aq-qula, with twelve squires holding his lead-
rope and seven sergeants-at-arms shooing people away to clear
space for him. That praiseworthy racer, the enormous Qula –
his coat like the feathers of the eagle-owl, his back piled with
richly ornamented saddle-cloths; let out to his ease on ground
strewn with sand and set to drink on lands strewn with wells,
distinguished by his mane erect as the onager's, rump round
and full like a drum – good fortune rested upon him; with ears
pricked up like candle-flames and upon his left flank a mark
Ayqojo had left where he stroked him with his hand, this was a
well-favored creature excelling all other beasts in form! Manas
had Aq-qula in peak condition; his soldiers too were stout in
their tightly fitted, gleaming gold mail-shirts.

His Forty Heroes now crowded in; Qïrghïl Chal roared, their
iron-tipped lances glinted, and the Forty gave a full-throated cry.
Eighty-four of Manas's warriors wore impenetrable corselets;
their glances igniting flames, like nothing else the world has ever
seen – all around them were red-hot coals. When Manas came in
among the feast-goers, they saw and understood that his exceed-
ingly forbidding air made him a lion among men.

Kökötöy's son Boqmurun the Snot-Nose, "It-Fazes-Me-Not"-Nose,* had that gyrfalcon of a creature, his *tulpar* Archa-toru brought forward, and had the call to prayer uttered; he presented his *tulpar* Archa-toru to Manas. Then he had a tawny-coated kid picked out and slaughtered for a sacrifice of thanksgiving, and distributed red gold coin as alms – the Forty Heroes, meanwhile, were careful not to disrupt the proceedings – and the poor appreciated the abundant donation.

Qoshoy, rocking atop his light-gray horse with his bright mail-coat stripped off to the waist and his white beard a-flutter, came to speak a wise word to that gray-maned ball of fury, to meet and exchange greetings with that chieftain, now that he had arrived. "God has honored us! Your boss has come!" he said to the people. "Let's give our greetings now to that world-wandering oath-breaker, bloodthirsty Manas the grim! Let's go on up to him – don't be put off by his terrible looks! We can't hang back and pretend he's not there. Come on, children! Don't take Manas lightly, while you fret that it's been thirty days since you got here and your feast hasn't started yet! He's a genuine kinsman of ours, they say; deeper than the sea, that bloodthirsty hero – and damned well blessed by God! They say he's a close kinsman, but that's neither here nor there – the fact is he's mighty damned powerful!"

Saying, "Come on, let's take some *bangzats* along and go meet that tiger, Baatïr Manas," Qoshoy of the Qataghan, Kökchö of the Qazaq, Töshtük son of Eleman, Jamghïrchï of the Eshtek, Baghïsh of the Jediger, Aghïsh son of Jetkir Biy, eloquent Ürbü, and Jügörü son of Qarashaq – those eight men, every one of them a ruler, every one a khan, went out to face him. The banner fluttered on their glinting crescent-moon-topped standard as they approached Manas's host, sonorously intoning the call to prayer as they went. Led by Qoshoy that whole company of rulers paid their respects to Er Manas with hands pressed tight to their stomachs; Qoshoy the giant and then the rest of them got down off their horses and stood before him.

Famed Er Manas gave a ringing "Salam!" to his elder kinsman, the white-bearded hero; dear uncle Qoshoy bellowed "Alik!"* in return.

Then Qoshoy spoke to Manas; his frayed temper showed in his strongly worded speech. "Well look who's here! Valiant Manas. Never before in the traditions of past nations, Muslim or heathen, have I ever heard of such a scandal as this! All kinds of people have passed on before us since our progenitor Adam; many a khan on his golden throne has passed on from this world – Adam's son Shish has passed on, and many, many people besides – Iskender, Sulayman* – this Kökötöy of yours, is he greater than they? Many a sultan, many a khan has passed on from this world, but never has there been a calamity such as this, never have the Muslims experienced such turmoil! The world be damned if anyone hears or sees a turn of events such as Almighty God has brought upon us here! That half-wit, brainless child, sowing his disturbances – Boqmurun can drop dead! Unable to make a go of it, he is determined to run his great fortune into the ground; there's hardly anything left of it now, anywhere. So today you happen upon the scene! Why are you so late, letting your people go to ruin? It's been a whole month that they've been saying, 'He's coming'! 'A month has passed,' they say; 'He'll come in a while,' they say – meanwhile the soldiers are looting the food! 'He'll come soon,' they say – meanwhile the grandees are looting the food! 'He'll come tomorrow,' they say; 'He's coming now,' they say – meanwhile the scatterbrains are looting and eating every kind of animal there is here! Now your people are saying, 'The Heathens have gobbled it all and bled us dry!' They are going out of their minds!" This is what old Qoshoy had to say to Manas. He continued: "Is it good planning if no one waters the crops that the peasants sow? Sultan Manas – head of the Muslim faith, as we like to call you – please see what I'm saying and speak to that unsteady lad. Aren't you outraged at this lad called Boqmurun? You advertise how great you are, but you've let a populous nation go to ruin; you advertise that you're the padishah, but you've let the whole nation go to wrack and ruin! Please listen to me, I'm telling you: *you* have brought about these difficulties, you have brought the sons of the Ughuz lineage to these dire straits! There's not a willow left in the denuded woods, not a beast left to slaughter for guests, not so much as a horse's mane left to ride! The people have gone quite out of their minds; many of them are flat broke from the way the Heathens gobbled everything and bled us dry! My valiant friend – how dare you arrive late!" All the leaders seconded this speech by the eldest of them, esteemed Qoshoy.

Your sultan, the battle-wolf, immediately replied: "You can't have fire without fuel and you can't have a shot without a gun; unless a man gets down to work, wealth is not going to settle on him. Dear uncle! Scrimping with cattle – who are you, Qarïnbay? I'll smash and I'll slash, and if the foe puts on airs, I'll fight him and have some recreation! It's up to me to judge the right moment to make the Qalmaq into an example for the whole world. Though there be no one left of the Kirghiz, I will put the plans I dream up into action, and take my ease! I'll surely test the Oyrots' strength doing it like that! I'll make valleys into hills; the plan I think up, I will carry out – and take my ease! I am a tall poplar rising up to the heavens; if God weren't pleased with me I would topple over. I am a steel-fanged lion, a dragon ready to pounce, a mighty poplar with golden branches rising up to the sky. Talk all you like, dear uncle, but a warrior must have honor. I have men assembled from all over the world, and right now I intend to gird myself and act in the name of honor! I have the hunger of a hunting lion!

"There's a thread to what I am saying to you, uncle. You said your piece, now don't worry about the cost! Can a hard stone be cleft with an ax-stroke? A stalwart warrior must face up to thick and thin. Don't dissuade heroes who are friendly to us from attending Kökötöy's memorial feast. Now, after the bright sun in the sky sets, dark night will come. Dark as it may get, the night does not last; a beautiful, splendid day does not last. Uncle, can't you recognize things of the next world by their features? For all this idle talk, who are you to say what the Almighty will bring about? Don't lose your head, and don't bemoan the cost! If it's a matter of resources we'll find them, and if we're really getting down to nothing then there's any one of the countless cities of the Heathens to be plundered.

"Now, as for that stinking yogurt, that moldy curd, Boqmurun son of Kökötöy! Whether in obedience to his command or on their own, his multitudes did not come out even the distance of four days' ride to meet me. Leaving me without an escort, as if he doesn't know his own lord – is he making himself out to be someone important, has he taken the title of lord? Not coming out the distance of five days' ride, not coming to meet me – is he standing on ceremony, or has he just turned into a shiftless good-for-nothing? Putting on airs, acting as if he has important things to take care of – that ill-bred animal! I'm going to have him seized in front of everybody and clapped in a halter; I'll cook him up a pot of troubles! I'll have him stood on his feet in the midst of everyone and his cheeks smeared with soot, and then I'll bring torments down upon his memorial feast and rob his encampment! I'll rain suffering upon his feast and sack his tribe!" Manas would not stop his abuse. He chastised Boqmurun like raging hellfire; his words created a panic. Having spoken, he had barely closed his mouth when that rich boy Boqmurun outfitted nine black horses in costly trappings and brought them to Manas as a present. That made the hero very glad that he had come, at last.

After Manas had met and exchanged greetings with the chieftains, he went to his lodgings. The great majority of Kökötöy's people, however, were disappointed not to have seen him. The maiden Torum's palatial white tent was exquisitely appointed: its trellis-frames and dome-poles painted to a high gloss, the reeds of its screens wound with silken batting, its covering of white worsted wool secured with gaily patterned straps and fastened down with wire rope. This very yurt the hero now entered.*

All the people from various lands, near and far, were getting bored and restless from having been at the feast for a month. It was for this reason that a great many of them mounted up to have some diversion by catching a glimpse of that lion Manas Baatïr. They completely surrounded that blessed hero; the high and the humble of this false, illusory world were passing in review, observing him. Six of Manas's squires mounted up and took swords and horse-lashes in their hands, and, splitting heads, spilling blood, shoving with their arms and jostling with their hips, the troops tried to form a protective cordon around

Manas. If you looked at that crowd, there were a damned lot of them surging forward; but even more were getting themselves clubbed. The strivers being clubbed on the neck saying, "Just give me a look at Manas!" were past counting, but even more were getting a bludgeoning; and past counting were those putting up with the bludgeoning just to keep straggling about. "You've been looking since this morning, stand aside now!" many were saying as they collared and poked and slugged each other. Some were even laying into each other with horse-lashes, saying, "Go on, get out of here!"; even so there were a few who came back and just put up with the lashings in order to get another look.

This went on for the time it takes to cook a pot of meat, until the squires' strength was at an ebb and they were quite exasperated at having to hold everyone off. "Get away, all of you!" they shouted, "If we let you, you would carry Manas off!" Then the mob calmed down and stopped pushing. "What's happened to my blasted mount?" men cried, for no one had kept track of the horse he had ridden in on. Around the maiden Torum's palatial white tent the soldiers in their great numbers billowed like waves. If you looked at the throngs of commoners descending on it, they seethed in masses; yet more than they were those who lifted the yurt's top felts to look in. The souls crowding in were past counting; yet more than they were those who shredded the skirts of the tent for a look – those piercing the felt walls were past counting!

As the people were thus occupied with their shouting and thrusting, Chaghïray, one of Alooke's cursed Heathens and a keen judge of warriors, said, "Let me go to this Burut,[1] this world-destroyer and padishah of the Muslims, Manas, and look him over, and appraise him – the secrets of his rage, the extent of his manly qualities." With these thoughts in mind that damned Heathen Chaghïray, full of cunning, came to perform his assessment.* Many people tagged along hoping to hear what he said. A big crowd followed him; guests at feasts and banquets only want to be entertained.

---

1.   "Burut" is what the Qïtays and Qalmaqs called the Kirghiz.

Chaghïray the Qïtay appraiser of warriors stepped up to the yurt and put his eye to a hole in the felt: he looked for mighty Manas, and right in front of him, before his eyes, whom should he see but the gray-maned one; right away his eye fell on Manas. At the very sight of him the Heathen's heart burst, and with a cry of "*Jabiniyin jaghï!*"* that vile Chaghïray fell down and died.

When the assembled crowd saw this, a lively chatter rose up, "The appraiser died making his appraisal!"

With no one leading it, this memorial feast of yours was fizzling. Manas had arrived in the evening. The next day just after noon, when the sun had just begun its decline, if you had looked you would have seen the best camels down on their knees and copper pots upended; chiefs, all of khanly bearing, their cloth-of-gold coats fastened tightly about them, and campaign-tents loaded onto black *nar* camel-bulls;* these Qara Kirghiz were past counting. Then, with Bay Jaqïp's red standard on its long pole of a padishah planted in the ground; the white banner tied on it unfurled against the sky, were you to have looked; and coming up behind to the sound of shawms, an army of forty thousand Kirghiz, tramping over the whole earth – Jaqïp's kinsman the powerful falcon Baqay was arriving; his army came on, larger than any other nation's.

The rich boy Boqmurun, his horse Maani-ker in peak condition, his figure handsomely clad in mail, asked Manas, "How shall I give this memorial feast? I have made ready every possible sort of necessity –"

9

Qongurbay, in a Huff, Demands Maani-ker from Boqmurun

"– You slay the spiteful; you yourself, hero, know how to arrange things." The two giants were having their consultation not on horseback but on foot. Er Boqmurun continued, "O my sultan, I have seen what a great crowd of people and how many different sorts of fighting men have come to this memorial feast. If I look west, at the end of Ulabas, there are soldiers filling the valley up to the ridge-tops opposite Qïzïl-qïya; if I look north, the valley of the Charïn is swamped with feast-guests; if I look east, the Ketmen range is solid armies, thicker than spiders, all the way up to the passes. That is the ground covered by this gathering of Heathens and Muslims." So said Boqmurun.

The two of them, the hero Manas and Boqmurun, together exclaimed, "Er Qoshoy will know what to do!" Then the imperturbable sultan Manas returned to his tent.

Not one of Manas's Alach soldiers, not one from the whole army that had come thronging in under the direction of old Baqay, had eaten any of the feast cattle; they had not so much as spoken of it. Each had with him his own animals for slaughter and paid no mind to the feast reserves; each had taken his place in their widely spread encampment. But all of a sudden, the Qalmaqs' champion, Joloy – Big Joloy, who smelled of grain from gobbling six *batman* of flour, who smelled of blood from slaying sixty giants at once; Big Joloy, who smelled of grain from gobbling seven *batman* of wheat, who smelled of blood from slaying seventy giants at once – the soles of his feet big as yurt-doors; unswerving before redoubtable foes – the boar of the Qara Qalmaqs – got hungry. Boqmurun, as you have seen, had summoned him peremptorily; he bears the blame for that! Among the teeming Arghïn-subun, that Joloy was a powerful giant. He had a father though there was no betrothal; he had a mother though there was no wedding. Our people have no fighter as tough as he! Enormously big around and clad in a coat of blue silk; wide in the middle but not tall, his face broad with a gloomy cast; an enormous enemy, hostile to the Faith, with a flapped fur hat on his head; he had six *jang-jungs* along with him to keep him company. (A *jang-jung* is a chief.) There was a horse-herd, Jangïbay, keeping watch with his lasso-pole; Joloy made this pole into a skewer, and made an unforgettable to-do for the person who presided over the feast.

Manas had arrived in the evening; the following day, just past midday, after Baqay appeared, they had raised the golden standard and started to kill the animals for the feast, and to make a sacrifice using the fattest beasts. Manas had a hundred sleek horses slaughtered and a hundred earthen hearths dug, and commanded that two hundred stalwarts should stand watch over the meat. The next day, late in the morning, he had another thousand hearths dug and a man placed at each hearth – a thousand honest guards; and a thousand herdsman's yurts set up to lay the meat in, with an old codger at the doorway of each one to turn people away. "Don't make the rice under-done or the meat rare, and do not slaughter a single lean animal! If the rice turns out under-done or the meat rare, or if you mix in lean animals, then keep out of my sight!" said gray-maned Manas. "Boqmurun, do not be offended with me tomorrow, or I'll bring torments down upon your memorial feast and rob your encampment! I'll rain suffering upon your feast and sack your tribe!" Manas was talking in that pique of his just as events were transpiring thus.

That Qalmaq, Joloy, had picked up the herdsman's lasso-pole and sharpened it into a skewer two fathoms and a span in length. This skewer was of birch. Joloy now left his camp, saying, "It's not that they haven't served us anything, it's just that the meat they did serve to me and my companions didn't fill me up. They're cooking meat right now, and sooner or later they're going to pass that meat around. Boqmurun, you sent your herald around with invitations, to say, 'Come to the memorial feast!' but I say you've left me hungry! I'm going to go eat some of that meat that's been laid in for the feast."

With his hat on his head and his *jang-jungs* at his side, Joloy headed to those yurts that had been set up, determined to eat his fill of meat at Kökötöy's memorial feast. The old men guarding the meat had blocked the doorways and were letting no one inside, so Big Joloy strode down the grassy mountainside to the hearth-pits and looked in the pot tended by a youth named Suqumbek. Inside the pot were boiling span-thick hunks of rib-fat and slant cuts of mane-fat. No one looked him in the eye, so Joloy got down on one knee and sat right at the edge of the fire-pit. Jabbering in his incomprehensible Qalmaq language, Joloy asked the lad, "Is your *maqan* done?"[1] The boy, unable to understand Qalmaq, looked at him inquiringly. Joloy stuck the sharpened skewer he was holding into one of the chunks of meat in the pot. The boy was now astonished, as Joloy, skewer in hand, speared and lifted up a piece of meat as broad as a platter.

"Stop! Don't do that!" said the little pot-watcher, and tried to grapple the skewer out of his hand.

At this the Heathen Joloy became enraged, and determined to eat all the meat in the pot and not leave one morsel. His eyes bugged out of his head, his chest hairs began to wriggle, his whiskers pricked up, and the hair on his head stood straight out. "*Ütügüngö shooday!*" he cursed, rushing at the boy with a spine-chilling look on his face; "*Amininge danim!*"* he cursed, grabbing him. With his left hand Big Joloy lifted him up and then slammed him down on the ground. Not a soul looked him in the eye, and he plopped that stalwart cauldron-guard right down on his rump. Now Joloy cast his gaze upon the cauldron full of meat; bending down on one knee, he used his skewer to spear chunks until it was full, though the meat was only half-cooked. Then with a "*Laaylama!*"* Joloy the strong-man drew the meat off all at once like shish kebab, and ate it up. Thus having squelched the lad Suqumbek that damned hero Joloy

---

1.   "*maqan*" means "meat" in Qalmaq.

wolfed down a whole cauldron full of flesh, leaving nothing uneaten. He wasn't full after the one cauldron, however, so he decided to eat a second. Joloy had drained all the savor out of the cauldron watched by the brave youth who now sat planted on his backside; the cauldron was totally empty, and Joloy now turned and headed toward another one.

But that lad, realizing a rampage was about to occur, cried out, "It's the Heathen Big Joloy! Sir, come here!" and called Boqmurun. At this summons Boqmurun made straight for the boy atop Maani-ker, who was in peak condition. Arriving on the scene he saw the pit-boys had lost a lot of their gusto, and the immensely large giant Joloy, having completely eaten up two cauldrons full of meat and leaving not a scrap – Joloy, whom no man approached at ease; his neck as thick as an ox's girth, the breath from his mouth like the blast of wind at a high mountain pass; his eyes as big as traveling-kettles, his chest like a table mountain, his hair like flaming reeds, his head that of an enemy who meant to do one harm – that Infidel stood right in front of the young Khan Boqmurun, staring at him.

Atop sleek Maani-ker, his mail-shirt sparkling, the rich boy Boqmurun laid into Joloy, shrieking like a white gyrfalcon as his anger poured out in rebukes: "Get out of here, you louse! Fie on your high station – go off and whine somewhere! Fie on your rank of *sungdung* – drop dead! Eating the meat out of the hearths – to hell with that humor, you're a dog I say! Eating the meat out of the fire-pits – you're a dog digging in the ground I say, and you should just die and go to hell! It would have been better if you had stayed in your tent and sent word to me that you weren't satisfied. You nuisance! If I haven't filled your belly, then please come to me; then and only then may you eat this meat that has been allotted for the feast. What, are you an idiot? This isn't the way people behave! You Heathen – are you an animal?"

As Boqmurun was speaking thus, despite the boy's exceptionally high status Joloy paid no attention to him. It did not even register that there was a human being addressing him; the giant Joloy's eyes were bugging out. You have to remember that at that moment Joloy was on foot, without a mount, and he did not understand Boqmurun's language; but the words did not even enter his ears. Joloy was as one gone mad, paying no heed to what the boy said; his eyes were riveted on the horse he was riding, Maani-ker.

What did the scandal-making giant Joloy, that conspicuous hero of the Qara Qalmaqs, have to say while looking at the horse ridden by Boqmurun, Maani-ker? "Are the insignificant Buruts, a nation of only a handful of tents, a horse-racing folk? Are there really such *tulpars* as these to be found among the Muslims? Apparently they do race horses; never mind the other Muslims, apparently the Buruts have raised this *tulpar*! Hooves of pure iron – that is a definite mark of a *tulpar*! Mane and tail-hairs like lance-tassels – if you look at his muzzle, it's like a marten-trap!* His croup high as a rammed-earth house – if you look at his ears, they are like the flames on large shrine-candles! Wild game on the ridges could get a head-start at the sound of his hoof-beats below on the steppe, and still not outdistance him! He's not one to thirst on a forty-day course; it would be a sin to tether that one – no need to hobble him at pasture! Race that one with proper training and the wind-spirits couldn't out-distance him! He sinks in the ground up to his fetlocks; jutting his chest like a stag's, stretching his croup, he flashes his eyes like a mountain ram's! Shanks like hewn beams, ears shaped like parrots perched in a garden – if a brave man raced him forty days and nights, that horse's spirits would only rise, all would be well! These insignificant Buruts who wield strapless polished lances – they don't have any enemies marching on them from afar. The Buruts have only a handful of tents, just a few fires – and yet they have this *tulpar* that far surpasses their standing. Surely God has cursed our *qalday*,* for we never acquired a horse like that!" That is what that damned Joloy was mumbling and muttering as he walked away.

The red-topknotted Oyrots' most powerful hero was Prince Qongurbay, they say, a towering prince of the Qïtay, the black-topknotted Heathens' brave Prince Qong, that grand prince whose courage exceeded that of old Khan Alooke and all the other Qara Qïtay. Joloy the strong-man went into the tent and presence of Qongurbay and said this: "See here, Qongur, you have no idea how they are treating us. Here we are arrived one by one, lying around like louts just glad to be fed, and unaware of the best things here. Here we are lying around in the way, just glad to get our bellies filled – preoccupied with eating our fill! But day before yesterday evening when Manas arrived, it just happens that that piece of carrion, Boqmurun, ordered his poets to sing and wittily praise Manas above everyone, then he sacrificed a kid for him and presented him with a choice gift, his *tulpar* Archa-toru. By making a gift of that horse Archa-toru he has inflated Manas's status. They say he's presented a *tulpar* as a gift, but in my estimation you are the mightiest; you are the khan of the world! Boqmurun rates you, and us who are close to you, no higher than cattle, for he has presented Manas with the *tulpar* Archa-toru, so say I.

"If you care for your good name, Qongurbay, understand this well. Today I went to the feast, and in due course came upon the cooking-pits, when across my path appeared a beast named Maani-ker, owned by Boqmurun. You have your Al'-ghara and Tor'-ayghïr – but you will be very sorry if you do not acquire that horse! Next to Maani-ker Al'-ghara is nothing. They say a horse's forelock falls in its eyes; I say, among the beasts of the known world there is none like Maani-ker! His intelligence is unique, like a man's it would seem. I tried to draw comparisons with similar horses, but that beast leads the world. I would say, for a worthy man confident of his powers, that is the horse to get! Let me describe his points to you accurately, then I shall go. This is a horse one would ride to Beejin having strapped on belly-armor and rounded Besh-qalaa; a horse that a *qalday* should ride having strapped on arm-guards and rounded Qara-shaar! This Maani-ker belongs to Boqmurun, but as I reckon him, he's a horse appropriate to you. Settle for nothing but Maani-ker! Insist upon Maani-ker, Qongurbay, or make that Burut feast-giver know unhappiness!" That is how Joloy described the horse; having spoken thus in his ardor he returned to his own tent.

Qongurbay's rage was no less demonic than Joloy's. "Very well, if that is the case, then summon the host of this memorial feast. Loyal Joloy has spoken well. I intend to get Maani-ker, by force if I have to. Debegi! Shïlqïm! Fetch that feast-giving churl!" Qongurbay commanded.

Six *jaysangs* headed by Debegi and Shïlqïm went to Boqmurun and said, "Qongurbay has summoned you." Leaving his yurt, Boqmurun went and arrived in no great hurry at Qongurbay's tent. The huge army of him they call Er Qongurbay was arrayed in perfect order. Boqmurun found him sitting by his fire, a huge man with a golden crown on his head. His face was like boiled lungs; his moustaches hung like horses' tails from a flagpole, but stiff enough to drill through wood. His eyes like filed iron, this Infidel had a nose like a landslide on a mountain slope. This ox-sized swine* had brows like molting vultures on a head like a charred block of wood. If you looked at his nose it was huge; his eye-sockets were deep as dug-out grain-cellars; the scum in his eyelashes was thick as huntsmen's soup.

Covered in a mail-coat of blue steel, he bristled like a lion in his rage at Boqmurun's entrance and searched for the words to utter: "You stinking yogurt, moldy curd, good-for-nothing coward! You said there would be cattle beyond counting for the first prize at Kökötöy's memorial feast. And you didn't just say that you would welcome all guests; you said you would sack me if I did not come. I don't think you could have put it any more strongly than that! Boqmurun, the time is up for you and your taunts; I dare say your innumerable words will cause you some pain! Our *tïytays* and *sungdungs* will sack you!" Qongurbay was on the offensive. "But I can quell each and every one of the teeming Infidels if you agree to what I say. If you ask me to hold them off, I will even assist you in putting on this memorial feast. I heard that you have in your possession a horse by the name of Maani-ker. If you are really giving a memorial feast for that deceased miscreant your father, then give me Maani-ker! You noted when Manas arrived, and you took what he said agreeably, did you not? You placed the *tulpar* Archa-toru before him as a present, did you not? Thus have you valued a prince of the Muslims above everyone else. If I am roused to anger, let there be no mistake: you shall die at my very own hands! You value a prince of the Muslims higher than me. If my frenzy comes over me, you shall die to little purpose!

You had better give me Maani-ker. If you do not give me
Maani-ker, you shall know misfortune! He is an animal one
would ride to Beejin having strapped on belly-armor and
rounded Besh-qalaa; a horse that a *qalday* should ride having
strapped on arm-guards and rounded Qara-shaar. With that
neck of his slender as a wether goat's, he is an animal to take as
a present next spring to Esen Khan. You have now in your pos-
session that beast by the name of Maani-ker. You had better
give him to me; if you do not, you shall know misfortune! You
shall be nobody to me; I will not eat the meat you serve. I will
bring torments down upon your memorial feast and rob your
encampment! I will rain suffering upon your feast and sack
your tribe!" Thus said Big Qongur – damn him! – the meanest
villain in all Qïtay.

Hearing which, Boqmurun was rocked back on his heels.
"You wish to take a horse," he said. "Let me take counsel, and
see about it. I have elder kinsmen; I shall go to my people and
consult them, and see. I shall sound out the people's dispo-
sition, and if they approve the idea, I will give Maani-ker to
you." These were the words that Er Qongurbay Baatïr heard as
Boqmurun the rich boy backed his way out.

Once astride his horse, Boqmurun was sunk in such deep dis-
tress that he did not know what to do, and was at a loss thus
all the way to Er Qoshoy's. Having arrived, Boqmurun told the
whole story to that old man of the Qataghan.

Your uncle Qoshoy too was taken aback. "Damn that big
Qongur of Beejin and his evil temper! God save us from that
cursed big Qongur of many-quartered Beejin! It seems he has
taken offense at the alacrity with which the Muslims bring gifts
to Manas and thus show their esteem. It would be useless to
withhold the horse, you can be sure of it. Doesn't he do exactly
as he pleases, that big Qongur of the Qïtay, damned well the
toughest of the red-topknotted Oyrot? Certainly there are those
in the crowd whose eyes have fallen upon that handsome racer
Maani-ker. I can just see that swine Qongurbay landing on his
backside from the sight, and saying 'I must get Maani-ker!' I
say fine, let's give him Maani-ker. Good-for-nothing Prince
Qong is nearly a padishah, after all. What is one horse to us, if

Bek Qongurbay requests him? It's time to give him up. Doesn't Qongur of the Qïtay slaughter whom he pleases; doesn't he do just as he pleases, that ruffian? Altogether better for you that your camp remain safe; next to that, cursed Maani-ker isn't worth the turd of a virgin mare. The earth submits to a horse's limbs; if the lowly earth had no master, whatever would? The sky submits to a bird's limbs; as the lofty sky has a master, so do many.* What is Maani-ker to us? It won't do to withhold him. This evil-tempered Heathen is a tiger in battle. If we don't present him with Maani-ker, the feast is not going to end well," said Khan Qoshoy.

He had barely closed his mouth when Boqmurun replied: "I will let him have the horse. I'd best be off, then, dear uncle. I must follow your advice." Er Boqmurun shouted to the companions who were with him, "To horse! I am parted from my poor, dear *tulpar*, which I had from my father!"

When suddenly, just as he was leaving, Er Qoshoy had an idea. "Let's not be hasty handing over Maani-ker to that scandalous Heathen Khan Qongurbay Baatïr. We had better not be skittish hosts, weak and easily taken in, for we would catch grief from that cruel Manas who would say, 'You gave away the horse without telling me!' Don't avoid Manas. Let us go to that lion of the Muslim chiefs and see what he counsels. If he approves of everything you have related, if he abides what your grandpa has to say, only then should we give Maani-ker to Prince Qong. Let's go to that hero now, not to stand in mute attendance but to hold counsel. If he finds the proposition justified, only then should we make the gift."

Saying this, Er Qoshoy then and there issued the command: Kökchö of the Qazaq, eloquent Ürbü, Töshtük son of Eleman, Jamghïrchï of the Eshtek, Baghïsh of the Jediger, Aghïsh son of Jetkir Biy, and the khan's maternal nephew Jügörü, made their stately way with Qoshoy leading them and a hundred troops apiece marching in attendance. All these chiefs great and small, young and old, approached the lion Manas Baatïr.

Looking for him they found that the hero had moved off with his excellent warriors some distance from the simple guests' tents at Kökötöy's memorial feast. And what an

excellent time they were having! They had plotted out and
drawn a huge playing-field for casting knucklebones, ninety
paces from edge to center, and the number of knucklebones
they had placed inside was eighty-three, in proportion to the
size of the field. The Forty Heroes were noisily knocking off
shots with Qïrghïl – Qïrghïl Chal, their leader – bawling out
directions as referee. It has been said that the memorial feast
for Kökötöy was a wonder to behold! For the pleasure of the
crowds at their feasting, the lion Manas Baatïr ordered eighty
dead-shot expert bowmen to put on a display of shooting,
while he beheld the scene of massed arrow-fire from a spot off
to the side of his pavilion. Your noble hero of the dragon-
whiskered visage lay stretched out, with his haunches resting
on a golden throne and a down pillow for his head – the war-
rior sultan, at the memorial feast for Kökötöy. Dazzling as a
watered-steel blade unsheathed, he reposed like a stalking tiger
that could seize Mount Qap itself and still have room in its
claws, that could be sated with nothing less than the whole
world. Thus he lay, sultan and warrior, as the players cast their
knucklebones.

When the leader old Qoshoy saw he was in a good temper,
he and the rest of the commanders of troops got down off their
horses and went on foot; giant Qoshoy went in front. Thus all
of them were on foot from the point where they rode in to
where they came into the hero's presence. Qoshoy gave a ring-
ing "Salam!"; the lion Manas Baatïr bellowed "Alik!" in return.

"Come, uncle! Welcome," said Manas, making a place for
Qoshoy and seating him with due ceremony and the polite
expressions dictated by tradition. The ways of etiquette differ
from preeminent warriors' air of toughness, and the ways of
khans differ from those of the normal run of folk who come to
a memorial feast to pay their respects; yet those khans found
themselves as if chastised by God, unable to face up to Manas
or even to say the first word.

So they stood there, nudging each other and saying "You
talk!" – and stood there, those chiefs, quite overcome with
dread, able neither to utter a word of address nor to get back
on their horses and ride away.

When the khans had stood there thus paralyzed and speechless for the time it takes to cook a pot of food, he who summers at Eki Kemin and keeps a pair of blacks trained, Er Ürbü, son of Taz, looked from side to side. "If one of you has a mind to, please speak," Er Ürbü began, casting glances at them. Only when it was clear that nobody else was about to do so, he said at last, "I'll speak, then." But, his nerve failing him, your Ürbü only managed to get out, "O Manas!" At that Manas did as he was wont to do when addressed by great men, to gauge them: he shot a glance at Ürbü. Fire flashed from his eyes and a terrible look of furor suffused his whole person. He fastened this gaze on Ürbü with the flames crackling from his eyes, and Ürbü, transfixed and gasping for breath, was rendered speechless. The illustrious chiefs standing by prodded him, thinking that God had stunned the brave man. But Ürbü had shut up tight, and after that no one in the group made a sound. Those powerful men stood looking at one another, tongue-tied.

Er Qoshoy frowned at Ürbü for stopping, and fixed his eyes on him. "Damn your father, Ürbü, you dog! May the earth swallow you up, Ürbü! Damn you, Ürbü, won't you say anything? And so what if you could blurt something out, after straining at it so long! Have you any honor left, if after standing there speechless you try to rouse me to do it, saying, 'Qoshoy, dear uncle, speak!'? Is it not I, Qoshoy, old but sturdy, erect as an old camel-bull, standing next to you? May God strike me down if I don't let bloodthirsty Manas kill you right here on the spot!" With these words and a twist of his moustache, Er Qoshoy well nigh pounded Ürbü down into the ground with his scolding; then having dismissed splendid Ürbü he turned in his vehement passion to face Manas.

"Ah, my colt, Er Manas, hero – listen please. That great evil-tempered *qalday* Qongurbay of Beejin, that great *qalday* cursed of his ancestors, Qongurbay of many-quartered Beejin, he of the vast armies, has taken umbrage, it seems; here he is arrived at the memorial feast, and he has thrown a tantrum, for no reason, directed at Boqmurun personally. He is saying that Boqmurun greeted you and presented you with that gyrfalcon of a creature, the *tulpar* Archa-toru; and that our wealthy host is playing favorites with those of the Muslim creed. He says that Boqmurun must give him Maani-ker, and if he doesn't he shall learn about duress. He says, 'If you have ceased to feel kindness toward me, then you shall surely learn about scandal; you are nobody to me, and I will not eat the meat you serve! I will wreak slaughter upon your encampment! Today, right now, I will sack your memorial feast!' This is what Khan Qongurbay has said, apparently. Your younger kinsman Boqmurun was in great distress when he came back. Now Boqmurun has told me everything and asked me what is to be done. He defers to the wisdom and counsel of us his elders – whether we should listen to that scoundrel and give up Maani-ker, for Qïtay is an enormous country which, though heathen, is ruled by a khan, and the people only love and care about making trouble. That is the gist of what we came here wanting to tell you. Should we give Maani-ker to Qongurbay or not? My rock of support, please give your answer!"

When noble Manas heard what Er Qoshoy said he was struck as if from above. Fire shot from his right eye; hot coals poured from his left; cannon-fire shot from the mouth of that mortified hero. He glared like a panther lying in its covert with curled tail and mottled coat ready to spring, like a tiger glimpsed in outline that emerges dreadfully into full view; nothing could escape in health from the onrush of one such as that! His features were quite apart from those of men; they were those of a lion.

Manas held the prerogative but made no answer to your uncle Baatïr Qoshoy, nor spoke so much as a word; instead he used a gong-mallet that he had been turning in his hands to strike a gold-rimmed drum. *Boom!* went the drum under the heavy blow, and the Forty Heroes, who had been engaged in their game of knucklebones, went off all in a body, not one of them dallying, to their tents. From these tents they now brought their armaments, and arrayed themselves with deftness that you would have to see to believe. The corselets they donned were of blue steel; He in whom they placed their trust was the One God. Beholding those Forty Heroes in their corselets, mail-shirts, and breastplates, one had to envision harm; their helmets of watered steel were enough in themselves to panic an enemy. From head to toe there was not a spot on them that could be pierced by lance or sword or bullet; an enemy who faced them in battle would be torn to shreds at once. They had just lowered over their faces visors of bullet-proof steel, when, at the next beat of the gold-rimmed drum, they leapt nimbly onto their horses in the blink of an eye, not so much mounting them as becoming instantaneously mounted. Their sway-backed racers were a delight to behold. The stalwart heroes clad in dark blue steel had their matchlock muskets loaded and the fuses burning as they fell in for counting-off, top marksmen and archers alike.

That horse which Manas had kept for a long time, he of the wide, lovely eyes – veteran racer, big Qula – was led in on a rope, stepping proudly, by the bustling master of the horse Joorunchu, and was brought before Manas. Joorunchu knew just how to get the great animal to storm along on the lead, fast as a speeding arrow, before placing him at the hero's disposal. At a bounding stride that angry lion of a warrior, your prince, leapt into the saddle without touching his feet to the stirrups of cast gold. Having mounted his horse, he spurred him to a gallop, pulled him up short and plucked his fearsome lance out of the ground where it stood planted. Then with a blow across the neck he drove Aq-qula into a lunging run like a lean hound and rode up to white-bearded Qoshoy.

"Alas, dear uncle, where are your wits? If anyone but you had said that – anyone now living – don't you know I would have taken his life? Don't you know I would have spilled his blood? You are saved by the fact that you are Qoshoy, whom I have respected since I was young, toward whom I have never harbored ill will. You are saved because you have grown too old to lay hands on! Why oh why would you say such shameful things? And where do *your* animals wander without their owner? When your poor Manas has died and gone off to the next world, please then go around and give gifts; but while Manas is still on his throne, please just count yourself lucky! I would almost say you held some grudge, but if that were true you would be better off dead. When your falcon Manas has died and gone to the Day of Resurrection; when the Infidels have divided up and rule the world and allow no one to make a sound, and ride without harness, then, Er Qoshoy, give away not only your horses but your daughters as well! When the Resurrection draws near and the Heathen's oppressions weigh heavily on you, please, give away your daughters. But now, as long as I am alive, please, rely on your Manas! Won't that Heathen who has raised his standard today seize from you what you guard most closely; won't he attack before we can make a move? Today it's Maani-ker – will he value him? Tomorrow won't he desire my horse Qula, and take him? You move so slowly! And then the next day won't he find a way to take Er Töshtük's Chal-quyruq? If the sons of the Islamic faith lose their best *tulpars*, won't they die? Don't camel-geldings rest at the top of the ridge – isn't a brave man miserable who is parted from his horseflesh?! If we allow Boqmurun to give up his horse without a fight, won't the trouble fall on us? In the afterlife shall not I, Manas land in hell? Please, do not say, 'I'll give up Maani-ker' until you have said, 'Manas has died'! And sooner than saying your hero has died, dear uncle, keep saying your prayers – may you die before you say that!" – This is how Manas addressed Qoshoy – "Where is that war-loving wild boar? As long as my brilliance shines like the sun, how can I give up my racer? This swine seems to be gaining power; it is time to contend with him in a race. If the Almighty gives me strength and power, I intend to make that Heathen a laughing-stock among all the people, and be on my way! As long as my radiance shines like the moon and the spirits of departed ancestors do not greatly chastise me, how can I give up my horse?* This boar seems to be getting bigger; it is time to deal with him! I intend to make an example of him for people to talk about until the end of time – and then be on my way! What power do we have to oppose fate? If death comes I must die!"

When Er Manas had spoken these words, he beat his golden drum and fired his musket Aq-kelte; the Forty Heroes, who had barely been able to stand still, came rushing on in a mob. Eighty-four of his warriors wore impenetrable corselets, and their burning glances ignited flames. The drums rolled, the camel-mounted guns thundered, the falconets roared, the

qoychaghïr-guns echoed. The Forty Heroes, who had barely
been able to stand still, rushed off in a mass toward the Infidels.
At the sound of their war-cry the enormous Muslim host all
mounted up; not one remained behind. They drove their lances
home; they smashed men's heads; the many who witnessed it
knew the Infidels had suffered a disaster.

Those luckless Infidels wound up in misery, deprived even of
their wits. Many were the Infidels saying "*Jabuu, jabuu, jabuu!*"
and running off en masse, while those outstanding, exemplary
heroes went coursing through their ranks, spearing them and
wreaking destruction as of the end of days upon their heads.
The Muslims in their hats of figured white felt and blue over-
tunics ransacked them from every side and ran on through them,
leaving swollen corpses as they passed. Many were those in
searing pain crying, "*Möndü, möndü, möndü!*"* and running off
by themselves, while those excellent heroes went chasing after
them, wolf-wise. The Muslims were like wolves attacking a
flock of sheep, dividing ones off and pursuing; the Heathens
were dying, cut down and flayed as they ran. They had to accept
their fate on the fly; those who had never seen such a thing saw
it now, on the run. The teeming host drove them in a chaotic
rout, chopping deep wounds in their heads with battle-axes,
slicing them through five and six at a time, gorging themselves
on the black blood with practiced skill, penetrating to the very
center of the press of Heathens.

Qongurbay Baatïr was in front of Qosh-döbö, greatly
aggrieved by the slaughter he was seeing; a sullen look spread
over his face like dark clouds. "If Manas is roused to anger,
what won't he do?" he wondered in his confusion. Then he said,
"This bloodthirsty hero is the sort to take us by surprise and
afflict heavy slaughter. I don't want any horse; this Manas is a
constant and perpetual scoundrel! I take back my wish to mount
a horse. Speak submissively to the eminent lion, Manas, and
present him with Qïl-qara – younger brother of my Al'-ghara –
that surpassingly handsome Qïl-qara – give him as a present to
Manas with all deference, and see if you can get him to stop
slaughtering the Qïtays." So said Prince Qong, that great lover
of disturbance – but when did he ever act but out of fear?

His forces had fled, disappeared, and were being chased down and ravaged by the sons of the Kirghiz. Red-topknotted Nezqara, poor fellow, took fright at the slaughter, as did Muradïl son of Qïrmuz, Ushang of the Qalmaq, black-maned Boroonchu, Oronghu of the Qanghay, and their elder, Alooke. They first heard the pounding of hoofbeats, and then brought Qïl-qara, a beast in superior condition, before Manas as a gift. The Muslims' falconets and matchlocks were loaded; their fuses were burning; but at the appearance of the gift the disorderly rout came to an end. With the sovereigns who were attending him at the memorial feast for Kökötöy, Prince Qong of the red topknot – that great prince of the Qïtay – had seen the slaughter and been brought to heel. Old Alooke went out in the lead followed by all sixty of their *jang-jungs*, and brought the gift before Manas. Intending to take a horse, Qongurbay gave one instead, and was sorely humiliated; he had not a shred of honor left to his name.

The thick dust dissipated; the distant fighting died down. Each returned to his tent; but the Qalmaqs and Qïtays who were scared out of their wits on the steppes were to remain there for two more nights.

That day everyone retired thus; next day at first light, as dawn was shooting forth its earliest rays, the Muslims made their great commotion with the call to prayer; then Kökötöy's blue standard was hoisted, its blue banner rippling and streaming. Everyone now mounted their horses and came on in a torrent. The eyes could not see across the mass of people, nor could words comprehend it. There were sixty armies there arrayed on either side of an open avenue; if you looked at the multitude they appeared more numerous than teeming spiders – the obsequies for the late Kökötöy fed and entertained many a guest! For the first prize in the horse race were posted eighty thousand horses, a thousand camel-geldings, also a hundred thousand sheep, fully nine thousand head of cattle – the grandees were overwhelmed trying to count all the animals! – as well as ninety yurts with otter-fur trimming around their walls, and if you looked inside, each one was occupied by a male slave and two lively slave-women.

10

The Horses Are Paraded; The Racing-Prizes Are Announced

The prize for the second-place horse – more takings to be won – was five hundred gelded camels groomed under the supervision of your grandpa Qoshoy the giant; plus forty thousand horses, four thousand head of cattle – many a man was overwhelmed trying to count all the animals! – fully fifty thousand sheep, and a yurt, occupied, if you looked, by a high-quality slave with a slave woman; that was the proclamation that was heard. For the horse in third place an enormous prize was posted: two hundred and fifty gelded camels, a yurt occupied by a couple of menials, twenty thousand sheep, and ten thousand horses to round it out. For the fourth-place horse, ten thousand sheep – this is how great the feasts were given by your dear old Kirghiz kindred to honor the dead! – a hundred and twenty-five gelded camels hobbled on their knees, five thousand horses, and a hundred cows. All these animals were tied up on level ground. Let me name the last prize so that we can get on from there: nine head of cattle, ninety sheep, a woman and a man. There was more than that; prizes for sixty horses after the first were posted that day. The holding of memorial feasts has been a sworn duty on all people of Kirghiz descent. If you figured how many horses would win prizes, the number came to sixty-one.

There were people of Jööt and Tarsa there; so many well-behaved people were there; Qïzïlbash, and people from Qïyba, who resembled no one else on earth; Orus, and Nemis – all the peoples of the world. Those of the Qïtay tribe were there as well, and a great gathering of Qalmaqs. All of the Muslims were there, even Imam Ayqojo of the Arabs. Crowds of people lined the parading-route; whenever that happens there is always such bother for the givers of feasts. Seeing this, none other than your dear uncle Er Qoshoy said to Manas, "Shall we parade the horses, then?" Yet so great were the crowds that even this word from Qoshoy brought on much ado.

For a payment of ten gold ingots and thirty large silver ones in consideration of his work of heraldry, for the job of making the announcement – plus six nines of horses – an appropriate sum, given his expertise – Ïrchï Uul son of Ïraman of the forty-knot tassel on the drawstring of his drawers, that fellow of the topknotted skullcap and effortless speech, mounted his horse and took along with him as his second Jash Aydar of the unruly forelock. Their instructions were to summon the entrants in a proclamation free of falsehood.* "Get your saddle-blankets on your horses and gallop them back and forth! Mettlesome youths are riding in the rout! If you've got a horse, get him in a lather! If it's a blooded horse, you know who you are! If it's a common nag, mount up anyway! You whose horses enter the race will be the fortunate ones, as if blessed on the Night of Power!* Tonight is that very night; tomorrow your horses will race; tomorrow is the time for getting horses in a lather!" The heralds made this announcement, and the people, young and old, made preparations.

Many were the spirited racers high in the withers and low in the back; many were the grand chargers that never tire at altitude and show not a sore after ninety days' riding; many were the thoroughbreds high in the back and low in the croup; but more than those were the choice *tulpars* that never tire on hilly ground and show not a sore after long riding, those celebrated racers bred for stamina with lungs like sieves and wings of copper, ears like cut reeds and hooves like pig-iron; and more than they were the coursers, celebrated gallopers bred for stamina, tireless tramplers. Many were the grand chargers covered in saddle-cloths of *torqo* and hung with nine amulets; many were the thoroughbreds pleasing to the eye in costly, figured saddle-cloths and hung with gay amulets. That day the people whipped up their hearts' desires, running heats with the horses, over and over again, to the annoyance of the trainers.

Then it was time to parade the horses. Like a flight of swallows, like swarming mice came the viers for glory; if you counted those horses they would come to fully two thousand. Seeing this, Er Manas thought: "This rabble! I should slaughter them all. For the horse race in honor of my dear Kökötöy they have tied up work-horses and nags to feed, which couldn't even overtake a yearling calf. They have set these hungry jades to pasture and are blocking the way for the true race-horses. This crowd is going to hold up the start of the race and bring down God's punishment on this people – they'll kill the jockeys! This blockage on the course will be the death of all those *tulpars*!"

The hero repaired to his tent mindful of the many services he had rendered on behalf of Kökötöy's memorial feast; now he called to his side that fine sultan, Almambet. "Exceedingly great is your art. Now listen to my instructions," said noble Manas firmly to Almambet. "Do whatever it takes, but change the weather, Almambet Baatïr. Qula, lean of rib – my choice *tulpar* Aq-qula, high in the withers, largest of all beasts, his spine sunken like the print of a rolling-pin amid his bulk – whether Qula comes in first in the race is white-bearded Qïrghïl's concern, but right now my great Qula has a whole day's reserve of fat on him. Do whatever you need to do to change the weather. All along the Qarqïra there are high slopes; exert yourself now, try and change the weather! The horses' fat should fit them snugly;* they need to be taut and trim in form. There are horses in good condition, but the thin ones all need to fill out!" This is what your lion, Er Manas, urged Almambet to do.

Almambet now began his conjuration. The idiom he used was from Qïrïm, but his art surpassed all others in the world. His pedigree was pure Qïtay, but his art was learned from many a place. He had spells written down to ward off demons, but now he recited a dark incantation by heart, in Qalmaq. He recited rapidly from the *Barayïz*,* from memory, faster now – forward to the end and backward to the beginning – prayers in Chinese, over and over. A grim look spread over the face of your Alma[1] as he plunged his weather-conjuring stone* under water.

In the blink of an eye, in no time to do this or that – and before the people had got their horses covered and laid up to

1. Almambet.

rest – rain began to fall all around, and hail came clattering down. The mountainsides were all covered with hail; a shimmering haze arose, and the sky blackened in the west, thundering and casting beams of bronze light. People and horses alike streamed at the nose from the sudden cold. The ditches became swollen; gullies and ravines were clogged. Eight times the flood from the skies turned to hail and back to drizzle; then an immense blizzard pressed down, and those who witnessed it were buffeted up, down, and sideways.

The rain that had fallen first had inundated men and horses all together; then the ice that fell froze the thin and weak animals to death. The better race-horses all hung their necks dejectedly, but on that day they came into their best, leanest shape; those coursers all took on a trim appearance, shapely and tucked-in, and ready to get down to business. That night many of the mediocre horses whose owners had nothing to cover them with, or even any idea how to find covers, went numb with cold and died. The *tulpars*, however, had kept the meat on their frames, and their ears stood up taller than ever on their heads. The coursers twirled, stamped, and dashed about headlong, leaving the earth cracked wherever their hooves touched. The hero Manas's horse Aq-qula lean of rib, that choice *tulpar* Aq-qula, was trained and ready and full of fire, nose-up like a roe-deer and agitated, longing to gallop. He now had fat for half a day's running on him; it was but a matter of bringing him to a lather once more and he would come into his full stride. The great horse Qula was lean and in peak condition.

That day they waited thus in the cold and frost. The following day at dawn, flies buzzed and birds flew about chirping; then a steady breeze drove the rising mist off the ground. Everyone came to the memorial feast now. Late in the morning as the day warmed up and Kökötöy's standard flew and its blue banner fluttered, Aydar gave a loud shout, "If you've got a horse, parade it!" swaying atop Quu-chabdar and making his way into the thick of the assembled armies to deliver his summons to one and all.

Almambet had altered the weather the evening before because so many were preparing to enter inadequate horses in Kökötöy's memorial horse race; but as everyone saw, and you have as well, that spelled the doom of many a horse. They died, and the owners thus deprived of their horses grieved and bemoaned their fate, saying, "They make us all gather here for a memorial feast, then they play nothing but low tricks on us! To hell with them and their feast! I don't want any of their prizes!" There was absolutely nothing they could do; they took the bridles off their horses. And it wasn't only the horses that had suffered; many a human being was wasting away.

Everyone was in a ruckus at the announcement that the horses were going to be paraded. The Qïtay were in one group, the Kirghiz in another, the Qïrïm in another, the Orus in another, the Ooghan in another; forming up in groups this way, the people filled the earth. Lances glinted everywhere; men's heads formed slowly surging black masses as the parade route was opened in the midst of the armies.

"Do we have the go-ahead, Buruts?" people asked. "The horses are all standing ready to be paraded now."

"Make way for the chieftainess of the Qanghay tribe!" Oronghu's mare Qula-bee, that grass-fed rack o' bones, went out to be paraded. The way they did things back in those days was to stuff half a thin saddle-blanket up a mare's backside to keep her from squelching at the rear like some lousy racing-camel when loping at a jog-trot. Following her, hung with golden amulets and marked by good fortune, his ears like candle-flames, that beast born of a whirlwind with a halter-worn spot on top of his muzzle, the well-favored animal with a mark on his right flank – that animal swift-as-an-arrow, Aq-qula now joined the parade. Following him, the answer to his owner's dreams, his stance in the rear wide as a notch in the mountains, the space between his legs wide enough for a man to walk under – stamping his hooves into the ground and tossing his bridle-amulets skyward, Ach-buudan now made his entrance – Joloy's horse joined in the procession.

When brave Manas had raged in his fury at that scandal-maker who demanded Maani-ker – when he had come crashing down on that prince Qong who put on the airs of a hero, Qong-urbay gave him Qïl-qara as a present, ran away without even

looking around, and crossed over Tötö pass – he got well away
from there! He found himself in a deserted place, unable to find
out anything about what was happening to his people, with no
news or even any way to get back to them. He spent two nights
there, in fear he would die of hunger out in that lonely spot, so
he dug up sow-thistle roots and ate six hundred and ninety of
them. His horse Al'-ghara was sweated out. White-bearded
Alooke sent a man out to search, who only barely managed to
find him. It was at the very top of a hill in the thick swamp of
Tötö that the scout managed with difficulty to locate
Qongurbay – and that is why Al'-ghara was not in the race.

Behind Ach-buudan, then, Bozkertik's horse Boy-toru joined
the procession. Following him came one still short of top condi-
tion that had spent fully seven years beneath the earth, and had
come back to the surface a mere seven days previous*: Er Töshtük's
horse Chal-quyruq of the seven lives, six of them already used
up, joined in to the sound of plaints and grieving.* Following him
was Muradïl's Qïl-jeyren, and following him was Muzburchaq's
Tel-küröng, and then came Er Qoshoy's Chong-sarï, and the two
blacks that Ürbü was racing, and Kökchö's horse Kök-ala.

The place where the horses were paraded was on the steppe.
It would be a lot of bother to mention all of the thousand horses;
suffice it to say that they paraded the horses and their number
came to a thousand. There had been some two thousand, but
the race had already brought the people sadness, for Almambet
had altered the weather. That doomed those who had no means
to keep horses properly; they searched for their animals sorrow-
fully, and some were even left without their saddles, tack, and
equipment – they lost everything. Your dear Almambet brought
great misfortune on the majority of the horse racers. Without
saddles they rode bareback with ropes passed round their
horses' lower jaws; this caused them no little resentment.

The horses were being ridden in procession and their number
was one thousand; now the questions arose, "In which direction
will they run?" "At which point will they turn for home?"*
"Brave Manas will have the answer," said all the Muslims and
Heathens. The elder of the Qataghan, Qoshoy, approved Manas
as the judge. "Tell us, hero, how long will the course be? You

know best, after all," they said. The people gathered round, and
the excellent princes who were Manas's peers in strength and
bravery conducted him into the midst. The lion Manas pondered,
turning things over in his mind. Before he could answer – before
he could say anything at all – he who resides at Eki Kemin and
keeps a pair of blacks trained, he of exceedingly crafty mind and
high-strung horses, Ürbü, hitherto unable to say what he wished,
suddenly said, "Manas!" then paused, unable to launch into his
speech. He had heard the rebuke Qoshoy had given him, had felt
that one's fury, and surely felt regret. But Ürbü had something he
wanted to say to bloodthirsty Manas, the presiding official.
"Men have striven before on long courses; celebrated *tulpars*
have raced before. Let them ride two days out and one day back.
I measured it today. The rest of you can hardly have anything to
add to that."

That is what Er Ürbü said, hearing which Manas flew into a
rage. Fire came out of his right eye and hot coals from his left;
bullets shot from his lips: "You rascally nit! – Slave! – Hold
your own memorial feast! Look – look – right here – look
Manas right in the eye, slave! You rascally, mangy-headed
slave! You know-nothing, drunken slave! Silence now! Since
when are you a holder of memorial feasts?" With these words
Manas took his big, knurl-gripped, knot-tipped horse-lash with
the tassel on its pommel and lead slugs in its core, swung it
around his right side, and putting his whole body into it struck
Ürbü on the crown of the head. His jaw was cut open; blood
flowed; the chiefs who love to vaunt themselves so highly to the
masses gave voice with their buttocks.

Swooning in shock, muddle-headed as a lackey, Ürbü had
been brought to a halt. Er Qoshoy, looking daggers, went right
up to Manas. "Hey, Er Manas, my colt, what's this temper
you're in? You don't think well of the high in rank and you
don't even look at the low. Whom do you think you have just
hit? You're one to strike Ürbü on the head! You're one to enjoy
swinging your arm! If I, Qoshoy, just happened to do some-
thing wrong, you would be one to strike me on the head. Even
if that is the way you treat people now, the time will come for
you to be humbled, my bloodthirsty hero. If Qoshoy rides in

anger, you'll be dead in a trice! Come now, have done with this
vein, my Manas. When they say, 'Manas! Manas!' you get all
puffed up; you swell up like a half-inflated goatskin bladder!"
Your uncle Qoshoy loudly scolded Manas, his white beard daz-
zling as his anger rose.

"Qoshoy is on my side," thought Ürbü. "If it comes to blows
with Manas, he will fight with me." Reveling in Qoshoy's words
and taking encouragement from them, that fellow, speaker of
eloquent words and wise counselor, champion of the Faith and
spiritual guide – Ürbü had this to say: "Sart of Samarqan,* Manas!
I shall cause you some pain, Manas! May the earth swallow you
up, you tawny-eared dog! Today I see the fleas you're shaking out
of your collar, Manas! Making yourself out to be master of the
world attended by your forty stalwarts, always putting on your
airs of toughness – you're one to swing your sword! One day
death will catch up to you; you'll find it in my battle-ax!"

That is what Er Ürbü said in his anger, hearing which the hero
Er Manas suddenly took on his lion-aspect. He glared like a pan-
ther lying in its covert ready to spring – if it happened once it
happened every time, his ire always led to action – like a tiger
glimpsed in outline that emerges dreadfully into full view with
curled tail and mottled coat; nothing could escape in health from
the onrush of one such as that! He lost his human form and
became like a reposing lion. Then with a beat of his gold-rimmed
drum he returned to himself. At the sound of the drum the Forty
Wolves at his side rained slashing blows on Ürbü, and were on
the point of killing him when your dear uncle Er Qoshoy, beside
himself at this predicament, said to Ürbü, "Don't talk that way,
or your anger will be the end of you! Don't let the Forty Heroes
butcher you. You mustn't become a sad story that's told until the
end of time! Bearing grudges is for Heathens; what on earth are
you playing at, Ürbü? Shut your mouth or the Forty Tigers will
be the end of you!" Your uncle Qoshoy hurried and put his arm
around Ürbü, and led him quickly out from the midst of the
army.

Reluctant to land a blow on Er Qoshoy, yet overcome with
rage and unable to repress his own anger – for who would be
insensible to the reproach of uncle Qoshoy's actions? – Manas

mastered the keen edge of his wrath; flames burned in his eyes, and he was filled with ire in every inch of his frame at the words Ürbü had said, like a tiger at the approach of autumn, like a bull camel at the approach of winter – it is not safe to be fixed in such a creature's gaze; you cannot stand too close. But in his perplexity his rage abated; your lion Manas hesitated and, in his amazement, conquered his anger.

Who could hold a look like that? – but he stayed still for the time it takes for a pot of food to cook. Only after that did Manas reply to the questions about conducting the race. "Our whole Kirghiz nation observes the customs handed down from our forefathers. Have sixty riders start the racing horses, and have them be nimble about it – crossing Chabdar pass, following the course of the Ile, keeping the jockeys close to the markers in that great valley and then letting them pick their own way to the end of Ulan. Türküstön* is the landmark of the world; it lies a world beyond! If you don't want to have them make two turns, then drive the horses outbound for six days as you go; then get a blessing from the esteemed shaikh of Türküstön – and, having heard his 'Allahu akbar', get back under way. On the horses' return path, six thousand men must go out with white flags in their hands to keep the horses on track and curb them from losing their way at night. Since you'll be driving them six days all the way to Türküstön, be careful in the night! Two days and a night on the way back, and the early-finishing racers will be here; only then let their owners lay hold of the chattels that have been put up for prizes! And let's have none of the constant love of disturbance from those uncircumcised carrion pricks, the Qïtays!" This is what Manas said.

The number of marshals was sixty. They took up their spiked lances and got under way with much shouting. Trustworthy men of high rank, they numbered many of the lords of the Kirghiz. Following them went six thousand escorts to keep the jockeys from losing their way. In the early autumn the nights are short, and the race was started on that very day, so those six thousand men went out to see the jockeys off and keep them from getting lost.*

And once the horses were run there was nothing more to

hanker for; having got the horse race started, the people all got down to feasting. The meat was done. The warriors were dismounted. Everyone, lofty and lowly, young and old, went to their places and got in their tents. That was when a great many here and there who were wearing thin clothes went around with hunched shoulders feeling quite cold.

All of a sudden the serving-boys appeared, bowing to everyone and carrying that lad Boqmurun's riches produced in the cities of Anjïyan and Tashken, golden ewers, more exquisite than any the people had ever seen, and basins of solid gold. The servants hunched over and ran from tent to tent, pouring water for hand-washing, and so every guest got a sense of Kökötöy's great wealth.

Now they spread out on the ground a dining-cloth, a single piece of *torghun*-silk so long that it was impossible for those in the tents, or even those outside on the dry steppe, to see from end to end of it. The one dining-cloth made do to seat that great multitude of people. If your grandfather Kökötöy's wealth wasn't such, then whose ever was? There was no one left who did not go to sit down, and the one dining-cloth fit them all in; there was no second one put down. Everyone – intimates, outsiders, elders – was shown great respect.

Boqmurun served every kind of food all up and down – he served sultanas whipped in milk – but Kökötöy's wealth held out, it was that abundant. Could something like that happen ever again in human life? The entire world took in the sight of Boqmurun Bek's deeds – how he spread raisins everywhere, how strong and tangy his kumiss had turned out – those were the deeds of your forebear. He served a glut of meat, and the guests who began to think of other things found still more meat being brought right to their chins. There was golden rib-fat, slant cuts of mane-fat – just imagine for yourself the splendor of it! They were passing dishes around in twos. Those lacking in hardiness were conquered by the excess and could eat no more, and a great many were those who packed up what they were unable to finish and took it home with them. So the people had their fill of food.

For the two days they were thus put at their leisure, that

giant, white-bearded Qoshoy, down off his horse and all afoot, served platters. Your dear uncle Qoshoy! He hitched up the two corners of his coat-hem and passed out dishes to the people. Manas mounted himself on that gyrfalcon of a creature, the *tulpar* Archa-toru, and went in among the feasters, asking people if they lacked anything and having dishes carried about as needed. Wearing a hat with the black part turned out and gently brushing his lash back and forth over his horse's croup, brave Manas presided from the margins. For two days and two nights he had the meat passed around to one and all, and the people had their fill of food; then the Muslims turned to reading the Qur'an.

11

Shooting the Ingot

"The people will get bored," thought Manas. "The horses will return after eight days; people are going to find the waiting tiresome. They mustn't sit around with nothing to do. They should limber up and compete at shooting the ingot." So saying, he had the spruces of Qarqïra chopped down – the tall ones, disregarding the short – and had a thousand logs thus collected. Driving the base into the ground like the central support-beam of a yurt, they joined six hundred of them together end to end and reared the pole up to the sky.

People who had no idea what was going on asked each other, "What are they doing?" To string up the ingot he had steel cables tied onto the pole. Now, Kökötöy had amassed much money, but since he had died his queen Külayïm was a widow. In his circulating gold funds there was one ingot worth the blood-price of a hundred men. This ingot they fastened to the steel wires in all its surpassing brilliance, and raised it up to that immense height, making the yellow gold into the prize. See what a challenge those heroes had – the ingot was secured with forty-two ties!

Now the heralds went about calling out the announcement, "Go to! Gallop on horseback and try to shoot it down;* that's the game of skill here! You skillful ones, take a shot at it; you others, forget about it! You marksmen, have a shot at it; you common soldiers, forget about it!"

Those who took up the challenge came from all different countries. There were dead-shot marksmen, there were expert shots with muskets, there were knowing shots with the bow and arrow. "You contestants – fire! You without weapons – sit this one out!" they called. A multitude from among the far-spread crowd mounted their horses and formed a body, marksmen loading their muskets, sharpshooters lighting their fuses. They formed up in groups of fifty to a hundred and rode at the ingot en masse, firing. But then they could not turn around; they were packed together in a great crowd and formed a vast, motionless mob. Some dismounted at the base of the target, and, straining with all their might to steady themselves against the upright as the crowd pressed in from all sides, they used the pole to sharpen their aim, and fired away again and again.

It was hard going for those marksmen. They had oiled all the guns and set their minds to shooting. There were falconets and *ochoghor*-pieces, cannons and *qoychaghïr*-guns. The match-locks let off their smacking reports; the shot that fell from the air was like a hail of blue lead dropping out of the sky with a crackle. The shooters made their fire rain from a blue sky, filling the spectators with astonishment and clouding the mountains and valleys with dust. Who put on such a spectacle? Your hero, Manas Khan! The rat-a-tat report of the muskets astounded people; at that time also the great mass of spectators was filled with consternation by all those uncircumcised pricks, the Qïtays and Qalmaqs, who were drawing their bows with all their strength. "There are so many people here that stray shots are going to hit us all of a sudden; we'll wind up dead in a trice!" thought your grandpa, old Qoshoy, as he stood directing everyone.

Indeed the audience sitting around was beginning to feel that it was time the ammunition ought to run out. When it did and the marksmen found they had no more powder in their flasks, the last of the ball and powder being shaken out, they stretched their necks out like swans and fired their last shots, then bent down and took their seats, the whole multitude of them having lost hope of felling the ingot. They had all fired at it. Falconets and cannon had been fired, but not a single ball had gone more than halfway up; not one had even come close to the ingot, not one of that great mass of gunners had even grazed it. The ingot hung there on its cords, untouched by all that ammunition, and the marksmen were sunk in dejection as they crowded around the base of the target. "If you've no more powder to shoot with, then mount up and move off!" your dear uncle Qoshoy was heard to say as he drove them along, and they withdrew from the target; "If you can't do any more, then move along!" the heralds were heard to say.

Just then word came from Manas, brought by his messenger, Prince Majik: "Heathens and Muslims – all you ordinary feast-guests – make room! All of you watch and wait, and you will see some entertainment!" This was the message that Majik, the hero's messenger, announced.

Princes and commoners alike were abuzz with excitement and swarmed up the low foothills; the common folk went further up the dark, spruce-clad mountainsides, the masses of them striving as best they could without a rest. Then they dismounted from their horses and took their seats all around.* From off to the side of the dense-packed soldiers, at the very head of the Qarqïra valley in the east, the hero Manas, the panther,* now mounted a horse, followed by all his falcon-like warriors. As he stood there thus facing west the falcon-like prince banged the drum with its rim of ruddy gold, and the eighty-four warriors clad in impenetrable corselets, their burning glances igniting flames, formed into two detached wings. The Forty Heroes who were Manas's companions had not a care for death, it seems. They loaded their muskets and set the fuses alight. As if on command those Forty Heroes drew up on either side, and in their midst sat Er Manas.

The numerous Alach looked on in amazement as another boom issued from Manas's drum, the muzzles of the heroes' guns seemed to piss fire, and eighty-four muskets went *Bang!* with a single report. Smoke swirled from the guns. The friends all shouted, "O! Allah!" and the Qalmaq officials all tumbled off their horses in shock, thumping down as if struck by bullets. The eighty-four, too, plopped down onto the ground. Only Manas remained erect, alone and towering over them; while he stood thus alone, his Forty Heroes who vaunted their own toughness lay on the ground as if dead. Manas atop his horse beat the gold-rimmed drum, and in the blink of an eye the numerous heroes lying there in a mass were totally remounted. It defies comprehension! Those excellent princes who had been stretched out on the ground mounted up again without even touching feet to stirrups; no one had ever seen horses being mounted in that way.

As the world's multitudes looked on in amazement, he beat the drum again. Qïrghïl Chal beside him, a spry old man, doing better than most, flung his ell-high hat up and sent it spinning skyward. From its high point in the air the hat began to fall back down, but as it was descending Khan Baqay, in a superb display of marksmanship, came forward and shot it. The bullet hit the hat in the crown and it was lifted up, and remained in the air a long time before again it turned and fell earthward; but behind Baqay Khan, Qïrghïl Chal, handy at every sort of undertaking, took aim and fired, and the hat spun skyward again. Again it came falling back to earth; and now Almambet came forward and fired one shot. – Who ever shot such as they did?! The hat never reached the ground; those Forty Heroes, sons of lions, never missed a shot! – Almambet shot with his *almabash*-musket, and the bullet hit the mark just as the others had, sending the hat upward to the height of a lance. Again it sank down, and Chalïbay son of Küldür came up behind and fired; next to take a shot at the airborne hat came Ajïbay, calmly and unhurriedly. The hat could not reach the ground. It hung and tossed about, and all the while those excellent heroes' shots never missed. Those sharpshooters loaded their muskets and set their fuses alight, and for the time it takes a pot of meat to cook they kept the hat hanging in the air with their gunfire, never letting it drop to earth. The lion Manas Baatïr sat and regarded all this until at last, when a time long enough for a pot of meat to cook had passed and the people were thoroughly astounded, he beat the drum, and the hat fell to the ground, completely riddled with holes. Back in their brave Manas's day, had the Qara Kirghiz a care in the world?!

Again their princely leader Manas banged the drum, and those eighty-four warriors, whose galloping horses trail fire, divided into groups of twenty-one and stood on all four sides – a fearsome sight. The prince again beat the drum, and Baqay,

on a swing-gaited gray ambler with his bright mail-coat
stripped off to the waist and his grizzled beard a-flutter – at his
side twenty companions, campaign-hardened tigers – charged
at that spirited glutton Qïrghïl, who also had beside him twenty
companions, dead-shot tigers. Those who stood witnessing it
could scarce keep their wits; old Qïrghïl let out a yell, a great
roar full of fury, and fell upon Baqay Khan. He met Baqay's
lance, which wounded him on the nipple. Qïrghïl Chal, who
vaunted his toughness so, went somersaulting off his horse; old
Baqay and all his companions were safe and sound. – Your
hero Manas amazed everyone with the terrible spectacles he
put on! – Not one of Qïrghïl Chal's companions was left peek-
ing up; not one of your uncle Baqay's companions came down
off his horse.

Manas paused, and beat the drum again. Whipping Sar'-ala
across the neck and "tucking away the falcon-hood,"* Almam-
bet Baatïr rode out and picked up each of Qïrghïl Chal's
companions as if bending down to pluck a hat off the ground,
and set him on his horse. He brought Qïrghïl Chal's men, sea-
soned and hardened as they were, back to their senses and
mounted them on their horses quicker than the blink of an eye.
Having displayed his prowess to one and all, Almambet moved
on from there and, reaching Baqay, who had already with-
drawn, he brought havoc down on him. Baqay had tumbled
Qïrghïl's men to the ground and they had been set up again;
and scarcely could they turn their horses' heads before Almam-
bet Baatïr, he of no little prowess, gave Baqay such a drubbing
that his dear uncle was turned inside out. Almambet and his
companions, skilled battle-tigers, withdrew without a scratch;
but now Ajïbay spurred his horse to a gallop, caught up with
them from behind, and thrust his lance into them, starting with
Almambet. All of them went crashing down off their horses
and lay stretched out on the ground. Behind them came Er
Baqay, who leaned down and picked up Almambet as if pluck-
ing a goat carcass off the ground,* and set him on his horse.
With your uncle Baqay in the lead his men left no one on the
ground; those who were watching were greatly relieved. Just
then Qïrghïl Chal of the grizzled beard came up behind Baqay

and thrust him into the dirt. And not only your uncle Baqay, the close comrades with him were not spared either; Baqay went flying off his horse and landed spread-eagle on the ground, and so did the others. Ajïbay appeared next and put them to rights, reseating Baqay on his horse and displaying a deft hand at it.

Manas, still standing where he was, gave a rap on the drum, and all around archers stood with their deadly bows and polished arrows, and – marvelous to behold – they nocked their arrows and let them fly, and those arrows passed over the whole of this inconstant, illusory world. After a while the hero Manas Baatïr struck the drum, and the Heathens watching there were sunk in bewilderment: *whoosh!* – arrows were drawn from the archers' quivers and driven home with such extraordinary skill that the topknots on the Heathens' hats were plucked off and sent flying. Everyone saw the arrows from the archers' quivers shear off the topknots on those Heathens' caps. Eighty warriors who had remained unscathed from the beginning rode up behind Manas.

Was it not time now for the Forty Heroes of high renown to display their skill? When the drum sounded again, they drew the swords from their scabbards. With their swords thus bared they lay down their dear lives and came at each other shouting. The crowd was amazed at their swordplay, for though they chopped at each other's necks they checked every blow. Sword slashed against sword, sparking red flames. The forty of them – lined up sword in hand, shouting and swinging and engaging in heated swordplay – astounded the whole audience with the masterful skills they displayed. They made not a crease in each other's flesh; not so much as touched one spot of it with their naked, watered-steel blades, though a suicidal massacre appeared imminent. For at least as long as it takes to cook a pot of food they slashed this way and that, sword in hand; those who saw the sight were quite dumbfounded at the powers of those Forty Heroes.

Then the eighty-four warriors came out to have some sport: if a welt appeared anywhere on him, then by the rules the man had to fall down. Some got their dander up even though they could not raise a welt on an opponent, and out of spite tried to knock their man over. – Never warming to the man they know, always hostile to each other; that is why this lineage of the Kirghiz has never increased! – Others were so fired with hate that they were trying to kill their man as they played, but try as they might they were unable to land a mortal blow. Also among the eighty-four were those thinking, "I'll put an end to this insolent slave!" but their intentions were thwarted by skillful parries.

When the people had been watching the combat for fully the time it takes a pot of meat to cook, the drum sounded again. Now with a great shout the warriors took battle-axes in their hands and laid into each other this way and that, with shields raised to meet every blow. Those watching were astounded at the way those Qara Kirghiz set axes to shields, sending sparks showering down to the ground. Muslims and Infidels alike stood and watched, utterly at a loss. "What men are these?" the great majority wondered, confounded and unable to absorb the variety of the drills on display. Dread Manas Baatïr's long-tutored captains could turn any foe they encountered into mincemeat.

As the day got on past noon, people remembered the ingot. No one from any other country had any bullets left; as far as the guests were concerned the ingot clearly remained for the taking. "Only Manas can do it," some said. "What will he do?" said others. "All that shooting and no bullets reached the target." "It must be set up too high." They stood in rows looking at brave Manas in wide-eyed wonder, all the Muslims and Infidels together, watching what would happen next.

Those foremost, splendid warriors – their jousting was of a different order! – the Forty excellent warriors with their red pennants and Manas their falcon, their sovereign, conducted themselves unlike the normal run of men. The Forty world-conquering Wolves of the iron-tipped lances tasseled in blue, sworn companions of that brave hero, stood in rows awaiting the signal. At the sound of Er Manas's crashing drumbeat, first Er Baqay of surpassing valor, whipping his gray ambler across the neck and tucking his white beard down the front of his shirt, aimed his musket Kök-chïbïq. As the old falcon-eyed warrior started out, the Forty Heroes let out a thunderous

cheer. There was a blue flash at the touch of the fuse; the mus-
ket Kök-chïbïq bore out its fire with a *Bang!* and one of the
ingot's cords snapped. Hollering at his own daring shot your
keen-eyed Baqay left the field.

Next came white-bearded Qïrghïl with a yell; his falconet
went *Bang!* and another cord snapped. After him without a
break came Almambet Baatïr. There was a white flash at the
touch of the fuse; his *almabash*-musket bore out its fire, and
one more cord recoiled with a twang. After him came Ajïbay,
then Chalïbay, one of the best marksmen, and Majik son of
Qaratoqo, Chalik son of Qambar, Satay son of the one called
Charghïl, Atay son of Shaghïl Biy, Ümöt of the Üyshün and his
son Jaysang – every one who rode out cut one of the cords. The
ingot had been raised to an immense height and secured with
forty-two ties; the gold ingot itself was the prize. Those tie-
cords were not going to stay whole but were being clipped off
one at a time, shot by shot. Next in turn came Qaraqojo of the
Arghïn, Boobek, Shaabek, and Shükürü – all of like mind and
in tune with Manas – then Altay of the Arban, Törtay son of
Dörbön, sullen Tölök the fortune-teller – each of these princes
severed a cord and moved off; then Aghïday the scapulimancer
whose predictions of future events always came true, squad
leader Toqotoy, Qalqaman who inspected the commoners, Ele-
man who oversaw the people; then those who were close
companions to Manas, brave Sïrghaq and Serek, indispensable
in a tight spot; then Qosh Abïsh son of Qonghuroo, young
Ïbïsh who inspected the troops, and Alaken son of Alïmshaa, a
real crack shot though but a boy. The lion Manas was there as
well, as were those who, when the army went campaigning and
made a long march in darkness, could follow a wolf's tracks
unerringly: Qadïr, Jaynaq, and Shuutu – they were eminent
marksmen; and those who, when the teeming Kirghiz army
went campaigning and made a march in the middle of the night,
would not stray from a fox's tracks, who thought nothing of
the night and never made a wrong step: Tümön, Jaynaq, and
Shuutu – they were marksmen through and through; and from
the Qazaq, Joorunchu, Qayghïl, Bögöl, Toorulchu, Kerben son
of Shïnghï, and Dörbön distinguished by his eloquence. Those

were all the Forty Heroes, with Qïrghïl and Baqay their seniors. They had each taken a shot one at a time, those lords of the Kirghiz descended from the progenitor Noghoy the giant – and thus cleared the field.

At the end came the lion Manas, who now commenced his shot at the golden ingot hanging in the air. Placing full trust in his God, he took Aq-kelte in his hand, slung on its gold-studded strap – Aq-kelte, unerring at close range or long, equalizer of near and far, its barrel and muzzle of finest steel, prodigious smoker, its lock of Ïspan make, fearsome of sight and true of shot – and headed towards the ingot. At a good distance, about the length of a horse-race course, the lion-hero brought his lash down on the racer Archa-toru, a horse not easy to train, and started off. Archa-toru ran headlong to within a short distance of the ingot; Manas raised his musket and blue smoke poured out, and out of the blue sky the ingot came falling down.

He had broken the pole at the base! That is how he put that problem to rest.* Manas fierce-as-a-white-goshawk had broken the timbers that had been lashed together and set up, putting an end to his enemies' wondering and filling his kinsmen's hearts with joy; he brought the ingot falling out of the blue sky and sent animated talk spreading through the crowd. Now Manas the lion spurred Archa-toru and raced in, and while the ingot was still whirling, before it had fallen all the way and come to a stop, the hero closed in at a gallop and, like a goshawk striking a lark, plucked it up and ran off. Who but the lion Manas Baatïr could have performed with such skill?

When they held the ingot-shooting contest at that memorial feast, everybody to a man was there: old Qoshoy of the Qataghan, and Kökchö of the Qazaq; Eleman's son Töshtük, Jamghïrchï of the Eshtek, Baghïsh of the Jediger, black-bearded Er Ürbü – all the while the commoners attending the memorial feast for Kökötöy and looking for entertainment went surging here and there. Kerkökül son of Kökmök, Janay son of Köchpös Bay – at Kökötöy's feast we saw and waited on many Türks from all over – many were the thoroughbreds in the race; many the pieces in Manas's armory; many the uncircumcised-prick-headed Qïtay. Many were the tough warriors from among the

Qïtays who had settled in at that feast and taken a sporting shot at the ingot: Qongurbay, and Muradïl son of Qïrmuz; red-topknotted Nezqara, black-maned Booronchu, Oronghu from the Qanghay, Sayqal the daughter of Qatqalang – let's mention each one! – Alooke of the Soloon, Joloy bad-tempered as a boar, Bozkertik of the Toqshuker, and Soorondük son of Solobo. That Tungsha Qïtay, Oronghu – one doesn't like to dwell on her! God knows how her part turned out. Oronghu was waddling about with the tresses at the back of her head sticking out like seventy mouse tails; but never mind them.* There is more to tell about the eminent Manas Baatïr. Listen to his story.

The Muslims who fill the earth had brought glory to God; did you not see with your own eyes how Manas swept that ingot from the earth? Indeed we ought to shout the praises of brave men who catch ingots in their hands! We Kirghiz have never forgotten our customs these one thousand and seventy years.* Our traditions have never yet disappeared. They have been retold continuously all that time; but their brilliance shone on one and all in the days of heroes! Manas roared out the war-cry, "Baabedin!" as he displayed the ingot in his hand all around. He had knocked the post down at the base, much to the chagrin of the teeming Infidels; the crash of the impact was still resounding in the ears of the sons of the Muslims when he brought the ingot and presented it to his burly elder kinsman, white-bearded Qoshoy of surpassing glory. "Dear uncle, take this!" he said. "You are my white-bearded elder, my khan, bulwark of the people; you are my cherished friend! Take this, and give me your blessing!"

To this honor that Manas had paid him your uncle Qoshoy replied, "Never mind that, my boy. Do not hold this one man so advanced in years, this old man at your side, in higher esteem than yourself. Take this first of all prizes of the feast, which you have won outright, and be off! If you like to shoot guns, then that's the way to shoot!" Thus your Qoshoy returned the honor.

While Manas had been shooting the ingot, Infidels had been promenading. Some of them had been present and some not; those who had not observed were completely ignorant of it.

Some were riding elephants, or if not on elephant-back then on rhinoceros-back – yes, there were towering heroes cutting a proud figure, not on horses, but astride rhinoceroses; the really big fellows, however, were the champions mounted on elephants, exceedingly cunning heroes who commanded thousands as easily as one man. The teeming, hulking tribes of the western nations were there: the khan Maamït Sultan and the giant Kötök – everyone you've ever seen or heard of was there – Kemel tense as a drawn bow – many peoples had come to the feast – Qaracha son of Suqtur – there are so many people in the world! They had to reckon that not many would ever excel Kökötöy's feast in hospitality and spectacle, nor was there anyone in the world to compare with that gyrfalcon of a prince, Manas.

The ingot-shooting having concluded, evening was coming on and many were realizing that they had never seen skill like Manas's. The people lay down to rest then and there. Dawn broke next morning to the sound of horns. As trumpets roared, shawms blared, and tambours beat rat-a-tat, Kökötöy's standard was hoisted, its blue banner a-flutter, and the enormous, dense hosts of Muslims and Infidels raised an ear-splitting din on every side.

12

Qoshoy and Joloy Wrestle;
Qoshoy Beats Joloy

Kökötöy's standard was raised with its rippling blue banner.
Ïrchï Uul son of Ïraman now cried out the summons. The people
were all heading toward an area where an arena was being
marked out; a huge crowd was already standing round, their
eyes filled with apprehension. Before anyone could say a word or
do anything, or even blink, Ïrchï Uul son of Ïraman of the forty-
knot tassel on the drawstring of his drawers, that fellow of the
topknotted skullcap and effortless speech, appeared mounted on
a horse with Jash Aydar beside him. These heralds called out in
stern tones to the whole assembly: "Muslims and Infidels, you
two peoples in your thick masses, obey the words of gray-maned
Manas at this memorial feast for Kökötöy! He cannot accept
contestants by tribe, or there would be difficulties with the great
number of them. He is not accepting contestants by clan and
inflicting countless multitudes of wrestlers on us. 'My people,
hear this!' he said. 'Let a true and willing champion from among
the Infidels take the field. If he's got the strength, let him beat his
opponent.' Manas commands you to listen! Our message is from
on high. The great masses of people assembled should not be
made to rue this feast; put up no ordinary man but an elite cham-
pion of champions. Someone who can smash the hard, black
stones in the earth to dust finer than clay – choose a man such as
that from your midst! Who can break iron bars like willow
switches, nearly keep his feet wrestling elephants and rhinocer-
oses, lay low and crush his enemies, and soothe his kinsmen's
hearts – let two such contestants come forward, one Muslim and
one Infidel, bull-headed heroes, unbeatable strong-men who fear
none in the ring and can defend their people!

"Now hear this: the winner gets the garner, and the loser gets nothing! The amount of the prize is six hundred horses and a hundred camels – But it's not enough, you say? – And two hundred head of cattle and five hundred sheep! Now all of you at Kökötöy's feast come together, and pick your champions to send out and wrestle in the arena! Let the loser lie where he's thrown and the winner bask in triumph!"

At that loud cry, the Infidels of the east and west all assembled. In an occurrence like none other at a feast or gathering anywhere in this illusory world, they were all united and joined as one in counsel to decide which one champion to put forward. Then at one edge of the Infidel mass there was a flurry of excitement and the crowd parted all in a tumble, and a space opened up between. There stood a sight to see – Joloy, the damned Heathen! A space opencd up in the midst and there at last we saw him, pawing up piles of dirt like mountains, flinging dust up into the air – Joloy, the cursed Heathen!

All the Infidels had ranked their wrestlers and this was their pick: if you looked at his nails they were like the claws of a white tiger; if you looked at his moustaches they were like water falling off the blades stuck round the hub of a mill-wheel. His size was immense, unique; the lenses of his eyes were big as cups. He had a father though there was no betrothal, it's been said, and there's no mistake there – he had a mother though there was no wedding; but our people have no fighter as tough as he! Wide in the middle but not tall, broad of face with a gloomy cast; a despicable enemy, hostile to the Faith; the brows upon his forehead like black dogs lying prone; an imperturbable giant with a head the size of a feasting-cauldron and hair falling in tresses down his back like horse-hair ropes. He was on the far side of forty, that scoundrel, with a body built like a tower, a yen to leave no opponent anywhere unfought, and ears the size of campaign-tents. This lone hero emerged from the Qalmaqs and stepped toward the arena. His ears were magnificent as shields; if you looked at the lashes on his eyelids they were like thorns sticking out of gut-membrane. Any opponent he got his hands on would be ground to pieces like oat flour. If one looked at his form, the span between his shoulders was a fathom and a half. A close and intimate friend of the khan, Qongurbay Baatïr, he had shoulders broad enough, were you to look, for two men to perch on; if you looked at his cheeks there was enough meat there for two grown he-wolves to gorge on. Joloy now made his slouching way forward, his bearing like something one would record in a picture, if one met him. The sockets of his eyes, were one to look, were like pits dug out for grain cellars; the scum in his eyes was thick as the soup that hunters boil down and dish onto plates; his calves big around as a bull's girth; the breath from his mouth like the blast of wind on a rather high mountain pass. If you looked at his arms they were thick as forty-year-old poplars; if you looked at his eyelids they were those of a deadly bird of prey; if you looked at the breadth of his chest it was like a mountainside; if you took in his whole mood, he resembled an enraged, gray-maned wolf! If you looked at his back it was broad as a horse-race course on the steppes; if you looked at his bosom it was as full as a teen-aged girl's.

Joloy now girded himself for the ring as the Muslims looked on with dread. Before anyone could say a word, that cursed Heathen had stripped and taken the field. There are those observant men who can hear from a distance if someone even whispers a proverb like, "A green poplar has no worth; the people have nothing but" – the people's keen appraisers knowing of all they see. The Infidels had sized up Joloy and were saying, "He'll definitely throw his man," but now the appraisers pronounced their judgment: "This is the most mettlesome hero the world has ever produced!" Bull-chested and quick with a rebuke, he had the look of haughtiness about him; his sword sharp and his lance well-planed, he had the look of a brave warrior about him; sparing with his thoughts, he had the look of toughness. There he was, then, the giant Joloy, his people's choice for the wrestling match. His biceps like camel-bulls' thighs, he had the look of a strong-man; and he had once defeated Muzburchaq, they noted, so he had the look of a winner; and, fearless of death, he had something of the beast about him as well.

A great many of the Qalmaq, Qïtay, Tarsa, and Jööt were standing around watching him and supplicating, according to their religion. Facing to the east they cried, "Heavenly god, help us!" and bowed to their gods. Those who saw Joloy trembled

at the formidable sight. He stepped into the ring and sat down,
roaring like a rutting elephant. Clouds of blue smoke poured
from his pipe with its bowl big as a brass kettle, and his raw
gullet and windpipe gurgled like rushing water.* The exultant
Infidels let out a deafening cheer. In his fury Joloy had sparks
crackling from his eyes. There he sat, massive, down on his
haunches, alone in the middle of the ring.

No one emerged to oppose Joloy from the sons of Islam. Not
one wretch championed the religion; instead they cowered and
hid. Your dear uncle Qoshoy cried out, his voice booming and
full of alarm, "One of you boys get out there! Beat that dog
and keep him from bragging!" Though soldiers stood dense as
hairs, there was no one to go down into the ring – but after see-
ing the formidable Joloy, after seeing what kind of hero he was,
would anybody want to get near him?

"That poor wretch is short on luck, the unbelieving, heathen,
shameless brute of a slave!" Qoshoy railed. "Look! Though of
khanly status, when his people wish it that swine is ready to
wrestle!"

Now Qoshoy went rocking along on a light blue-gray ambler,
his white beard a-waving, to speak face to face to the towering
leaders of men and the mightiest bruisers, and hear their answers.
"Er Chegish, son of Joodarï, enemies bleed at the sight of you!
You're a likely fellow, you've got an extraordinary build. You're
the khan of Jazïyra and Jemsi. What if you go as our champion?
What if you go and wrestle with Infidel Joloy in the ring?"

Your uncle Qoshoy had barely finished speaking when Chegish
replied, "I'm not getting near Joloy, that cursed Heathen." That
was his answer to Qoshoy Baatïr, so your dear uncle left him
there.

"Abdïraman, son of Sayat of the people of Qabarïsh, only
son of your father! Here's how things stand right now. It's time
for those who profess Islam to show some courage. All the Infi-
dels are rejoicing and saying, 'Our Joloy is the strongest!'
because Joloy went out as their champion."

His answer to Qoshoy was, "I'm not getting near Joloy. I
can't go up against the likes of him."

Your dear uncle's white beard dazzled as he spurred his light blue-gray horse to full gallop and left him there. Next he came to Kerkökül, but when your dear uncle pulled up and asked him, "What about you?" his answer was, "I'm not getting near Joloy. I'm not going to fight with someone like that."

And so your uncle moved on; coming to brave Jamghïrchï Baatïr, he asked, "What about you?" but the answer came, "I'm not getting near Joloy."

So your uncle left him there and came to Ürbü son of Taz, the mighty paragon of the Qïpchaq. "How about you for our champion? To the victor go the spoils!" said Qoshoy.

Ürbü was quick with his tongue, as he had been since youth. He said, "Alas dear uncle Qoshoy, where is your mind? That colossal Joloy, that rogue who has entered the ring, has biceps the size of rawhide jugs – see, that's why he's gone out and sat down in the ring so calmly! In what way do I match him? His calves are as big as children! If I'm the one to go out there, uncle – ho! then our strength must be at a low ebb. His biceps are like camel-bulls' thighs, his moustaches like ax-handles; that sack between his legs could hold a saber. If he happened to get his hands on me there would probably be nothing left but wisps so tiny they would get lost up a fox's nose. That brute has thighs as big around as inflated goatskin bladders, a bag of ballocks like a leather pail, veins in his buttocks big around as my wrist, and flesh on his temples bulging like tubs. If we look at the shape of his arms, they are like old poplars; he's got sinews thick as herdsmen's crooks; if you look at his ballocks they're like three-span carved bowls. You see me; don't insult me with your idle words!"

Hearing this, your dear uncle Er Qoshoy said, "Such a little devil! Has this one no shame?" and left him there. Then he came to Er Kökchö. "You, who summer in the Sarï-arqa and lead the Qazaqs on their migrations, you who keep Ker-töböl trained and in fine fettle at the hitching-post, decapitator of enemies who threaten – you, Kökchö, have been one of the foremost Qazaqs. You have always had a certain energy about you. Now Joloy has gone out to wrestle and steal his enemies' honor. The Heathens are ready to humiliate us if their champion wins the match," said your uncle Qoshoy.

Stalwart Kökchö too sought to get out of it. "I may puff out

my chest, but I'm timid to the core, just a poor wretch. Dear
uncle Qoshoy, what is this you're saying, that I'm strong, trying
to whip me up? It would be worse for my name, and worse to
hear, if they said, 'Kökchö of the Qazaq went out and the Qal-
maqs' bruiser Joloy slammed him to the ground'! I won't go
near a battle-wolf like Joloy. He's a dog that can't be filled
though he gobbles six *batman* of grain, a dog that leaves no
opponent in good health; a dog that can't be filled, I say, though
he gobbles seven *batman* of flour; a dog, I say, that leaves no
enemy in single combat standing – Big Joloy, who smells of
grain from gobbling wheat seven sacks at a time, who smells of
blood from slaying seventy giants at once; Big Joloy, who smells
of grain from gobbling wheat six sacks at a time, who smells of
blood from slaying sixty giants at once!"

This is what Kökchö said, and it made your dear uncle
Qoshoy very angry all of a sudden. "Kökchö, you dog, a curse
on your father's grave! May the earth swallow you up! Damn
you, Kökchö, what kind of talk is that? Don't you know that
all the sons of the Muslims, lofty and lowly, young and old, and
the other peoples' observers are standing around watching and
listening? Don't you know they can hear what you say? If there
were a brave man willing to go down in the ring and he were a
Muslim, wouldn't his heart burst? How could a champion will-
ing to enter the ring even dare to, after getting frightened at the
things you're saying? Those are very bad things you're saying.*
If you don't want to go down, then don't go down. – That life-
less stare of yours! – If you refuse to go down, don't spoil it for
the others!" Thus rebuking Er Kökchö and spurring his light
blue-gray horse into a caper, Er Qoshoy went on his way.

Next he came to Er Töshtük. Attending Töshtük was a thick
gathering of the best of the Qïpchaqs, who were just then say-
ing to him, "You, Prince Töshtük Baatïr, are the youngest of
nine sons, the darling of your father Eleman, a servant of the
Almighty, with all kinds of people under you; uncle Qoshoy
could scarcely come to you?"

But Qoshoy said: "Joloy the damned Qalmaq, as those who
were cut off from the Muslims are called, whose forefather was
Manghul, who grinds his opponents into flour and knows the

cursed Infidel rites by heart, has gone out as the Heathens' champion, and those who have looked him over apparently hold out no hope of beating him. Er Töshtük, will you enter the ring against that worthless Heathen, that faithless wretch? Don't refuse and destroy our honor! Don't lose to that abominable Joloy and bring affliction on all the Muslims!"

When Qoshoy said this, Er Töshtük, despite the great distance he had just traveled, was unable to say no. So as not to refuse his esteemed elder's request, he said, "Many a time I have found myself horseless and on foot, wrestling many a powerful opponent. I have fought *divs*, *peris*, and *jinns*. Who dares to underrate Töshtük, victor in those contests? Does the moon flee from the stars? On Köyqap, while spending time away from the Kirghiz, I fought many a man, many a giant; I faced *peris* and put *divs* to death. The heathen race of *peris* have been my enemies for many a year. There's nothing I haven't seen and no enemy that's defeated me, though they fairly teemed. In my weary state, returned as I am from my journeying, just seeing your face has banished my cares! – just hearing you speak! I was parted from my own, dear uncle Qoshoy, but I see you and I am well again. Meeting you is my happiness; that one they've set up in the ring, Joloy, shan't make me lose heart! I will sacrifice myself to God; no man in this world lives on without dying. My wish was to return safely to my people, dear uncle; now may your wish be fulfilled! You are getting on in years, so I accept your charge." That is what Töshtük said, adding, "I have no regrets in life."

Qoshoy the khan heard him and saw his courage. He met Töshtük's bold gaze and scrutinized him carefully. Then he shook his head. "Töshtük, my boy, listen to me and listen well. You have reached unreachable lands and crossed many waters – rivers, the whirlpools of the salty ocean, and the greatest waters on earth; raging torrents of mud; the northern waters seven years' journeying across; the conjoined waters seventy years' journeying across. While absent from your people for seven years you made a journey of seventy years, and have endured many years' sufferings. Töshtük, my boy, don't say you'll enter the ring with Joloy! The Zïmïrïq itself has tucked you under its wing and flown you a year's distance in a day. Muslims and

Heathens never belonged to a single religion in the regions you have visited, yet the flesh of any son of Adam goes for a thousand gold pieces a dram. The Creator has helped you, and you have returned alive. Now you are stringy and emaciated; you've got barely any blood left in you. I don't think your strength will be adequate to wrestle with that Qalmaq," said Qoshoy, and he passed on from that place.

Brave Joloy was still sitting there in the arena as before. – How can I be silent about what was seen by all? – A hero appeared, Kökqoyon son of Kökbörü, and uncle Qoshoy rode over to him. With folded hands he greeted Qoshoy and received greetings from him in return. "O my foal, Kökqoyon! The red-topknotted Oyrots and the Qïtays are feeling their oats. They have forwarded a champion, a khan, but a simpleton: Joloy the scourge of the Qalmaq has taken the field. How about you, will you be our champion?" This was old Qoshoy's message.

"Think about it, uncle," said Kökqoyon, "Who could give me the strength and courage I need right now? If I am thrown by that scoundrel the Heathens will rejoice at our misfortune. Aren't you stronger than I am? If my strength is the size of a leather jug, yours is like a well-soured leather kumiss-vat!" So said Kökqoyon.

Your dear uncle Qoshoy moved on, saying, "Qoyon, child, you're no good." Going through the thick of the crowd, he made for Aqbay. Qoshoy sized up his character and found he was like a young goat gamboling on the cliffs; he sized up his courage and found he was like a spring shooting out of the rocks. The charismatic Er Aqbay had eyes that flashed like lit candles and brows black as if engraved. His age was seventeen; from his head small as a camping-kettle hung tousled black hair. Qoshoy came up to him and asked, "How about you, my boy?"

It was this little charmer, full of ardor, who said yes: "I don't have it in me to run from anyone; it's not in my makeup to refuse. If it's the wish of all these people who are waiting, then I have no intention to run. What will be will be, I don't care! If I have to go then I'm on my way; if I have to go down in the ring, I'll go down," said sweet Aqbay.

Only then did Er Qoshoy look and see what the lad had not

revealed: the shapely, fifteen-year-old, delicate-fingered, luxuri-
antly tressed, duck-necked, dainty-headed Zïyandash, daughter
of Taanas Khan. "I see you've married yourself a beautiful wife,"
said Qoshoy. "You've been going around thinking about getting
on her all the time, and you've become stringy and emaciated;
your flesh is ropy and lean, and you've got barely any blood left
in you. Sweet Aqbay, you won't have the strength to wrestle
Joloy. Your calf muscles haven't filled out yet; you aren't old
enough to be a champion. Your heart muscle hasn't filled out yet;
you aren't old enough to be the attacker. You've got hatchling-
down on your forehead and mother's milk on the roof of your
mouth. You've still got cradle-down on your belly; you're not
ready yet. You still haven't fully developed your toughness and
strength, and you've got newborn-down on your buttocks.
You're not old enough to go down in the ring; you're not even
old enough to break a branch off a tree! We mustn't let the giant
Joloy, who is at the peak of his strength, rip your arm off, and
make the Muslims enter the ring to defend you in such numbers
that they knock into each other and start fights themselves! We
mustn't let Joloy hew your leg off, and send all those Muslim
bystanders into their own ruckus! The one they call Joloy is an
immense bruiser; in war he has felled many an enemy. Do not
think he'll be easy, don't make sport of that Heathen! My boy, if
you face him, do not imagine you will emerge in good health.
And don't covet the prize!"

With that your uncle passed on until he met Muzburchaq
son of Buudayïq. Your uncle Qoshoy went up to him and asked,
"How about you?" but Muzburchaq said, "I don't have the
strength anymore; I'm not young anymore. I'm not getting near
Joloy, that Heathen with the cruel ways. Could anyone survive
in the arena with Joloy Baatïr?"

Your uncle Qoshoy moved on, fretting as he went, and drew
near Manas. To the celebrated, foremost hero, him whose skill in
lance-combat was a thing apart; to the Forty Heroes with their
red pennants, whose deeds were a thing apart; to his falcon, sov-
ereign Manas, Qoshoy now went, rocking atop his gray ambler
with his white beard all a-flutter. The majestic Er Manas gave his
greeting, and your uncle returned it. "That shameless Heathen

slave, grim hero of a slave, faithless wretched slave, poor unfortunate slave Joloy the giant, son of Keder, is down on foot and has gone out as the Heathens' champion. From the sons of the Muslim faith, however, from the servants of the Faith, no champion has gone out to face him. The sons of chiefs have all lost heart and held back, and the commoners have fled looking for shelter. No one has gone out to oppose that scandalous Heathen. Though cruel, you have always been a hero, always of surpassing courage. That piece of carrion Joloy has already entered the arena and sat down, and made everyone here lose heart. I am getting on in years, and stiff. I move like a doddering old camel-bull. I don't want to go up against that Heathen. But you, though cruel, have always been a hero, always of surpassing courage. If you do not go up against that Heathen the panther Joloy Baatïr, who else would cross him?" This is what Qoshoy said, hearing which Manas fumbled for words.

"It is well that you have come! What you have said needed saying. If I ever hold back from the Heathen, I'll take the blame! – Let me answer your question, dear uncle Qoshoy. When I am mounted on a horse I am a born death-bringer, a bullet, but I have always been useless on foot. Among the sons of the mountain Kirghiz I have always been quick-tempered and unrestrained. Brave Qoshoy, my tiger, if I am thrown I get hurt, but if I make the throw the foe gets hurt. Old Qoshoy, understand what this bloodthirsty hero in front of you is saying! For the sake of honor I'll gird myself, for the sake of the spirits of our departed ancestors I'll strip down and go out and wrestle their champion, and if I go I'll throw that dog down. But if afterward I'm splay-legged and have an awkward seat on my horse, if I have a tender seat on my *tulpar* and can't stay upright, how am I supposed to take up my lance and go out jousting? If I have a friend in the Lord God, and if the strength I always have holds out, I'll win both – the jousting and the wrestling; but people will have tantrums, saying I didn't forward a competitor from their midst. If it comes to fighting I will win, but people will murmur slanders, saying I wanted the prizes." That was Manas's answer.

Your big uncle Qoshoy was quite overcome with his cares,

and gave a loud cry. This is what your old grandpa had to say: "Not one strong man has come out from the Qara Kirghiz, from the sons of the Muslim faith, not even a slave, to champion the religion! Not one valiant giant or rock-ribbed man of courage or fierce man of grim resolve; and the poor have run off seeking shelter. No one has thrown that blasted dog! I encouraged everyone, but no matter what I said, they wouldn't listen; none will throw that raging slave! They said, 'May blood fill your filthy mouth and an unhappy day be yours, may sand fill your blasted mouth and a joyless day be yours if the luckless Muslims all flee from that Joloy! You are the master of the commoners; though you are old, you are a giant.' They wanted me to fight that scandalous slave, but they didn't get me to do it!" As your blessed uncle reflected on what he had just said, his whole body swelled with pique; he twiddled a ring on his saddle-bow as he stared at the ground.

At last that panther Manas Baatïr understood what was rankling Qoshoy; from the way he flapped like an aroused hawk and pawed like an enraged panther Manas guessed his inward state. He went over and stood beside good-natured Qoshoy Baatïr. "Don't go setting snares for rooks," he said, "don't make that mean rabble out to be strong-men. And don't let the Heathens and Muslims standing around demean you. But now you have come to me, dear uncle, dear elder, and what you say is true. You are getting on in years and stiff, and you move like a doddering old camel-bull, but if you do not go up against that Heathen, or if I, Manas, your closest friend and bloodthirsty wretch do not wrestle Joloy, then will anybody go near him? If so would Joloy leave him in one piece? In fact there is no one to face him; the Muslims of the world have no one to rival him. They think only of their deaths, but their eyes have no life in them! I see them all as if they were drunk – them and their words. There is going to be fighting at this feast, and it is going to require a different kind of khan. Uncle Khan, if you don't enter the ring yourself against that scoundrel Joloy, if you simply accept that we've been bested by Infidels, you might as well say we've forfeited and recognize him as champion. If your heart isn't up for going out and wrestling, you might as well drive the prize-herds in for him!" That is how the lion Manas Baatïr finished speaking, hearing which Er Qoshoy's thoughts came together.

"Alas, this world! Just living day by day your strength leaves you. There are so many different people filling the face of the earth, and so many of them are here mingling about; I said to myself, the memorial feast for Kökötöy is a sight to see, with all the *divs* and *peris* and *jinns* and sons of Adam of all kinds and every origin mingling together. I said to myself, the people of the felt tents are at the peak of their influence; there are more khans than commoners. I look and I see such a great multitude of people covering the earth. The great are more numerous than the small, and there are such a lot of different tribes that I should not like to have to count them. And this, my brave Manas, is the state I am in, white-beard that I am, when you lay troubles upon me! My woes are many and my pains severe. The affliction they call death is a wrought-iron cage with no exit, and by now your uncle here has been humbled by age.

"If it were long ago when the Heathens and Muslims were equals* on the broad face of the earth, and your grandpa Qoshoy were just starting out – if doughty Qoshoy were twenty-five and this very same feast were going on and Joloy crossed my path, even with a head made of stone he would not be in good health upon leaving my hands! If I met him at thirty-five, wouldn't I be the man to ruin him? Would I be outclassed by that dog? If we were charging each other with lances and fighting up hill and down dale, or if we were locked in a clutch and throwing kicks, wouldn't I be the one to leave him the worse off? Would I be outclassed by that constantly farting dog? If I had reached only forty-five years of age and we were fighting with iron-tipped lances and the jousting got hot, would I spare his black head, wouldn't I be the one to turn things hotter still and make him spew the food he'd eaten from his mouth? Would I be outclassed by that raving slave? If I ran into him at age fifty-five, would I be the man at a loss for tricks? Wouldn't I be the man to find a way to baste him into a hole in the ground? Would I be outclassed by that raging slave? But now that your uncle's strength has left him, now that thirty years of regrets have passed me by and I have lived to be eighty-five – now, my brave Manas, you tell me that my people all of a sudden desire something of me. It seems to me this terrible world of falsehood is pretty fickle!

"I'll be no comfort to the Heathens, I'll be no disgrace to you, my brave one; I'll bring no shame upon your people. Is there blood anywhere that cannot be spilled; is there a soul anywhere that shall not die? That one of whom you speak, who has brazenly entered the arena and is sitting there, Joloy – is he not a knave?! Since that piece of carrion, that slave, that icy wind from out of the clouds has sat out there all this time, though I am old, I say, whatever will be will be; I'll take the risk. I won't stay, I'll go!

"But I have something I want to say to you. God knows whether I shall return from wrestling that Heathen having shamed myself; but I tell you I shall certainly bring shame on myself if I spread my legs too wide apart. To my great sorrow and sore regret I have a misfortune from which I am never parted though my black beard has gone white and I am grown old, and that is that my wife has always been incompetent. It is her handiwork that makes the puttering sound around my backside. My trousers are made from the hide of a lean goat – a curse on her father's grave! – that apparently lay steeping until the curing-bath dried up, and the leather with it. So her tanning-work turned out stiff, and her kneading made it crinkle. That damned giant Joloy whom no horse can lift and who goes on foot, had better not grab these trousers by the crotch and rip them in two, for then your uncle will surely be shamed! I don't want to be embarrassed by going out and wrestling that big fat slave; I don't want to have to cover myself up from going out to fight that big gawky slave. My dear, bloodthirsty Manas, my trouble-making oath-breaker, the crowd is dense – have a look! Please call your khans and tell them to come here; please find me a pair of trousers* somewhere that will fit me. Is there a pair of pants among our people that will stretch to a stop but not split, that don't take up too much room, that stretch when you pull them and snap back when you let go, that hug a man's midsection when you tie the narrow waistband tight?"

When old Qoshoy had finished saying this, he stood and looked around. Sanjïbek of Qoqon in his buff leather pants turned his horse to go when he heard Er Qoshoy's presumptuous words, but Er Manas, catching sight of him, ordered, "Get over here, you piece of carrion!" Sanjïbek turned and went before him. "How about this man's pants, will they fit you, uncle?"

"My famous hero, my little foal, I can see his pants are of buff, but when you ask will I try them on I have to see how they are made. Won't my heels get stuck in them? If I thrust my legs in them, won't I certainly tear them open? Baatïr, notice things before you speak. They aren't going to fit me," said your uncle Qoshoy.

Standing to his right happened to be noble Kökchö Baatïr. Your uncle the terrible Qoshoy cast his eye over him. "You with your embroidered hat, your trousers of yellow buff, the metal trinkets on your belt-pouch tinkling from a silken sash, your copper boot-heels capped in gold, Er Kökchö son of Aydar Khan, you fancy milksop! I've heard tell from caravaneers and others who've seen, that your spouse Aqerkech is a knowing seamstress. Come, Kökchö, little bridegroom – give me your britches!" said Er Qoshoy.

Kökchö lord of the Qazaq whipped his pants off and said, "Here you are, dear uncle Qoshoy," holding out and handing over their vast bulk.

The lord of the Qara Kirghiz, that wrestler of fearsome rage your old uncle Qoshoy stepped into the right leg, but not even terrible Qoshoy's calf would fit. He stepped into the left leg, but his heel got stuck.* Sweeping the pants back off his shanks, he held them up in his hands. "The woman, feeble Heathen who made these – if I don't slash her on the right cheek! If I don't pierce her ankles and hang her upside down, and shave the right side of her head! If I don't beat her and throw her down in my yurt, force her to ride a blood-bay virgin mare,* and clothe her in felts! If I don't take her, and scour and roam the land of the Alach people from end to end until I find her father, and hand her back to him! – And if some strapping young fellow doesn't take her to wife all over again!

"Kökchö, you haven't a drop of fleet-footed-by-night, laughing-and-racing-about-by-day, stealing-about-in-secret, calling-on-maidens-and-ladies youthfulness left in you. You've no sense today, wearing a pair of pants skin-tight as horses' rectums! If you were to compete against a foe, ride into the

arena and joust with an enemy, you are just the sort to land on
your elbows in a twinkling – you'd get knocked down right
away! – and then get ganged while you tried to mount your
horse. You would fear for your life if you faced a foe. You are
not one of the skilled lance-fighters, and I am not the person
you could give your pants to, not the one who could fit into
those sorry breeches. Though he is dried out, Er Qoshoy has
shanks thicker than weed-stalks!" Just look at how distressed
your uncle was when he had said that! "You and your damned
pants, get out of here and stay out!" he said, and wadded them
up and hit him in the head with them. It cheered the hearts of
those who saw it for Kökchö to be deflated so.

No wrestling breeches had turned up for Qoshoy to wear,
and he was vexed. With no pants to fit him he was at an
impasse – this fleeting world passes on, but your grandpa
Qoshoy was at a standstill. Just then the spirits of departed
ancestors intervened to help. – If they do not help, what ever
gets done? – Manas, ruffled as a hawk and bristling like a pan-
ther, came up to Qoshoy and spoke to him. Brave Manas Baatïr
had found the solution that eluded them. "There is the one
called Qanïkey, the noble. From her hands have issued a pair of
ibex-leather trousers. We had packed and hidden them away
and were saving them for campaigning, but Ajïbay and Chalïbay
are always speaking so highly of them. Please have them
brought here and try them on, hero, so that we can have a look
at them. If any trousers are going to fit you, it will be those,"
said brave Manas. But he did not finish there; he continued to
praise his wife without end, coaxing and cajoling.

"Ajïbay and Chalïbay," said Qoshoy at length, "Bring the
pants, I want to know if this is true or just idle talk. Manas,
right on this spot I want to see how handy your wife is." When
Er Qoshoy had spoken, Ajïbay and Chalïbay followed his com-
mand and drew up their horses, turned over the cushion that
padded one of their saddles, picked up the ibex-leather breeches,
brought them to Qoshoy, and handed them over. Qoshoy the
giant – blast him! – got down from his horse and stood there on
foot. He stepped into the right leg, but not even his calf would
fit. He stepped into the left leg, but his heel got stuck. Then as

he tried to work himself into the pants, he could no longer pull his legs out.

He signaled Ajïbay and Chalïbay with his eyes. "You two fellows, come sit over here," he said. "Find a way to get these on me. If these tight pants I've been given don't fit me, then he of the faultless decrees whom no one perjures with impunity, he whom his Creator supports, He of unequivocal dominion to Whom none equivocates with impunity – whom God supports, Manas the grim, must not see. This must not be the ruin of his newly arrived bride. He must not slash her on the right cheek and mar her radiant beauty, drag her out of the yurt, shave the right side of her head, force her to ride a blood-bay virgin mare, and clothe her in felts. He must not take her and scour and roam the land of the Kirghiz from end to end until he finds her father Qara Khan, and hand her back to him* – Qanïkey must not be made to rue the Kirghiz! Her palate is etched and her throat marked with eloquence; any sort of thing she undertakes, Allah Most High prospers it, and those who do her wrong do not succeed. Her curses never err; may the children of the Qara Kirghiz avoid the curse of that queen whose bride-price terms set all women at naught; may that sad day never befall them! You two fellows come sit over here. Find a way to get these on me or there's no telling what will happen." That is what Qoshoy said.

The two giants, Ajïbay and Chalïbay, quietly reined in their hurry as they went over to your uncle Qoshoy, one on the right and one on the left. "These pants have got to fit!" they said; they both had the desire, for if they didn't fit, the lion Manas Baatïr had just the demon touch in him to do what Qoshoy had said he would. Thus those poor fellows pulled, unable to make progress in fitting Qoshoy into the pants nor able to free his shins.

Just as they were really getting into it, on the far side of the crowd, he of the dragon-whiskered visage, the keen-eyed gyrfalcon of a hero, cast his eye over at the Muslims' champion. He immediately spurred his horse and rode over to him. "Really, the pants for Baatïr Qoshoy won't fit him?" asked Manas. "This is what these two swine get up to, with all their praises! I never should have got mixed up with Qara Khan's daughter Qanïkey. A wretch like that – if I am angered I will kill her and whoever is around her – never mind that she is my wedded wife, that I undid my bright mail-coat and stored it in her yurt, that I tethered my horse to her manger; I would sooner the musket Aq-kelte with its blue-sparking fuse shot her, than see Qanïkey's face or enter her house again!* Uncle, what are you doing sitting there and looking at that thing you call a pair of pants?"

When he had said this the lion Er Manas jerked those tight pants, which would not fit over the gigantic Qoshoy's legs, and pulled them right off. As he was turning to leave he cast a glance at Ajïbay and Chalïbay. "You two slaves have been the ones praising these pants from the very beginning. That was your fault! I won't kill Qanïkey, but my name is Manas the Bloodthirsty and I have an insatiable appetite for blood. I won't leave you two scandal-making slaves alive!" said Er Manas as he turned his horse and left.

Watching him, Ajïbay jumped to his feet. "Damn his high rank! If only I had that high a standing, then just let the bullies try to pillory me! This world could do with a lot fewer heroes and famous strong-men, and the ones we've got can take their capricious notions to hell! They should die in childhood! What mortal man should have to endure such a litany of contempt?"

Qoshoy had been unable to draw up his sprawled legs or even to open his eyes. He lay prone, saying nothing in reply to Manas, unable even to call him to a stop. Thus your uncle Qoshoy lay there.

Ajïbay and Chalïbay were both stupefied as well. Death seemed to descend on them; the two of them were plunged into darkness, unaware of the world.*

In this state of perplexity something dawned on Er Chalïbay, and he said, "Say, Ajïbay, those are no ordinary breeches. Qanïkey did not just do a modest job on them. When the world in front of me was invisible it came to me again.* It was six years ago all told, if one were to think back, since what I am talking about came to pass; and a full twelve years since the very inception of the making of those tight, ill-fitting pants. Qanïkey sent a party of sixty crack-shot hunters headed by Abïke to the yonder side of Anjïyan, on the hither side of Ayïm Münsök, where there was an ibex on Dangdung-bashï – a goat of the dark cliffs as yet unseen by hunters. So as not to mar the skin she had them shoot it through both eyes; then for the drying she had the hide rolled up tight and hidden in a chest of freshly hewn wood, away from the rays of the sun.

"Nor did Qanïkey neglect the tanning. With perfect discernment she placed the hide in a copper pail of water, had apple bark added to it, and let it sit to ferment for six months. Shaghïl the Sart in Anjïyan sold her the dye for it, women did the cutting, and maidens cunning with the thimble did the sewing. No one but cunning mistresses worked on it; ninety maidens headed by Aruuke daughter of Qayïp Bek spent nine days in biting patterns into the leather with their teeth. Such elegant patterning has never been seen before; the variety of work that went into the making of the pants has never been known before. If you tried to see the fineness of the stitchery you would be unable to make it out; the seams have been made invisible with thread plaited snake-belly fashion.* The tooth-marked patterns are of double-gutter form; the lining sewn inside is of *buulum*-silk.

"Thinking, 'Without toughening, a lance-blow could pierce the leather, then all this work would be for naught,' Qanïkey had hardened steel filed down for quilting into the leather,* and seventy enormous strong-men drafted into service to work over that blasted pair of pants like none other. Then that queen herself oversaw the application of the colors. So far as rating its qualities is concerned, a bullet fired from a modern musket with painted stock would not pass through the leather; a glowing coal of meadowsweet-wood placed directly on that blasted pair of pants would not hole them. No one has been found who can fold them up; knowing seamstresses who see them sing their praises.

"Saying, 'Let my esteemed elder Qoshoy wear them, for I am longing to have a child, and his blessing would help me,'* she intended them specially for your uncle Qoshoy. She did not make this fact known among the people, though it was no secret that it was an extraordinary pair of leather breeches. So she told me to give them to uncle Qoshoy; though not knowing if that would come to pass or not, she had measured the pants more or less in such a way that Manas could wear them as well. Ajï, you are a highly respected person – not a common hat but a crown! – please go to Manas Baatïr and ask him to give us the breeches."

Ajïbay was thrown off guard when Chalïbay put it this way, as he had already experienced before how Er Manas had become exceedingly domineering. But Ajïbay agreed to Chalïbay Baatïr's request. "Let's go, whatever the consequences," Ajïbay said. "Let's press on for the sake of the people. Let's both go to Er Manas together and ask for those pants. If it makes the blood-thirsty hero angry and we meet our deaths, then we die; we'll ask for those pants back, and if he turns and sees the light then we will obey his orders. But, Chalïbay, don't you go talking your clever talk! Don't push me up to that madman and then back away. This is hard for me, so stay with me, friend."

They went to Manas. With hands pressed together and beseeching eyes bright as a hare's, both talking over each other, they said, "Baatïr, please give us the leather breeches you've got in your hand –"

"Just as Allah shows kindness in every way towards men, just so –"

"Give back the breeches; it is my one unfulfilled wish –"

"What I heard from the very start was that the knowing bride Qanïkey produced those pants –"

"And apparently right from the start she said that Baatïr Qoshoy should wear that very pair –"

"She said it would stand her in good stead in one respect if he was pleased with her good offices to him –"

"It seems that she considered how he is a father to the Muslims, and listened to people who had observed his stature and gait and knew what size he was, and made the pants to that measure –"

"– hoping that through his pleasure with her good offices she could obtain his blessing as a young wife and thus conceive a son –"

"– was apparently what she was thinking while she made the pants!"

"All along, from the very beginning, this has been the good news in store for Kökötöy's memorial feast. So, since no wrestling-pants can be found for him among the people, and we are at a dead end –"

"– since no one else's leather trousers will fit him, and we are at a loss for what to do –"

"– give us the pants, Baatïr. Other pants won't fit over your uncle Qoshoy's shanks, and have split," said Ajïbay in conclusion.

As he watched them Er Manas gave the pants he was holding in his hands a wrenching twist. "Damn you and your pants," he said. "Take them and get out of here! I am shamed by another, my enemies' hearts are assuaged, and you still praise these pants!" He fixed Ajïbay and Chalïbay in a wild-eyed, wrathful stare. "Do not toy with Manas! And do not think you will remain in good health if these pants don't fit Qoshoy!"

When Manas had finished berating them Ajïbay and Chalïbay took back the leather breeches. Then they looked at the place where the legs joined: the hip section was gathered up in a bunch, all the way down to the legs. If one examined them closely, they looked as if they had been rolled up for packing, a curious sight for those that saw them.

Ajïbay said, "The stitching!"

Chalïbay said, "The gusseting!"

Qaratoqo standing by said, "This is a piece of exceedingly fine workmanship!"

"What a pair of pants Qanïkey has made that's put the people in such a buzz! Let's see if they're well made, and let our detractors be buried. Let's not anger bloodthirsty Manas, but they have to be parted or split. Come over here, Chalïbay," said Ajïbay. They sat down together and grasped the breeches across the hip section, then put their colossal strength into pulling, while bracing against the soles of each other's feet, until *R-rip!* the seams gave, and widened out.

What fine apparel we saw! They slathered rubber cement all up and down the gaps, and the seams closed right up without a trace, completely undetectable. Ajïbay was relieved; when he stretched the breeches the seams gave about a span.* Back he went to old Qoshoy, elder of the people, and gave him the goat-skin breeches. "Try these on, uncle," he said, "We are all out of strength now, so please do as we say."

Bear in mind, this man was a giant. The people's champion

thrust in his right leg, and it was as if a child had taken his father's pants and stepped into them; they hung flapping around him. Qoshoy the old hero, toughest wrestler of the Kirghiz, thrust in his left leg, and it was as if a boy had taken his elder brother's pants and stepped into them; they reached up to his full height and hung flapping around him loosely. He suited up, cutting a fine figure with the pipings luffing gently about. Your uncle Qoshoy rejoiced, and rolled the right leg all the way up to his burly thigh. Then your stalwart uncle thrust his right arm down that leg and turned it to the right, and stretched the leather straight out; when his arm returned to his side the leather sprang back and hugged his flesh. Was not that blasted pair of pants a superior piece of workmanship? He rolled up the left leg and pushed it up to his burly thigh. He thrust his left arm in and turned it to the left, and stretched the leather out on that side; when his arm jutted out perpendicular to his side, he let it down and the breeches returned to their original shape, all the while giving off stretching and scrunching noises. You see the quality of those breeches!

A roguish smile played across your grandfather Qoshoy's face that sent his long moustaches darting upward. He vaunted himself and belted up, then lumbered off to see Manas, holding the pants out at the sides as he walked along. "My bloodthirsty Manas of boundless wrath, my trouble-making oath-breaker, there is no lack of skins of every kind on the face of the earth, yet now that I have got to know this leather, all the rest pales in comparison. Someone has brought out all the virtue of the hide and worked it to perfection. What sort of person made these ibex-leather breeches, these pants with such a cunning fit? Who worked them? Who grooved them with her teeth? Just tell me what went into their making," Er Qoshoy asked, and immediately Er Manas answered:

"I can tell you who worked them and who grooved them with her teeth. Your young lady remains childless, however; when will her shame be redeemed? It was your young lady Qanïkey who worked them, over a year and a half; Aruuke daughter of Qayïp sat grooving them with her teeth for a month and a half. The face of Qanïkey who made them grew pale as she worked without a break from that day to this; the teeth of the lady who patterned them became ugly and yellow.

"You, old man, have sacred powers. What could not come to pass if you gave your blessing! In her trouble at not having given birth, in her pining for a child, she thought, 'Let my uncle the hero see these breeches, then he will bless me.' Please believe what I say, uncle; if you had not come to the memorial feast, I was planning to send them to you in care of a passer-by."

Hearing this, Er Qoshoy asked, "Where is my child Qanïkey?"

Sashaying gracefully and curtseying down to her knees, Qanïkey stepped forward. Your dear uncle Qoshoy the giant examined her with a prophetic eye. "Good for you, my brave hero! This child Qanïkey is like a glowing-hot coal; finer than she simply does not exist wearing the white scarf of matrimony! But the hair on the nape of her neck is woolly, which means that after you have passed on she is fated to suffer with hard work and servitude.* Let the notables come hither!" he shouted.

All the children of Islam came and planted themselves there. Many an elder came and stood along with the vast multitude and the preeminent sons of Türk; all the common folk went as well to see what was going on. Your dear uncle Er Qoshoy wound a hasty turban around his head and invoked the Creator with loud sobs and open palms; then the rest of the people uttered their noisy benedictions. Many were those who gathered together there; according to the majority, this is what Qoshoy said:

"Allah, grant my wish: that this woman should bear a child, not a girl but a boy, not a bear but a lion! May he conquer those he fights and trounce those he wrestles. May he rule the sons of the Muslims but leave them untrammeled, a hero who sets the sedgy banks ablaze, whom no man surpasses; who sets the fields of feather-grass afire and gladdens his kin. May he spill blood in still waters; may his potency spread to the people. May he spill blood for water, spite the arm for the coat, cut off the head for the hat, and pierce the eye for a length of cloth! Those he catches – let him rake them like coals! Those who tangle with him – let him file them down like iron! If Qanïkey bears a son after all, let his name be Semetey!

"The child of lady Aruuke – let him be his true companion and like-minded supporter, and let the child's name be Külchoro! Let them gad about together, Külchoro's goat-sallow bush to

Semetey's willow tree! And as often as he climbs a mountain ridge let God be a friend to Semetey! Let him bloody his white watered-steel sword; when his wrath has come upon him let him slay Abïke, Köbösh, and Khan Jaqïp! Let him bloody his blue watered-steel sword; when they have tried his patience to the end let him slay the Forty Companions! Let him hone his black watered-steel sword; when his anger is upon him let him slay Khan Qongur!"* And just as Qoshoy at length blessed her, so everyone standing round* added their blessings – the earth shook from the noise as from a peal of thunder.

Now look as your uncle, having uttered his blessing and passed his hands down his face in supplication, began to walk; having lodged his blessing on Manas Baatïr's behalf, your grandfather Qoshoy strode along and came to the arena.

Joloy had taken up position and was sitting there, big and solid, silent and immobile. To him your dear uncle Qoshoy now turned, his eyes burning like a tiger's. Er Qoshoy advanced a few steps into the ring, stopped, and stood still. "The sons of the Muslims are few and the people of Heathendom are hostile. Good fortune is with the Heathen, for at this time among the Muslims not a noble could be found with the courage to trade blows in the arena. In younger days, starting with my bouts against the giants Aqdöö and Kökdöö, I fought, and yielded my honor to not a soul; now I am responsible to the whole nation.

"I've got a spine that's been thrashed by cudgels. However much I've been cut by swords, my sorest regrets are when the Kirghiz people weep. I've taken battle-ax blows to the head, but now there is no partner among the Muslims to walk beside me. If I look at myself today, my eyes are starting out of my head, my body is hunched forward and my neck crooks backward. My spine is swollen with yellow lymph; the spaces between my back-bones and ribs, I should think by now, are brimful of the dropsy; and I say the yellow fluid has filled the joints of my hip-bone and tail-bone too. My people have a wish all of a sudden that I wrestle with the Qalmaqs' champion, Joloy the giant gone-on-foot. So I stand here having placed my trust in the One God, bent in the middle and burning with the pains of old age.

"Boys! Come here, five or six of you, and walk on my back for me. Give it a good trampling! See if you can make this poor old puckered wretch's body into a cushion," said your dear uncle Er Qoshoy with a cherubic look. Then he lay his large, handsome body down and stretched out to his full length, his eyes reddening like a lion's.

Some commoners standing by watching made ready to tread on him; seven men from among the armor-bearers went out in a knot. Your uncle could hardly feel them. "What, are they all dwarves? Keep them coming!" he scolded. A knot of nine more men got ready and made for Qoshoy, and mounted his back without a pause.

"Stomp with all your might!" said your uncle as he bore all sixteen of those men on his back. "Stomp! Put all your heart into it! What are you doing, you scurvy little boys? Stomp for all you're worth!" Er Qoshoy shouted.

Qamanbek son of Jüzgön – he was a Qalmaq – wondered, "What has happened to Er Qoshoy? The sons of Türk have gathered together; what are they up to?" He got in among the crowd, and what he said reached the ears of the people: "These chattering Buruts! In all the world I have never seen such a nation lacking in shame. All on their own they are kicking and crushing the sickly old man! That old man's luck has surely run out. All on their own they seem intent on trampling him to death! Thus surely our eminent hero Joloy will beat him?" Qamanbek was heard to say.

At that Er Qoshoy cried, "Enough, boys!" He was irritated at what Qamanbek had said, and with a quick lunge he regained his feet. Those who had been walking on his back rolled right off and crashed down, like children who have climbed up onto a grown-up. The wrestler Qoshoy of the Türk, swaying just like a bull *nar* camel, his grizzled beard a-flutter, stripped to the waist for his bout and walked slowly out.

Joloy the damnable giant, also on foot, made ready to close with him; flames poured from his mouth and sparks flew from his eyes. To grapple with him was to lose blood; to look at him was to lose courage; those who saw him rise thunderously to his feet flinched from head to toe. He taunted Qoshoy: "Quit the high and mighty act! Your black beard has gone white and you are in the twilight of your life. Your end is drawing near; your grizzled beard has gone white and there is no strength left in your joints. Your death is close at hand and is sure to arrive soon, and when it does your honor will flee; how could it not? For your young people were unable to come forward; there was no better choice than you in your dotage for their champion in the ring. To my eyes, that was a curse on you! My name is Joloy; enemies run from me in fear. What man can approach Joloy? What mortal, having approached, can prosper? My Qoshoy, I will surely win if you have a thousand lives in you; I will surely gorge myself on your blood!"

When Joloy had spoken your dear uncle Qoshoy's anger rose. "A curse on your father's grave, Heathen slave – you faithless, wretched slave! That was your dim-wittedness talking. In the valley of Ükürchü, beside Üch-qapqaq, at Üyshünbay's feast, I beat you to within an inch of your life and left you tied up by your tent – I remember it to this day. On Balchaqay pass where you boasted of the size of your encampment and made much of your grandness, I defeated you in a contest of oratory; then we took to fighting for real and had at each other like hungry wolves, and I wrestled you off your horse. I tormented you all the way to Qulusun and got you two-up in front of me in my saddle. Why are you talking to me in such a temper, like someone who does not know these things? My swine, it has always been I who have gouged you in the eyes, I who have brought you to ruin, so think before you speak! In a valley of the Qulja mountains,* at Qutmanbay's feast, Qaldar the Qazaq chief was there and you picked a fight with me in front of everyone; that was the time you coughed up blood. Do you say that wolf-like Qoshoy has somehow changed? – Is there no end to the shit you eat! Wherever we have fought, we've wrangled back and forth but I have always been the winner. You, Joloy, have always been the booby! When did strength come to you? This asinine talk from you! – Here I come! What are you going to do?"

Qoshoy thrust out his forearm – the Muslims prayed, "Let this not end in disgrace for Qoshoy!" – and Joloy grabbed hold of it tightly. Qoshoy jerked his arm away. The champion of the followers of the black cult, Khan Joloy, had taken a firm hold, and the saintly Er Qoshoy had freed his forearm with one pull – but Joloy peeled the skin from his arm and held on to it. Then your dear uncle Qoshoy took the Qara Qalmaqs' and Qïtays' acclaimed champion by his strong forearm, and with two tugs Er Joloy just managed to free it – but the skin of the arm peeled off and stayed with Qoshoy.

Joloy the giant withdrew, uttering prayers in Qalmaq. He had an image of pure gold; he bowed before his idol and returned to the ring. Your dear uncle Er Qoshoy had remained there, also steeling himself. He bowed down and touched his head to the ground and let the tears flow in torrents. They both were recalling times past when old Qoshoy and big Joloy had grappled in hand-to-hand fights.

The Qalmaqs' champion Joloy caught hold of your uncle and swept him up in the air. Your uncle had a hold on Joloy as well, though, and would not let go. Your dear uncle Qoshoy's strength swelled in him when his feet made contact with the ground again; his soles came straight down, and the earth beneath them cracked out to the circumference of a spread-out colt's hide. Your uncle had kept his footing. Now look at his power: using his grip on Joloy, he shifted him and raised him up off the ground. After spinning him around in the air he let the world-famous champion of the Qïtay fall head over heels – but the rascal regained his footing and landed upright; the ground where his soles crashed down erupted in a plume of dirt.

And that is what they did for a long time – bat each other into the air like balls, incessantly. They were like cannons firing at each other; there was not a son of Adam who would go close for fear of getting caught up with those two. Those who watched were astounded. Black clouds of dust rose up and obscured the view for many Infidels and Muslims alike. The teeming armies could not be seen in the enveloping dust.

Everyone had started talking, saying, "We can't see the game!" when suddenly Almambet Baatïr had an idea. The excellent hero plunged his weather-stone under water, and in the blink of an eye a multitude of clouds appeared and formed into a dark bank that spread over the people like the dome-felts of a yurt. Black rain and white hail poured down, then stopped. Seeing this, everyone was astonished; then the wrestling was again the only thing to marvel at as the rustling wind died down, leaving no more dust hanging over the earth. Joloy and Qoshoy were visible once more in the arena.

Hounding and hurling each other about as the teeming crowd recoiled, yet unable to make a throw, like the vanes of a millwheel, heaping pain on one another, all that day they circled around, shrugging off death. Even in their anger the two giants brought their utmost skills to bear. They strained against each other like great bulls until their pants rode down their backsides; their holds drew blood; their blows raised clouds of dust. People were beside themselves in suspense, saying, "When is one of them going to make a throw?" On and on the heroes wrestled, jerking each other up and down, while the crowds of people were left to marvel. Counting on their own honor, they leaned into each other, collar bone to collar bone, their heels pulverizing and rending the earth, raising mountains of dirt and curtains of dust; the ground beneath their feet became a pit, and a haze hung in the sky. Onlookers trembled when the two struggling giants roared like lions. Neither was able to throw the other; success remained just out of reach.

Dusk was coming on, and the day was flying. How did your grandfather Qoshoy fare then? By means of Almambet's weatherstone the black dust that spread over everything had been cleared. When the sky filled up with a tumult of stars and the middle of the night arrived, Joloy's voice could still be heard, roaring – a spine-chilling sound to those that heard it. People were saying, "When dawn comes we'll have light" – "The Heathen Joloy is going to throw old Qoshoy Baatïr" – Everyone present had given up all hope in their champion down in the ring, Qoshoy. "Why has his voice gone silent?" – "His strength has left him," many were murmuring.

Several thousand riders had clapped rumps to saddles and lit candles, and all the lanterns were brought and lit. In the flickering glow, were you to look, the warriors were seething like worms and completely filled the limitless steppe. Among the mingling multitudes there were standards fixed in sixty locations so that people could see and recognize them. Everyone was standing around in a daze watching the two champions

Joloy and Er Qoshoy wrestle in the arena, so if no banners had been erected it would have been no surprise if many had lost their way and gone missing at that feast; had there been no crescent-moon-topped standards it would have been no surprise if people lost their way and went missing.

When midnight had passed and dawn was approaching, Qoshoy's voice could be heard clear as a bell: "O Allah!" he yelled. "Joloy's hands are some kind of poison!"* Your dear uncle Qoshoy had that yellow lymph pooled up in his spine, and Joloy was squeezing his back. Fighting and wrestling had always been your dear uncle Qoshoy's occupation since his youth; now Joloy's strength was penetrating to the discs of his spine. However it was that the "poison" in Joloy's hands worked, under his grip the pooled-up lymph popped out and ran down Qoshoy's sides. Joloy chafed at him, raking back and forth, but his grasp was like a pleasant caress on your dear uncle's buttocks. "Harder, you dirty dog!" said Qoshoy, wriggling around.

When dawn broke and sunrise came on like a parting seam on the horizon, behold, were there ever such wrestlers in this world as they – Baatïr Qoshoy, and Er Joloy of the Qalmaq tribe – the best of their two peoples, Muslim and Infidel!

"Majestic Aalï, my lion, support me! Be my support on this path," Qoshoy's voice was heard roaring out.

"The old codger's got his strength back," said the Infidels, and it made them shudder.

The two of them had begun wrestling the previous day right at noon, and everyone was amazed that they had wrestled the day away and that neither one had been thrown down by nightfall, and then a night had gone by as well. They had been wrestling for a day and a night without a throw that whole time, and now the next day had come. When the sun had cleared the horizon and it was getting close to noon again – just look at your uncle's heroism as he struggled away! – Qoshoy's attention began to flag and his sight grew dim; his eyelids drooped and fluttered, and a feeling of peaceful slumber came over him. From time to time he would say, "Harder! Keep working those muscles on either side of my spine," as he drifted into sleep.

Joloy noticed this. The previous day that scoundrel had

planned some mischief. Where all the strong-men had gath-
ered there was a boulder about the size of a small yurt that
they had thrown around for exercise. Joloy had it in mind that
someone who struck that rock would be in a bad way, so he
was going to carry your dear uncle Qoshoy over and beat him
against it.

He picked up Qoshoy of the grizzled beard in his arms, but
Er Manas saw him do it and raised the alarm. "Uncle!" he
shouted, "Your honor is slipping from your hands! This will be
the end of your ardor! Qoshoy, old man, open your eyes! What
evil has afflicted you? You're letting that swine get the better of
you and handing the glory to the Heathens! You're giving the
tribes of the Muslims a bad name!"

The voice of the brave hero Manas, whose deeds excelled
those of men, the lion-tempered, the enigmatic, his visage ter-
rible when angered, his eyes terrible to behold, his words
terrible when spoken in anger, traveled through the air and fell
upon the ears of your uncle Qoshoy. "Manas's voice rises
higher; he screams great screams in agitation. Whence does this
brave hero give voice in his rage?" thought Qoshoy.

Do not imagine that your distinguished uncle was a push-
over! By the time his eyes had opened all the way and he had
come to his senses, the Heathen Joloy was just about to beat
him against the rock; Joloy had him wound up like a ball of
yarn and was getting ready to batter him. Awake now and with
his eyes open, your old uncle Qoshoy jerked and spilled himself
out of Joloy's grasp. His full strength had returned, and as his
feet touched the ground your dear uncle Qoshoy the giant's
fury was rising – In times past at feasts and funerals there had
been no wrestling in the ring or hog-tying the loser! – Now
your dear uncle Er Qoshoy set his arms to bear the load,
grabbed hold on either side of Joloy's pants, and fixed his mind
on lifting the giant. With his right foot your uncle executed a
face-to-face back-heel swipe, and before the eyes of all raised
Joloy the champion as if uprooting a mountain. He lifted and
tossed him to the ground, and the multitudes were witness to
God's punishment of Joloy.

As Qoshoy began to walk away and was stepping over Joloy's

head amid cries of "You hobbled him!" – "I was afraid he wouldn't manage!"* – "You fettered him!" – "You flung him down!" – "My worries are over!" – and they were jostling your uncle all around, Joloy took the ibex-leather breeches that Qoshoy had received from Manas by the shanks, and was about to peel them off down to the ground.

The brave fellow Manas, with his horse-lash gently brushing back and forth and his hat with the black part turned out, said, "A curse on your father's grave, Heathen slave – you faithless, wretched slave, you've been thrown and that's that! What are you doing reaching for my uncle?" and he swung his knurl-gripped horse-lash with the tasseled pommel and the core of blue lead shot around his left side, and let it fall on the Heathen with a chop. The skin over his ribs parted; his blood poured out onto the ground. The lion Manas Baatïr's strength was seen by all; Khan Qoshoy freed himself from Joloy's grasping hands and left him.

The Muslims made an enormous crowd, all buzzing with joy; every Muslim was shouting to the heavens in praise of your grandfather Qoshoy Baatïr. Then the call went up and down, "Hoist the champion!" and their champion Qoshoy was lifted, and those who saw it were astonished. – How could they not be overjoyed? – Troops came flooding in.

The excellent Er Aqbay, his mind clear and forceful as a rock-bound spring, his temperament in every way like a young goat gamboling on the cliffs, his eyes flashing like lit candles – if he had no honor, who had? – lifted up his gigantic elder kinsman, your dear uncle Qoshoy. Er Aqbay put his head between your dear uncle's legs and lifted him right up like a six-year-old child – the multitude saw this! The Muslims lifted Qoshoy up and ran him around and brought him back, and paid him honors. After-ward a great many of the feast guests would not stop at that: they put a gold crown on him and seated him on a throne, and proclaimed old Qoshoy the people's chief. Having thrown the Heathen into ignominy, old Er Qoshoy was covered in glory.

Then they drove the prize in to your uncle Baatïr Qoshoy, and everyone came, and the excellent Er Qoshoy stood and counted the cattle, and gave them to the poor. He counted them all up, leaving out not one beast, and divided them among the unfortunate. From seeing that, all the nobles got the idea to give aid to the poor; likewise they became more accustomed to taking a brave stand against the Infidel.

All the Muslims' troubles were over. They rejoiced at their victory in wrestling, and a great many of them cavorted boisterously, the way people do in such circumstances. As that was going on, he of towering acclaim, the lion, your grandfather Baatïr Qoshoy, letting his white beard wave as he rocked atop a gray ambler, got things running again. Here is how:

"Muslims, Infidels, everybody!" he shouted, "If you know what's good for you, let's have no more yelping, let's have no more hollering! Let's have two mangy bald-heads from the two sides down here in the arena, and let's have them come out to the middle and butt heads together!"* For the prize he led in ninety horned cattle and arranged them, and tied up nine camels. "Let the victor take these!" he said, and drove in ninety four-year-old sheep as well.

Mardïkeleng the mangy bald-head went out and entered the arena. The sons of the religion of Islam, having no one with the mange to send out, stood rooted without moving. Jash Aydar went galloping about and stopping here and there, shouting, "There's the cattle for the taking!" and talking it up, but not one person went near the Heathen Mardïkeleng. Meanwhile the sun was setting, gliding under the earth.

"No mangy bald-head has come out, so take the prize!" your dear uncle Er Qoshoy cried in a loud voice. We have seen all kinds of sports, and here seems to be one where the Heathens could win with great competence. The Oyrots succeeded here, just as if they were spurring horses to a gallop amid a din of shouting, and sending columns of dust rising up to the sky, and winning a mass of loot. Horned cattle and camels by the hundred, sheep by the hundred – pay attention to the great quantities at the feast given upon the death of Kökötöy!

The sun reddened and sank, and everybody disbanded. By the first light of dawn could be seen the multitudes of people spread abundantly everywhere, and nine white camels tied up.

13

Oronghu Untethers the Camels; The Mangy Bald-Heads Fight *

Of white camels without blemish there were nine, by common consent; and nine black camels besides, and of other camels there were nine tawny-red *nars*; to these were added three race-horses, making thirty animals all told. "Let's have two people out here, one from the arches and one from the poles – one from the women and one from the men, and let the people watch! Let the woman be the ewe and the man be the ram, and let him plumb her backside for the delight of the spectators! Let the woman be the heifer and the man be the bull, and disport themselves here in the midst; and for letting us watch them do it they can take this loot! Let the man be the stallion and let the woman come whinnying like a mare; and this will be the people's entertainment for today! Let the woman be the camel-cow stepping along, and the man be her bull – let's have him cover her, no stalling now! Let the whole world see it – camel-woman down on all fours* and camel-man pressing in, and let the onlookers satisfy their curiosity!"* came the announcement from the herald.

Manas the excellent hero let it be known that he would kill any Muslim who took part. Riding Qalqaman's black steed – that black with the excellent points, like wings for a skirmisher – armed with steel, dressed in a campaign-tunic, bobbing like an aroused hawk, bristling like an enraged panther, straining forward on his black mount with elegant upturned toes on his boots and a slender lance – what a little angel atop Too-qara! – with a sword jingling on his belt and a battle-ax clinking at his side, growling with menace to do harm to any Muslim who took part, Er Manas thus made his presence known.

The common people had been thoroughly dismayed by the proclamation. They said, "It would be a shame on the Faith; how could the Faith abide someone with no shame? How could we be forgiven the dishonor? Even if it were ninety camels – or nine hundred – how could we live with ourselves? How could we strip and go naked as our mothers bore us?" The Muslims were standing and talking thus in their bewilderment when, wide-eyed, they beheld such a scandalous proceeding among the Infidels.

There was one named Oronghu, a disgraceful Heathen, her slot running like a spring in a gully; her clitoris like a large pot on a stone trivet, and around it, hair – a full donkey-load in all, were one to look. That slot of hers looked about a fathom and a half, with down on the lips; the hole itself was six spans and four finger's-breadths exactly. If a man said, "I can manage that, more or less," in-and-out he'd go, and be completely spent to satiety. The soles of her feet were like broad shovels; her two breasts, were one to look, were like dangling camels' hearts. She had a head that caught the eye, like an upturned kettle; a crotch like a green mountain hollow, and hair that was going gray, for she was between fifty and sixty years old. Oronghu waddled out with tresses like seventy mouse tails at the back of her head, were you to look; in her excitement this Heathen's eyes were stretched open as big as ponds. This wretch came to the arena, raving as one possessed by a *jinn*, with eyebrows like burnt thickets on her head like a charred hill. The sockets of her eyes were like pits dug out for grain-cellars; her nose huge, the scum in her eyes thick as soup, her shins like poplars in every way; the nipples on her breasts like six-pot gruel-vats, only bigger; the scarf around her hair broad as a flag; her two lips, were you to look, were stretched out like rawhide belts; if you looked at her two cheeks, there was enough meat there for two wolves to gorge on. This one made her dainty way out, swaying like a raving elephant. Following her came old man Mardikeleng.*

These damnable Heathens stood to gain a nine of camels and a hundred and one sleek cattle.* One the ram and the other the sheep – at Kökötöy's beautiful feast – would that were all to say about those fools! Mardïkeleng got that thing of his erect just so, like the ridge pole of an open-sided cowshed, with Oronghu as his heifer, and everyone got an eyeful. That mangy bald-head Mardïkeleng became the bull, bellowing and sticking it every which way with each step. Then he seemed to think better of it. "Let me see if I can just flick her," he thought, and rushed up on her from behind with a loud cry. But as he approached, Oronghu crouched on all fours, head down, and that blasted Keleng's thing stood up tall, and he mounted her stallion-wise. "Damn their eyes, the Heathens!" said the Muslims who were there, and they ran away in all directions. He thrust in to her swollen place, and yellow sperm poured out. Keleng was the camel-bull, and he had her down like a camel-cow, covering her all over. The Infidels were mad with delight at the sight of their private parts, while the Muslims, not wanting to see, scattered up to the hollows on the high, green slopes.

Then poor Oronghu spoke: "Oy, people, a tender lot you are! You're not even one freckle better than what the two of us just did! – Pinch your lice and you'll crush them! – You people standing there watching, where ever would you have come from if not for that? These loins of mine bore Qongurbay and Joloy both; why should I be ashamed? Muradïl son of Qïrmuz Shaa, red-topknotted Nezqara – these loins of mine bore them." Slapping her rotten vulva in a rage, she said, "Alooke and Boroonchu – these loins of mine bore them! I am not the least bit ashamed. Alooke of the Soloon, Bozkertik of the Toqshuker, Soorondük son of Solobo – these loins of mine bore them. Before whom should I be ashamed? These loins of mine bore Qongurbay and Manas both; I will absolutely not be shamed! Töshtük son of Eleman and Jamghïrchï of the Eshtek: these loins of mine bore you! My loins bore the warriors of this motley world; bore the nations that are spread over the many lands. I am not at all ashamed. Sarï Döö of the Saqalat: these loins of mine bore you!"

That damned swine spoke, slapping her cunt with the palm of her hand as she heaved and bustled along into the presence of the khans; after her the rascal Mardïkeleng sauntered up. Oronghu faced the *beks* with that place of hers flapping and gaping between distended lips; old man Mardut walked behind with a big, bobbing weapon, the foreskin puckering up in wrinkles. Having left him, damned Oronghu puffed and pranced just so, like a real cow. The old bachelor Keleng stood erect as ever; he was holding up.

Now Oronghu went crouched down on all fours to untie the camels from the dug-out place where they had been tied up. She pulled out the camels' pegs* as the people stood around her and watched, and managed to get six, working her way along like that. As she left the arena with her animals, the Infidels erupted in loud cheers and lively, joyous chatter, bragging as if the loot was theirs: "They got the loot!" – "Take that, Muslims – you got nothing!"

This competition had got under way in the morning, and for those who observed Mardïkeleng and Oronghu, it was a scene that would never leave their minds. It was the torrid dog days of summer,* and the day was getting on towards noon; see what nasty goings-on can happen and be ended before noon! The people had barely turned around after all that when there came another announcement: "Heathens and Muslims, now hear this!"

14

Manas and Qongurbay Joust;
Manas Lances Qongurbay

Kökötöy's standard had been hoisted, its blue banner rippling; multitudes on horseback poured in from all around. "Let heroes select choice steeds and mount up; let them don tunics of gold-shot silk and strive in their strength; let them submit to their fate, even unto death; let them pick up lances, take the field, and joust! The Muslims and the Infidels have had their quarrels and their cunning tricks; now let their greatest, leading jousters – fellers of foes with lances, burly-armed strong-men, wise captains; the great and pure ones, never mind the small and mean; with aim keener than a marksman's, who send ordinary foes recoiling; good-looking ones – let those heroes come and joust! The winner gets the garner, and the loser gets nothing!" was the summons.

They had a hundred grand chargers tied up, and of ordinary horseflesh another nine hundred head driven in and added to those. (So it is widely renowned: A thousand horses! Where ever have they posted a prize like that? – At Kökötöy's memorial feast!) All the heralds, led by Qoshoy, circulated the announcement to khans and chiefs.

Alooke called his people to listen to what the Qara Kirghiz had been saying since former times:* how all those of "contrary" religion had gone to Qïtay, and how the vast Qïtay populace, flowing and rippling like waves – Orus, Nemis, all of them – were prepared for defense; and how the wealth of those "damned" people of Qalmaq origin should be broken up, and how from the very beginning they all tried to "create trouble"; and because of their consummate industry their herds had grown till the world could no longer hold them, and they piled gold up into mountains and strung their tie-lines with precious stones, and they squandered their silver; and the people of the great country of the Muslims had all armed themselves and taken counsel, and would surely put forward a certain Manas, because he was such a bully; and he had a wise counselor and co-religionist, a certain Qoshoy who was descended from Qataghan, and this tribe originated with Ughuz, and they were all related. Manas, Alooke said, was devoid of ill luck, without blemish on his person; and his past deeds were so great, Alooke considered, that the wives of their people of the old religion* are about to become widows. He spoke of their umpire, Qoshoy, and reckoned that since Mardïkeleng the mangy bald-head had won a certain amount of wealth, and Oronghu had won her loot, Qoshoy had likely set these people's* sights on giving a hard joust and winning it for themselves.

"All kinds of bouts are already past, and in every one was seen great prowess; but this one, I fear, is a narrow path leading a brave man to death. At Kökötöy's memorial feast we have witnessed the best: the most dexterous experts at jousting,* the young besting the old, the noble besting the lowly, the shaman besting the madman, the stone besting the brick. It looks as if the Muslims have many tents-that-don't-flap-when-the-wind-blows: many heroes who have sought death and not found it; heathens sparing with their thoughts;* arbitrators wise in their decisions; captains in control of their people; champions who do harm to their opponents; victors who smash contending enemies' heads like apples! When Manas goes out he trounces us all: you saw when he shot the ingot! I've had my fill of his prowess. Let us pool our best weapons and find and equip our own stalwart hero. Let us pick out our best brave warrior, and, if we meet with success, gobble up those horses that have been posted for the prize!" Alooke their most senior leader counseled them thus.

Then Bozkertik stood up and spoke: "O people!" he said. "From the Qïtay we have Prince Qong, a great prince known the world over, and he is skilled in lance-combat; he can lance a pearl. Muradïl son of Qïrmuz Shaa is exceedingly bold, but young. Red-topknotted Nezqara by now is past it, poor fellow; his moustache has gone roan and white roots have appeared in his forelock. Ushang of the Qalmaq is this very day at the peak of valor. Since our people are in this strait, shall we not send him?"

Old Surqan of the Qalmaq rebutted him vigorously: "We have entered only Qalmaqs so far, and it will not be fair to everyone if we enter no Qïtays. We sent Joloy out as our wrestler; the other side has that bully Manas.* Joloy got thrown in the ring and his good fortune disappeared. But there is the brave Chanaq Choyun, son of the Qïtay Jangshaa –"

When Surqan said this, the assembly asked, "Which one is Choyun Baatïr?" He had a huge dark-bay horse and a nature different from other men; ears the size of campaign-tents and a nose that flowed like a spring; his horse stout, his stature short – here was one of their strong-men; but they decided that despite his considerable strength he was fainthearted.

Another said, "I think relentless Manas the Kirghiz is going to joust, and try in any way he can to kill Alooke's son. That in a word is his desire and that alone his intention." But no one could think of anybody besides Qongurbay to take up an iron-tipped lance and spur his horse to joust, no one who could go against Manas as an equal.

Another said, "We must acknowledge that as things stand now, there is simply no brave warrior among the people called 'Infidel' who can take the field against the Muslims. Let us hang back and send no one out; to hell with them and their joust!"

All the Heathens, young and old, talked back and forth: "If those that fear death hold back, then no one else will go" – "If those whose death is near hold back, then no one at all will go" – so the people of the old infidel religion wrangled with each other, while the warriors tried to get out of it.

When he heard all this, Alooke's son Prince Qong became angry: "Are there people among you who live two thousand years without dying? Won't God punish the Qïtay who flees when beset by a Kirghiz? Are there those among you who live so long without dying? Won't God punish a *qalday* who flees when stopped by a skirmisher? Death may be upon me, but let the earth swallow me up if I run away! What kind of madman says that Manas will go out to the joust? I have been standing and observing along with the rest of you since morning; though disgusted I have stood fast, and I contend that gray-maned Manas the bloodthirsty will not enter the joust. In truth, of course, only God in heaven knows

whether Manas will go out, and who will unhorse whom. If
Manas goes out to the joust, you can try to tie me up but I will go
out; if that bloodthirsty hero goes out to the joust you can try to
surround me but I will go out. Heathens,* why do you think a
Türk is going to unhorse a Qïtay?" This is what Qongurbay said.

Then they saddled and outfitted a great black horse that had
not been raced, and with old Alooke in the lead the teeming
Qïtay bystanders came crowding in before Qongurbay in their
massed multitudes, all the unbelievers – the Saqalat and Shibe
gathering together – and the endless throngs of Infidels were
amazed by the excellent Qongurbay and his arms.

The head of his foe-frightening lance was a fathom and a half
of watered steel that would as soon butcher a body as poke a
wound and, were its wielder moved to wrath, could pierce a black
stone; its tip wrought into a wolf-tongue point and then quenched
in venom, it brought joy to him who wielded it. The pennant
affixed to this lance was a motley of sixty colors – yellow, blue – a
Heathen driven to anger has no lack of magnificence! To the
gray-maned hero's rear hung an *almabash*-musket rifled with a
spiral inside, whose shots meant death; its barrel and muzzle of
finest steel, it stole the good health of the targets of its aim. Those
lacking the training kept their hands off; shots from this gun flew
the distance of a horse-race course, and a foe thus hit would
embrace the dirt. Its loud report shook the earth and toppled
mountains. Deadly, it had a ramrod of brass and a golden ham-
mer, and a foe thus hit would be transfixed. Big ugly Qongur
poured shot into this old war-musket, preparing himself step by
step for combat. The Heathen added to his equipment by strap-
ping on a saber with a black steel blade thick as a finger and a
recurved point. The next weapon he got ready was a crescent-
moon-bladed battle-ax with double recurved points, its surfaces
etched with elegant tracery, hafted on *sabïl*-wood; a blow of that
ax would not land uselessly, and one struck with it would not
regain health. Next to the saber in its gold-capped scabbard he
fixed this ax.

Qalcha[1] was eager to start. His mail-coat and breastplate

1.   "Qalcha" is a nickname of Qongurbay.

tokened readiness for war, and clad in his wide trousers magnificent Qongurbay was all put together for the combat. But the other day he had been caught suddenly unawares; never imagining that so many of his people would be killed and set to flight headlong, never imagining that he, an invited guest, might be killed, he had fled in a great hurry without a single weapon on him. The ruefulness Qalcha felt made his eyes burn as if with billowing flames; he knew that the moment had come, and if Manas took the field for the joust, he would fight him. The enormous disgrace he had brought on himself filled his whole frame with wrath and steeled his sinews for a row with Manas the bloodthirsty; he gathered up his anger.

He possessed a mail-coat of pure gold, but it barely matched the size of his body; so instead he put on hardened iron. He prayed to his idols and girded himself in the wrought iron, his face darkening with rage as he spread the corselet over his chest. Loaded up with blue steel, Prince Qong strutted. See his true nature from that – from the outward aspect of the iron corselet, that blue-gray battle-garment that now covered him! The stalwart hero Qongurbay raged like a blue-gray tiger and invoked his god of the blue heaven. That blue-gray corselet with its generous skirts, tough enough to stop a lance, had nine button-holes and nine laces with which that great powerful wild boar of a hero, that glowering wild boar of a hero armored his whole frame, doing up the buttons from top to bottom with practiced skill. Qalcha's visage was terrible: like boiled lungs, with moustaches stiff enough to drill through wood; eyes red and fearsome as iron, nose sheer as a mountain slope. Broad of breast and thick of chest, Prince Qong was world-renowned for his strength from of old.

His anger rising, he mounted his huge, fine, high-strung black horse Al'-ghara with the Qïtay-style saddle and trappings. And now look what he did: he spurred Al'-ghara swift-as-an-arrow to a lunge, and with his war-musket slung on his back and his blue lance in his hand he went capering left and right, up and down with a magnificence that astonished onlookers; with Al'-ghara he cut an enormous figure terrible to behold. He loomed atop his great black horse with the haft of his mace jutting up, holding the slender lance in his hand; with gold-clad brass heels on his elegant Chinese boots; with his sword jangling at his belt and holding aloft his formidable yet graceful blue lance; with his brilliant dagger jingling at his side, growling like a hungry lion, his blue pennant streaming. Enemies who beheld such magnificence would avoid approaching!

Now, having readied himself, his one desire was to exchange lance-blows with Manas. He had been caught off guard some days before and had been shamed for it; now his vexation was unbearable, and he was determined to set matters right.

"There's a hero filled with fury!" – "Qongur has come out to the joust!" said the people who were circulating about. Your uncle Qoshoy was there as well. "Qongurbay has put on all his armor, bowed to his idols, and outfitted his horse Al'-ghara!" – "Big Qalcha with the bulging eyes* has readied himself and is about to enter the joust!"

"It looks as if Qongur has headed out to joust, and he looks as if he could knock even Rüstöm Dastan* himself to the ground with his breath! We saw him with our own eyes just now, clad not in shirt and drawers but in steel, and fitted out in every way to attack the Muslims, joust or no. Qoshoy, dear uncle, try to understand: he has his war-musket Aq-jökör slung on his back and a ten-fathom lance in his hand, and today his manliness fills his tunic to bursting!" This is what Qoshoy heard from a certain Alashbek, who came riding up with the news. "Please understand," continued Alashbek, "He is the khan of all Qïtay, a formidable warrior they say, and this Qara Qïtay khan looks angry."

Rocking atop his gray ambler and with his white beard all a-flutter your dear uncle Er Qoshoy now went straight to the Qïtay throng and headed into their midst. There stood Prince Qong, mad as a *nar* camel-bull, raving about his honor and blowing hard for a joust. Then he stopped and stood still, stuffed a hand-ful of tobacco into the copper-bowled, gold-stemmed pipe he held, struck steel to tinder, and gave the pipe a gurgling suck. Smoke billowed from his mouth; sparks crackled from his eyes.

Your old uncle Qoshoy went to black-maned Boroonchu and said, "Tell me what's going on here. Who is your contestant in the joust?"

To old Qoshoy's question Boroonchu answered, "Does a

ninny get the job done? Does a coward take the field? If you have pitched your tent for the tourney, then know that the hero Khan Qongurbay is ready for the joust. Whichever Muslim may enter the arena, Qongurbay shall be the one to face him." This was Boroonchu's answer.

Bolting off on his gray ambler and sending billows of dust rising up in his tracks your uncle Qoshoy returned, but without a glance at any of the sons of the religion of Islam, at any of the upstanding servants of the Faith – none of them was to your stalwart uncle's liking. Heroes, strong-men, he passed them by; your grandpa Qoshoy was headed for that hero Manas the brave.

When he arrived Qoshoy spoke in a loud voice: "Bad luck! Ah, little foal, Er Manas, listen to this! That great tormenting *qalday* Qongurbay of Beejin, that great damnable *qalday* Qongurbay of many-quartered Beejin, has suffered disgrace and is angry about it. He has bowed before his idol-shrine and outfitted a fearsome black horse; by the look of things, the whole of Heathendom picked him by acclamation. He has readied himself, mounted his furious steed Al'-ghara, put on a glinting, gold-adorned helmet and is glowering with spite, spoiling for a joust. He says, 'You can send a giant of your heroes, you can send a walker of your horseless wretches – he can come out riding an elephant if he wants, but I will have my way with him! If a thousand come I'll slay them! Whoever comes out spoiling for the joust, I'll do the chop-and-gobble on his life! Send him out riding a rhinoceros, I'll slaughter whomever I find!' This is what he has said in his affliction, for he is sorely vexed. The other day you fought him when he demanded Maani-ker, and brought disaster down upon him, and that caused him offense. That faithless, wretched slave, that shameless Infidel slave, that swine, seems to bear a grudge; and he intends to overcome his opponent and sow quarrels. He says he'll contend with the Muslims, make hidden what is known to all – 'I will get what I want!' he says. He'll bring grievous strife, but he says, 'I'll get my revenge!' Warlike Qalcha, Prince Qong, is filled with rage; his eyes are aflame.

"My bloodthirsty Manas of the many scandals, my troublemaking oath-breaker, I am getting on in years, and stiff. I move like a doddering old camel-bull. I don't want to go up against that Heathen. But you, though cruel, have always been a hero, always of surpassing courage. If you do not go up against that Heathen the khan Qongurbay Baatïr, who else will face him? He has laced up his gray tunic and hefted his steel-tipped lance. I went to have a look at him and take his measure, and he is surely the cause of the Heathens' rising confidence today. He has strapped on a black watered-steel sword, and anger covers his face like roiling rain clouds; the Infidels are all convinced that no one can beat him. He has fastened a battle-ax on his belt that was made with balanced haft and a blade quenched in venom; he appears to all the Heathens to be invincible. He has slung on a war-musket and cheered the people's hearts. His great black horse swift-as-an-arrow sends the earth flying apart with its hoofbeats, and the Heathens are encouraged. With his mace at the ready he seems no longer human, but paces like a lion. He has mounted his horse, and from every indication I can see, that damned Qongurbay is angry! What are you going to do, brave hero?" said old man Qoshoy.

When the lion Manas Baatïr heard this, flames shot from his eyes; Qoshoy's words filled him with a fury that burst forth from his person. High of brow and narrow of head, he was strong in every inch of his frame; with its high-bridged nose, thick eye-lashes, and piercing gaze his face struck terror. Wide-mouthed and deep-eyed, broad of jaw and long of chin, thick-lipped and dark-eyed, his features were those of a warrior. Broad in the palms and generous, attended by success in every undertaking, his features were those of a hero. Broad of breast and thick of chest, wide in the back and narrow in the hips, he was in the prime of his fighting powers. His face terrible with raging ire, heedless of death, he had the bearing of an elephant. That tiger-necked, thick-armed hero, with massive shoulder blades and a heart of stone, with eyes sparkling under heavy lids – right then at the peak of his valor – enjoyed renown in his time! Wolf-eared, lion-browed – behold, the incomparable Manas!

He paused before answering Qoshoy, the anger overspreading his frame, the piercing gaze in his eyes flaming like coals from amid his craggy features. Then he roused like a blue-gray

wolf: "Unlucky Muslims! Stupidity has always been our fault.*
If someone had said before that Qongurbay would enter the
joust I would not have set my sights on the racing-prize and
would not have run the great, powerful, spirited horse Qula.
Don't I have that much sense? With the horse Aq-qula beneath
me and the corselet Aq-kübö about me, with a look of terrible
fury on my face and a polished lance in my hand, if this venge-
ful Prince Qong himself were to cross my path, I would dispatch
him with a single stroke and be none the worse for it! But since
that is not to be, come, call forth all your wisdom. All the horses
are racing now; find and make ready one horse for me to ride,
uncle!" This is what the mighty warrior said.

So Qoshoy Khan looked over the horses. A great crowd of
people stood and watched, asking each other, "What kind of
horse do you think he will like?" as others touted the adroitness
of their mounts and spurred them on with blows of the lash in a
galloping procession before the eyes of stalwart Qoshoy.

The common people saw Qalqaman's black steed, and liked
him; but old Qoshoy said, "You Qara Kirghiz do not know
how to appraise animals. That one is stricken in years; he
would run away at the sound of a loud shout. There is some-
thing about him that is not entirely horseflesh, a temper like
wild game, it seems – but if you look carefully for his weakness,
you see that he has been raced out. He's broken down up top,
his heart is not up for jousting, and he's spindly-legged. Your
brave Manas musn't ride such a spooky horse; if he does, he
shan't beat Khan Qongurbay." Qoshoy waved him on, and the
peevish black went past.

Then there was Er Ürbü's animal. Ürbü son of Taz had a pair
of blacks; the more mettlesome one he had toughened up and
entered in the memorial horse race, but that left the tempera-
mental one. "Dear uncle, what about this one?" Ürbü asked,
bringing him up.

"He's got every sign of a well-endowed horse, but in compe-
tition he'll give out; there is a weakness about him. Do not
imagine that the Heathen Prince Qong will be an easy oppo-
nent! Never mind this one; don't ride him," said your uncle
Qoshoy, waving him on for all to see.

Among those called the Dumara, which was one of the tribes of the Kirghiz, there was a hero named Altïn Kökül. He had a bay horse with a star on his forehead, huge for his breed and full of fire, and a blood-bay, also with a star and a bearing altogether different from other horses. Altïn Kökül had raced the blood-bay, but the bay remained in his string. "Will this one suit, uncle?" asked hearty Kökül as he approached.

Your dear uncle Er Qoshoy, horse-appraiser to the Muslims, cast a cold eye over the bay and announced, "Now this one's got some marks of a *tulpar*. But be that as it may, he will easily tire. If he were ridden in combat with the Heathen, in four or five passes he would stop in his tracks, it looks to me. As a foal he was not kept tied up and he suckled his dam dry, so he's no good. He's got a lump of fat the size of a fist at the apex of his stomach, and if that happened to melt, he would come to a standstill; he's no good. Prince Qong would maim your hero Manas in a trice. This one mustn't be ridden either. That Heathen called Qongurbay is a formidable foe, a caged black tiger!" Qoshoy sent that horse away.

The taut steed Sar'-ala was a real pet, with the points of a hare about him; Almambet came dashing up atop lean-crouped Sar'-ala. A number of the people standing by asked, "What if Manas rides him?"

Manas answered that question: "Whoa, people! Sar'-ala is an animal from the herds of Qambarboz that has never been lassoed; he was designated as an undefiled sacrificial victim for men bent on campaigning, and for any women who greatly fear for them in their fighting and striving in dire straits. Therefore he was always coddled, and is too plump. When the fighting gets hot, he is likely to err; if I have to joust long, he is likely to give out."

The people didn't like the idea either, and said, "Once Almambet gave up his horse he would be on foot, and how would that be? For Almambet it would be unseemly!" Qoshoy waved that horse by.

After him, were you to look, came Alïmsarïq mounted on one of Khan Kökchö's animals: Alïm Biy had in hand the black with-a-blaze Jar-mangday and was running him in the procession, and all the people turned their attention to him. As soon as Er Qoshoy saw him he said, "Come over here." Sariq went to him.[1] "You, Alïmsarïq," he said. "Dismount from your horse and come here. My boy, give us taut Jar-mangday for the joust. This black with-a-blaze has the dread features of a hound. Were you to ride him on a six-month siege of Beejin through brain-boiling heat and the thick of battle, or gallop him for forty days, he would not show fatigue nor any red sores gall his back. High in the withers and low in the croup, he could ride through a conflagration without breaking a sweat; he'll stand at pasture unhobbled, yet fleeing game couldn't outdistance him; he could ride through desert without thirsting. And here is another auspicious feature: this striking vitality of his is at its peak. Good fortune is inscribed upon his brow. His ears are like candle-flames; he is a horse that rouses to the din of the crowd, with marks of a *tulpar* as well!"

Having said this your dear uncle gave orders for Jar-mangday to be brought and saddled and outfitted. They put Aq-qula's huge saddle-cloth* over him, and suddenly that taut devil looked rather mean. The front of the saddle-cloth rode up on his withers and the back drooped over his croup, making him look quite small. On top of that they put the high-bowed Mongol saddle, and then Aq-qula's harness. They found, however, that they had to shorten the crupper and the two girth-straps, big and small; each of these was taken in by two spans and four finger's-breadths. Jar-mangday born-of-a-whirlwind flung his mane above his ears as the harness was arranged and the outfitting seen to perfection.

Manas the panther then sat atop him filled with ardor for battle. He tucked his shirt into his ibex-leather breeches, then to brace his trunk drew on a strong corselet of lark's-eye mail – that is its rings of Chïyïrchïq gold were like small birds' eyes, so that it was cold-proof on a blizzardy day and water-proof on a rainy day. The lark's-eye rings shimmered, the hen's-eye rings rustled, their mesh too fine for a mosquito's snout to penetrate, too dense for a gnat's snout to pass – you couldn't see your

1. "Alïmsarïq," "Alïm Biy," and "Sarïq" are all forms of the same hero's name.

hand through it if you looked at high noon! – this lark's-eye mail-coat had a collar of yellow gold, and toggles all of gold. Proof against bullets and lances in his estimation, with short sleeves up off the elbows, this golden corselet is what Manas now donned, crying "Give me strength and power!" and making a reverent supplication to his God. Next he put on his head a helmet made by Döögör the smith with four separate chin-strap rings, a spike wrought into a taper like the throat of a ewer and fastened on top, a yellow gold jaw-guard chased all over with designs, and a steel curb fixed all around it; this helmet he pulled down until it covered his ears completely.

And so Qongurbay and Manas fought each other with lances at the memorial feast for Kökötöy. Qongurbay was ruler of the Qïtay from the Tungsha Beejin tribe; his ancestor was Pang, who ground into meal foes that crossed him.

Raging like a mad tiger, crazy as a camel-bull at the approach of winter, your brave Manas girded on his weapons. Then he uttered a supplication to Shaymerden, "Departed spirits of Aziret Aalï, esteemed lion, and of martyred warriors, come, support me!" On that day your brave lion made ready his borrowed soul, saying, "My Allah! By your leave," as Ayqojo of the grizzled beard spread open his palms and let the tears pour, and the Muslims of the seventy tribes let out a cry so loud that it shook the earth. Your prince made many pine with regret. As the brave lion mounted his horse, spurred it forward into long strides and headed out, the lions Baqay and Er Töshtük wrapped the white cloths around their heads and went beside him as seconds.

That great Prince Qongurbay who ruled the lands of Qaqan was a capable prince in everything he did; the horse he rode, Al'-ghara, was a beast distinguished in grandeur. Now Prince Qong was all clad in iron and looking like Rüstöm, and he and his horse Al'-ghara were the most fearsome sight in the land; in his corselet and astride his horse, that Heathen looked like Mount Qap, and his face was a torrent of fury. The Muslims who beheld his valor were quite undone, saying, "Whoever picks a fight with him shan't remain in good health!"

All the Infidels gathered before their idol of cast gold, Alooke Khan's talisman, and intoned, "*Laaylamaluu!*"* – they did not know that these things had led them astray and that they were placing their hopes in the devil.

Qongur astride his horse took his lance in his hand, and the assembled crowds of the Qïtay began shouting and yelling and cheering him as he rode away. Golden helmet flashing, pennant on lance-tip streaming, the great goggle-eyed Heathen Qalcha came bursting forth atop Al'-ghara and entered the arena. The excellent Er Manas emerged from the Muslim ranks riding Jar-mangday, terrible to behold. Seconding Prince Qong and jutting their necks like cockerels came Bozkertik and Budangchang; a multitude of voices bleated like sheep, "Let my Prince Qong return safely!" as he entered the arena.

As soon as they saw each other they whipped their horses and – Allah knows how much of this is truth or lies – the two giants strained forward to the impact. The dazzling lances were set for combat, their pennants streaming and their tips flashing. Both heroes ignored other targets and aimed to pummel the point between the two eyes, where they could drive their destructive lances through. In a flash the impact sent their knees buckling up off their *tulpars*. "One of them is not going to survive," the onlookers said in despair. But the lances wobbled as they hit home, and although they had gauged for the eyes their lances went crashing into the bowls of their helmets and slid along their jaws in passing.

Er Qongur went barreling off toward the Muslims in a rage; Khan Manas was in a rage too as he drew near the Infidels. Your magnificent prince wheeled around, the whiskers on his face standing erect as he besought Shaymerden. The magnificent but damnable Er Qongur wheeled from the side of the Muslims, and striking his black horse with his lash he charged back toward your brave Manas. "May our prince find his strength!" cried the Infidels.

Brave Manas urged Jar-mangday to a gallop, his lance flashing as clouds of dust billowed behind him. Placing full confidence in his honor, he thought nothing of the outcome for his own borrowed soul; instead he was thinking, "The arch of a Qalmaq's saddle rises just to the apex of his heart; the edge of his golden saddle is at the tip of his breastbone" – thus Manas was gauging his aim. In just the same way, Er Qongurbay the Infidel was thinking, "The arch of his golden saddle rises right to the apex of his heart, the deadly spot; he will die of a lance-thrust there," as he charged to meet Manas. The two combatants had at each other mercilessly with their lances; the shafts trembled against their huge bodies, and the horses they were riding sank down on their haunches like dogs.

Gripping the horses' manes, they swung hard at each other with maces, but amid all the clanking the two giants remained unhurt. Steel struck watered steel, showering their two bodies with sparks and cinders; the onlookers were beside themselves. When their work on each other had reached a certain point, they redoubled their efforts and hacked with sabers, again and again, the red sparks igniting here and there into flames. Next they took battle-axes in their hands, thinking, "The crown of his head is the spot," and, "Will he ever tire?" and in their exasperation swung at each other's heads. Steel met watered steel and their helmets started off their heads, raining sparks that burst into flames.

As the crowds stood and watched, their combat devolved into a clutch. Saying, "Not like that!" and, "Scuffling isn't fighting!" the lion Manas Baatïr's elder kinsman Baqay and Er Töshtük got hold of him and brought him away; Bozkertik and Budangchang got hold of Er Qongurbay Baatïr and brought him away.

Those standing close by looked on dumbstruck as the two heroes regained their composure. "The joust!" they cried as once again they set to. First, sheer of nose and red of eye – what I am saying is common knowledge – great Qongur of the Qïtay let out an ear-splitting shout as he turned in his fury, the damnable Heathen. Then the black with-a-blaze and the dread features of a hound, Jar-mangday, beat his hooves into the earth and tossed his bridle-amulets skyward, and sent clouds of dust wheeling up behind him as the lion Manas applied the lash.

With a flash of his lance Manas fell upon Qongurbay, but like one gone mad Qongurbay struck him above the arch of his golden saddle, right at the apex of his heart. Er Manas's haunches started up out of the saddle and his feet slipped from the stirrups, and he was barely able to rein up as poor Jar-mangday dove past headlong; but then the hero recovered.

Qongurbay, as he bore away at an angle, had a lock of hair dangling free below his ear. "That is the edge of his helmet," thought Manas, "and beneath it will be the base of his skull." The solid covering of iron was parted there, giving a view of Qongurbay's head just behind his ear and above the collar of his mail-coat. Manas fierce-as-a-white-goshawk fell upon him from behind and drove his lance in under the edge of his foe's helmet. The lance pressed into the skull, and Qongurbay, one so ready to boast of his own strength, went flying off Al'-ghara! He fell; his head plowed into the dust with the lance still jutting out; the skirts of the blue tunic he wore under his mail-coat were splayed out on the ground like the wings of a butterfly. Blood poured from the base of his skull, and with it, the strength of that hero, who had striven so hard, ebbed from his body.

As Qongurbay crept on his belly his black horse Al'-ghara pranced away from his grasp, and the gray-maned hero who had knocked him silly secured the horse and did not give it back. The Muslims rejoiced at Manas's victory and made lots of noise, raising cheers of "Aziret!" and cries of "Noghoy Khan!" The happiness of a great number of guests at the feast was secure now; the Muslims were celebrating, as they all had seen and marveled at their hero's valor. Fired up by the war-cries, Töshtük son of Eleman and Jamghïrchï of the Eshtek rode on either side of Manas stirring up a boisterous hullabaloo.

The prize amounted to nine thousand head, of which nine hundred were camels. Manas was the giant of that age; he gave four thousand head of horned cattle and camels to Qan Qojo, telling him, "Take these"; then he distributed the remaining five thousand to the people, saying, "Let the poor and the indigent have them." The Infidels had been humiliated; Manas had thrown their khan Qongur, who had borne him ill will, into the dirt. The tribes of the Muslim faith were eased in their hearts. These are things that have been done and handed down from olden times when Qazaqs and Kirghiz hold memorial feasts. The Forty Heroes called the Qïrq Choro were all khans to a man. Manas had taken the field at noon and amazed everyone by his deed. Now there will be another sport, and the people are gathering to watch.

Wrestling on Horseback

Kökötöy's blue standard was raised with its streaming banner, and Ïrchï Uul son of Ïraman shouted out the announcement: "The Muslims shall sit this one out! Let an Infidel from the west and a Qïtay, two Infidels, face off and wrestle on horseback! Let the more dexterous rider win, and show us a stoop from the saddle like a game of buzkashi with a goat!" Thus the call went out. Ninety horned cattle and camels and five hundred sheep were posted for the prize. Ninety horned cattle and camels, and five hundred sheep – feasts like Kökötöy's memorial do not happen anymore in this world!

The exceedingly numerous Infidels of the west were dashing here and there excitedly just as Shandöögör emerged from among the Qïtays, a man of the Tungsha Qïtay tribe in the land of Tüp Beejin. Shandöögör came out mounted on the younger brother of Ach-buudan, Quu-chabdar, capering and spoiling for a knock-down drag-out; thus Shandöögör took the field.

Immediately following him – though sad to say, if you visit the Infidels in the west today you will find many who have never heard of Kökötöy's memorial feast! – Chïnoonchük the Döböt hero took the field. Those who beheld him were stunned out of their wits: his lower lip hanging out heavily, his upper lip pendulous and ponderous; his two big ears flapping down and nearly covering his shoulders, he rode on Qoy-toru. When they saw he had courage, those people of the west made a great din. With ears big as campaign-tents, eyes big as traveling-kettles, and the face of a madman, he donned an iron corselet as he besought Laaylama, pulling the mail over his bare body; sparks leapt from his eyes like flying tinder as he rode into the arena and under the gaze of the limitless throng of worthies.

Spurring Quu-chabdar to a run and sending mountainous clouds of dust roiling up, Shandöögör made his charge. As the two clashed, Chïnoonchük thrust out his arm first; the two wrestled atop their horses, now clutching, now untangling, neither able to get the upper hand. Sixty times they grappled as the multitudes of the people of the west murmured with a dull roar and set the black earth trembling with their shouts. What people do for honor! The Qïtays yelled on their side, joined by the Qalmaqs.

The world is full of people, but when those two giants wrestled all the people lost interest. Dusk fell and the day ended. And what about those wrestlers? Cherry-red blood poured out from under their gripping hands. The old man Küshöng went out to break it up; Aqbay the Kirghiz went as well when he saw where Küshöng was headed.

"Shandöögör! That's enough, my boy," said old Küshöng.

But just as he was getting hold of him and turning him around, Aqbay said, "Don't stop, grab him!"

The champion from the Beejin side had calmed down and started to move away, but before he could even say, "I'm off," Chïnoonchük of the west pulled him down off his horse. And so the land of Qïtay was defeated when its champion was brought down.

"Evening has come, dinner is served!" cried the heralds, but the Kirghiz and Qïtay will remain on bad terms until Judgment Day; their spite stems from that. Along the banks of the Qarqïra and in the valley of the Qara-suu, by Qaynar-qashat and Üch-bashat the people were ranged. On one end they stretched to the Ketmen mountains and on another to Qïzïl-qïya; if one looked on one side they reached the pass on the road to Aghïyaz, while if one looked north there were troops ranged all the way up to Chabdar pass; on another side they stretched to Tötö pass.* Other peoples accepted hospitality from the Qara Kirghiz, but those Qïtays bore a grudge over what Aqbay had said. Where the Muslims were camped they passed out the meat of foals suckled on young mares; to the Qïtays of Qaqan–Chïn they gave only pure white fat rendered from beef and mutton. The Muslims had pallets and covers of *torghun*, *tubar*, and *shayï* silks; for the people of the west they only boiled and served strong tea. Eating off by themselves, all the sons of the Kirghiz slaughtered horses and passed around the fat, and everybody was served mutton. That is how your departed ancestors provided for so many guests when they decided to hold the memorial feast for Kökötöy.

They slept that night, and then it was dawn.

16

The Finish of the Horse Race

The horses had been started on a race course that was six days outbound, and the people had been waiting for seven days. Everyone was in great excitement, as this was the day they mounted up for the finish.*

"The home stretch takes two days!" – "We have to get ready today!" they said, scurrying and crowding about in a hubbub: "Come on! Mount up! Let's go!" The people called the alarm, and formed into many little bands so that the face of the earth was full of riders.

The great prince Qong of the Qïtay silenced the red-topknotted Oyrots and gave orders: "Now that the horses are approaching, give full vent to your hatred! No one gets out of this. All of you, young and old: if one of the Muslims' horses comes, then every single one of you – stop him from getting through and knock him over! No one try to get out of it – bring down those horses! Are not our encampments near by here? Would we not be damnable wretches if we let these insignificant Chantuus[1] win the race? If one of the Chantuu horses comes as a reminder of the pain we have been suffering lately, go right out against it, block its path and knock it over!

"Listen to what I am saying now, these Buruts who have long been under our sway* are bringing us to grief. Listen, they are marrying their daughters around and giving memorial feasts for the whole world in honor of their dead. They are acting as though they are independent and full of prowess; they act like Töshtük and Manas. And they act as if they were simply rolling

1.   "Chantuus": Chantuu is what Qïtays called Muslims.

in bounty! We didn't finish off Qoshoy of the Qataghan before;* now he comes here, and we see his strength! And after him will come his children. The servant has grown clever, and Türkestan is a big country. The mountain-dwelling Kirghiz are becoming the equals of the Qïtay empire, and will one day surpass it; the Qïtays' kindled fire will one day be extinguished. The champions of this world will find their places in the next, and depart; the silver-winged white gyrfalcon will search the earth, and dust will obscure the sun. I fear, in the end, that the Kirghiz of Türkestan will terrorize the world; I fear they will attack Tüp Beejin.* We must spoil their memorial feast, sow quarrels, topple their horses – punish them! Starting now we must fight them – crush them! We must tear down their cursed houses to the foundations! All of us, young and old, great and small must raise a commotion! We must subjugate them under Qïtay rule! We must destroy their gardens, make ashes of them; ruin them! We must fling to the ground their eminent men who hold their heads high!

"The numerous Kirghiz in our realm inhabit the vast lands above the Altay. In Qumul, Chaghan, Aghïlïq, Emil, Bökön, Taghïlïq and Sïyabush there are Qalmaqs; among the Qalmaqs, Ushang and Qaramar have been harassed by the Chantuu. People, consider well: the two rivers Urqun and Ertish – those are in Qalmaq territory, as are the desert of Erime and, to the south, the lake at It-ichpes. In all of these places the population is Qalmaq. And then a few Kirghiz so-and-so's come, and they think they can do anything they like?! Let us turn their memorial feast into a torment and make them a laughingstock! Let us turn their banquet into a hell and bring torment upon their rabble!

"Let us slaughter their people and not let them multiply – wipe out the arrogant Chantuu and be done with them! If we do not take this bold step they will sell your sons in Urum, sell your daughters in Qïrïm, and inflict their doings on the rest of the world! Let us pluck them by the handful while they are young – nip them in the bud! Let us not let their young daughters grow up, for from one of those will grow three, and from three will grow a hundred! Who among the teeming people of

Qaqan is there to snarl at the Qara Kirghiz? – Surely the people of Qaqan are the ones to uproot their charred stump!"

When Prince Qong had done speaking, red-topknotted Nezqara, Ushang of the Qalmaq, black-maned Boroonchu, Sayqal daughter of Qatqalang, Alooke of the Soloon, Er Joloy ill-humored as a boar, Bozkertik of the Toqshuker, Soorondük son of Solobo, Bedööng of the Chïrash, Ködöng of the Daghïr, and all the lords of Qïtay mounted their swift horses and held council, the Qïtays cajoling them to go and face the Muslims in battle. Qongurbay, for his part, had made up his mind and was ready to stride forth. A deputation under Bozkertik went to Oronghu and Joloy and the Qalmaqs under Suqal.

Everyone there attended first to the counsel of Ushang, elder of the Qalmaq: "If one of their race-horses appears and we block its way, grief will come of it. The Kirghiz and Qalmaqs must not kindle the fires of disaster by unsheathing their swords and coming to blows; the enemy must not gain satisfaction from the Qïtays' misfortunes. They must not drive the remaining Qalmaqs into exile and trod the lands of your tribes all the way to Qaqan. The Qara Qïtay tribe must not be allowed to sit by with its pretense of fairness; in promoting a massacre of the Kirghiz, Qïtay has designs on both the Qara Kirghiz and the Qalmaq. If swords are going to be wielded against the Kirghiz, it is the Qalmaq who will be forced to do it, and if the sons of Türk lock horns* we shall find ourselves estranged from the spirits of our departed ancestors. We should not agree to this. If the Qalmaq agree to the plans of the Qïtay, we shall face a Qara Kirghiz tribe that is brimming with courage. They will not stop their slaughter until Judgment Day, and they will gouge out the eyes of the Qalmaq Heathens who remain!"

Thus Khan Ushang began, but an impure spirit had conquered Joloy and he did not let Ushang finish: "These Buruts here invite us to their memorial feast, and then when we come they heap troubles on us; they have vexed us to the point of ruination! How could I call them kindred?* *Apsap shooday!* If I don't thrash these *aminine** Buruts! You come with your biased words, playing at trickery, but it is the Qïtay who will be my kindred. We have mixed and loved, knotted our horses' lead-ropes together, grieved for our dead and delighted in our living; when one was stooped the other was a support. How am I supposed to depart from the Qïtay and desire the Kirghiz? How can I depart from Qaqan and desire the Qazaqs? Once Khan Qongurbay has spoken, I lay down my life!"

The others stood around agonizing. "If our first ancestor was Türk –" they puzzled, but could not for all their concentration figure out what to do.

Oronghu and Joloy both refused to bicker with their countrymen. After his joust with Manas, Qongurbay wanted revenge on those who called his religion "contrary" and said the devil had tempted the Qïtay. Manas had slammed him in the back and vanquished him. Joloy had entered the wrestling ring and been thrown and humiliated by Qoshoy the giant. Because of that, Joloy obstinately resisted Ushang and went with the Qïtays; and because of that the Qalmaqs were divided and punished by God.

Mounting their horses, the teeming Qïtay who crowded Chabdar pass set out, spreading over the land. Orus, Qïtays, and Qalmaqs joined together and made for the appointed location; people of the Tarsa, Jööt, and Saqalat readied themselves for the end of the affair, the arrival of the race-horses.

The place where the horses had been turned around was beyond Türküstön, at Quu-jeken island. There the sixty marshals halted all the horses in the race, standing in a row to block their way; then they pronounced a blessing. That place called Quu-jeken was a low-lying, marshy area near the Sïrdarïya river about half a day's ride from end to end, and along its whole length the marshland was full of wild geese.

Now, you may say that the horse you are riding is valuable to you just because you can ride it, but that would be wrong. When you hear why I say this you will laugh. When the jockeys got under way, those horses they were riding showed what thoroughbreds they were. As they came to the cranes and geese in the marshes of Jekendi, those cranes and geese were killed as they took flight, trampled in great numbers by the speeding horses. Then the sixty marshals of the horse race came up behind and loaded their horses with the birds, as many as they could carry. Some of those goose and crane carcasses had broken necks; some others had broken wings. The sixty riders who came from behind gathered a great many of them. It is impossible to tell whether this is truth or falsehood, but such is the acclaim of Kökötöy's feast down to the present day. The celebrated *tulpars* flew like birds as they pounded over the trail; like swift white gyrfalcons striking ravens close to the ground, the excellent *tulpars* flew like the wind and trampled those birds; the excellent racers overtook even God's birds on the wing.

The jockeys gave their mounts free rein and whipped them left and right with their lashes; they had run all over this woe-begone world, and now, from their start in late morning they reached Qara-qum at the end of Ulan by that evening. There, the six thousand escorts were watching out for the horses to put them on the route and keep them from ducking to the left or to the right. Until the count of exactly one thousand was reached and that many horses had gone by, they formed the route for the race to pass, and only then, as your forebears have told it, did they themselves get under way to chase after the racers; the six thousand escorts stood by as the racers passed, and waited and watched to see that all of the horses made it by safely.

Next they came to the flowing Ile river, with the Qapal mountains on the other side. (It is well for you to hear the meaning of the name Qapal: in the time of the prophet Musa his people wandered there, though there was no report of it; and they said, "We have grown indifferent to this false world," and the word "*qapïl*" stuck there.)[1]

The horses were all coursing through the big valley, making their way along the broad Ile. As they neared Chabdar and began to ascend, towering Aq-qula, high in the withers, largest

---

1.   " 'We have grown indifferent to this false world,' and the word '*qapïl*' stuck there": "indifferent" is *qapïl* in Kirghiz and "this false world" is *qapïlet*. The literate poet Saghïmbay recognized the related Arabic forms *ghufl, ghaflat, ghafal* in the etymology of the Kirghiz words *qapïl, qapïlet* – to which he imaginatively sound-matched the place name *Qapal*.

of all beasts and with the spine to carry his extraordinary bulk, and lean of rib – the choice *tulpar* Aq-qula – suffering in the black sweats that wetted his whole body and streamed off him in his supreme exertion, with steam shooting from his nostrils and water pouring from the folds in the pits of his forelegs – sprouted and spread the wings that lay on his sides, and the ground under his hoof-beats was rent with holes deep as hearths. His sword-steel bit dangling low, Qula massive-as-a-racing-camel flew like the wind, hunching into the climb. At the sight of him in the distance, the common folk gave up hope of winning the first prize – Aq-qula was trailing behind seven other horses! He whizzed like an arrow; his jockey's sleeveless gray jerkin was whipped to shreds from the hems and nearly blown off; the rocks thrown up from his hoof-beats whistled up to head height, loud as shots from a camel-mounted gun.

In the lead, were you to look, Joloy's horse Ach-buudan was covering the course well ahead of the excellent *tulpars* and the rest of the pack. Next came Töshtük's horse Chal-quyruq, who had seen the region of Köyqap and the land of the teeming *peris*, and had suffered many sore hardships and torments at a wizard's hands; who had endured unendurable outrages and difficulties at a trickster's hands; who had come to grief and discontent from the massed *divs* and *peris* of Nurghabïl – that beast had come through it, albeit bereft of six portions of his life-force; and now Chal-quyruq of the seven lives flew like a whirlwind. That sufferer of grief and discontent bereft of six of his lives ran on relentlessly; having that day spent the last of his fine fettle, he relied on a sole remaining life.

Thinking, "If only I could overtake Ach-buudan and make it to the feasting grounds quicker, arrive in the lead of all these excellent racers and topple Kökötöy's standard!" – the horse Chal-quyruq gave a burst of speed, and Joloy's horse Ach-buudan was soon left far behind even Chal-quyruq's dust-cloud.

Ach-buudan surged onward, the foam from the poor animal's mouth flecked with blood, the rocks struck by his hooves flying and tumbling skyward. He had a whole day's sweat left in him; Joloy the giant, in his ignorance, had not sweated him out properly before entering him in the race. His tail was wrung out to a fathom's length; sweat poured from his sides; his ears lay back like a hare's, and the hollows of his hooves flipped skyward in his all-out gallop.

He was making it a hard-run contest, coming up alongside Chal-quyruq, when, were you to look, behind him Qoshoy's horse Chong-sarï, hunched up like a hungry mountain sheep, bunched up like a hungry polecat, tossing his mane-braids to the sky, dust puffing from his jockey's jerkin, was coming up galloping full-tilt. Behind him came Budangchang's horse Sal-qara; behind that one right in line came Muzburchaq's Tel-küröng; behind him with long, bold strides came Kerkökül's Ker-qashqa, who had been none too lean at the start, an animal of extraordinary build, his stance in the rear wide as a notch in the mountains, the space between his galloping legs wide enough to fit a loaded camel. After him, were you to look, came Qarach's horse Jar-qïzïl; after him Alooke's Nar-qïzïl;* next came Kökchö's horse Kök-ala ridden by a sly jockey with tears streaming from his eyes. He fancied himself a horse-trainer. For Kökötöy's memorial feast he had kept Kök-ala to an intensive regimen and got him too lean; but, too clever by half, this jockey was thinking, "I trained him too hard – I took Kökchö's advice and am the worse off for it!"* Next in line and keeping up was Qalqaman's Qaz-qara; behind him came Sultaqan's Taz-qara, Chegish's horse Sar'-ala, Aghïsh's horse Qar'-ala, Köchpös's horse Chabdar; following him, at a run, came Baqay's horse, then Ümöt's horse Jar-qïzïl, and keeping up behind him Bar'-qïzïl, the horse of Baqcha Biy, a lord of the Qïtay, they say. Then came Baghïsh's horse Sur-kiyik, Shïghay's horse Aq-moyun – the sporting was world-class at Bay Kökötöy's memorial feast! – Atalabek's Aq-jambash, Sïnchïbek's Sar'-qïzïl, Chïnoonchük's Chiy-ala – one could go on, there were so many horses that people at the end of time will be telling this story! – there were prizes for sixty horses, a lavish garner for those that won them – fifty-nine – sixty – you people keep count! Last of all came Oronghu's Qula-bee, a hard-running mare that – poor thing! – fell behind to take a drink, and with that lost her stamina and ended up in sixtieth place. But leave off with them now; there is something to tell about that racer that had pulled away into the lead, so listen to that report.

Qongurbay had set off and crossed beyond Chabdar leading his Qïtay subjects, and had come to the course of the broad Ile* where the Sarï-jaz valley lay near the Qoroghotu and Qosh-köl. As Qongurbay watched he saw thick dust rising over Qoroghotu and Qosh-köl, and then the haulers-in* became visible at Suuq-döbö. The horses, rimy with salt and trailing steam, came on amid the noisy clamor of shouting. In front was Ach-buudan, behind him Chal-quyruq. Going downhill Chal-quyruq outstripped him bounding like a roe-deer; on the uphills Ach-buudan – the cussed temperament of that racer! – took the lead. Behind those two, bruised and blistered, Qula was now catching up, his beating hooves sinking pastern-deep in the ground, his chest jutting like a stag's. Er Manas, spying his horse, placed his trust in Allah; but earlier and unbeknownst to him, it transpired that Prince Qong, that great prince of the Manju realm, had led a group of forty-two Qïtay to make an attempt to bring down Aq-qula.

Two *jaysangs* were sent and placed on either side to block the way; but the lion Manas's horse Aq-qula was in a great heat, and by stretching out his stride bounded right over the two *sungdungs* on the road. At that Qongurbay took off, spurring Al'-ghara to a gallop,* thinking, "If I can just catch up mounted on Al'-ghara! If I can just get Manas's horse Aq-qula in a head-on collision, that will be the last we see of him!" Qongurbay set off thrashing at his mount and covering himself in dust. Manas too raced to get there, spurring Archa-toru to a gallop and sending clouds of dust swirling behind him. Just as Qongurbay and Al'-ghara were overtaking Aq-qula and were about to crash into him and send him toppling, Manas swung his tassel-pommeled horse-lash with the knurled grip and the core filled with blue lead shot around his right side, and, saying, "What are you doing with my horse, Heathen?" he struck Qongurbay on the head. Dust flew off his flapped fur hat, his jaw was ripped open and blood spurted out; he lost consciousness. Poor Prince Qong who thought so highly of his own manliness flung his arms around his horse's neck in a stupor. The wound on his jaw was deep; the blood flowed down in ropes.

Just then Aq-qula surged past, and Almambet Baatïr ran up,

yelling, "If you want to mistreat a horse, that's not how you do it – this is!" and struck Joloy's horse Ach-buudan on the head. Ach-buudan stumbled and sank and barely recovered his footing while Chal-quyruq ran past; somehow he managed to bounce back and start on the course again, but not before three horses had gone by him.

"*Ütügüngö shooday!*"* Er Joloy cursed as he hounded Almambet. Your Prince Qong had said, "This is how to bring down a horse," and had his try at toppling Aq-qula, but Almambet turned it to his detriment.

Khan Almambet said, "What were you playing at, Heathen?" and left it at that – he was not one to linger – and rode off.

That Infidel Joloy nocked an arrow in his deadly bow, thinking, "I'll shoot him," but Chubaq son of Aqbalta saw him do it. Pulling from his belt the battle-ax broad as a door, he struck surly Joloy atop the head; the blade landed, and Joloy aiming his bow was parted from his senses. The bow fell from his hands, and Big Joloy bitterly forsook his soul. When he turned and looked behind, the Forty Heroes with old Qïrghïl in the lead were coming on in force with such vehemence that were his head made of stone they would surely kill him. At the sight of them Big Joloy ran away and rejoined the Qalmaqs, who had been sunk in disputes since he ignored Ushang's counsel.

The lion Manas, the white-bearded elder Qoshoy, and all the rest watched as sixty horses went by them. That the first prize went to a Kirghiz was clear to Manas; the hero now turned his full attention to managing the horses of the other nations and their prizes. "To conduct the horses at the finish you need to be vigilant," he said to the sixty men. These were the things that the lion Manas Baatïr had to do as judge. "When a horse comes flying in, conduct him," he instructed the sixty, and that is the reason why racing-prizes are still called "*dayek*."[1]

Giving orders to hold the crowds of troops back, having all

---

1. "'When a horse comes flying in …' … racing-prizes are still called 'dayek'": "comes flying in" is *dayar kelse* in Saghïmbay's phrasing, to which he makes an imaginative connection here with the unrelated word for "racing-prize," *dayek*.

the finishers inspected, conferring prizes on each one, having herds formed up as he moved from place to place – he had had prize-herds set by the Chelek and the Charïn, and others had been lodged along the banks of the Üch Almatï and in the valley of the Üch-bulaq. The prize that was to go to the garner of the last-place horse's owner was a great quantity of sheep crammed onto the middle slopes of the mountain up toward Qïzïl-qïya pass, and that is how people in later times came to call that place Sarï-tologhoy.[1] The race-horses' owners rushed about and kept the lion Er Manas completely tied up and harassed, and it was in milling about with them that the hero found himself detained.

---

1. "Sarï-tologhoy": *sarï tologhoy* means "tawny, trampled ground halfway up a mountainside."

The Qïtay–Qalmaqs
Make Off with the Prize;
The Ensuing Battle

The Jööt and the Tarsa and the Qalcha were there – innumerable well-behaved peoples. Arab, Ajam, Atalat – you know their illustrious origins. The Ïndï and the Saqalat – to the mindful observer, all of those peoples' stories fix on a prophet. Then there were the Orus and the Nemis, and the innumerable Qïtay and Qalmaq. Manas was counting up and conferring the prizes for the horses that had finished the race, and when he had done with the counting and had the crowds sent away, it was no longer early; it had grown quite late. Only then could stalwart Manas spare the attention and go to Qara-suu at Üch-bulaq, the place where he had had the first prize laid aside and secured.

When he arrived there, Manas saw that sixteen of his companions were lying vanquished, their heads split and their faces battered, and the prize-herds were stolen. The Qalmaqs were responsible for that mischief; they had driven the animals away without a trace.

From among their khans, Prince Qong of the Qïtay, Muradïl son of Qïrmuz, red-topknotted Nezqara, Ushang of the Qalmaq, black-maned Boroonchu, Sayqal daughter of Qatqalang, Alooke of the Soloon, Er Joloy bad-tempered as a boar, Bozkertik of the Toqshuker, Soorondük chief of the Soloon, Qaracha and Qïchar were there. "Come what may," said Qongurbay, "today's order has arrived as if from Esen Khan himself. Drive off the camels and make the calves whine, drive off the meaner cattle in bunches, drive the horses off neighing and if you see their minders, sound the signal! Drive the foals and yearlings with shouts, make the steppe boil with dust, drive the lowing cows along! Our horse deserves them, so we'll take them!" said Er Qongurbay as he set the raid in motion. "Drive the bleating sheep along; drive their herders on the steppes helter-skelter amid cries of woe! First came Aq-qula, then Chal-quyruq after him, then my horse* came third in line!" – He gave his sovereign command, and for Ach-buudan who came in third the whooping Qïtay chased off the herds for the first three prizes.

Seeing this happen and much surprised by it, the youngest of nine sons, Eleman Bay's darling son Töshtük uttered entreaties to the Creator and rode out yelling to meet them; the force of the four myriad men he led sent the dust swirling up in the air as that tiger Prince Töshtük went to block the way and keep the raiders from getting through. Four myriads are forty thousand, but the Qïtays were beyond number, and their leader was gigantic Qongur; they just battered their way onto the Ters-mayoo road. (That river was called Ters-mayoo before Manas was born, when Tekes Khan ruled there; then when Manas conquered Tekes Khan the name Ters-mayoo fell into disuse and it was called Tekes. Manas's uncle Baqay had said, "Now the wonderful land of Ters-mayoo shall be called Tekes until Judgment Day. Whenever the Qalmaq contend with the Kirghiz they shall not be able to flee very far away, for this land shall remain a part of Alach." Thus Baqay had pronounced back then.)

Now the Qïtays had made an audacious attack and stolen the prize-herds at the memorial feast for Bay Kökötöy, and Er Töshtük had crashed in and caused a disruption on their path; but the Qïtay people seethed and teemed like flies, and went rumbling on, saying, "Why should we give up the prize? – Let's take it all and get away safely home – We raced real *tulpars* – Our prizes don't belong to the Buruts; as long as Qongurbay and Joloy answer for us, we'll plunder to our hearts' content! – We'll wreak a heavy slaughter and take those scoundrelly Chantuus' daughters as our gifts! With our lords' license we'll plunder them into a rumpled mess! We'll take those beaten Buruts' sons as our gifts! We'll shatter the door-frames of their yurts, make their young lads weep, and set their virgin mares kicking away off the mountainsides; shatter the trellis-frames of their yurts, make their young ladies and maidens weep, and set their mares kicking away off the high, grassy slopes; turn their lasso-poles into meat-skewers, and make it an affair they will never forget; turn the wall-felts of their yurts into under-blankets for our saddles and slaughter every single one of them; turn the dome-felts of their yurts into under-blankets for our saddles and slaughter them, leaving none to thrive! If our gods aid us, we will make bloodthirsty Manas's blood flow like water! We'll rip him open at the ribs! See if we don't make the sons of the Kirghiz suffer! See if we don't toss them before we let them take Ach-buudan's prize! Let's take the whole prize and divide it up among the soldiers! See if we don't engage bloodthirsty Manas who lords it so in single combat! They invited people to this feast, but it turns out they only invited them to make fools of them. All along we had heard, 'No one in the world has ever seen a heathen like Manas before.' Samarqan and Qoqon are faraway lands, but we had it on reliable authority from innumerable multitudes of other nations. Right in front of us, in Turpan, there are the eastern Kirghiz who are subject to bloodthirsty Manas; Ajïbay's people are there, as are Qutubiy's. The time has come that this raving Kirghiz could ignore the mighty Qïtay!* But until tomorrow evening when we cross over the boundary of the Muslims' lands, until we pass beyond Tersmayoo and manage to reach the two confluences at Echkilik as a company, let us drive the cattle along, and if we happen upon any Chantuus let us tie every one of them up and lead them off; but once we have passed beyond Ters-mayoo let us make an end of any captives by slitting their throats like sheep!" Having conferred like this they made for Baqalïq. Leave the Qïtays and Qalmaqs on their way now, those Infidels who took counsel to massacre the Kirghiz.

Having distributed the prizes, the hero Manas arrived in the evening and found the lasso-poles lying broken, everything clean muddied, and sixteen of his greatest heroes wounded and on the point of death. Some of the Noghoys, fearing for their lives, had got away and hidden in the stands of birches when the Infidels pummeled the descendants of Noghoy. The tribes of the Muslim faith were left in a rumpled mess; some escaped into the stands of spruces around Qarqïra, exhausted and unable to overcome the Qïtays, and heedless of the fallen.

Before sunset Er Boqmurun arrived. He left the hero Manas in charge of everyone else and led his own host on the march, raising Kökötöy's standard as they set out in pursuit of the Infidels.* When he reached the Almaluu river he came upon Er Töshtük. Boqmurun had a hundred thousand troops with him; his strength, were one to estimate it by eye, was greater than a mountain.

When Ushang Baatïr saw this, he said, "I'm not fighting them," and departed on his own with his force of thirty-five thousand. The giant Joloy who vaunted his own toughness so was irritated, and that ignited his temper: he took forty thousand of the Qïtays, and with fifty thousand of his own troops fearlessly plunged ahead in pursuit of Ushang. Stirring dust up to the sky, their lances tied with pennants, those Qïtays came on a-whooping and the Qalmaqs came on a-hollering. Seeing this, Budangchang and Ushang beat a retreat, but the Qalmaqs in pursuit overpowered their ninety-five thousand and plundered their horses and equipment. Night had already fallen as this was going on and the Qara Qalmaqs were breaking apart; they were still breaking up amid thunderous din the next day.

Dawn broke and sunrise came on like a parting seam on the horizon. Your Manas was saying farewell to the dispersing guests and seeing them on their ways home. In the evening he came and addressed his people, the lofty and the lowly. You will marvel at what he said. "Though they are Qïtay they are a mighty nation, a multitude of scoundrels teeming in masses. Though they are Qalmaq they are a nation with a khan, abundant too in their masses. The Qïtay have a separate origin from the scoundrelly Qalmaq who range within my borders like giants; the Qïtay of Qazïlïq are separate from the scandalous Qalmaq who range within my realm like giants. I thought, 'They will be our kin one day'; I thought, 'Their power will wane'; but while I was thinking about my hospitable duties, it turns out that that damnable dog Joloy was wishing for war. I will give him what he wants, and if my Creator shows me friendship, I will stretch Joloy's hide upon a rock! I will see every hostile Qïtay defer to me; I would sooner die than surrender the prize for the horse race! I would rather you said, 'Manas has died' than 'Manas has given up the prize'! Children of the Muslim faith, bless me!"

When he had finished saying this the excellent Manas Baatïr called for Er Töshtük, but Töshtük had already gone off in pursuit of the Infidels Qongurbay and Joloy. Baghïsh of the Jediger had just won a prize; he arrived just then from the camp where he had been given accommodation. "They have stolen the prize! The Qïtays have foiled the Kirghiz and got away!" they said.

The moment he heard this Baghïsh flew into a tirade. "What a disgrace!" he shouted, flinging diatribes like rocks. Yelling and storming, with his golden-crescent-moon-topped standard he set off with seven thousand men. Aghïsh went with him leading two thousand, and Aqbay took along his force, and they started on the Tekes road trailing the Qïtays; Qoshoy of the Qataghan heard of this and took eleven thousand soldiers. Thus the eminent heroes got under way and joined up over the course of the night, assembling an army past counting.

Budangchang and Ushang both had come upon their Qïtay enemies at Kendeger ravine, and were in the process of parting company with them; when they saw the Muslims approaching, every last one of them fled. Ushang came out on the right, wailing, "Joloy did us in!" That day Er Qoshoy let his white beard wave and his gray ambler sway, out at the head of the soldiers, and the lions Töshtük and Boqmurun were there at your uncle's side.

When the sun rose again and cast shadows in the mountains, a great multitude rallied. Gray-maned Manas had arrived with racers and thoroughbreds fitted out in costly trappings and ridden out in front by mettlesome youths; he had Aq-qula with him on a lead, unsaddled. Almambet, Sïrghaq, and Chubaq, his lions, rode around him; Ajïbay and Chalïbay – unharmed for now* – and that gyrfalcon of a hero, Qutunay, made their stately way in company with Er Manas. Tips of lances glinted, soldiers' heads flowed like a river; with Prince Manas in the lead the heroes' cavalcade ground the earth to powder as they rounded the right flank at full strength and ran head-on into Budangchang and Ushang on the move.

"You are about to see God's will! If the hour of your death has arrived, you will embrace the earth and die! If Allah Most High so orders, you will witness what that means! You have combined our prizes with your herds, but it's a fool's errand for you to separate them now!" So said Manas.

"Baatïr, our home is at Sümbö!"* the Qalmaqs said.

"Then I will ride there with your herds right now, and make love to your Qïtay wives!" When Manas had made this reply, his pursuit force banded together and started off, sending dust wafting up into the air.

The Qïtays and Qalmaqs raised a great clamor as they rode ahead, nearing Qulja. The mountains on the south side of the Tekes valley continue until they communicate through a pass with the Altay mountains, but our story takes us elsewhere: on the north side of the valley the mountains end and give way to an area of steppe. They followed the Tekes river, circling and feinting back, until they came to the end of the mountains and ran up against the river by Kürköö and Küyük. Then they rollicked along the Qundaq river impetuously, making lively chatter, "We've got away!" – so they thought; but just as those Qïtays and Qalmaqs of alien religion made their way along there with their black-topped standard, raising a clamor as if they were on migration over easy terrain, the Kirghiz army arrived and surrounded them, and those whooping Infidels' black souls met their undoing.

Earlier Joloy had sent a messenger home to announce in the Qalmaq country that he had returned. To Jumabek son of Asqar he had said, "Don't stay here, go now, and have my encampment at Chanaq descend from the mountains and greet me on the way. Have my beautiful wife Qïyash come out to meet Khan Qongurbay Baatïr; have them slaughter a great number of hogs and cook the light marrow with rice – they must do it now! Have them serve liquor – the strongest kind;* have them load the field-tents onto the camel-geldings!" Thus when they had lifted the prize with Prince Qongur in the lead and set out for Tötö, he sent his man Jumabek ahead with that message. Jumabek rode through the night, driving his horse mercilessly, and brought the people down from Chanaq. They descended to a hollow sheltered by Ubang mountain just this side of Qulja, and filled the banks of the Qurdum river with their encampment.

"We have massacred the Kirghiz," was the news being spread around the land meanwhile. But among the forty tribes of the Qalmaq were many elders, wise men, who said, "The people have made this hasty trip in vain, because as long as the lion Manas is alive he will not simply allow us to take those herds." Animated discussions ensued. Joloy, refusing to accept what they had said, set off after Jumabek.

For the time being there was no breach between the Qalmaqs and the Qïtays, and their commoners drove and pastured the animals together, crying, "We stole the prize!" and puffing themselves up like heroes. Prince Qong was in his field-tent, and Nezqara Baatïr was in his; Muradïl son of Qïrmuz Shaa, Oronghu of the Qanghay, Sayqal daughter of Qatqalang, and the hero named Chïlantuu were there as well – a profusion of nothing but faithless Heathens. On their right flank, in the south, high mountains loomed up; when your ruffians had come to the level ground was when their enemies caught up with them from behind. Their trumpets roaring, shawms blaring, and banners streaming, with gold-topped standards glinting and musket-fire rumbling, the innumerable descendants of Türk came on in a mass and full of stratagems. For two full days and nights they had marched without a stop. The Infidels had begun to gloat, "We've eluded them!" – and just as they were saying that, God sent them their punishment: six teeming hosts of the Muslims fell upon them helter-skelter. The Qïtay army consisted of four hundred thousand soldiers, but at that moment the Kirghiz army was as vast as the world itself.

With a forceful attack the sons of Alach began the battle. "*Jabuu, jabuu, jabuu!*"* cried the mob of jabbering Qalmaqs, taking hold of their horses and flinging on their saddle-blankets as the teeming Muslims came at them from all directions.

When they saw what was happening and the battle thus begun, the Qïtays' mood turned ugly; galloping madly about, great multitudes of them were crying, "This scandal is Joloy's doing! Just when he's disappeared, the Kirghiz come and slaughter the Qïtay!" The Qïtays started collaring the Qalmaqs and yelling "*Taa! Taa!*" – when they say "Taa" it means "Strike"* – and the dust filled up their eyes.

The Kirghiz of the forty tribes poured in, wreaking heavy slaughter amid a great din. Lance-tips were planted in chests; battle-axes clove Infidels' heads; swords fell on necks. They set those unsuspecting wretches moaning, "Ah, woe!" – lancing the ones at lance-distance and butchering with swords a few who came in close enough. Exchanging musket-rounds, those Infidels and Muslims were awash in blood up to their sides; those fated to die were parted from their souls and fell sprawling to the ground. Much was the plunder the Kirghiz drove off.

"It's not far now to the populous land of the Qalmaq," they reckoned. "We shall enter it tomorrow, and be on the border of Beejin" – "To the north is the land of the Zubun Qalmaqs, the unsuspecting wretches!"

With entreaties to the One God the Kirghiz rode manfully across the border. They made those self-conceited *beks* bend over, then bludgeoned them on the head with maces; they laid a great many of those princes on their bellies. Many of the careless Qïtays who could not manage to mount a horse or find any place to hide saw the spiteful rage in the Muslims' eyes and perished, stabbing themselves with their own daggers. And more than those were the ones who already had stabbed themselves and crumpled over, and lay dying; more still was the number of those hurriedly running up and down looking for a place to take shelter, and finding none; no one who was mounted and in flight answered anyone else's call for help. Those clamoring Infidels who managed to get away found themselves stuck on the point of land at the confluence of the Qurdum river. There, rather than die in a rout – rather than watch the Kirghiz ravage them and die at sword-point; rather than see the Qazaqs' fury and die under the lash – they fled to the river's edge, fell, and smacked into the water. More than those were the ones who had realized there would be no escape now that the Muslims were riled, and had flung themselves into the raging rapids and were being borne along; more still was the number of those going along trying to save their borrowed souls.

Six hundred thousand Muslims had taken up that hue and cry against no few Infidels, whose white-bearded elder was Alooke, the aged khan. Almambet reached Alooke's tent and rained torment after torment upon his soldiers' heads; with fifteen thousand of these soldiers Alooke beat a retreat and headed up the mouth of a defile in the mountains.

An army of one hundred fifty thousand remained under Muradïl and Prince Qong – astride Al'-ghara and with his watered-steel sword hanging at his waist – and red-topknotted Nezqara. Qongur was the greatest warrior among them. Joining those three came Oronghu in her ungainly fashion sending dust rising into the air; the tail of her mare Qula-bee taut-as-a-bow was cocked up as she flew along, and the mare was squelching and farting out her womb, for it had not been plugged up. Oronghu's hair was going gray; she was between fifty and sixty years old. In her left hand she held a bow broad as an ox's girth – Qula-bee taut-as-a-bow ran like the wind that blows on a mountain crest – Oronghu sallied forth in a fury; she was not one to be lazy when talk turned to combat – and in her right hand that Heathen held aloft a lance of ninety arm's-lengths. With Oronghu they made four.

Er Qongurbay Qalcha's eyes burned like flames as rage overspread his frame; the time had come for that scandal-maker Qalcha to show his courage. He rode onto the field of single combat with a yell, raising his ancestral war-cry "Chïlaba!" and saying, "By your leave, hero!" as he emerged alone from his army.

Now Boqmurun Baatïr came, saying, "Let me at that dog and I will die with him!"

"If you want to go, prince, then go," they said, and gave their leave.*

Like a young tiger prowling the thickets, Boqmurun went out raging for a fight. He donned a coat of mail and put a helmet on his head, then readied his weapons, took up his iron-tipped lance, and besought God for help: "All in vain to have done them honor! The tears never dried from my eyes. Those goddamned Heathens, I kept paying them respects and they kept flaying me! I have passed so many days in toil leading the nation, so many days in labor leading the people, and Qong-urbay has never let me rest an elbow on the ground nor granted me a wink of sleep, never allowed me to stretch my limbs nor my head to touch a pillow! The contempt this dog has shown me! Who could bear the outrage?"

With a rigid lance in his hand and Al'-ghara in fine fettle beneath him Qongurbay raged like a blue-gray tiger. He donned his corselet of blue steel and drew his helmet down over his head. Then, calling Nezqara to his side and taking up his deadly lance, he let Al'-ghara cavort as he rode out onto the field. Many a Muslim was sunk in consternation at the sight of him. He called out loudly to his deity: "*Laaylamaluu!*" Prince Qong the khan shouted. Clad in a helmet like an iron yurt-dome, raging and roaring like a lion he came on.

Nineteen-year-old Boqmurun saw the whole proceeding. He said, "This is what I have wished for. This is the moment for the sons of the religion of Islam to show their courage! I have watched that one, that scandal-loving schemer of the Qara Qïtays, lifter of racing-prizes – that one is simply mad! Riding Maani-ker I infiltrated their army last night* and observed that Joloy has gone missing. Who else is there but I myself to approach that rogue Qalcha? Let me take the risk and go face him! Won't the spirits of our departed ancestors punish me if I let that brutish idiot take the prize-herds? Is my horse not a racer, if I weaken and need to escape? O people! Loose Maani-ker swifter-than-an-arrow on that clumping Qalcha! Won't blood be spilled if God Most High decrees it? Won't armies pelt against one another if the enemy is engaged? If the Creator so orders that delay should give way to action, shall I not beat that ferocious fellow who has taken the field, that great prince caparisoned in gold, Prince Qong?"

As Boqmurun spoke these words steam rose from his body and rays of light shot from his face as off the surface of ice. As he made ready to ride out, Er Qoshoy looked him over quickly and said, "Stop! Your calf muscles haven't filled out yet; you aren't old enough to be a champion. Your heart muscle hasn't filled out yet; you aren't old enough to be the attacker. My boy, don't be led out by your racing heart; don't hand victory to that vengeful wild boar and disgrace yourself! If you should be suddenly parted from your honor, or if you should happen to die, all the orphans and widows of your homeland will come to grief. Many are the encampments under your rule that are weakened now. They have lost their strength; you proposed to hold your memorial feast, and they are left without a hair from all their cattle. Do not head onto the field! Qongurbay is known as a warrior of exceptional heroism; he is of singular strength, a caged black lion, they say! He is filled with lust by the very mention of campaigning, a hot-head of a kind you certainly are not. Even brave Manas has not defeated him.* Do not fight him, I forbid you!"

When Boqmurun heard what Er Qoshoy was saying, he spurned him. It could hardly have been otherwise, he was so angry and full of passion. "Ach, please, dear uncle! Where are your wits? Does the Almighty not mete out death? Is a person ever parted from the Almighty's doom by empty words? Does God not mete out fate? Is a person ever parted from God's doom by prattling? Not a soul dies but in the manner ordained; not a single khan dies in possession of his throne. Death comes but once, not every month. What son of Adam does not die? A person who is immortal – what a sight that would be! Who ever refuses the command of Allah Most High? Dear uncle, wise Qoshoy, did your wits leave you when your beard went white? The word of Allah Most High is fixed throughout the world. Death is not some poor stinker sitting around at home; it is not someone such as you or I who see but know each other not. Death walks beside you, together as one with you, yet you do not see. Have the accurate words of the prayers and rites not yet fallen on your ears?

"I invited all the sons of the Kirghiz to this feast for the dead, and as many as came have shown their strength; then this rascally dog starts complaining at being unhorsed by Manas in the joust. He looks to his advantage from having his home and lands nearby with Qalmaqs all around, and from belonging to the great country of Qïtay. Do you not see his disgraceful behavior, the violence he commits in his vainglory? You, man of the Qataghan, though old you are a hero; do not begrudge me, Kökötöy's only son! Let me die for honor's sake! Let me try to make a charge at that goggle-eyed Qalcha! Dear uncle Qoshoy, bless me, and if my death comes let me die!"

When Boqmurun had spoken these words your dear uncle Er Qoshoy gave him his blessing. "Almighty Allah, support him!" said Qoshoy Khan.

Meanwhile Manas had been thinking hard, "The teeming Qïtay are surrounded, and for making off with my prize-herds Khan Qongurbay Qalcha has brought disaster upon himself; but there is no one among the Muslims to go up against that scoundrel Qalcha. A *peri* would go, or a *jinn*, but will any mortal man face Bek Qongurbay the *qalday*? Besides myself who will go?" As he said this Er Manas as yet had nothing to do with Boqmurun's setting forth or with Qoshoy's attempt to protect him; no one had any knowledge of what Boqmurun was doing. So Manas had the bit removed from the mouth of his horse Aq-qula swift-as-an-arrow and had him watered at a pool. He girded his immense frame, loading his legs into ibex-leather breeches. He laid a saddle-cloth – proof against hot coals on a dash through fire, proof against bullets fired in close ranks – on that horse, then had the high-bowed Mongol saddle brought. Er Manas Baatïr's crystal-clear eyes kindled as he tucked his shirt into his breeches, braced his trunk, and let his courage mount to the heights. The hero was ready, and turned his thoughts to waging war.

Brave Manas was just saying, "Allah Most High, support me!" and mounting his horse, when Joorunchu of the Qazaq rode up.

"Boqmurun has mounted Maani-ker," said Joorunchu. "When your grandfather Qoshoy tried to stop him, he scorned him. Boqmurun son of Kökötöy has donned a steel corselet and entered the field of single combat." This was the news he brought, hearing which your lion Manas was taken aback.

"What on earth is that trickster up to? To be so froward and rowdy he must have taken personal offense; he must be furious at that Heathen who keeps flaying those who pay him respects. But is that not the way of this false world, good deeds repaid with evil?" To that Er Manas added, "God's decrees are firm; he who resists them is half a man."

Then he said, "Bring me my horse!" They brought Aq-qula, and your lion Manas Baatïr loaded on his gold-adorned weapons, rage flowing from his lips and sparks shooting from his eyes. He roared like daytime thunder and glowered like dark of night; anger played over his face, and the hair on his body stood up bushy enough to spin yarn for five pairs of stockings.

The Forty Heroes, senior among them Qïrghïl and Baqay, were astounded at the hero's ardor. The tribes of Qïr Ughuz origin – Kirghiz, Qazaq, Dumara – stood watching them, as did that gyrfalcon Töshtük of the Qïpchaq, Joorunchu of the Qïzay, and Qoshoy of the Qataghan. That gyrfalcon Ürbü of the Qïpchaq paragon of olden times, held aloft the flapping standard, and the two sides, Muslim and Infidel, formed up in ranks and approached one another.

On that side, from the army of the Qalmaqs and Qïtays, Qongurbay came out, the dust rising from his tracks as he set his horse Al'-ghara a-capering and careering back and forth. Then Boqmurun emerged on this side with Maani-ker in top condition, his figure handsomely clad in mail.

"Though I gorge on black blood I cannot be sated! Can it really be? Boqmurun has come out alone to meet me in single combat!" With that shout Qongurbay charged, his pennant blowing in the wind.

Boqmurun, cool and composed, reined up opposite. "My cause against him is entirely just," he said to himself. "After he stole the prize for the horse race I was stung to the core." Then, shouting, "Allah Most High, by your leave!" and, "Heathen, this shall not go well for you!" the orphan hefted his lance with its silken pennant, and in the blink of an eye Maani-ker swift-as-an-arrow had covered the distance.

The young lad Er Boqmurun aimed his lance for the heart. Maani-ker was a racer, of course, and Prince Qong was a bit too slow in bringing his lance into position for a thrust at Boqmurun. Never before had that great prince seen such a thing happen; he hefted his lance, but before he could set it, Boqmurun struck him on the chest. The lance thumped into his mail-coat in a solid, resounding hit.

Fire shot from the eyes of Prince Qong who thought so highly of his own manliness, for here was Boqmurun, astride Maani-ker – Boqmurun, a warrior now and full of valor! What did Er Qongurbay say? "You thrust your lance out of turn, you pitter-pattering rascal – but you'll pay for it now!" Qongur brought his lash down on his black horse and made for the lad at a gallop.

Boqmurun couched his lance against his side without paus-ing to judge the distance. Prince Qong was dazed from the first lance-thrust, and that great prince who vaunted his own tough-ness so among the red-topknotted Oyrots was finding his seat in the saddle as he rode, his face swollen with rage; but while he was still fidgeting in the saddle Er Boqmurun was upon him. "There's his vital spot," thought Boqmurun, "below his blad-der, where his trousers hug him," and there he drove his lance home again.

The first time Qongurbay had emerged unscathed, but with this thrust he received a deep wound from groin to anus. See what Allah decreed! That sheep-faced one with the air of a wolf, Boqmurun took his polished lance with the wolf-tongue point and parted Qongurbay's groin from his tailbone. Boqmu-run had first girded himself for battle that very day, and here he was bathing that scandalous Qalcha's posterior in blood.

Qongurbay could not regain his strength to return to battle. Blood poured and spluttered out of him; his determination was shattered. But his iron corselet protected all the parts it should, making them proof against lance-wounds. "I'll just get in my saddle," thought Qongurbay and raised himself up.

With Qongurbay's backside thus raised in the air, Boqmurun thought, "There's his vital spot," and landed him a bonus stroke. The lance ran Qongurbay through; blood filled up his black Qïtay-style trousers. Suffering torments in this fashion, great goggle-eyed Qongur had given up his good name. He turned his black horse's head and retreated toward his army, but Maani-ker caught up with him sprinting like a hare.

Boqmurun sized up his target and decided, "There's his mortal spot, between the upper edge of his corselet and the bowl of his helmet – the base of his skull is wide open," and he thrust his lance. It caught on the collar of Qongurbay's mail-coat, and he flung his arms around Al'-ghara's neck, the blood pouring down in ropes over his back.

Qongurbay beat a retreat, and Nezqara, who had accompanied him on the field, swung his sword at the lad Boqmurun with a shout. For Qongurbay's pains Nezqara slashed not at his body but at the lance instead. The shaft was severed from Boqmurun's grip; thus Nezqara repaid the scorn Er Qongurbay had been made to swallow. Er Manas saw this happening, and his heart ached in sympathy for Boqmurun. Striking Aq-qula with his lash, "My Forty Heroes, curses on your fathers' graves! Are you totally beaten already?" he called, and with a cry of "Allah!" he set off, urging Aq-qula to a gallop as dust swirled behind him. Nothing of your lad Boqmurun's lance remained but the stump in his hand. See what sport your forebears got up to!

The Forty Wolves who attended Manas, his sovereign retinue, charged helter-skelter, churning dust up into the air. Out onto the steppe at Chatalaq they went – just let those discontented Qïtay try to escape disaster! Careering along on his gray ambler, dust billowing up at his back, Qoshoy entered the fray, and along with him came regular troops in a tremendous wave. Spurring Chal-quyruq to a gallop and sending dust swirling up behind him, Töshtük now entered the battle. Memorial feasts today end in rows, but just remember, people – that whole business was handed down from your forefathers!

The Qalmaqs and Qïtays were heedless and in no temper to turn back. They left the herds they had plundered on the steppe; with no plunder at all they met with cruel misfortune. Qongurbay managed to get away, but Nezqara made an easy mark and fell captive. Sowing strife had been their intention, but that day the bird of happiness flew from the Infidels' heads and their lucky star fell to earth. Battle-axes crunched into their heads; when the Infidels showed their horses' rumps and fled, lances landed square on their backs and swords landed on their necks.

Some lost heart and went limp, their breasts awash in blood; others, already dead, went stiff. At this point it turned into a slaughter as of docile sheep. Ketelik lies above Qulja, at the back of the Altay mountains – but why should we deal in empty words? – the Muslims fell in behind the Infidels, many of whose souls came to mishap. Few escaped that onslaught. Horses stood about dragging their lead-ropes while their masters lay on the ground going rigid. Blood was pooled about where it had spilled; many were those who lay soaking in it. Fugitives had got away, but the enormous herds of animals had all fallen into the hands of the Kirghiz. Horses moved about dragging their lead-ropes, and the nation who started the brawl remember it. How could they not remember? Er Qongurbay, wounded, escaped to Qaspang; all the while that he had thought, "I've stolen their prizes, I'm great and powerful!" his own miserable fate was sealed, and the Muslims utterly massacred the Qara Qalmaq people.

Qoshoy interceded, "Stop, children! They are our kin, but they will have nothing to do with the language we speak, which has led to this accident."

"We will not stop for you, uncle! They have treated us with contempt," said the Forty Companions, and with their elder Baqay in the lead they set out to attack Joloy at Chatalaq.

"Listen here, boys!" said the lion Manas; "Careful now, follow me, and not too fast," and he jogged off astride Aq-qula.

Joloy had reached Uluu-özök on his way to meet Qongurbay and unite their hosts and herds, and after getting his people together and ordering them to make camp, he set about pestering them. "We'll leave before dawn for the rendezvous," he said, and much more than that.

With his wife at his side, at the head of his hearth, he had a fire lit and sat warming himself as he boasted to her: "What was I supposed to do with that scum? Bloodthirsty Manas the Burut was ravaging the people to ruin, but I spelled his fate out for him, didn't I? There is no doubt his luck ran out thanks to me. I took big advantage of those Muslim Kirghiz, and not only that: we brought home Aq-qula's racing-prize! I slew Manas's forty retainers – shrouded in red blood that lot who vaunted their toughness so. Those Kirghiz so certain of a Day of Resurrection – let their wives and daughters weep! What was I supposed to do about their contempt, their audacious violence? They despise the Qalmaq religion and think their own religion is all there is. And that beggar they call Manas – the way he talks! What can I say about it? 'My creator is God!' he says. 'You do not obey God, so He will throw you into the deepest hell! Hell is hotter than fire,' he says. He deludes the people, telling them to abandon their 'heathen' ways. And that tribe of roughnecks the Noghoy have even found themselves someone they call a prophet. For that they bring scandals down on people who just want to live in peace. But I got back at that bloodthirsty Manas, that world-wrecking oath-breaker, didn't I? I slew his forty retainers and made their wives and daughters weep; shattered the door-frames of their yurts and made their young lads weep! My soldiers plundered and destroyed those feast-giving Buruts. What was it if not a destruction? Only after I attacked with my army did the chattering Qïtays give them a nice plundering. They drove off their bleating sheep and clapped fetters on their shepherds; drove off their lowing cows and sent their herders along with blows and punches; lifted every last one of their horses and moved them off without so much as a shot fired or a bow drawn. We made them anguish for their unguarded cattle; we robbed them of their strength. We left them not a yearling of their shod beasts nor a sheep of their branded beasts, and drove them all here!"* Thus Joloy sat by the fire warming himself and boasting to his wife, incautiously, unaware of what was about to happen. His words were reassuring, and thus his arrival resulted in a full camp. Try to imagine, people, the others who inhabit this world!

Everyone in Joloy's camp, young and old, came and sat around listening, but his knowing wife with second sight, Ayghanïsh by name,* said, "My accursed Joloy! Clearly you shall come to ruin in the end. Every one of the heroes you are thwarting is from the teeming Alach. You are belittling Manas, but Manas is not a warrior to be taken lightly. Those who quarreled with the religion of truth and parted from their kin in the time of the prophet Musa remained in that state, and took the name Qalmaq; but you never leave off your quarreling!* The world has become fodder for Manas, and his deeds are as balm to the people. If he but droops when riding out, those helping spirits the Forty Chilten are there to succor him. You are blaming Manas, but in my estimation you yourself are a good-for-nothing devil!

"Where is Beejin, and where is your land? You place your hopes in the Qïtay, but where are they, and where is your country? You alienate your own kin and act beastly all the time, but you are tying up your own sound head for the slaughter! You see your kin as enemies, but your luck will run out and you will die. In my estimation you are abusing that prince of the Muslims. You rate the Kirghiz as enemies and want the Qïtay for kin, but the Qïtay don't care about you at all, and even if they did, they would not side with someone like you now against Manas. You are called a Qalmaq; though your ancestor was Manghul, your quarreling has never stopped!"*

When Ayghanïsh had reached this point in her tirade, Joloy said, "A curse on your father's grave, woman! How dare you yelp at me and call me a Heathen!" And see what he did after that: he picked up his lash, and having picked it up he struck his wife on the back with it. She hunched over and ran out.

Meanwhile someone had halted his men and stood opposite Joloy's tent to ascertain what sort of temper he was in and to listen to what he was saying. As Ayghanïsh ran out, Joloy chased after her – and a battle-ax came down and felled him right on the spot! As Joloy plunged over and embraced the dirt completely unconscious, the lion Manas gave a loud yell to his troops, "Charge!" The mobs that were lying in ambush stirred columns of dust up to the sky as they cried, "O Allah!" and their shouted commands rang out. Drums beat rat-a-tat; guns shot bangety-bang; bullets thumped into the Qalmaqs all over their bodies, making them squelch with blood; the Muslim army made a dull roar as six hundred thousand soldiers overran them in swarms from all sides.

"Not to kill, boys!" yelled Baatïr Qoshoy, making a huge noise. This is what their elder, white-bearded grandpa Qoshoy, was yelling about: "Though bad may come of it, do not finish them off, boys! Though they may continue to be our enemies, we will just have to see about it; how could it end well for us after we massacre them? Take their cattle but leave them alive. You can do a lot without committing sin; poke out that scoundrel Er Joloy's eyes!" Having said this Er Qoshoy set about separating the two hosts.

The lion Manas Baatïr, like a lone thief, had stolen up to that Joloy by himself; he had heard all he could take of those boasts of Joloy's. He had landed one stroke of his battle-ax and split open his head, and was on the point of delivering the death-blow when his dear uncle Er Qoshoy called to him, "Spoils, hero! Present him to me as a gift from the spoils!" and thus got Manas to spare his life. Joloy lay snorting where he had fallen, his blood gurgling from the wound.

They raided the Qalmaqs of Jardaq to their hearts' content. There were thirty thousand tents of people. That is how things were done when the eminent hero Manas was alive: white banners on red standards and a loud noise and commotion; blue banners on red standards and the blue sky resounding with the great noise. That is the outcome Joloy saw when he stretched his neck out like a crane's: they drove off his black-tailed *nar* camels, and greater was the number of his snarling women that they led off in bonds; they drove off even more red-tailed *nar* camels, and even greater was the number of his teeming girls that they led off in bonds; more still than those were the gowns of *torqo* they put on, each worth a thousand gold pieces. The horses they lifted from just one valley were past counting, and more than those were the amblers they drove off; more still were the buried ingots they scoured out of their hiding places in the side of the cutbank; more than those were the *buulum* and *buta*-silks they folded up, saying, "Look at the stuff they've got!" and more than that was the haul of chests they packed off on top of camels.

The Qalmaqs took flight across Chardaq pass headed toward the Altay mountains and toward Emil and Dardaq. Those subjects of Qïtay who tried to escape by crossing into Kirghiz territory fell into the hands of the Kirghiz. White-bearded Qoshoy and your dear uncle Baqay were there, and said, "Do not take their lives!" Those old men had to pull attackers off

victims and separate them. "They were our kinsmen originally!"
they explained. "They didn't understand, what are you doing
killing them? Ach, the damned simpletons!" So they left them
alive but gave Joloy's people a beating.

Then they rested for two days and had a feast, and ate their
fill of food. They spared the lives of the Qalmaqs they had
raided. "It was all your own doing, and so you got a beating,"
was what they were told by your uncle old Qoshoy and the rest
of the white-bearded elders.

"They could still die by some mishap," they reasoned, and
decided, "If they are left completely destitute then it might hap-
pen that they starve," so they took only the Qalmaqs' animals
and left them their grain. But there were a great many survivors,
and those perspicacious heroes were moved to sympathy, so
they also gave up one milch animal for every two tents of Qal-
maqs. Some got milch mares, some camels, some cows; and then
they took the innumerable herds and departed from Qalmaq
territory.

Having humiliated their Qongurbay and raised a nice scab
on the sinews of their Joloy's neck with a battle-ax, Khan
Qoshoy of the Qataghan, Kökchö of the Qazaq, Töshtük son
of Eleman, and Jamghïrchï of the Eshtek – the four heroes who
had directed the memorial feast* – returned home safe and
sound. Manas was in the lead and all the heroes rode in atten-
dance on him; Qoshoy was the elder of the people. All who had
tried to meddle with the Kirghiz had been humbled. At the
mere mention of the name Manas, the yellow went out of all
the Qalmaqs' and Qïtays' faces.*

Notes

I
Kökötöy's Deathbed Testament

p. 3: *Babur Khan . . . Jaqïp's son was Manas*: Saghïmbay's account of Manas's genealogy goes back to remote legendary times. Much of this depth may have been the bard's own innovation. See the comparative note, "Manas's genealogy and the Kirghiz" (pp. 288–9).

p. 3: *got into a sore fight with him*: The fight between Manas's son Semetey and Chïnqojo takes place long after the action of this epic, after Manas has died.

p. 4: *Tulus from whom he took the river*: The Talas river is meant. In an earlier episode Saghïmbay claimed that the river's name originated from that of Manas's conquered foe.

p. 4: *emerged from the Altay . . . came charging down the Chüy valley*: Manas's movements mentioned here are the subject of earlier episodes of Saghïmbay's expanded *Manas* plot, before *The Memorial Feast for Kökötöy Khan*.

p. 5: *his uncle, his aged grandfather, Kökötöy*: These are terms of respect for an elder and are not meant literally. On the relationship between Manas and Kökötöy see the comparative note, "Kökötöy's relationship with Manas" (p. 289).

p. 5: *gray-maned*: This heroic epithet, usually applied to Manas, alludes to the mane of a mature male wolf.

p. 6: *my wife Ayïmkül*: On this woman and others named later see the comparative note, "Kökötöy's wives" (p. 289).

p. 7: *the Kirghiz of the six fathers*: This is not a known grouping in traditional tribal genealogies; Saghïmbay merely used the phrase to indicate the magnitude of Kökötöy's rule. In Kirghiz society communities were defined by genealogical descent from male ancestors. To express a leader's power in terms of the size of the population under his control, one could invoke the depth of shared ancestry of those related clans. "Six fathers" means that Kökötöy's Kirghiz subjects reckon common descent from six generations back, from the same great-great-great-great-grandfather.

p. 9: *don't have me shaved with a saber or washed with kumiss*: These two ancient-sounding funerary details also form part of Kökötöy's last behest in a nineteenth-century version of the epic (*MKNB*, ll. 56–7). The alcohol in kumiss would have acted as antimicrobial treatment for the lengthy interval before burial favored by Central Asian nomads.

p. 11: *Itaalï, the women of whom are human, but the men dogs*: In Saghïmbay's fanciful description of the Itaalï he may have been making use of the exotic name of Italy and the Italians. The peoples and places he names in association, Arabs, Mïsïr (Egypt) and Qudus (Jerusalem), confirm that he was imagining points west. Medieval accounts by the Italian travelers in Inner Asia John of Plano Carpini and Marco Polo of dog-headed people (though not dog-headed Italians!) circulated in Russia in Saghïmbay's time, and may have come to his notice via Central Asian orientalist circles.

p. 14: *a Ninety*: An offering of ninety horses is meant. For the Kirghiz, a "nine" of animals on the hoof, such as nine horses or nine camels, was a traditional form of a gift of honor, an offering, or a prize. Saghïmbay, intent on depicting the magnificence of his epic world, sometimes increased these quantities to nineties, or even ninety thousands.

p. 14: *the qibla*: The *qibla* is the direction from any point on the earth toward the geographical center of the Islamic world in Mecca. Sharia instructs Muslims to bury their dead in graves consisting of a rectangular pit at the bottom of which a niche is excavated on the side nearest the *qibla*. The body in its winding-sheet is placed in the niche on its right side, facing the *qibla*, and sealed in with bricks, then the grave is filled with earth. Here Saghïmbay (expressing either Kökötöy's confusion or his own) conflates the *qibla* orientation of the niche with the position of the body laid on its right side.

p. 15: *my wives*: The word translated here and elsewhere as "wives" in relation to Kökötöy is not formed as a plural in Kirghiz and can also be read as "wife." Kirghiz custom permitted a man to marry more than one wife simultaneously. See the comparative note, "Kökötöy's wives" (p. 289).

p. 15: *the elk*: The Eurasian elk is meant, the animal called moose in North America.

p. 17: *my dear Qanïshay*: The identity of this woman is ambiguous, either Boqmurun's bride, whom Kökötöy has already mentioned but not met, or a wife of Kökötöy with the same name, co-wife of Külayïm. See the comparative note, "Kökötöy's wives" (p. 289).

p. 17: *Oyrot with their red topknots*: The Oyrots' "topknots" reflect a system of insignia for official ranks in the Ch'ing dynasty, where the color of the finial on the wearer's hat indicated his rank or grade. In the eighteenth and nineteenth centuries the historical Kirghiz had seen Qalmaq leaders wearing such rank buttons, and some Kirghiz chiefs had received them from the Ch'ing as well.

p. 18: *gray hill*: The Kirghiz called an elevated place used for single combat by champions of opposing armies a "gray hill."

p. 20: *Those to the west will scorn you ... Our Lord is the creator, and no one else made us*: Saghïmbay places Christendom in his epic world.

p. 23: *he leaves no child*: Saghïmbay says literally "he leaves no child" when we have seen above that Kökötöy has daughters and – what matters for purposes of inheritance – a son, Boqmurun. Yet the statement bears a kernel of truth, as does Kökötöy's remark below, "I adopted the son of a spirit." See the comparative note, "Boqmurun son of Kökötöy Khan" (p. 292).

p. 24: *See that he doesn't try to breed his young ewes*: The Kirghiz original says literally, "See that he doesn't try to milk his lambs"; Saghïmbay's telegraphic phrasing leapt over the interval of time it takes for young female lambs to become mothers and produce milk.

p. 25: *my dear Ayghanïsh and Küljar I leave behind*: On these women and others named previously see the comparative note, "Kökötöy's wives" (p. 289).

p. 25: *I adopted the son of a spirit*: Boqmurun was Kökötöy's adopted son. See the comparative note, "Boqmurun son of Kökötöy Khan" (p. 292).

p. 25: *being Kirghiz by nature they must not remain as Qalmaqs*: Here Saghïmbay makes one of his plays on the term *Qalmaq*, which Central Asian Turkic peoples supposed came from their word *qal-* 'to remain', as if the Qalmaqs were those distant relatives whose ancestors had rejected Islam to remain heathen.

p. 25: *from the bride's legs and the shepherd's staff*: This is a Kirghiz proverb. A family's fortunes are said to come from these two things: the shepherd's staff, meaning how well he tends the flocks, and the bride's legs, meaning whether her arrival will bring happiness and progeny to the family. There was an old custom that on her first approach to the encampment of the bridegroom the bride must dismount from her horse and walk on her own two legs.

p. 27: *However much the expenses come to ... no one will be saddled with the cost*: Here is a first inkling that Baymïrza's report to Boqmurun on what Kökötöy said in his last testament includes ideas not explicitly expressed by Kökötöy. Baymïrza's own concern for reducing expenses has led him to distort Kökötöy's words, but not simply to call for modest observances, which Baymïrza wants. It would have been possible to quote Kökötöy's words selectively to justify such modesty. The disregard for costs that Baymïrza reports in Kökötöy's speech appears to be part of Baymïrza's manipulative attempt to cast doubt on Kökötöy's soundness of mind, which he continues to do below. Of course, Kökötöy's testament had in reality been contradictory and confusing enough that Baymïrza's caution seems not unwise. In the nineteenth century as well the epic bards had depicted controversy between Boqmurun and Baymïrza over the finances and fate of the bereft tribe in the face of Kökötöy's last testament. Saghïmbay's dramatization here is particularly creative. See the comparative note, "Kökötöy's testament" (pp. 290–91).

p. 28: *Qozu-bashï and Qopo*: Qozu-bashï, a pasture on the north slopes of the Ala-too range, and Qopo, a valley to its north, were favored as choice grazing grounds of this vicinity since at least the sixteenth century; here Saghïmbay contrasts their abundant herbage with a pair of pastures he imagines to be more frequented and thus not as nourishing for the herds.

p. 28: *The camels should have no rings put in their noses*: For caravanning.

p. 29: *the Qïtays are going to steal ... see what that will get them*: Here Baymïrza is overstating what Kökötöy said in his testament, but it resonates with the development of the plot. See the comparative note, "Predictions of trouble" (pp. 292–3).

2

Boqmurun Journeys to Consult Manas after Kökötöy's Death

p. 33: *Boqmurun Journeys ... after Kökötöy's Death*: The placement of headings such as this one appears to have been affected by the pace of work in the recording sessions. Saghïmbay likely forged ahead in singing a new "chapter," and the scribe only managed to write in the heading at this point.

p. 34: *My cattle of four kinds*: The nomads' traditional five kinds of cattle are here reckoned as four: horses, horned cattle, camels, and sheep plus goats.

p. 34: *Make it surpass all the world's memorial feasts*: Boqmurun is engaging in his own prevarications. Less artfully than Baymïrza above (pp. 27–9), the words Boqmurun puts in Kökötöy's mouth describe unambiguously the lavish observances that Boqmurun seems to want. His appeal to Manas is for help in stewarding the wealth that will be necessary to cover the outlay. See the comparative note, "Boqmurun consults Manas" (p. 293).

p. 35: *Musa ... Ïysa*: Saghïmbay gives the Arabic-derived Kirghiz names of the Islamic figures Moses and Jesus, drawing a religious distinction between those of the "religion of Ïysa" or Christians on one hand, and Muslims and Jews on the other. The ethno-religious and geopolitical divide between Muslims and Christians was a concern in the Russian-colonized Islamic Central Asia of Saghïmbay's day. Saghïmbay's point in these words spoken by Manas, that there are differences in religious doctrines, sets up Manas's instructions to Boqmurun on how to conduct proper obsequies for Kökötöy.

p. 35: *It has been only a short time ... Ayqojo ... customs surrounding death simply haven't arisen yet*: Manas's statements, "It has been only a short time since we entered the religion of Islam" and "customs surrounding death simply haven't arisen yet," appear to be Saghïmbay's way to head off Islamic doctrinal criticism of the funerary rituals to be depicted below. They display variance from sharia, particularly with respect to the timing of the burial (delaying longer than absolutely necessary) and the general pomp.

Ayqojo 'Moon-Khoja', a saint named in the nineteenth-century epics as well, was responsible, in Saghïmbay's telling of an earlier episode, for converting Manas to Islam.

3
Boqmurun Sends Out the Announcement

p. 39: *Boqmurun Sends Out the Announcement*: The placement and syntax of this heading allow one to read it as a clause linking the last words of Part 2 with the first words of Part 3, which suggests that Saghïmbay may have uttered it in performance. A more descriptive heading for this part would be, "Boqmurun Conducts the Burial, Two Feasts and Horse Races in Honor of Kökötöy." Though lavish, the feasting in this section, at Tashken, is but a prelude to the grand memorial feast at Qarqïra.

pp. 41–2: *sheep ... Goats ... without a care in the world*: The comparison of high-maintenance sheep and worry-free goats is based on realities of life for herding people.

p. 42: *Qara-qulja is a narrow place*: The valley of the Qara-qulja, headstream of the Chatqal river, evokes the uttermost cranny of mountain pasture that a ruler of Tashkent could fill with cattle without having to send them over a high pass.

p. 44: *Now let's try and list ... the companions of Manas*: In cataloguing Manas's Forty Companions Saghïmbay often got very close to forty names. This was not a given for a good oral bard; in the nineteenth century the lists, even at their stateliest in the form of invocations, were much shorter. When they are named, Manas's closest friend and companion Almambet and his close kinsman and ally Baqay are normally thought of as separate from the Forty, since those two ranked well above the ordinary companions.

p. 44: *the name Serek*: The origin of the hero-name Serek is uncertain, as is Saghïmbay's point in alluding to its meaning.

p. 45: *Tashken ... some distance from the town walls*: In this paragraph Saghïmbay appears to construct an incomplete bridge of thought connecting a political nuance about the status of the ruler of Tashken with a description of nomad guest accommodations. The point may be that Manas would expect only to be put up in a yurt outside the walls of Tashken, since while Kökötöy was alive and on the throne Manas had not conquered the city for himself.

p. 45: *wands of fig-wood in their hands*: The wands of fig-wood in the mourners' hands may reflect a mourning custom of bending down the twig-tips of fruit trees, recorded in mid-nineteenth-century Kirghiz epic (*MKNB*, ll. 166–9) as well as in a lament sung by Saghïmbay at the memorial feast of a real chief in 1912.

p. 48: *keperet ... buraq at*: Saghïmbay, who had some Islamic education, uses language in this paragraph that is rich with the vocabulary of burial ritual. For translations see the comparative note, "The burial and the fortieth-day feast" (pp. 294–5).

p. 49: *a legacy that has come down from him*: In a sense the legacy of this legendary singer, Manas's companion Ïrchï Uul, stretched to Saghïmbay himself, who was a sought-after performer of funeral laments. The rich garner that Ïrchï Uul 'Singer Boy' gained for his short lament sounds like a sly dig by Saghïmbay at patrons who rewarded him less for longer compositions.

p. 50: *came to Kengdi-badang; on the mountains north of Anjïyan*: Andijan (Andijon, Uzbekistan) is farther away from Tashkent than Kanibadam (Konibodom, Tajikistan), so the positions of the two mentioned places in relation to the finish line of the race at Tashken do not make sense in this passage, even allowing for an exaggerated scale.

p. 52: *try to pay attention ... you mullahs who are recording Manas*: Saghïmbay admonishes his scribes while singing.

p. 54: *Thirty of his menial bond-women ... Kökötöy's wives had become widows ... when someone had died ... scandal for the Kirghiz*: In this passage Saghïmbay seems to converse for a moment with the audience in the act of performance, as the scribe dutifully kept writing. Thus Saghïmbay's words in the apparent exchange have become part of the text of the epic. At issue were the Kirghiz words used to denote slaves, an area of vocabulary that, by 1925, was supposed to have been in disuse after six decades of Tsarist and Bolshevik prohibition of slavery. There was no gender-neutral word in Kirghiz available to mean "slave," which seems to have put Saghïmbay in difficulties with his intended counts. The first word he used for the thirty slaves put up as prizes, *chor*, means "bond-women" or "slave-women," but the bard then went on to specify that the thirty slaves included fifteen women (*küng*) and fifteen men (*qul*). By this point he was apparently in conversation with the audience, who may have shared his diffidence about the exact terminology, if not indeed about the whole subject of slavery. Saghïmbay also thought better of the allotment of those thirty slaves as the first prize, a level of luxury that might make the scene seem even more scandalous; a little later he says that they were "apportioned out for the next nine horses." The bard's compositional difficulties show that this bit of narration probably was not traditional (there is no echo of it in the mid-nineteenth-century texts), but rather part of Saghïmbay's own creative efforts to embellish the grandeur of the traditional epic.

The seemingly non-sequitur remark about Kökötöy's widows amid the discussion of slaves actually evinces a large household suddenly no longer in need of the labor (and, perhaps, female companionship) provided by the slaves to the deceased head of the family. Without touching the widows' own slaves, the heir could take the opportunity afforded by the man's death to give the unemployed menial slaves away as prizes at the feast games, burnishing his prestige and further relieving himself of the on-going expenses of their upkeep. This is perhaps what "all the sons of the Kirghiz" used to do, if they possessed slaves, according to Saghïmbay in this aside.

p. 56: *tenth was Or-qïzïl ... Sïnchïbek's*: This is the second horse named Or-qïzïl mentioned; above (p. 51) there was one that belonged to Jügörü.

p. 59: *Suu-samïr ... Sayram*: The places mentioned in this paragraph, lying within a radius of about six hundred kilometers from Tashkent, describe an epically large area of pastures available to the ruler.

4
Boqmurun Assembles the People and Takes
Counsel on Holding Kökötöy's Memorial
Feast

p. 63: *all kinds of groves . . . lots of space*: Guests arriving at a town with insufficient indoor accomodation would be bedded down in the surrounding orchards and groves.

5
Boqmurun Sets His Entire People Migrating
and Goes to Qarqïra to Hold Kökötöy's
Memorial Feast

p. 67: *moderately wealthy men*: The term was familiar to the Kirghiz from the vocabulary of communism in the 1920s, which had been translated from Russian into their own language for propaganda purposes. In this rare instance where he used a term from contemporary affairs, Saghïmbay's intent seems to have been ironic.

p. 67: *the young ewes he had left unbred*: The Kirghiz text speaks not of unbred ewes but of unmilked lambs; see p. 241 above (note to p. 24).

p. 68: *the hand of Manas in the goings-on*: Saghïmbay reminds the audience that Manas had counseled Boqmurun on planning (pp. 35–6 above); however, that counsel as narrated by Saghïmbay did not extend to these preparations for the grand memorial feast.

pp. 68–9: *This cavalcade . . . thundering herds of horses*: On the route to the feasting ground at Qarqïra see the comparative note, "The feasting ground, Boqmurun's itinerary, and timing" (pp. 297–8).

p. 69: *Eshik and Türgön . . . sending men on ahead earlier*: Saghïmbay implies here that the migrating nomads have their planned grain harvest brought in at Eshik and Türgön to take along as provision for the feast.

6
Bokmurun Mounts Aydar on Maani-ker and
Sends Him to Invite the People

p. 76: *lungs like sieves*: The image in this phrase, literally "sieve-lunged" in the original, refers to a round sieve of very large diameter, of a sort used to process bulk grain. The basis of the equation seems to be the untensil's great size.

p. 77: *If you do not come to my feast I'm going to get nasty*: Boqmurun's threats to his invitees are a fixture of the traditional epic. Though grotesquely harsh and violent, the threats were not pure hyperbole; the success of the memorial feast was a high-stakes, serious affair for Boqmurun. See the comparative note, "The invitations and threats" (p. 295).

p. 78 *shatter the door-frame of your yurt*: An attacker's act of smashing the door-frame of his victim's yurt has long-standing existential significance in Inner Asian traditions. Mentioned in the nineteenth-century *Manas* epics and as early as the thirteenth-century *Secret History of the Mongols*, it was a poetic way to communicate the utter destruction of an enemy house and people.

p. 78: *trample . . . underfoot like felting-wool*: Felt is made by laying out an area of unspun wool on a mat, rolling it up, and stepping on it repeatedly.

p. 79: *second to none*: The original says literally, "his face untouched by clods," i.e. clods thrown up by the hooves of faster horses than his.

p. 83: *Joloy and Ushang . . . Let Joloy train up Ach-buudan and choose a jockey*: This invitation and the accompanying threats begin in regard to two Infidel chiefs, Joloy and Ushang, but by the end it is explicit that the addressee is Joloy alone. Saghïmbay is attempting to bundle Ushang, a hero new to the tradition in this telling, into a speech relating to Joloy. Similar doublings-up occur in the invitations that follow.

p. 88: *By the time nine months had gone by*: On the timing of the feast and its preparations see the comparative note, "The feasting ground, Boqmurun's itinerary, and timing" (pp. 298–9).

p. 88: *out to the distance of second cousins*: The Kirghiz expression in the text literally means "sons of three fathers," which in this context means descendants of Boqmurun's great-grandfather. This is not a great distance in the Kirghiz reckoning of relatedness; the audience would imagine this set of family members as those who would be "at home" for a large party prior to the arrival of the actual guests. See pp. 239–40 above (note to p. 7).

7
The People Arrive at Kökötöy's Memorial Feast

p. 94: *on the point of executing the lad there and then*: The harsh treatment for Boqmurun's herald is found in the older tradition as well. See the comparative note, "Manas's companions' cruelty to Jash Aydar" (pp. 295–6).

p. 95: *casting knucklebones*: The game of *ordo*, where players use the blocky knucklebones of cows and sheep as pieces, is laid out and played somewhat like marbles, though on a larger scale, and the bones are thrown rather than rolled. It was and is a favorite pastime of Kirghiz boys and young men; Manas and his companions play it in the nineteenth-century epics as well.

8
Manas Arrives at Kökötöy's Memorial Feast

p. 98: *held aloft sixty jaysangs*: The Qalmaq *jaysang* was a military officer; what is held aloft here are apparently the banners of sixty units commanded by *jaysangs* previously taken in battle.

p. 99: *Boqmurun the Snot-Nose, "It-Fazes-Me-Not"-Nose*: Saghïmbay's play on Kirghiz words here comes through clearly in English thanks to the coincidence that the pairs of words in play actually rhyme in both languages. The text reads:

> *Kökötöydün Boqmurun,*
> *köngüldö qayghï joq murun.*

There are no fixed rhyme patterns in Kirghiz epic poetry, though rhyming effects occur frequently.

p. 99: *Salam . . . Alik*: The greetings draw on the Arabic exchange *Assalāmu ʿalaykum! – Wa ʿalaykumu ʾs-salām!*

p. 100: *Shish . . . Iskender, Sulayman*: Seth; Alexander; Solomon.

p. 102: *The maiden Torum's palatial white tent . . . the hero now entered*: Given the presence at the feast of Manas's chief wedded wife Qanïkey (narrated later on) this scene where Manas is given lodging in the tent of a maiden is incongruous, though it has traditional roots. See the comparative note, "The hospitality Manas receives at the feast" (p. 299).

p. 103: *a keen judge of warriors ... came to perform his assessment*: The *sïnchï* or appraiser was an important expert who scrutinized weapons and armor, horses, hunting birds, and other valuables that could be taken and distributed as war booty – and the qualities of warriors themselves. Speeches describing inspections by *sïnchï* were widely heeded; an example in this poem is Qoshoy's appraisal of horses before the joust (pp. 195–7).

p. 104: *Jabiniyin jaghï*: This phrase is Saghïmbay's imagining of the foreign language spoken by Chaghïray.

p. 104: *camels down on their knees ... campaign-tents loaded onto black nar camel-bulls*: The scene described here suggests that many guests had rapidly judged the feast to be a dud and were getting ready to leave before it properly began. Baqay's arrival presently, not Manas's the previous day, seems to have got the party going.

9
Qongurbay, in a Huff, Demands Maani-ker from Boqmurun

p. 109: *Ütügüngö shooday ... Amininge danim*: These phrases are Saghïmbay's imagining of the foreign language Joloy speaks, based in part on obscene words in Qalmaq.

p. 109: *Laaylama*: The term, a divine name invoked by Heathens, may reflect *Dalai Lama*.

p. 111: *his muzzle, it's like a marten-trap*: The image of the horse's gracefully proportioned head is suggested by the elongated triangular profile of a deadfall constructed of two logs for fur trapping.

p. 111: *our qalday*: Qongurbay is meant.

p. 113: *swine*: Swine were abhorrent to the pork-avoiding Muslims.

p. 115: *The earth submits ... so do many*: Although traces of these lines are found also in a mid-nineteenth-century version of the epic (*MK*wr, ll. 819–21), Saghïmbay's symmetrical formulation (after the emendation of one vowel) captures the underlying stoicism of the thought better than the earlier bard's lines.

p. 120: *my racer ... my horse*: Manas (or Saghïmbay) seems to be forgetting that Boqmurun's horse is at issue.

p. 121: *Jabuu ... möndü*: These words are traditional Kirghiz impressions of Qalmaq "gibberish" based on Qalmaq words.

10
The Horses Are Paraded; The Racing-Prizes
Are Announced

p. 126: *For a payment of ten gold ingots ... a proclamation free of falsehood*: The herald Ïrchï Uul is such a highly paid official at the feast because he has to remember and accurately recite the details of dozens of prizes amid a throng of people who could raise disputes if a prize given at the finish of an event differed from the one announced at the start. Ïrchï Uul's second, the young messenger Jash Aydar, perhaps is due a share of the honorarium at the commencement of the horse race for his having successfully journeyed and summoned so many worthy guests to enter their racers. Saghïmbay, in his prime, was in demand as a herald at memorial feasts.

p. 126: *the Night of Power*: This is the Muslim holy night commemorating the revelation of the Qur'an to Muhammad.

p. 127: *work-horses and nags ... The horses' fat should fit them snugly*: The differing intentions that Manas expresses to himself and to Almambet would both be served by a spell of bad weather: the excess of weak horses would be made unfit to start, and wellconditioned horses would be brought into the peak of leanness for racing. These calculations and Almambet's use of weather magic to achieve the results are new to the tradition with Saghïmbay's telling.

p. 127: *Barayïz*: The divine precepts of Islam (known as *farā'iḍ* in Arabic), which summarize Muslims' duties for right living as commanded by God, are here used by Almambet as magic spells. The extraordinary mixture of Islamic faith with other religions and sorcery in this incantation shows Saghïmbay's venturesome and at times irreverent creativity.

p. 127: *weather-conjuring stone*: Such stones were fixtures of Inner Asian weather magic.

p. 130: *seven years beneath the earth ... seven days previous*: Er Töshtük's adventures in the underworld with his horse Chal-quyruq were legendary in Central Asian Turkic cultures. The epic formula "who had spent fully seven years beneath the earth, and had come back to the surface a mere seven days previous" appears above in reference to Töshtük himself, in the scene where the hero makes his entrance (p. 92). The "seven days previous" makes no literal sense by now, a whole month having passed at the feast. Traditional audiences of oral composition in performance received the formulaic content of such expressions with no apparent contradictions in their literal sense.

p. 130: *joined in to the sound of plaints and grieving*: The plaints and grieving seem to be a further allusion to the underworld adventures just mentioned, specifically the loss of six of Chal-quyruq's lives. However, grammatically it is the steed itself that is making the plaints and grieving. Horses with human speech and emotions are rare in Kirghiz epic poetry, but are more common in the south Siberian traditions with which the Er Töshtük legend shares some of its plot.

p. 130: *At which point will they turn for home*: A Central Asian horse race was run on a simple out-and-back course; besides the locations of the start/finish (naturally situated by the feasting ground) and the turning-place, fixed layout was minimal.

p. 132: *Sart of Samarqan*: See the comparative note, "A traditional epithet of Manas" (p. 301).

p. 133: *Türküstön*: This is the city of Turkistan near the Syr Darya, now in Kazakhstan.

p. 133: *The number of marshals was sixty . . . keep them from getting lost*: The sixty men tasked with managing the race carry lances to fence in the horses as they line up to start. In actual races there were said to be an average of three marshals per hundred entrants. The image of a starting line the length of sixty lowered lances conforms with the enormous scale of this make-believe feast. The marshals then rode after the pack and assisted racers in trouble. The six thousand escorts went out to line the route of the home stretch, which was run partially in darkness over the last night of the race, according to Manas's plan.

II

Shooting the Ingot

p. 137: *try to shoot it down*: In a version of the actual game similar to what is described here, the crossbar of a pole about ten meters tall had several long hairs from a horse's tail tied to it, which were used to hang an ingot of valuable metal. Marksmen tried to sever the hairs with their shots, and the shooter who cut the last tie and brought the ingot to the ground won it as his prize.

p. 139: *the common folk went further up . . . took their seats all around*: The spectators have spread up the hillsides to get a clear view.

p. 139: *Manas, the panther*: The term "panther" in this translation stands for a Kirghiz word, *qabïlan*, that may signify a tiger, a lion, a leopard, or some other large predator. It is an appellation of heroes, mainly Manas.

p. 141: *tucking away the falcon-hood*: The figurative expression, taken from hunting with birds of prey, means a preparation for swift, decisive action.

p. 141: *as if plucking a goat carcass off the ground*: Such a maneuver with a goat carcass was familiar to Saghïmbay's audience from buzkashi, a game that is well known in Central Asia today. However, that sport is not narrated in the *Kökötöy* epic (either in Saghïmbay's or in the nineteenth-century versions); heroes did not play all the same sports as common herdsmen.

p. 145: *put that problem to rest*: The problem was that the ingot had been secured with forty-two ties; each of the Forty Companions severed a tie with his one shot. This left two cords holding the ingot, and Manas the last marksman.

pp. 145–6: *everybody to a man was there … but never mind them*: The catalogue of heroes in attendance that crops up here seems little motivated by the plot, and may have been Saghïmbay's way of re-engaging a flagging audience or summarizing the setting for an important person who had just arrived at his performance. See the comparative note, "Catalogues of heroes and peoples" (p. 291).

p. 146: *these one thousand and seventy years*: The chronological reference is obscure. By reckoning back from the performance date of AD 1925 in the Gregorian calendar, 1,070 years previous was 855, a date fairly close to the conquest of the Uighur Kaghanate by the Kirghiz in 840. Published orientalist scholarship on the role played in that event by the medieval Kirghiz of Siberia could have reached Saghïmbay in some form, and the ethnic name shared with the poet's own people may have been the basis of the idea in this allusion (though the Siberian Kirghiz were not Muslims). The Kirghiz words for "one thousand and seventy years" scan better in the line than would "one thousand and eighty years" or "one thousand and eighty-five years," which suggests Saghïmbay may have first sung the line around 1910 and left it unchanged thereafter.

12
Qoshoy and Joloy Wrestle; Qoshoy Beats Joloy

p. 152: *blue smoke poured from his pipe ... windpipe gurgled like rushing water*: For Muslim Kirghiz, whose tobacco use was restricted to snuff, the rough breathing of smokers was distinctive of Heathens.

pp. 153–4: *Such a little devil ... Those are very bad things you're saying*: Qoshoy's sense of outrage is at such vaunting of Joloy being heard coming from the mouths of Muslim heroes, Ürbü and Kökchö.

p. 160: *when the Heathens and Muslims were equals*: On Muslim and Infidel heroes' ideas about their relative power see the comparative note, "Opposed world-views and looking-glass enemies" (pp. 307–10).

p. 161: *a pair of trousers*: The Kirghiz word translated here as "pair of trousers," *qandaghay*, denotes trousers made of ibex hide, a tough, soft, elastic leather favored by hunters and sportsmen.

p. 162: *his heel got stuck*: There were two styles of wrestling breeches in Kirghiz epics. The older style was the *qandaghay*, cut from the chamois leather of the ibex and designed to fit the wearer's legs as closely as possible ("that stretch when you pull them and snap back when you let go," p. 161), to deny the opponent the advantage of a hand-hold. A newer design trend called for such a voluminous expanse of material that the wearer's opponent gained no mechanical advantage even if he could – and he certainly could – get a hand-hold. Saghïmbay's narration inherits the tight style of breeches from earlier tradition but plays with aspects of the baggy-legged style, as here with the trousers that Kökchö had on for everyday wear and lent to Qoshoy.

p. 162: *force her to ride a blood-bay virgin mare*: A way to shame a woman was to make her ride on a blood-bay mare that had never foaled.

p. 164: *He must not slash ... hand her back to him*: It makes little sense in the narrative for Qoshoy to employ the exact same run of threats twice in rapid succession, first above positively toward Kökchö's wife, then here forbidding the same actions toward Qanïkey. See the comparative note, "The wrestling breeches" (p. 303).

pp. 164–5: *if I am angered I will kill her ... than see Qanïkey's face or enter her house again*: On Manas's egregious condemnation of Qanïkey see the comparative note, "The wrestling breeches" (p. 303).

p. 165: *plunged into darkness, unaware of the world*: On the death-like trance and vision see the comparative note, "The wrestling breeches" (pp. 302–3).

p. 165: *it came to me again*: The word translated as "again," *jangi*, also means "newly, for the first time." Given the uncertainties in this passage in the original language, Saghïmbay's intent is difficult to determine. The information being introduced here, the steps in Qanïkey's manufacture of the breeches, was openly talked about in the mid-nineteenth-century versions of the epic; thus the tradition, at least, suggests that the knowledge came to Chalïbay "again."

p. 166: *thread plaited snake-belly fashion*: Plaiting of the type called *jïlan boor* 'snake-belly' is the weave ordinarily used for the rawhide quirts on horse-lashes, about one centimeter thick. Its evocation here as a method of plaiting thread for invisibly fine seams reinforces the extremely high level of workmanship on these breeches.

p. 166: *hardened steel filed down for quilting into the leather*: Quilting iron filings into cells in double-layered leather garments was known in the late nineteenth and early twentieth centuries, but the sport for which such garments were made was jousting, where the filings would damp the impact of a lance-thrust. Such a garment did not allow much range of movement; as Saghïmbay says, it could not be folded, though the working-over by seventy strong-men may be the poet's epic notion to restore flexibility.

p. 166: *Let my esteemed elder Qoshoy wear them ... his blessing would help me*: On Qanïkey's wish in the context of Saghïmbay's narrative design see the comparative note, "The wrestling breeches" (pp. 302–3).

p. 168: *They slathered rubber cement ... the seams gave about a span*: The stretchy property of modern rubber cement presented Saghïmbay with an opportunity to play up the doctoring of the seams of the breeches to give Qoshoy a better fit and greater freedom of movement in wrestling.

p. 170: *fated to suffer with hard work and servitude*: Qoshoy alludes to Qanïkey's hard times after Manas's death.

pp. 170–71: *Allah, grant my wish ... let him slay Khan Qongur*: Unfortunately no recordings of Saghïmbay's version of *Semetey*, the sequel to *Manas*, survive. The plot points from that epic alluded to here appear close to the nineteenth-century tradition. There Semetey does have Külchoro for a companion and does kill Abïke and Köbösh, the treacherous half-brothers of the late Manas, and Qanïkey herself kills Manas's father Jaqïp, who took their side. Semetey also kills his father's Forty Companions, a spiritual disaster for him. He does not, however, kill Qongurbay in the nineteenth-century texts.

p. 171: *everyone standing round*: The original text says, "the Heathens and Muslims standing round," but this could not be the literal sense when Qoshoy's prayer has just invoked the future slayer of the Infidels' chief hero. The phrase "Heathens and Muslims," in the context of the great gathering at Kökötöy's memorial feast, suggests "everyone standing round," in a looser and narrower sense.

p. 173: *In the valley of Ükürchü ... In a valley of the Qulja mountains*: The identifiable places that Qoshoy mentions in his taunt are located around the border between the Kirghiz and the Qalmaqs, not far from Qarqira.

p. 176: *some kind of poison*: Poison here means something painful, or a strong medicine, in an ironic sense; Qoshoy perversely gets some benefit from Joloy's grips.

p. 178: *I was afraid he wouldn't manage*: The original means literally, "I was submerged in a feeling of regret over unfulfilled desires."

p. 179: *two mangy bald-heads ... butt heads together*: This was an actual game.

13
Oronghu Untethers the Camels; The Mangy Bald-Heads Fight

p. 181: *Oronghu Untethers the Camels; The Mangy Bald-Heads Fight*: Though it is announced in the heading, a contest of mangy bald-heads does not take place in this part, just as it did not in the last; also a game takes place in this part that is not mentioned in the heading.

p. 181: *camel-woman down on all fours*: Camels copulate in a kneeling posture, and the Kirghiz word here refers specifically to the position of the camel cow during mating.

p. 181: *let the onlookers satisfy their curiosity*: Like head-butting above, the game played here had a real basis, though it was more for onlookers' amusement than for the contestants' glory. See the comparative note, "Sex games" (pp. 304–5).

p. 182: *Mardikeleng*: This character, who earlier had stood unchallenged for the mangy bald-heads' butting contest, appears in this scene to an extent that reveals the satirical sense of his name. *Mardikeleng* (not found in the nineteenth-century epics) is a Kirghiz rendition of the Persian *mard-i kalān* 'huge man', here obviously 'well-endowed man'.

p. 182: *a nine of camels and a hundred and one sleek cattle*: This reckoning of the prize is quite different from what was just posted above; bards (and heralds) strove to avoid such errors.

p. 184: *She pulled out the camels' pegs*: The traditional game called for the nude female contestant to untie the camel's rope at the stake with her teeth; Saghïmbay thus implies that Oronghu pulled out the stakes with her teeth instead.

p. 184: *the torrid dog days of summer*: On the timing of the feast see the comparative note, "The feasting ground, Boqmurun's itinerary, and timing" (p. 298).

14
Manas and Qongurbay Joust;
Manas Lances Qongurbay

p. 187: *Alooke called his people to listen ... since former times*: The structures of speeches in this parley among infidel heroes present textual problems that nevertheless show Saghïmbay's skill at creating scenes that were new to the epic. See the comparative note, "Infidels' counsels" (pp. 305–7).

p. 188: *the old religion*: What is meant is the religion of the Heathens, which predated the appearance of Islam.

p. 188: *these people's*: Alooke refers to the Muslims as "these people."

p. 188: *we have witnessed ... experts at jousting*: We have not literally witnessed jousting yet, as that event is just about to begin.

p. 188: *heathens sparing with their thoughts*: From the present perspective of non-Muslims, the Muslims are heathens.

p. 189: *We sent Joloy out ... that bully Manas*: Saghïmbay inappropriately places Manas in the previous day's wrestling-bout instead of the Muslims' victorious champion, Qoshoy.

p. 190: *Heathens*: Here Qongurbay calls his hearers, his own co-religionists, heathens, perhaps with some disdain in the Muslim Saghïmbay's idea of the scene.

p. 192: *Qalcha with the bulging eyes*: Qongurbay's by-name Qalcha is also a pejorative word in Kirghiz for facial features marked by the high-bridged nose of the Qalcha or Pamiri ethnic group. The imagery works best on the level of emphasizing the hideous countenance of the foreign enemy; *adïrayghan* 'with bulging eyes' enhances the basic grotesqueness. Saghïmbay seems to be the first epic bard to use the by-name Qalcha for the khan of the Qïtay.

p. 192: *Rüstöm Dastan*: Saghïmbay inserts a learned allusion to Rustam of Iranian epic (*dāstān*).

p. 195: *Stupidity has always been our fault*: This opinion sounds more like an early twentieth-century Muslim's than a traditional Kirghiz epic hero's. Saghïmbay speaks ruefully from his knowledge of the contemporary world where Heathendom eclipsed Islam. See the comparative note, "Opposed world-views and looking-glass enemies" (p. 309)

p. 197: *Aq-qula's huge saddle-cloth*: Apparently Aq-qula was outfitted and entered in the horse race with lightweight saddle and tack, different from the war equipment being brought out now.

p. 198: *Laaylamaluu*: This is another form of the divine name Laaylama.

15
Wrestling on Horseback

p. 204: *Along the banks of the Qarqïra ... stretched to Tötö pass*: To the extent that the place names are known, much of this delineation of an expanse of territory wide enough to hold a multitude of people is quite realistic.

16
The Finish of the Horse Race

p. 207: *a race course that was six days outbound ... mounted up for the finish*: Seven days having elapsed, at this point the spectators begin to snap out of their leisurely feasting rhythm and get ready for the main spectacle, the finish of the horse race. According to Manas's plan, the race course was measured at six days' running outbound from Qarqïra to Türküstön, then back over the same ground faster for two days and a night to the finish (the implied speed of the racers is exaggerated in line with the enormous distance). Nights were spent resting between day stages, until the last, when the racers ran through the night to finish in the morning. Racing at night was only possible near the finish, where escorts with flags could ride out from the feasting ground and line the route to prevent jockeys' straying from the course. The escorts had already gone out at the start of the race, and presumably took their time to set up the home stretch.

p. 207: *Buruts who have long been under our sway*: On Muslim and Infidel heroes' ideas about their relative power see the comparative note, "Opposed world-views and looking-glass enemies" (pp. 307–10).

p. 208: *We didn't finish off Qoshoy of the Qataghan before*: This apparently alludes not to the wrestling match that Qoshoy won in this poem, but to past conflicts where Qoshoy led Muslim forces against the Infidels.

p. 208: *I fear they will attack Tüp Beejin*: Qongurbay's fear anticipates the sequel to *The Memorial Feast for Kökötöy Khan*, the epic called *The Great Campaign*, where Manas's forces attack Tüp Beejin.

p. 209: *if the sons of Türk lock horns*: In this epic, the Qalmaqs are understood to be among the sons of the Türks. See the comparative note, "Opposed world-views and looking-glass enemies" (p. 309).

p. 209: *How could I call them kindred*: No one has asked Joloy to call the Buruts (Kirghiz) his kindred in so many words; nevertheless he is rebutting an explicit proposition made in this parley: the idea of ancient kinship between the Qalmaqs and Kirghiz, which was disrupted by the difference in religion. Joloy's words hark back to that plane of kinship through the ancestral Türks. See the comparative note, "Opposed world-views and looking-glass enemies" (p. 309).

p. 209: *Apsap shooday . . . aminine*: Joloy speaks untranslated words in his own language, as Saghïmbay imagined it, based in part on obscene words in Qalmaq.

p. 213: *after him Alooke's Nar-qïzïl*: Above (p. 212) Saghïmbay said Aq-qula was following seven other horses, which ought to put Aq-qula, not Alooke's Nar-qïzïl, next after Qarach's Jar-qïzïl.

p. 213: *I took Kökchö's advice and am the worse off for it*: Saghïmbay has observed the less than trusting relations among horse owners, trainers, and jockeys: any one of these with a losing horse can always think of one of the other two to blame.

p. 214: *the course of the broad Ile*: The locations mentioned so far correspond to the lower Chu, not the Ili.

p. 214: *the haulers-in*: Blatant interference by supporters was permitted, including having mounted men pull a horse ahead of others. Here the leading horses' haulers-in have gone out from the finish line to meet their racers and are now doing their work at the front of the pack.

p. 214: *Qongurbay took off, spurring Al'-ghara to a gallop*: This seems to be inconsistent with the scene above where Manas took Al'-ghara away from Qongurbay and did not give the horse back after defeating him in the joust.

p. 215: *Ütügüngö shooday*: Joloy speaks untranslated words, in Saghïmbay's understanding of obscene words in Qalmaq.

17
The Qïtay–Qalmaqs Make Off with the
Prize; The Ensuing Battle

p. 220: *my horse*: Qonghurbay (or Saghïmbay) seems to be forgetting that Ach-buudan is Joloy's horse.

p. 221: *this raving Kirghiz could ignore the mighty Qïtay*: In the Qïtay view, the Kirghiz display a new arrogance. See the comparative note, "Opposed world-views and looking-glass enemies" (p. 308).

p. 222: *Er Boqmurun ... set out in pursuit of the Infidels*: Saghïmbay, unlike the bards in the mid-nineteenth century, found ways for Boqmurun to act heroically at the end of the epic. See the comparative note, "Boqmurun's final act" (pp. 310–11).

p. 223: *unharmed for now*: Earlier Manas had threatened to kill Ajïbay and Chalïbay over the affair of the wrestling breeches (p. 165).

p. 224: *our home is at Sümbö*: It is not clear why this should be the Infidels' one reply to Manas's imminent threat. It may have been an appeal for clemency by the Qalmaqs based on the sanctity of the Buddhist monastery at Sümbö near Qarqïra. The monastery existed until 1864, when it was sacked and burned by Kirghiz and Qazaq raiders.

p. 224: *slaughter a great number of hogs ... liquor – the strongest kind*: The Infidels have missed their pork and hard liquor while being entertained at the Muslims' feast.

p. 225: *jabuu*: This untranslated word is a traditional Kirghiz representation of Qalmaq "gibberish."

p. 226: *when they say "Taa" it means "Strike"*: The Chinese word *t'a* means "Strike!" as an order to administer corporal punishment. Saghïmbay may have learned this during his stay in China as a refugee.

p. 227: *gave their leave*: It is not said in the text who gave Boqmurun leave to go out and challenge Qongurbay. The plurals "they" and "their" are not explicit in the text either.

p. 228: *I infiltrated their army last night*: This is news as far as the text is concerned, because Boqmurun's reconnaissance has not been narrated. See the comparative note, "Boqmurun's final act" (p. 311).

p. 229: *Manas has not defeated him*: Manas has defeated Qongurbay twice: in the rout of all the Infidels after Qongurbay demanded Maani-ker from Boqmurun, and one on one in the jousting match. However, the poet means here that Manas has not defeated

Qongurbay in battle, which the Kirghiz text expresses as a verb distinct from "to rout" or "to beat at jousting."

p. 235: *drove them all here*: Joloy, having taken a different route home and not seen the fighting that has just taken place, is unaware that the stolen herds will not be arriving at his encampment; they have been abandoned by the Infidels and recovered by the Kirghiz.

p. 235: *Ayghanïsh by name*: The name Ayghanïsh is different from the one Joloy used above for his wife, Qïyash, in his message of instructions to his encampment. If Saghïmbay has not simply made up two names for this minor heroine in two different places, he may be intentionally distinguishing two women by their descriptions, Qïyash "beautiful wife" and Ayghanïsh "knowing wife with second sight." In his own epic in the nineteenth century Joloy has two wives, but their names are different from these, they have a close relationship, and they are not distinguished by the attributes "beautiful" and "knowing."

pp. 235–6: *Those who quarreled . . . remained . . . but you never leave off your quarreling*: "remained" is *qal-maq bolup*, the verb form *qal-maq* 'to remain' being to Kirghiz understanding of the origin of the ethnic name Qalmaq; "never leave off" is *qal-baghan*, with the same verb root. Ayghanïsh's pun implies that "Qalmaq" (as if from *qal-maq* 'to remain, leave off') is something of a misnomer for Joloy.

p. 236: *though your ancestor was Manghul, your quarreling has never stopped*: This sentence, a seeming non sequitur, is a pun similar to the one on *qal-maq* 'to remain' explained in the previous note. The ethnic name Manghul 'Mongol' can be understood in Kirghiz as if it consists of the words *mang + qul* or *–ghul*. The second element means "slave"; the first means "hashish," or "confused, indecisive," and is the basis of a number of Kirghiz idioms such as *mang bash* 'dull, stupid' (literally 'hashish-head'). Saghïmbay implied that Manghul meant "addle-headed slave" or "slave to hashish," "hasish addict," and thus the contrast between the quarrelsomeness of Joloy and the drugged passivity of his forebear makes ironic sense.

p. 238: *the four heroes who had directed the memorial feast*: These heroes have not been named as directors of the feast until now. See the comparative note, "Four directors" (p. 311).

p. 238: *the yellow went out of all the Qalmaqs' and Qïtays' faces*: A racial stereotype regarding the skin color of East Asian people is the least problematic of alternative readings of the text.

Introduction to a
Reading of the Tradition

FUNDAMENTALS OF THE PLOT

The plot of the traditional epic *The Memorial Feast for Kökötöy Khan* sat at the juncture of a tangle of tense problems. In its most basic and perhaps original form, the epic's dilemma was a perennial one facing the successors of a deceased Inner Asian nomad chief. They could hold the tribe together by distributing wealth generously among the people (anticipating that poor nomads, if uncared for, could easily move off to seek better fortunes elsewhere), or they could spend modestly and husband the herds and other resources for several months in order to build up a lavish spread and a rich prize purse for the dead leader's great memorial feast and games. The latter option was not a frivolous one, nor was it a measure aimed primarily at mass amusement. Feasting was a political as well as a ritual activity, where the future status and even independence of the tribe could be decided by the number and status of the chiefs – relatives, allies, or foes – whom the president of the feast persuaded or commanded to attend. Even more than hospitality and ritual, the principal attractions inducing these personages to show up were the sporting contests, especially horse racing. This offered guests a chance at the prizes and, intangible but even more important, prospects for winning vicarious glory through the exploits of their choicest horseflesh. The feast's president, and by extension the tribe, stood to gain the high repute of having sheltered and regaled all the powerful guests, a form of prestige that had strong political overtones.

Thus the fiscal problem facing the dead chief's successors was stark: either spend on behalf of the common folk to keep the departed leader's hard-won polity together, at a cost to the impression one could make on one's chiefly peers at the feast, or save up for a rich feast in anticipation of a boost in external standing, thereby possibly alienating the base of common labor and military support upon which local power rested. An idealized solution to this problem was a special kind of leader: a hero. The *quality* of heroism in Inner Asian nomad thought thus provided a way to resolve the problem of *quantity* in the political economy surrounding the successors of a dead chief. This may help to explain why the Kirghiz have a large-scale, complex epic about a memorial feast. In Saghïmbay's version of the epic, when Boqmurun prepares to invite the other heroes to the great memorial feast, he says, "Of all my obligations, this is the most important" (p. 70). But the structure of the epic built up from there rises far above this basis.

I have spoken of the dead chief's successors in the plural up to now because orderly transition of power was not assured. In theory, and on the surface, a militarily talented, charismatic son, brother, or paternal uncle of the dead chief was the likely favorite to succeed him. In practice, beneath the regime's façade, claims were often complicated. Dynastic chronicles and heroic epics had their different ways of dealing narratively with the complications. A literary work from Inner Asia that falls somewhere between those genres is *The Secret History of the Mongols*, where the dangers of the orphan Temüjin's period of minority are similar to those implied for Boqmurun: clansmen descended and usurped the family's property, nearly extinguishing the prospects of the future Chinggis Khan.[1] In *The Memorial Feast for Kökötöy Khan*, the khan's orphan son Boqmurun is adopted, apparently too young either to rule or to manage his father's enormous wealth, and brotherless. In short, the situation could not be more precarious – nor could it promise a greater narrative payoff if the orphaned hero were to succeed. There are other epics in the Kirghiz cycle that deal with the rescue of a late khan's imperiled house, but in them the rescuers are the women who have married into the family.[2] The plots of those epics show how little help could be counted on from the men, even were a mother to look to her son, the heir. But *The Memorial Feast for Kökötöy Khan* deals differently with the danger, for these were also the conditions where a trusted supporter of the ruling clan would step in as regent. Kökötöy Khan's trustee, Baymïrza son of Bay ("Rich-Noble son of Rich") plays that prosaic role, but so unsatisfactorily that young Boqmurun has an opening to act on his own. With dire straits like these for a premise, dramatic happenings were sure to follow.

1. *The Secret History of the Mongols: A Mongolian Epic Chronicle of the Thirteenth Century*, ed. and trans. Igor de Rachewiltz (Leiden: Brill, 2004).
2. "The Birth of Semetey" and "Semetey," in *MWR*.

INTRODUCTION TO A READING OF THE TRADITION   263

The epic's moral mechanism had other tensions as well. Boqmurun's minority was not a mere legal hindrance; there were foreign dangers that called for the sound policy and heroism of a mature khan. Blocs and fault lines of power defined the geopolitical space that the Kirghiz occupied in the eighteenth and nineteenth centuries. The main features of this historical landscape were the divisions of Inner Asia among Muslim Turkic nomads in the west, Buddhist Mongol nomads in the east, Irano-Turkic Muslim townspeople and farmers in the south, and newly expanding Russia, an Orthodox Christian power, encroaching from the north. In Kirghiz epic, the world of heroes – people who mattered – was basically divided between nomadic Turkic Muslims and nomadic infidels identified as Qïtay and Qalmaq, or Sino-Qalmaqs, to use Arthur Hatto's term. The Turkic Muslims sometimes drew spiritual power from holy men based in the Irano-Turkic oases and, more vaguely, in the Arabian heartland of Islam. The Sino-Qalmaqs had an imposing empire and were sometimes joined with a new-fangled sort of infidels, the Orus or Russians, in the Kirghiz' imaginings of an ominous dual front of unbelief.

Identity claims that transcend the tribal level are one of the strongest catalysts of heroic epic poetry. The Kirghiz and other Central Asian Turks had in common the peerless epic tribe the Noghoy to face the world. Supratribal epic identity also included an ingredient of stark opposition along religious lines, mirroring the confrontation of the Franks with the Moorish and Saracen infidels in the French *chansons de geste*. The Kirghiz heroic tradition had its border epics that worked out the meaning and limitations of the religious difference between Muslims and infidels. Two of the border epics recorded in the mid-nineteenth century (the story of Almambet and the story of the Közqamans) show, with logical precision, how difficult it was to tell good people from bad people where blood relations and religious affiliations complicated the geographical dividing line. *The Memorial Feast for Kökötöy Khan* (literally) approaches the border differently. It takes for granted the political, religious, and ethnic definitions that the line imposes, and shows a realistically messy interaction between antagonistic forces who try, for the sake of honor, to come together in peace at the very place where the two worlds touch.

Nor did the fault line of ethnic and religious geopolitics (for want of a simpler term) encompass all that was at stake for the Muslims. The two parts of the world were not evenly matched. Under the lens of this epic, the Sino-Qalmaqs preserved an imperial status much loftier and more dangerous to Central Asian Muslims than actual Mongols and Chinese in the mid-nineteenth to the early twentieth century. At least in the version recorded in 1856, the Sino-Qalmaqs hold some kind of political sway over the Noghoy, whose old guard at times seem careful not to upset the arrangement. This irritating political subordination to the Sino-Qalmaq raised the question in the epic thought-world of the nineteenth-century Kirghiz, whether it was better to live on in détente with the hated infidels or to risk a bold power-play aimed at deliverance. Here is where Boqmurun's vision of his own incipient heroism had the potential to turn the ritual occasion of the memorial feast into a political coup and a chance for a secure future.

The plot of a romance would trace the hero's adventures on his path to achieving the desired outcome. But this is a heroic epic, so what is at stake is not a quest for fulfillment but the struggle for existence itself; and as surely as there is a diversity of agendas, there will be no formula for reconciling them. As we have seen, heroism was the potential solution to a fiscal problem of managing resources; but heroism itself became a problem as chiefs' competition brought the whole system to the limits of stability. Heroic epic poetry was the crucible in which to test those limits.

The political circumstances implicit in *The Memorial Feast for Kökötöy Khan* make its plot one of the major meditations on chiefly competition within the Kirghiz epic tradition. In turn the poem belongs to a small summit of heroic epics on this theme worldwide. The *Iliad* is a condensed story of the effects of the wrath of the paramount hero, Achilles, toward his over-king, Agamemnon, who is a lesser man. Similarly, the *Nibelungenlied* deals with a mismatching of strengths and statuses, but pits the wives and close allies of Siegfried and of Gunther against each other over a long period of time, with inevitably tragic results. Although the plot of *The Memorial Feast for Kökötöy Khan* is neither as exquisite nor as decisive as either of those poems, nevertheless it excels by the welter of heroic counterpoints that it boils down into the fraught scenario of a momentous truce between enemies at the border, moreover where chiefs in each opposing camp are locked in their own contentions.

It was implicit in the nineteenth-century versions of the epic that Boqmurun needed to plan and preside successfully over his father's anniversary memorial feast in order to live down the childhood name Boqmurun 'Snot-Nose' (a nickname given to ward off evil), and to gain the name and status of a grown-up hero. When we recall that the "hand" Boqmurun had been dealt included bad cards for being an orphan, an only son, not the natural-born son of his late father, and a minor, we can see that he already faced stiff obstacles to his heroic enterprise. All the more so when the others against whom he had to struggle were enormously formidable. These adversaries were, for preponderant political reasons, the Sino-Qalmaq heroes, backed by their heathen empire and commanded by their paramount leaders, the Qïtay Khan Qongurbay and the Qalmaq Joloy Khan. Delicate, peaceable, make-or-break dealings with a maximal, irreconcilably opposed adversary on the very border between two worlds is a sophisticated form of rivalry not normally found on the résumé of a young hero just starting out.

Indeed, Boqmurun's task appears to have been too great for him. The field of his rivals at the feast also included the heroes on his own side. Using his good sense and policy to convince them of his greatness was just as important as it was to use his power and largesse to convince the infidels. But the potential challenges on the Muslim side go deeper still. Boqmurun and Manas, though on the same side, had different agendas. In the nineteenth-century versions, Manas quickly usurped the predominant role as soon as he appeared at the feast; by the twentieth century his predominance was never in doubt. Boqmurun disappeared long before the climax of the fight waged by Manas and his comrades against the infidels. Saghïmbay, out of affection for the lad, gave Boqmurun a small part to play in the last battle, but he still ignored him in the dénouement and gave him no portion in the harsh terms that the Muslim heroes imposed over the vanquished Sino-Qalmaqs. In *The Memorial Feast for Kökötöy Khan*, Manas closed off Boqmurun's path to success.

One can view Boqmurun's and Manas's relations simply in terms of their interactions on the plane of the epic plot. But since we are dealing here with an oral tradition from which we possess several different expressions of the story from different times, we can also examine the historical meta-relationships between the characters as figures on the plane of tradition. The formation of the plot in the nineteenth- and twentieth-century versions may make more sense if the texts represent stages in a process of absorption, where the arc of Boqmurun's claim to heroic status through presidency of the feast was subsumed within the expanding orbit of the ascendant figure of Manas. The relationship between Boqmurun and Manas – both as heroes on the plane of the epic plots they share and as figures on the plane of the oral epic tradition that somehow caused their paths to cross – is one of the most enigmatic problems of understanding *The Memorial Feast for Kökötöy Khan*. It is not entirely clear why Kirghiz audiences have had such enduring affection for Boqmurun, but the effect is that the tradition has arrested his development, since the mid-nineteenth century at least, in a sort of limbo between fully realized heroic existence and annihilation in the glare of Manas's star. Thus it is possible to discern in the epic's prehistory evidence of a stage of composition where an independent epic of Boqmurun was swallowed up by the Manas cycle. How that older story of Boqmurun went, if it existed, we cannot know for sure.

A brief summary of the different framing members of the plot of *The Memorial Feast for Kökötöy Khan* will accentuate the multitude of weighty problems wrapped up in the showy, rather loose-looking package of the epic. Fundamentally, an Inner Asian nomad chief's death created problems of political economy: whether to husband resources to keep the population together, or spend lavishly on the memorial feast to gain the upper hand with other chiefs. The solution to the problem of quantity lay in the application of heroic quality. Kökötöy's death naturally raised concerns of dynastic succession and the secure sequence of power, which Boqmurun's various vulnerabilities did little to quell. In the specific historical circumstances affecting the Kirghiz, problems of ethnic and religious geopolitics arose as well. On the strength of historical memory, the infidel Sino-Qalmaqs exerted some influence over the Muslim Kirghiz and their earlier exemplars in epic, the Noghoy. The question thus became whether to continue in détente with or even in outright submission to the Sino-Qalmaqs, or to maneuver for political advantage. To make such an attempt by means of the "diplomacy" of a grand memorial feast and games at the border was an extremely risky undertaking, for the very reason that heroes compete with one another and cause trouble, both on and off the playing field. Tensions across the divide were exacerbated for Boqmurun by the dual potentiality of Manas's presence within his camp: the Muslim supreme hero could be both an integrative and a disruptive force. But neither version of Manas's nature helped Boqmurun. Whether by integrating or disrupting the scene, Manas would overshadow the young hero. And Manas managed to do both, reaching both poles of his potentiality. Boqmurun, on the other hand, was finished.

The historical range of the surviving texts tells us that the multilayered plot of *The Memorial Feast for Kökötöy Khan* was a source of recurrent fascination for patrons and audiences of Kirghiz epic poetry. Part of what they relished were the dense fundamentals provided by the tradition, but the energy of a very good bard could lift up the ponderous timbers of the traditional plot and remodel the creative tradition for a new generation. That is what Saghïmbay did. In order to appreciate fully the achievement of a classicizing artist like Saghïmbay, one must start with the tradition he worked in. The nineteenth-century Kirghiz epic texts thus form the foundation, and their context is the intellectual landscape surrounding the epic tradition.

The rest of this Introduction examines two things in greater detail, the intellectual landscape and what Saghïmbay built on the foundation of the nineteenth-century epics. After sections on the culture and history of the Kirghiz, memorial feasting, the epic tradition, the bard, and how he remodeled the tradition, a series of comparative notes confronts Saghïmbay's *Kökötöy* text with the two versions from the mid-nineteenth century. The notes show where Saghïmbay's distinctive narrative design lent its own form and energy to the inherited epic. At these points we can perceive facets of the poet's genius, as well as his limitations, and glimpse the intertwined workings of tradition and innovation.

CULTURE AND HISTORY

The Kirghiz were traditionally nomads, or mobile pastoralists. Their way of life revolved around tending flocks and herds of hoofed animals on horseback as they followed annual rounds of migration to grazing grounds that greened up in different seasons. The meat, milk, wool, hides, and brute labor of their herds of the "five coats" – horses, camels, sheep, goats, and horned cattle – constituted their principal economic resources. Horses were especially prized. Every aspect of the breeding, training, riding, and outfitting of the horse, every point of its physiognomy, and its uses in war and sport, were subjects of uniquely developed nomadic art and science.

The Inner Asian mobile pastoralist way of life was further distinguished from that of settled people by its social structure. Nomad families reckoning their relations by patrilineal descent were organized into named groups or clans, several of which together would constitute a tribe. Men of the most prominent lineages decided matters of governance and war. The power of the chiefs of the clans and tribes was the real organizing principle of society. Chiefs achieved their rank and power by exploiting a flexible toolkit of political claims, including seniority within the lineage, leadership in war and law, and the ability to neutralize rivals through open contest and intrigue. The idiom of kinship was the main means of expressing social reality, and it was fluid. Clans and tribes thought of themselves as groups of families related by descent, but in actuality they could consist of numerous elements bound together not only by patrilineal kinship but also by the charisma, wealth, and leadership of chiefs. Weaker and poorer nomads, escaped captives and slaves, and those dissatisfied with their lot in life could, with luck, find a new identity within the orbit of a new leader. The allegiance could even be confirmed with a genealogy, the fictive nature of which would over time be lost to memory.

When presented with external threats or opportunities for plunder, confederations of nomadic tribes came under the sole leadership of a powerful chieftain, or khan; that military title could become royal and hereditary. The khan's encampment was an epitome of the nomadic social order it secured. At the center stood the large yurt covered in white felts that served as the khan's court and residence, or *ordo* (from which comes the word "horde"). Around the *ordo* stood the yurts of the khan's wives, the senior wife's standing closest of all to the khan. Ranged in their yurts around the ruling family, the khan's companions pledged to sacrifice everything for him in war, both personally and in command of their troops, and were richly rewarded with plunder. If they felt slighted, they might leave or rebel, both options carrying great risk. (The spatial arrangement and political fragility of the khan's court encampment are in the symbolic background of the popular game *ordo*, played by throwing animal knucklebones as strikers to dislodge knucklebones set up at the center of a circular arena.) The yurts of the multitudes under the khan's rule then spread out widely over the available ground, grouped by clans, from nearest to farthest roughly in order of seniority.

Beyond the encampment (or a city where the chief had his seat) lay the pastures, and perhaps a bit of cropland tended by the poorest of the poor, who lacked the animals to join in the regular migrations. Traders came and went over local tracks that linked up to form a transcontinental network; these "Silk Roads," as well as expansive conquests by steppe nomads, ensured that the seemingly isolated reaches of Inner Asia were anything but.

The Mongol Empire founded by Chinggis Khan (d. 1227) set a template for sovereignty in Turkic Inner Asia that lasted for centuries. Yet while Uzbeks and Qazaqs recognized khans who traced their descent back to the Mongol "White Bone" or royal lineage of Chinggis Khan, groups such as the Kirghiz and the Noghay did not (the *Qara* that sometimes precedes the name Kirghiz means black, or plebeian). In terms of political history, the Kirghiz' lack of a White Bone clan is an indicator of their unimportance; yet the reverse side of that notion is the fact that they never admitted a supra-ethnic line of khans into their society or saw themselves as ruled by such khans. Khans for them were rarities chosen in times of war or danger. Their geographical situation in a mountainous region of Central Asia, the condition of their relative insignificance, was also a refuge that guaranteed the luxury of living outside the Chinggisid political dispensation. Their perch in the mountains, from where they could look down on the vast tableau of shifting nomadic polities on the steppes, may have lent the Kirghiz some part of their imaginative gifts in the narration of heroic epics.

The high Tien Shan, Pamir, and Alay mountains where the Kirghiz lived were difficult, though not impossible, to cross. Since the sixteenth century, Kirghiz chiefs gained power when they were able to control the complicated routes to and fro. They profited when caravans sought access to roads between Tashkent and the cities of the Ferghana valley (mostly in present-day Uzbekistan) on one side of the mountains, and Kashgaria over the passes in East Turkestan. They vied with each other for control of the choicest pastures in the region, the land of Jeti-suu, "Seven Rivers." Their fierce autonomy in remote mountain terrain may have been one reason why many Kirghiz became recognized as Sunni Muslims later than other Central Asian Turkic peoples, starting in the seventeenth century.

The *Manas* epics display the religious prejudice of the convert. The basic motivating antagonism of the epics pitted Muslim Turkic nomads, the "us" of us-and-them, against neighboring infidels: the Oirats, nomadic western Mongols whom the Kirghiz called Oyrot or, usually, Qalmaq (they were Buddhists, though the Kirghiz could not care less), and the Qïtay or Chinese (imagined as nomadic tribes to make them worthy foes). This situation broadly recalls the position of Central Asian Turks in the face of the Junghar Empire of the Oirats, which expanded at the expense of Qazaqs and Kirghiz in the seventeenth and early eighteenth centuries. The Ch'ing dynasty of China conquered the Junghar Empire in 1755, massacred its people, and extended political and economic patronage over numerous eastern Kirghiz chiefs in the aftermath; this control ebbed in the early nineteenth century. Ch'ing domination weakened Qalmaq remnants and migrants in the region, though some of their chiefs held Ch'ing army ranks and commanded cavalry on the border. The Kirghiz' bitter memories of oppression and war at the hands of the Qalmaqs, combined with the alliance they supposed existed between Qalmaqs and Qïtays, gave the Kirghiz epic tradition a tensely wound mainspring of hostility, if not a precise mechanism of accurately remembered incidents.

Drawing Kirghiz contempt rather than heroic antagonism were the Sarts, settled Turkic and Tajik folk of the Central Asian towns and oases, fellow Muslims, who traded in needed goods and grew essential crops, but who could not put up a creditable fight as far as the nomads were concerned. Nevertheless, in the early nineteenth century the Sart and Ghalcha (in Kirghiz: Qalcha) troops and artillery of the Khanate of Khoqand (Qoqon), a regional competitor to Bukhara ruled by an Uzbek dynasty from Ferghana, advanced rapidly into the Tien Shan and the Chu valley. By the 1820s Khoqand had constructed forts deep inside Kirghiz territory. From those strongpoints the khanate levied tax on Kirghiz chiefs, after which the control of the Ch'ing, outmaneuvered and distracted by Muslim revolts, vanished in the areas that eventually came under Russian rule. In northern and higher-elevation areas of Kirghiz territory, out of reach of Khoqandian and Ch'ing domination, political power was fragmented. The epic tradition flourished under the patronage of warring chiefs. Beginning in the 1850s, when Russia under the Romanov tsars advanced its army, the best in the region, southward in search of a secure imperial frontier, unstable Khoqandian control over northern Kirghiz chiefs gave way. By 1867, the chiefs were firmly under Russian rule. Soon Russia liquidated and annexed the Khoqand Khanate. For the Kirghiz within the new Russian border, the formerly multipolar sphere of their external politics was transformed into one of uniform Tsarist colonization.

A Khoqandian military adventurer, Yaqub Bek, crossed the Tien Shan and in 1867 established a Muslim state in Chinese Turkestan, fueling the ardor of Muslims in the region for a reckoning with the Infidel. The Ottoman Empire and the core lands of Islam within its borders were remote from Central Asia. Rather than performing the haj, many Central Asian Muslims made pilgrimages to saints' shrines closer by; the majestic tomb of Khoja Ahmad Yasavi in the city of Turkistan (in Saghïmbay's Kirghiz text: Türküstön) was one of the most important pilgrimage sites in the region. In the late nineteenth and early twentieth centuries, mullahs promoting modernized Islamic education among the Qazaqs and Kirghiz espoused ideas based on new scholarship about the ethnic unity of Turkic peoples from Siberia to Turkey. The ideology of pan-Turkism that grew from those ideas was an influential but short-lived element of minority nationality policies in the twilight of the Russian Empire and the early years of Bolshevik rule; parts of Saghïmbay's *Kökötöy* text reflect pan-Turkist thinking.

Belek Soltonoev, a Kirghiz historian of the late nineteenth and early twentieth centuries, wrote a caricature of the social conditions of the pacified, colonized Kirghiz that helps to evoke the period of archaism into which the heroic epic tradition had permanently subsided:

From that time [1867], the free-roaming Kirghiz could no longer engage in the raiding that was their specialty. They felt constrained by the orders that they could no longer cross the bounds of their assigned *volost* lands to other places. It was as if they had been imprisoned in cages or had entered a dark tomb: the hated way of life of the townsmen, "flightless chickens and immovable houses," which they had always feared and avoided, bowed them to the law of the colonizers. From that point, the children of the Kirghiz began to ride in carts, calling them four-legged, wooden horses.[1]

Among those formerly free-roaming Kirghiz were the chiefly patrons of epic bards, former leaders of war-bands. Our bard Saghïmbay, a child of the new cart-borne generation, did much to keep alive the Kirghiz' sense of past horse-mounted heroism through his mastery of the art of epic poetry. But the coupling of life and art at the heart of the heroic epic tradition had been undone by history. The tradition began to change with the times, as epics always do.

MEMORIAL FEASTS

In descriptions of actual memorial feasts it is possible to glimpse in miniature a feast like the one the Kirghiz imagined for Kökötöy in epic. Saghïmbay was a famous herald and singer at feasts, memorable events where he lived and saw things very close to what the epic heroes lived and saw. He put his all into *The Memorial Feast for Kökötöy Khan*, a poem that was for him a lens on his own experience.

In the Tsarist era large memorial feasts drew thousands of people and featured sporting highlights that were remembered for years afterward, though the chiefly political subtext became obsolete under colonial rule. Demoted in terms of formal power, the chiefs tried to use memorial feasts to hold on to their social prestige and influence.

The most important memorial feasts were given for prominent men. Following the rites for burial and on the fortieth day after death, the grand memorial feast was traditionally an anniversary event, but the interval could be shorter or longer than one year. The preferred time to hold the feast was in the autumn. A council of the close male relatives of the deceased decided on the date, the place, whom to invite, and the amount of cattle and provisions needed for hospitality, as well as the total size of the prize purse, including specific enumerations of the top prizes for the main horse race. Relatives and dependents of the clan

1.   Belek Soltonoev, *History of the Kirghiz* (Bishkek: Arkhi, 2003), p. 378, in Kirghiz.

were required to set up numbers of furnished yurts, give up their ani-
mals for slaughter, and receive the guests. (The chief's survivors reckoned
all this wealth and effort to be theirs.) Inside the yurt of the deceased,
his close female relations kept up continuous lamentations beside his
personal possessions.

The biggest of the horse races covered a course twenty to thirty
kilometers, or sometimes as much as fifty kilometers, out from the
feasting ground and back. A great anniversary memorial feast given for
a Qazaq around 1862, attended by about five thousand people includ-
ing neighboring Kirghiz, culminated with the horse race on the fourth
day. Prizes had been posted for the ten leading horses. The first prize
was fifty head of assorted camels, horses, cattle, and sheep, and a small
yurt with all the furnishings, before which sat on horseback a girl
dressed in bridal costume – herself a part of the prize. The tenth prize
was five horses. There was a parade of the entrants before the start.

While the race ran, other games would be played. Wrestling on foot
and on horseback, shooting down a suspended ingot, and jousting
were all popular games becoming of warriors. These were spiced with
now long-forgotten amusements like the one where a naked woman
tried to win a camel laden with valuables by untying its tether with her
teeth, or the spectacle of bald men with scabby scalps butting heads at
a full run.

At the climax of the race, as soon as the pack of leading horses was
spotted in the distance from the feasting ground, a wild cavalcade of
the racers' owners and supporters would ride out to them and drive
their favorites on with whistles, shouts, thrown rocks, and lashes from
their horse-whips; some pulled exhausted finishers in with ropes. (The
Kirghiz word for the home stretch, *süröö*, means "dragging.") The fin-
ish itself might erupt into a riot in which spectators made off with the
winnings. The owners of the best horses knew they were competing
for nothing but fame.

But by the end of the nineteenth century the Kirghiz and Qazaq
tradition of giving memorial feasts was nearing the end of a long
decline. High-handed guests who perceived slights to their honor
started fights and feuds. Russian and native commentators in the press
decried the vainglorious waste of money, yet hosts, in their efforts to
stretch the appearance of extravagance, posted cheaper prizes. There
were reports of prize-animals being sold by their winners on the spot
for the price of their hides; other hosts demanded their largesse back
after making the show of bestowing it.

One of the last Kirghiz attempts to revive the custom was the great
memorial feast put on in October 1912 by the sons of the famous chief

Shabdan Jantay uulu (*c.*1839–1912), at Shabdan's home pasture in the Little Kemin valley. The widely advertised, lavish event lasted six days and at its height drew an estimated twenty thousand to forty thousand people. There were numerous games and horse races, the longest on a forty-kilometer course with a first prize of five thousand rubles. Saghïmbay was one of the singers present. Affairs were mismanaged, however, and the crowd dwindled. Chiefly organizers had succeeded in pocketing much of the wealth intended for the prizes, which they had amassed through mandatory contributions from the common Kirghiz under their control. The two contestants in a jousting match received serious lance wounds, which put an end to the games; they later died. In anticipating a boost to their social prestige that never materialized, the deceased chief's heirs miscalculated the continued relevance of the custom of holding memorial feasts. The age of heroes was over, and by the time Saghïmbay sang his *Kökötöy* epic in 1925, memorial feasts were virtually a thing of the past.

THE EPIC TRADITION

An oral epic poem is not merely a text. For the bards, patrons, and audiences who create them together in performance, epics are events, which can be shaped to fit their needs. The characters, themes, incidents, plots, descriptions, even minor phrasings of the traditional stories are known to all, and are expressed by the bards from performance to performance in varied combinations of traditional verbal formulas. The passing down of this word-stock from master bards to pupils went on for generations with no written aids to memory, only gradual alterations in the stories as changing times brought new tastes and new ideas.

The interplay of tradition and creativity and the synergism of bard and audience were immediately apparent to the linguist Wilhelm Radloff when he wrote down epics performed by Kirghiz bards in the 1860s. Radloff's insights became a cornerstone of the study of oral poetic traditions:

> The bard's inner disposition depends on his existing stock of formulas, but . . . this is not all that is needed for him to sing; he still needs an external incentive. Such encouragement naturally comes from the group of listeners around him. The bard strives to gain the approval of the crowd, and as he is interested not only in glory but also in material benefit, he always seeks to conform to the audience around him. If they do not ask him to sing a particular episode, he begins his singing with a prelude

meant to introduce the listeners to the gist of his song. He knows how to get his listeners in the mood by artfully interweaving verses with allusions to respected personages in the audience before moving on to the song itself. When he concludes from the cheers and shouts of the audience that he has gained their full attention, he either proceeds directly to the action itself, or gives a quick sketch of certain events that preceded the episode to be sung, and then begins the action. The singing does not move at a constant tempo. The excited approval of the audience keeps spurring the bard to new efforts, and at the same time he knows how to adapt the song completely to the circumstances of the audience. If rich or eminent Kirghiz are present, then he can work in skillful praises of their lineages and sing the sorts of episodes that he surmises will draw the approval of the notables in particular. If the listeners are only poor people, then he will not hold back from inserting cutting remarks about the arrogance of the rich and eminent, and indeed the more applause he garners from the audience, the more he expounds. This bears comparison with the third episode of *Manas*, which was intended to insinuate itself perfectly to my tastes. However, the bard knows very well when he has fallen off in his singing; should there be any sign of fatigue in his listeners, he seeks once more, by working up their highest passions, to increase their attention and thus to elicit a burst of applause, then suddenly breaks off his singing. One can only be amazed at how well the bard knows his public. I myself saw how one sultan leapt up suddenly in the middle of a song, tore the silk robe from his shoulders, and with a cheer threw it to the bard as a gift.[1]

This was the performing art that shaped Saghïmbay's *Kökötöy*, though knowing his public meant something different to Saghïmbay. He dictated much of his *Manas* not in front of rapt or restless crowds, but before folklorists who had the novel intent of collecting a complete text.

Action in the poems, not identity or ideal, was the foundation of heroic character. The Kirghiz epic tradition was not interested in heroes who always won out or foes whom everyone expected to be beaten.

1.   Wilhelm Radloff, *Samples of the Folk Literature of the Northern Turkic Tribes*, vol. 5 (St. Petersburg: Imperial Academy of Sciences, 1885), pp. xviii–xix, in German. Radloff's statement that one of the epics he collected "was intended to insinuate itself perfectly to my tastes" refers to "The Duel between Manas and Er Kökchö; The Marriage, Death and Return to Life of Manas," where Manas submits to the Russian tsar. Radloff believed the bard took him for a Russian official (*Samples*, p. xiv); Hatto sees a possibility that the bard already had practice with the theme of Manas's submission to the tsar (*MWR*, pp. 73, 443).

Manas died multiple times in the nineteenth-century epics; Joloy, his infidel enemy, enjoyed heroic courtesies in the older bards' hands, especially when he was killed. Muslimness was not the be-all and end-all of the Muslim heroes; there is even an epic that tells how the converted Oyrot hero Almambet found his Muslim preceptor Er Kökchö to be a lesser man. Heroism was the only kind of status that mattered; sovereignty, on rare occasions when it is mentioned, is more a matter of set decoration than characterization.

In the mid-nineteenth century, the plots of the epics were tensely rigged workings-out of crucial problems of the heroes' existential commitments. A special kind of heroic action that helped the older bards structure these plots were the "highly charged narrative ganglia" that Arthur Hatto called "epic moments," gestures or scenes redolent of the irreducible selfhood of heroes and heroines as they faced the world.[1] An example of an epic moment from the *Kökötöy* poems of the mid-nineteenth century is Boqmurun's announcement of the long itinerary of the migration he will lead to the feasting ground (*MKNB*, ll. 373–81). This act was what prompted the chiefs to raise Boqmurun up as khan, though his work as a hero was only beginning. (The nature of this epic moment was muffled in Saghïmbay's reconfigured plot with Manas on the ascendant.)

Manas's fragile lineage had its most reliable and effective champions in the women who married into it. In the nineteenth-century epics about the generations after Manas, the fortunes of the lineage lie in the careful hands of Qanïkey, Manas's widow, and Aychürök, wife of Manas's son Semetey, who is widowed before the end.[2] The version of *The Memorial Feast for Kökötöy Khan* narrated by Saghïmbay is unusual in Kirghiz epic for its dearth of important heroines. The tradition's generally rich and varied female *dramatis personae* are represented here only in brief appearances. The impressive heroine Qanïkey has only one scene, and although it is an important and consequential one in the context of Saghïmbay's overall narrative, she does not have much to do, and nothing to say out loud.

Heroism was not merely a combination of strength, power, and bravery, though those traits may come out. Where their fates are all that matters, heroes and heroines appear largely self-motivated. If their interests enlarge beyond what we might diagnose as egoism, it is to

1. A. T. Hatto, "General Introduction," in *Traditions of Heroic and Epic Poetry*, vol. 1, ed. A. T. Hatto (London: Modern Humanities Research Association, 1980), pp. 4–6.
2. "The Birth of Semetey" and "Semetey," in *MWR*.

serve the lineage or a friend, not to be savior or protector of a common weal for its own sake. Defending the nation is a motive imposed on epic heroes after the fact by the politics of more worldly times. Saghïmbay's *Manas* displays the beginnings of this motivation. In contemporary independent Kyrgyzstan, where the national polishing has gone further still, the stern, ruthless *Qanqor* 'Blood-drinking' Manas of Saghïmbay's day has become *Ayköl* 'Great-hearted' Manas of propaganda and civics curricula.

Oral heroic epic poems are not history, yet wherever they exist, a person interested in history will find them difficult to ignore. This is because heroic epic is existential in nature. The heroes' problems refract the bards' and audiences' understanding of their collective struggle for existence. Four poems from the mid-nineteenth century may be called border epics for their preoccupation with heroes' lives lived along and across the frontier between the Muslims and the Sino-Qalmaqs.[1] The real border and the epic border reinforced one another. Equally important but with subtler historical significance are the epic tradition's preoccupations with power and vulnerability. Boqmurun's predicament in *The Memorial Feast for Kökötöy Khan* is of this kind. For the Kirghiz chiefs in the mid-nineteenth century, the vicissitudes of a fragile lineage were powerfully evocative of their precarious footing in the world. It was these chiefs' patronage that gave the oral epic poetry of the time its existential edge.

There is refracted history also in the imagined ethnic identity of the main heroes of the Kirghiz epic tradition, the Noghoy. The power and even some of the named members of the Noghay Horde, a tribal confederation that controlled the Central Asian steppes in the fifteenth and sixteenth centuries (also known as the Manghit Yurt) inspired celebrations of nomadic warriors in the heroic poetry of different Turkic steppe peoples. By the late eighteenth century, the Kirghiz had borrowed elements of this cycle from the Qazaqs, forming the nucleus of the epic tradition witnessed today. Qoshoy, Kökchö, Jamghïrchï, Manas, and other heroes got their names from the Noghay cycle, though the epics that the Kirghiz bards created are widely recognized as unparalleled. Kirghiz bards and audiences, in possession of a great epic tradition, had no difficulty accepting the non-Kirghiz descent of

---

1. The epics are "Almambet, Er Kökchö and Ak-erkech; How Almambet Came to Manas," "Köz-kaman," and "Bok-murun" (the last a version of *The Memorial Feast for Kökötöy Khan*), edited and translated into English in *MWR;* and an earlier version of the *Kökötöy* narrative by a different bard, *MK*NB. In this book "Bok-murun" is referred to as *MK*WR.

their heroic paragons. Arthur Hatto likened the high esteem paid to the epic Noghay by Turkic nomadic peoples to the diverse Greeks' celebration of Achaean heroes in the Homeric epics. Saghïmbay or the folklorists who commissioned and transcribed his *Manas* seem to have been responsible for giving the main Noghoy heroes new ethnic identities to suit the times.[1]

The poems show profound concerns with actual geography. Kirghiz nomads knew a great deal of highly contoured terrain first-hand, and integrated additional geographical knowledge from reports of other herders, raiders, and traders in distant regions. Few epic traditions in the world could rival the realism (mostly) of geographical knowledge put into poetic form by the Kirghiz. This knowledge, alien to maps or two-dimensional imaginings, was embodied in movement. Heroes' itineraries, particularly in the mid-nineteenth-century epics, were passages of elevated style and interest. Itineraries could even encapsulate a form of heroism in themselves, becoming epic moments, as when Boqmurun announces the grand itinerary to the feasting ground. In a nineteenth-century version of *Kökötöy*, as the assembled Noghoy chiefs raised Boqmurun up as khan for his brilliant planning, the audience too would have cheered the young hero's mastery of the route and timing of a major nomadic migration through their intricate mountain homeland.

The geographical space depicted by Kirghiz epic bards was not an evenly objective map but rather a factor in their exclusive understanding of Muslims' place in the world. The border epics mentioned above are based on the understanding that since the Islamic faith is a defined community of people, and a people occupy territory, then the limit of that territory is a limit of human sympathies as well. Recently hemmed in by infidel Russia and China, nursing old wounds of Junghar oppression, and far removed from religious power places in the Near East, Kirghiz epic bards as Sunni Muslims imagined their home heroes surrounded by a horizon that challenged their existence. *The Memorial Feast for Kökötöy Khan* is in one sense an extended rumination on Muslims' place within that horizon.

The surviving records of the Kirghiz epic tradition can be ranged by their dates into three main eras: the Heroic Period until the mid 1860s, the Twilight Age from the late 1860s to the early 1920s, and the

---

1. Resolution on this point is complicated by the fact that the pages of Saghïmbay's *Manas* manuscripts show evidence that certain ethnic terms that the bard used in his narrative were obliterated and replaced later. See p. 286 below.

Classical Period from the early 1920s onward. (The earliest bards mentioned in oral histories are said to have been active in the latter half of the eighteenth century.) In the Heroic Period, the politically fragmented Kirghiz tribes were led by chiefs who had to wage war to hold power. *The Memorial Feast for Kökötöy Khan* was recorded from two different bards' performances in this period, in 1856 by Chokan Valikhanov, a Qazaq prince and officer in the Russian army who heard the epic performed by the bard Nazar Bolot (d. 1893), and in 1862 by the Turcologist Wilhelm Radloff, who did not name the bard whose version of the epic he wrote down. In addition to the epic he titled "Bok-murun," Radloff recorded six other epics about Manas and his son Semetey and grandson Seytek, and two separate epics about Er Töshtük and Joloy Khan.

The records of the briskly told epics of the Heroic Period have an average length of about 2,200 lines, which would have taken about two and three-quarters hours to sing (though some of Radloff's texts may be on the short side). One or two epics would thus have made up an evening's entertainment, and a performance of the whole repertoire including *Manas* and *Semetey* was said to require several days. The plots feature strong, nuanced moral arguments punctuated by epic moments.

The Kirghiz chiefs submitted one by one to the tsar, the last in 1867, likely the year of Saghïmbay's birth. In the Twilight Age from the late 1860s to the early 1920s the Kirghiz continued their epic tradition while living at peace under Russian colonial rule. It was during this time that Kirghiz literati wrote down the earliest known epic manuscripts to be recorded within their culture. The textual records, though scanty, suggest that changes were occurring in the tradition. The plots lack the strongly interlocking structures and epic moments that characterized the Heroic Period epics. The figure of the paramount hero Manas was slipping into archaism; in his place the younger generation favored the epics about his son Semetey. Some bards of the era (and still today) positioned Kökötöy's memorial feast as a flashback within the plot of *Semetey*, in order to showcase one beloved remnant of the *Manas* cycle. Yet a resurgence of interest in *Manas* seems to have occurred late in the Twilight Age, early stirrings of classicism that culminated in the meeting of Kirghiz from different regions of Russian and Chinese Turkestan after the 1916 rebellion.

The imposition of Bolshevik power in Russian Central Asia raised the state's awareness of the political relevance of non-Russian national cultures, and this generated an interest in Kirghiz epic poetry. The newly focused official attention brought on the Classical Period of the epic tradition, when literate interests became a center of patronage of the epic bards. The current of classicizing activity that mainly concerns us here occurred within the Soviet Union and later in independent Kyrgyzstan. Another current had been under way in China from the early years of the twentieth century, where the Kirghiz poet and amateur folklore collector Balbay Mamay (1892–1938) used a library of manuscripts and books he had amassed to conceive of a complete *Manas* epic. It was, however, Saghïmbay's landmark composition of his complete, unified *Manas* narrative, the first of which a record survives, that marked the beginning of the Classical Period. Its creation was the result of individual effort rather than official fiat, so the significance of the transition to the Classical Period can be appreciated through the story of its founding bard.

THE BARD SAGHÏMBAY AND HIS MOMENT

Saghïmbay Orozbaq uulu ('son of Orozbaq'; his name is also written as Sagymbai Orozbakov) was born in a valley northwest of lake Issyk Kul; according to his stated age of sixty-three near to his death, the year was 1867. His father Orozbaq, a member of the Moynoq clan of the Sayaq tribe, had been a witness to many historic events in the turbulent final years of the Kirghiz chiefs' independence, and served as a trumpeter in the retinue of a powerful chief of the Sarïbaghïsh tribe, Ormon Khan (d. *c.*1854). Ormon had a fearsome reputation as a tyrant; the parallels with Manas's formidable character are suggestive, and Saghïmbay may have perceived them in stories he heard about Ormon. Both of his parents died when Saghïmbay was about thirteen.

Saghïmbay began performing epics at about the age of sixteen, learning from a number of leading Twilight Age bards: Aqïlbek (*c.* 1840–*c.*1926) whom Sagïmbay rated the highest of all the bards he had heard; Tïnïbek Japïy uulu (1846–1902) who was generally held to be the greatest bard of his day, from whom Saghïmbay heard "the whole poem" for the first time, and who enjoined Saghïmbay to sing *Manas* "purely, without adding anything," and whose *Manas* "pure as colostrum" a contemporary observer distinguished from Saghïmbay's inflated performances; Naymanbay Balïq uulu (1853–1911) who lived in the Chu valley and served in a Solto chief's camp, where Saghïmbay later received a generous welcome; Shapaq Rïsmende uulu (1863–1956) from whom Saghïmbay learned the *Great Campaign* episode; and Alïsher, Saghïmbay's elder brother. Saghïmbay in turn influenced Shapaq, his near contemporary who outlived him by many years; the literate bard Bayïmbet Abdïraqman uulu, also known as Togholoq Moldo (1860–1942); Ïbïrayïm Abdïraqmanov (1888–1967; no relation to the preceding) who became his scribe and friend; and his own son, Amanqul. Like other bards, Saghïmbay claimed to have first received his gift of epic singing in dreams. Even awake he would see visions of Manas's cavalcade in the distance. Though many bards' dream-summonses come from Manas, Saghïmbay's came from a vision of Manas's son Semetey. Throughout his life Saghïmbay was more famous as a singer of *Semetey* than of *Manas*.

Saghïmbay's repertoire was more diverse still, and won him renown in a number of oral genres, including folktales in prose, topical poetry, lyric poetry, and love poetry. He was a sought-after performer at feasts, including memorial feasts for chiefs and rich men, where he not only sang laments for the deceased but also acted as herald and even instructed the bereaved women and girls in how to sing their laments. He was known as a healer as well.

Two more circumstances in Saghïmbay's intellectual biography help us to appreciate his *Manas* text: literacy and exile. Saghïmbay could read. The religious language in his epics reflects the four winters' schooling he had as a child. Beyond this, his *Manas* shows that he got access to a great miscellany of information about the world, either from reading or from talking with educated people.

Saghïmbay was swept up in the mass dislocation of Kirghiz who were forced to flee into northwest China after the bloody, disproportionate Russian suppression of the 1916 Turkestan Rebellion. The period of approximately one year that Saghïmbay spent with his family as refugees was a time of intense activity in the epic tradition. Crowds of uprooted and idle Kirghiz nostalgic for home heard *Manas* performed by a convocation of bards from all over, and Chinese Kirghiz took note as well. The *Manas* tradition seems to have experienced a ferment. Numerous manuscripts of *Manas* versions were taken down and changed hands. The Chinese Kirghiz amateur folklorist Balbay Mamay was particularly active at this time; he was among the aficionados in the audience at a *Manas*-singing competition between Saghïmbay and a Chinese Kirghiz bard.

The surviving texts of Saghïmbay's *Manas* came into being after he returned to his homeland, which not long afterward passed under Bolshevik control. The collaborator who initiated the recording of Saghïmbay's complete *Manas* was a teacher and folklore collector of

Bashkir Turkic origin named Qayum Miftaqov (1882–c.1948).[1] When Saghïmbay happened to visit the south shore of lake Issyk Kul where Miftaqov was working as a school headmaster in November 1921, it soon became apparent to Miftaqov that this Kirghiz singer was a possible source of the entire story of Manas, a collecting opportunity Miftaqov apparently had never been presented with before. Though the two men talked about the idea, the recording did not begin immediately, as winter was coming on and Saghïmbay had to get home over the mountains to return his borrowed horse. During his spring expedition in May 1922, Miftaqov came upon Saghïmbay in summer pastures at Kök-torpoq above the Narïn river. He wrote:

> We've found Saghïmbay. They had slaughtered a sheep for him at one tent, and he was singing *The Memorial Feast for Kökötöy Khan*. We too had come to hear *Manas*, so we told him to continue singing. Everyone sat listening without making a sound. The audience were like ants all around the tent. The profound content of *Manas* along with his pleasing voice and music drew everyone to him like iron filings to a magnet.[2]

The collaboration between Saghïmbay and Miftaqov's team began soon after. Among the Kirghiz apprentices who joined the team, the teacher Ïbïrayïm Abdïraqmanov was a talented scribe. He soon took charge of transcribing the Saghïmbay sessions, as Miftaqov recalled:

> After slaughtering a sheep to Manas's departed spirit according to folk custom, I had Ïbïrayïm, Saparbay, and Chaki Qaptaghayev sit around me in front of the gathered people, and setting a pillow on my legs and a tray on top of that, I began to write. After writing a few pages, I passed the pillow and tray to Ïbïrayïm, and watched him write a few pages. I very much liked his cursive hand.

Another apprentice scribe added:

> One of Ïbïrayïm's advantages is that he writes Arabic script extremely fast. Because Saghïmbay was not accustomed to reciting for dictation, we

1. A manuscript by another early scribe who recorded parts of Saghïmbay's *Manas* in the 1920s has come to light in *The Epic of Manas: The Manuscript of the Manas Singer M. Mergenbaev*, facsimile, transcription and interpretation, ed. Kadyraly Konkobaev et al. (Astana: Ghylym, 2019), in Kirghiz.
2. *Mso a*, vol. 1, p. 36.

could not keep up with his recitation. Only Ïbïrayïm was able to keep up as he wrote down what was recited.[1]

Saghïmbay did not always sing at a rapid pace. He sometimes paused in thought, or revised a previous day's narration after dreaming it differently overnight. He was used to interacting with his audiences, and he did the same thing with the folklorists he now faced. In his *Kökötöy*, he tells "you mullahs" to pay attention (p. 52), and seems to engage in a momentary back-and-forth with them over obsolescent terminology (p. 54); the folklorists' words are not recorded.

The collaborators set about methodically toward the goal of recording the entire *Manas* text from Saghïmbay. The work went slowly due to insufficient financial support and organization. The bard was living in abject poverty when the project started, and his situation did not improve much, despite small donations the folklorists gave him from their own pockets. Saghïmbay kept at the work out of friendship with Abdïraqmanov, his closest collaborator. The two traveled to Tashkent in 1925 at the summons of the Soviet Turkestan government's scientific research arm, but their appearance generated little interest and no funding. Saghïmbay got an upbraiding for his slow working pace; Abdïraqmanov later learned that the experts burned the transcripts they made of Saghïmbay's singing, preferring to search for a bard from a different tribe. Back home in the mountains, Abdïraqmanov tried to encourage Saghïmbay to finish his *Manas*, but the bard was heartbroken. They worked on as best they could, moving from place to place, always in need. The work became monotonous. Instead of appreciative crowds, for hours on end Saghïmbay faced the lone scribe, albeit his friend and partner. The later parts of the narrative, including *The Memorial Feast for Kökötöy Khan* (recorded in October 1925) are said to have suffered in quality from all the strain.

Saghïmbay was sick with a neurological disorder, and by 1925 his powers of memory and stamina had begun to decline. He stopped singing *Manas* in the latter part of 1926; the last lines that Abdïraqmanov wrote down, after the very end of the narration, were Saghïmbay's blistering complaint about the bad faith, ill treatment, and lack of support the two faced from state officials in their years-long labor.[2] Returning home after parting with Abdïraqmanov, Saghïmbay could not remember his wife. In 1929, afraid of falling

1.   Kuttugaly Ibraimov, *Ybyraiym Abdyrakhmanov* (Frunze: Ilim, 1987), pp. 12–13, in Kirghiz.
2.   *Mso a*, vol. 8/9, pp. 633–4.

into the hands of Bolshevik agitators who branded him an adherent of the old chieftains and the old religion, he moved to the shore of Issyk Kul near his birthplace. His health improved, his neighbors adored him, and he began to sing again for a while, but by the following spring his health declined and he took to bed. He spent his last painful weeks gripped with visions from *Manas*, rambling incoherently, rising at times from his bed to say, "Look how many people have gathered, don't you see, they're putting on Kökötöy's memorial feast!" In May 1930 he was taken back to his longtime home, the high, windy Qochqor valley. Upon arrival there he took a drink of water from the stream and died in the cart he was riding in, aged sixty-three.[1] His *Semetey*, for which he was particularly famous and which he most enjoyed singing, was never recorded. Talantaaly Bakchiev, a present-day *Manas* singer and scholar, and thus an authority on the strenuous labor of the bardic art, has declared that Saghïmbay gave up his life in reciting his *Manas*.

Narrating a full-length epic biography of Manas had likely not been attempted before Saghïmbay, particularly for the purpose of writing it down. Saghïmbay's painstaking work over several years to unify the sprawling plot lines of the epic cycle, add supplementary material, and get the whole thing committed to writing was an unprecedented and influential achievement. The fact that the initiative for the project came from a folklorist outside the tradition, and that Saghïmbay collaborated with an evolving group of patrons and scribes, makes the work more complex to analyze, though no less Saghïmbay's own masterpiece. Miftaqov and Abdïraqmanov not only succeeded thus in salvaging *Manas* for the embryonic textual archives of the new Soviet scientific establishment; they also enabled the artist to conceive and construct as if from the ground up a new, unitary epic vision. Saghïmbay's artistic innovations are of a kind well known in world literature where conscious collaboration between oral poets and ethno-nationally minded folklorists produce works to suit the needs of modern audiences. These intellectual interventions in epic poetry are as old as time (the Finnish *Kalevala* is a well-known example), but few traditions besides the Kirghiz afford such a clear view of the who, what, when, why, and how behind the metamorphosis of oral heroic epic into folkloric national epopee.

Contemporary critiques survive that show that Saghïmbay's exuberant inventiveness was not to the taste of some connoisseurs. One, the Kirghiz historian Belek Soltonoev (1878–1938), who heard

1.   Raisa Kydyrbaeva, *The Bardic Mastery of the Manas Singer* (Frunze: Ilim, 1984), p. 43, in Russian.

Saghïmbay perform *Manas* several times, even wrote indirect criticism of Qayum Miftaqov, the initiator of the Saghïmbay recording project, subtly implying that the Bashkir outsider had failed to discern Saghïmbay's tendencies to over-inflate his narrations. After Soltonoev died, his criticisms of Saghïmbay lay unpublished and forgotten for many decades.

But Saghïmbay's text began to fall short of other, tougher standards. By the early 1930s the Soviet Union's shifting dogmas on thorny questions of national cultural identities completely overwhelmed the normal public life of the Kirghiz epic tradition. Religious, national, and "pan-Turkic" elements in the epics came under harsh scrutiny, and were found in particular abundance in Saghïmbay's *Manas*. Sayaqbay Qarala uulu (also spelled Saiakbai Karalaev, 1894–1971), a farm laborer who was a loyal and active communist, worked with the approval and support of the state to become the most famous bard of the Soviet era. The first project to record Sayaqbay's *Manas* in writing began in the year of Saghïmbay's death with sessions that ultimately came under the management of Saghïmbay's friend, the bard and master stenographer Ïbïrayïm Abdïraqmanov. Sayaqbay narrated *Manas* several more times over the decades for recordings, including audio and film. His monumental *Manas* lacks the broad, eclectic, religious world-view of Saghïmbay's version, which should have made its wide publication in the Soviet era less problematic. Yet Saghïmbay's version remained the preferred standard in the Soviet era, requiring arduous abridgments before it could be published.

In China, where literary impulses in the tradition had been felt early, the bard Jüsüp Mamay (1918–2014), initially trained by his elder brother Balbay, created his own enormous *Manas* cycle in the 1960s (and again, after the text was destroyed in the Cultural Revolution, in the 1970s and 1980s) using a combination of oral and written composition – in some ways a cousin of Saghïmbay's *Manas* from a parallel realm of classicism and communism.

HOW SAGHÏMBAY REMODELED
THE TRADITION

The unity of Saghïmbay's narrative structure seems to have lent it an almost physical strength to uphold massive accretions of narrative expansion and ornament. We can measure the overwhelming scale of Saghïmbay's additions by comparing the length of his *Manas* with the epics that survive from the nineteenth-century Heroic Period.[1] Saghïm-bay's version totals over 185,000 lines, nineteen times longer than the 9,400 lines of Radloff's nineteenth-century *Manas* texts. Saghïmbay's combined narrative would have taken approximately 200 hours to perform straight through. Where mid-nineteenth-century bards had narrated *The Memorial Feast for Kökötöy Khan* in about 2,000 to 3,000 lines (entertainment for half an evening to a full evening), Saghïmbay luxuriated in a telling that was more than 13,000 lines long and would have taken about sixteen hours to perform.

Saghïmbay's innovative narrative design captured, for the first time that is known, a long story arc in which Manas's life served as the focus of a grand super-narrative of ethno-religious struggles. Saghïmbay built connections of cause and effect, of foreshadowing and retrospective, across the episodes of Manas's life, weaving into a single narrative numerous epics that before that time had been separate members of a cycle.

In Saghïmbay's telling, Manas grew up to be the unifier, liberator, and martial paragon of the Kirghiz people. He converted to Islam as a youth, ended his near relations' long sojourn in the Altai mountains, and brought them together to reconquer the Tien Shan mountain homeland from which they had been driven out by the expansion of infidel Qalmaq and Qïtay. The reconquest of this territory by the Kirghiz left their Qïtay and Qalmaq foes with scores to settle. These came to a head in the later episodes of the narrative, where Manas was in charge of both the Muslim Turkic allies' defense against infidel incursions and climactic campaigns of plunder and conquest inside Qalmaq and Qïtay lands.

The overall plot of Saghïmbay's *Manas* text comprises ten episodes. The first four episodes represent Saghïmbay's most extensive individual contributions to the narrative, featuring his foreshadowing and bridging episodes that undergird and motivate the heroes' actions in later episodes: (1) The birth and childhood of Manas; his first clashes with enemies; his election as khan; (2) His battles in alliance with Qoshoy against enemies; (3) His campaign to the Tien Shan mountains to liberate the land of his ancestors; (4) Migration of the Kirghiz, led by Manas, from the Altai mountains to the Tien Shan; victory over the Qïtay Alooke Khan; victory over Shooruq. Only a tiny portion of the incidents in these early parts is known from the mid-nineteenth century.

The fifth through the eighth parts correspond closely to the plots of documented epics from the Heroic Period, and thus constitute the

1. On the periodization of the tradition see pp. 277–9.

core elements of the cycle; the ninth part also relates to the known Heroic Period epics in so far as its plot constitutes a massive outgrowth of the final action of the eighth part: (5) The story of Almambet; (6) Manas's marriage to Qanïkey; (7) The intrigue of Manas's kinsmen the Közqamans, who were raised in Qalmaq territory; (8) Kökötöy's memorial feast; (9) The great campaign to Beejin. A final part (10), about Semetey's birth, Manas's departure on the haj, a raid by the Qïtay on Manas's defenseless realm, and his punitive campaign, death in battle, and burial, bring Saghïmbay's biography of Manas to a close and prefigure the rise of Semetey.

One innovation by Saghïmbay or the folklorists who transcribed his words was so influential that it is seldom acknowledged. The reidentification of the preeminent Noghoy heroes as Kirghiz was a fortuitous step that ensured the epic of Manas would survive and gain new relevance in Kirghiz Soviet national culture. On the pages of Saghïmbay's *Manas* manuscripts, particularly in the *Kökötöy* volume, some (but not all) instances of the name *Qïrghïz* (Kirghiz) have been written in over an obliterated original word. In some of these instances it is possible to discern traces of the name *Ughuz* (Oghuz) or *Alach* (Alash) or *Türk* beneath the overwritten *Qïrghïz*. This suggests that Saghïmbay had used ethnic vocabulary suitable to him and his audience, and later changes to the manuscripts leveled the diversity of terms, putting the Kirghiz in the foreground. Ïbïrayïm Abdïraqmanov's hand is identifiable in some of these alterations. In other parts of his *Manas*, Saghïmbay explains the origin of the Kirghiz via the ancestor Ughuz Khan; those manuscript pages seem to be untampered with.[1]

Saghïmbay was inclined to show more of himself in his poetry than the mid-nineteenth-century bards, and it is fortunate that the poet thus revealed has wit and charm. His appreciation for the beauty of nature was undoubtedly inspired by the untold time he spent traversing his mountain homeland on horseback. A lyrical image of the rays emitted by a low sun from under the cloud cover of a sudden storm, "The mountainsides were all covered with hail; a shimmering haze arose, and the sky blackened in the west, thundering and casting beams of bronze light," concludes with the rueful comment of one who is all too experienced at being caught out by bad weather: "People and horses alike streamed at the nose from the sudden cold" (p. 128).

Saghïmbay's outlook comes across as a humble optimism tinged, sometimes irreverently, with religion. He even verges on inter-confessional

---

1.   *Mso a*, vol. 6 suppl./7, pp. 167, 268–9; vol. 8/9, p. 495. See Qïr Ughuz in the Index.

philosophy, as when he comments on a scene of venal behavior by mullahs: "First one encounters the sharia; higher than that is Truth, and higher still is the Way; crowning them all is Knowledge. Those who know, know that much!" (p. 48). When Boqmurun is on the point of being forced to present his beloved heirloom steed Maani-ker as a gift of honor to Qongurbay, wise old Qoshoy does his best to soften the blow with a stoic aphorism: "The earth submits to a horse's limbs; if the lowly earth had no master, whatever would? The sky submits to a bird's limbs; as the lofty sky has a master, so do many" (p. 115). In other words, everyone is doing someone else's bidding, know your place in the world.

Indeed, Saghïmbay's humanism is tempered with a fatalism that reveals not only his piety but also his long experience of suffering. The world he knew best was that of ordinary people, whose acceptance of poverty and oppression he depicted with no sense of injustice; the abused were as fixed in their fate as the rich and powerful were in theirs. When Boqmurun has cartloads of coins from his late father's treasury thrown out by the handful to the common people, they are reduced to grubbing in the dirt and fighting each other over the meager gain (pp. 51–2). One suspects that Saghïmbay saw scenes like this at feasts he attended. This prevalent world-view is remarkable only by historical contrast, given that Saghïmbay's *Manas* was recorded in the early years of the Soviet Union. We know from a funeral lament the bard composed "On Comrade Lenin" that the optimistic formulas of communism did appeal to his sense of hope, though most of the thought on display in his *Manas* would be impossible to reconcile with Marxist–Leninist ideology.

There is humanism too in Saghïmbay's ability to joke about people, from the highest to the lowest. When Qoshoy finds himself at a loss with no wrestling breeches to wear, "this fleeting world passes on, but your grandpa Qoshoy was at a standstill" (p. 163). Yet the bard, like many of the heroes, had a mean streak; the poem is fraught with rough mockery, and to the very last line Saghïmbay was able to tap depths of bigotry to which purveyors of incipiently national epics have always been prone.

COMPARATIVE NOTES

The Memorial Feast for Kökötöy Khan is a well-known epic poem popular in the Kirghiz bardic repertoire even today. It is the only *Manas* poem that was recorded in two different oral versions in the mid-nineteenth century, several years before Saghïmbay was born. Comparing these two versions, the oldest ones known, with Saghïmbay's can tell us a great deal about all three poets' oral knowledge and creativity, and Saghïmbay's innovations in particular. One of the versions was performed in 1856 near Qarqïra by the bard Nazar Bolot and was written down by or for Chokan Valikhanov, a Qazaq prince, Russian army officer, and folklore collector; it consists of 3,251 lines. The other co-version of our text was recorded in 1862, probably in the same general area as the first, by the Turcologist Wilhelm Radloff from the oral performance of a bard whose name was not recorded but who definitely was not Nazar Bolot; it consists of 2,197 lines.

Possessing a set of three different texts of the traditional narrative to compare, we can begin to deal with them efficiently by using clear and concise labels. MK signifies *The Memorial Feast for Kökötöy Khan* in general, irrespective of or generally comprising the specific texts that survive. The texts are labeled MK*NB* (the MK of Nazar Bolot),[1] MK*WR* (the anonymous MK recorded by Wilhelm Radloff),[2] and the text translated in this volume, MK*SO* (the MK of Saghïmbay Orozbaq uulu, 1925). Headings of notes below are arranged by the page numbers of the passages in MK*SO* to which they relate; if the discussion in a note ranges widely in the translated text, the page numbers in the heading represent one of the first important passages. Passages in MK*NB* and MK*WR* are usually quoted from Arthur Hatto's translations, though in a few cases I have changed the translations to reflect my different interpretations.

Manas's genealogy and the Kirghiz (p. 3)

Manas's genealogy was neither deep nor stable in the nineteenth-century MK tradition, as bards drew differing accounts of his lineage consisting of only a few generations. The genealogy in MK*SO* shows considerable depth in remote legendary times, a sign of innovation in

1.   In Hatto's 1977 edition of MK*NB* he labels the poem *KO* ; at that time, the attribution of the text to Nazar Bolot was not confirmed.

2.   Hatto labels this poem both *BM* ("Bok-murun") and, following Radloff, I, 4). Hatto also published two comparative analyses of the structures of MK*NB* and MK*WR*: A. T. Hatto, "Kukotay and Bok Murun: A Comparison of Two Related Heroic Poems of the Kirghiz," *Bulletin of the School of Oriental and African Studies* 1969, (Part I) 32, no. 2, pp. 344–78; (Part II) 32, no. 3, pp. 541–70; and Appendix 2 in MK*NB*, pp. 249–54.

the tradition. A much fuller version of the genealogy than the one given in *MKso* occurs in the opening lines of Saghïmbay's full-length poem on the birth of Manas. Names of personages and lineages here that might have chimed in Saghïmbay's mind with historical or legendary antecedents include Babur Khan, Buura Khan, Noghoy, Qara Khan, and Ughuz Khan. In Saghïmbay's account of the genealogy, Qara 'Black' Kirghiz, an ethnic label introduced by Russians in the nineteenth century, gains a look of ancientry through the association with Qara Khan, a traditional ancestor of Manas the Noghoy since the nineteenth century.

Kökötöy's relationship with Manas (pp. 4–5)

Saghïmbay had narrated the events recapitulated here – how Manas's distant relative the aged Kökötöy had acquired the throne of Tashken by overthrowing Esen Khan's viceroy Panus Khan with Manas's help – at length in an earlier episode, but there is no evidence that this narrative was known in the nineteenth century. With this invented prologue, Saghïmbay's version brings Manas's growing predominance in the traditional story of Kökötöy's memorial feast onto the level of explicit plot logic, as if Manas's long-standing regard for Kökötöy were his motivation for presiding over the feast when the time came.

Kökötöy's wives (p. 6)

In separate passages Saghïmbay names several women dear to or left behind by the dying Kökötöy, sometimes two together in one verse: Ayïmkül (p. 6), Külqanïsh (p. 13), Qanïshay and Külayïm (the latter possibly the same as Ayïmkül, p. 17), Ayghanïsh (possibly the same as Qanïshay) and Küljar (p. 25). Only Külayïm receives more than one mention, once as "his queen" (p. 137). The woman Kökötöy refers to as "my dear Qanïshay" (p. 17) could be one of his wives or his new daughter-in-law, Boqmurun's bride (p. 8). Thus there are from three to six named wives of Kökötöy in the poem; they take no part in the action. The names have jingling, stereotypical meanings (Ayïmkül 'Lady Flower', Külqanïsh 'Flower Queen', Qanïshay 'Queen Moon', Külayïm 'Flower Lady', Ayghanïsh 'Moon Queen', and Küljar 'Flower Beloved'). The nineteenth-century epic texts record no wives or widows of Kökötöy, by any name or number. From these facts it is apparent that Saghïmbay ornamented his ample narrative design by introducing these insignificant characters and giving them names that were new to the epic tradition.

Kökötöy's testament (pp. 6–25)

For about 1,200 verses at the start of the poem, about 9 percent of the text, wealthy Kökötöy utters his last testament, making a long, contradictory list of prohibitions and commands about the rites and the correct amount of expenses of money, goods, and livestock. Beginning at page 7, Kökötöy tells his survivors not to spend lavishly on the burial and public observances, going into great detail about what they should not do, and not to send heralds out with announcements to an endless run of such-and-such people in some-such land ruled by so-and-so hero. Then he reverses, and issues commands for what he does want, seemingly just as extravagant. The pivot occurs as he plans his burial (p. 14); the issue of what constitutes a seemly outlay for the final obsequies over his earthly remains seems to pry open his mental purse. Announcing, "Let my riches be used up; let the people know I have died!" (p. 15), he makes his behests all over again, but in even more elaborate form and changed into what he does want. Vacillations between do's and don'ts recur throughout.

Saghïmbay makes use of the contradictions in Kökötöy's testament later on, from which we may be assured that they were part of the bard's narrative plan. Baymïrza, who has the responsibility of relaying Kökötöy's wishes to his absent son Boqmurun, justifies his own miserly attitude by interpreting Kökötöy's words as senile ravings; Boqmurun in turn is able to point to the positive behests as his own justification for spending generously.

This is one of many ways in which Saghïmbay's narrative design resembled the traditional plot (Kökötöy's testament is given and wrangled over in MKNB, ll. 45–258), while also greatly elaborating on it. The spirit of Saghïmbay's elaboration itself seems to have roots in controversies over chiefly funerals in the nineteenth century. The Tsarist Russian administration that ruled in the Kirghiz homeland since the 1860s sought to curb the power of the tribal chiefs and prevent them from putting on expensive memorial feasts. In their anti-feasting policies, Russian officials found allies in a new wave of Muslim imams and teachers who spread Islamic teaching among the Kirghiz during the late nineteenth and early twentieth centuries. Feasting was a traditional practice of nomadic Muslims that the new champions of religious norms would not abide, and Kirghiz were enjoined more than ever to bury their dead without extravagant observances.

We can be confident that Kirghiz connoisseurs of epic in Saghïmbay's day would have been familiar with the hints-to-do-the-opposite trope of modesty in Kökötöy's last testament. A Kirghiz oral history preserves a famous example of this very thing happening around the death of a powerful chieftain. Before he died in 1858, Borombay of the Bughu tribe, a loyal subordinate of the tsar, told his people not to hold a horse race at his memorial feast, or build him a tomb, or allow his women to go into mourning and scar their faces. His inner courtiers were upset, and a poet in his circle sang a rejoinder, imploring Borombay to abide by tradition.

This concern did not appear in texts of the *MK* tradition until much later, in *MKSO*. There, Kökötöy gives contradictory commands to Baymïrza both to be sparing and to be unstinting with his wealth after his death; Baymïrza interprets the testament according to his own miserly inclination. In *MKNB* (which was recorded two years before Borombay's death and, coincidentally, within his clan), there are economic concerns, but they are characterized differently. Kökötöy commands that his tomb be erected, that there be feasts and racing, and that his people be held together; the regent Baymïrza is unmotivated to put on the feast, preferring to live on in luxury at the expense of Kökötöy's estate. Boqmurun then upbraids and effectively usurps Baymïrza to get the feast plans going (ll. 247–58). The changed cultural climate under Tsarist rule may have affected Saghïmbay's narration of Kökötöy's testament, the policy that he described Baymïrza adopting afterward, and Boqmurun's handling of the wishes of his father and his regent.

Catalogues of heroes and peoples (pp. 17–24)

The catalogues of heroes and the itineraries linking their residences are the main features that make Kökötöy's testament so strikingly long in *MKSO*. Catalogues are an important resource in epic narration. More than mere lists, they are a means for the bard to convey mastery of large amounts of traditional knowledge and thus to enhance his standing with the audience as an expert narrator. They may also help the bard to get control over a difficult stretch of narration, or to coax a distracted audience into receptivity. In the nineteenth century, catalogues of heroes were rife with cyclically allusive epithets, something of the nature of "hyperlinks," where cognoscenti in the audience would recognize discrete incidents in the tradition from their mentions in association with the hero, heroine, or horse being catalogued. In this fashion catalogues could even be a sub-entertainment of their own, as for example Boqmurun's invitations in *MKNB* (ll. 531–820) and *MKWR* (ll. 25–174). Saghïmbay, on the other hand, padded some of his catalogues with enormous amounts of novel information. This is understandable if we remember that Saghïmbay could read and was a highly curious compiler of knowledge. Faced with awareness of the vastness of written knowledge, he may have used catalogues like the ones in Kökötöy's testament to display the relevance of the oral epic tradition.

Boqmurun son of Kökötöy Khan (p. 23)

Saghïmbay's narration says literally that Kökötöy "leaves no child" when he means that he leaves no son, and even that understanding is embedded in knowledge that is unspoken. Two subtle layers of meaning underlying this statement, which would have been clear to the Kirghiz audience, raise questions for us. First, what of the daughters of Kökötöy whom Saghïmbay already mentioned briefly? Even though it is technically wrong to say that Kökötöy's wives "never gave birth" (earlier Kökötöy said, "I have given away daughters as brides in eleven lands, so my eleven sons-in-law are all over the world," p. 7), the girls simply did not count in the matter of childlessness being discussed here, because in this patrilineal society, only males could inherit property; married daughters were no longer members of their birth families in this respect. So a second question arises, what of Kökötöy's son, Boqmurun? Here Saghïmbay's statement "his wives never gave birth before they reached old age, so that he leaves no child" (son) makes sense from the standpoint of the epic tradition. Kirghiz audiences knew that Boqmurun had been born the natural child of the hero Er Töshtük and a *peri*, and that Töshtük had left him on the steppe, where Kökötöy later found him; Kökötöy, lacking sons of his own, adopted him (as Kökötöy says later in MK*so*, "I adopted the son of a spirit," p. 25). Kökötöy's death when Boqmurun was so young (in the nineteenth-century versions he was clearly a child) left the vast wealth vulnerable to the very sort of contentions and appropriations that Kökötöy describes.

In MK*NB* Boqmurun is explicitly raised as khan in Kökötöy's place after he plans the migration to the memorial feast all on his own (ll. 268–381), before the real action begins. This shows that the main motivation of the story, as described above in Fundamentals of the Plot, was for Boqmurun to attain not khanly rank, but something more: heroic standing.

Predictions of trouble (p. 29)

Baymïrza puts interesting words into Kökötöy's mouth in reporting the content of the testament to Boqmurun. Kökötöy did not, as

Baymïrza says he did, predict the troubles that will arise at the feast: "the Qïtays are going to steal the first prize of the thoroughbred that comes in first place in the race," and a bit later, sounding even more oracular, "Invite those seeking vengeance, let them attack my people!". The Kirghiz audience knew those results were coming, however. Saghïmbay knew they knew, and took the opportunity to work the predicitions into his characterization of Baymïrza's deviousness. Baymïrza implies: Who would want to throw a feast where such terrible happenings were anticipated? Saghïmbay here opens a window through which the seasoned audience could gain extra enjoyment of their own knowledge of the epic. This is but one example of Saghïmbay's artistic generosity toward his audiences and his need to be in "conversation" with them and with the oral tradition they shared.

Boqmurun consults Manas (pp. 34–6)

Saghïmbay's conception of Manas's involvement in the planning of the feast is innovative. In the nineteenth century Boqmurun did not consult Manas on his plans or even expect that Manas would predominate. Instead, Boqmurun made his own plans, and Manas took the lead upon his arrival at the grand memorial feast. In Saghïmbay's narration, there is a plausible justification for Manas's involvement when Manas recalls, "Kökötöy blessed-by-Qïzïr was someone closer to me than my father" (p. 35). There is also Manas's stated intention in the prologue to Kökötöy's testament, where Saghïmbay says, "Manas made every effort in giving his memorial feast" (p. 6). This was a tellingly false attribution of the planning to Manas, but a true sign of the completeness of the tradition's acceptance of the Manas figure's takeover of the proceedings.

Manas's harsh disdain for Boqmurun (p. 35) was traditional, appearing in the nineteenth-century versions of the poem as well. In those texts it makes more sense, however, since Manas was not described as friendly with Kökötöy as he was here, and Boqmurun's first meeting with Manas does not occur until the latter's arrival at the feast, the invitation to which has made him angry.

The burial and the fortieth-day feast (pp. 39–56)

There is a subtle difference between the advice Boqmurun requests of Manas in their interview and what Manas actually advises him to do (pp. 34, 35); neither point is dealt with in the mid-nineteenth-century versions of *MK*. Kirghiz custom recognized three main funeral observances: the sharia burial as soon as possible after death, a feast forty days after to send off the departing soul, and a grand memorial feast, the ritual end of mourning, customarily on or about the anniversary of death. Kökötöy's instructions, to which Boqmurun alludes, concerned the burial and the grand memorial feast. Manas seems to limit his advice to the plans for the burial and the fortieth-day feast, which, according to his thinking, should be combined. The incongruity may be part of Saghïmbay's design to provide fuller justification for Manas's effective takeover of the memorial feast proceedings. If audiences preferred the thought of Manas stepping into the role with good cause, Saghïmbay seems to point to Boqmurun's extravagant spending in the days after Kökötöy's death, which culminates in the fortieth-day feast, as a sign that Boqmurun was not financially prudent enough to carry out his grand plan.

Part of Saghïmbay's motivation to portray fulsome details of Islamic burial ritual (p. 48) may have been to preclude criticism of the delay of the burial for nearly forty days. This interval was in line with older local customs, but was seen as impious by Muslims from elsewhere, of whom there were growing numbers among the Kirghiz in the late nineteenth and early twentieth centuries. Moreover, Saghïmbay may have depicted Boqmurun holding the burial a little before the fortieth day in order to give Boqmurun a modicum of independent decision-making in the direction of greater piety; it was Manas's advice that the burial should not take place until fully forty days had passed.

The words Saghïmbay uses to depict the burial rituals, derived from Arabic, sound unusual in the context of the Kirghiz epic tradition. They may even have had an abstruse ring to some members of Saghïmbay's Kirghiz audiences, who would have looked to Saghïmbay as an authority on the basic concepts of the religious life of Muslims. Below, the same portion of the paragraph with the untranslated burial terms is shown with English equivalents given in brackets.

Then Boqmurun awarded his *keperet* [donation to the mullah for performing the ritual atonement of sins] by driving in two hundred thousand sheep and tethering ninety thousand cows, and had fully forty-one mullahs recite the *janaza* [funeral prayer], and had the *buraq at* [horse as a gift to the presiding mullah] fitted out. A crowd of friends took hold and carried the *tabït* [bier]; then he made the *bidiya* [donation from the chattels of the deceased for the atonement of his sins]. For the *salootu namaz* [prayer of solace] and the *janaza* [funeral prayer] the people stood shoulder to shoulder in row after row until you could not see the other end; a shout from one side of the crowd would not be heard on the other. They recited the *namaz* [prayer] and the *tekbir* [glorification of God] without *sajide* [making prostrations], and fitted out the racer named Chong-toru as the *buraq at* [gift horse to the presiding mullah]. (p. 48)

The words *keperet* and *bidiya*, similar in meaning to *dooron*, the word Kökötöy used in his testament (p. 9), signify donations from the property of the deceased aimed at the atonement of his sins, or in payment to the mullah who performs the ritual atonement. Bowing and prostration to the *qibla*, called *sajide* in Kirghiz, is required in daily Muslim prayers, but is prohibited in prayer at burials.

The invitations and threats (pp. 77–87)

Boqmurun's harsh threats to the chiefs he invites to the feast have traditional antecendents (*MKNB*, ll. 531–820) and traditional motivations. One was narrative characterization: a hero will boast so, confident both in his power to make good on his threat and in the expectation that the invited hero will choose to attend. (The heroic ethos permitted no empty threats.) There is a subtler matter of social and political context as well. Nothing could be left to chance when the candidate–chief organized his predecessor's memorial feast. He had to attract a large and prestigious list of guests; their presence validated his candidacy for the succession and thus supported the political transition brought on by the former chief's death. One could not assume that an invited nomad would go out of his way to attend merely out of feelings of sympathy, conviviality, or sportive enthusiasm. Other gatherings held by the tribe followed the annual calendar and thus had a more predictable base of attendance, but a feast occasioned by a death had no traditional, seasonal motivation; the host had to bring it into being by virtue of the deceased's reputation and by force of will. Faced with these requirements, the candidate had to persuade or, to be on the safe side, command and threaten his fellow heroes into attending. See p. 261 above.

Manas's companions' cruelty to Jash Aydar (pp. 94–5)

The sense that heroes of Kirghiz epic could be severely cruel has emerged clearly in the text. The scene in which Manas's close companions Sïrghaq, Serek, and Chubaq nearly execute Boqmurun's herald Jash Aydar dramatizes this cruelty for the first time. Jash Aydar's offense is no more than to have repeated the peremptory words Boqmurun instructed him to use, but the companions will not allow anyone to

address Manas in that way and live. Manas saves the wretchedly beg-
ging Aydar at the last moment, gaining credit for both the magnanimity
expressed by him and the severity expressed on his behalf.

There were antecedents to all this, more violent versions of the
encounter in the nineteenth-century texts. In *MKNB*, Manas is touchier
than the companions in *MKSO*. Jash Aydar invites Manas respectfully,
even adding, "'Please to direct my Feast!' said Bok-murun." Angry at
being disturbed and at Aydar's too-demanding conclusion, "On my
return from this place, what answer am I to give to my lord Bok-
murun?" Manas flies into a rage, and commands his companions to
execute Aydar. The herald narrowly saves his own life with eloquent
begging; Manas releases him to go on his way with threats to Boqmu-
run for having dared to invite him (*MKNB*, ll. 946–1111). The bard of
MKWR displayed even more brutality. Manas's companions carry out
his order to kill the herald – tying him down and trampling him under
their horses – for the lesser provocation of having interrupted him while
he was losing at chess (ll. 258–338). Professor Hatto has emphasized
the significance of this action: "Needless to say, the killing of an envoy
was a crime of the first order on the steppe." The fact that Boqmurun
does not avenge the killing marks him as a heroic nonentity in *MKWR*,[1]
a fate in keeping with the development of the tradition. The harshness
of the scene seems to have weighed on the *MKWR* bard. He holds some-
thing back as if out of guilt by association: when Manas orders his
companions to do the deed, he does not call out their names in the tra-
ditional catalogue–summons.

The scene in *MKSO*, though within the range of past tradition, has
lost the thread of logic in Saghïmbay's busy hands. The bard ignores
the fact that Boqmurun sent an invitation to Manas to attend the bur-
ial (p. 39), presumably using peremptory threats that Manas himself
advised him to use (p. 35), and that Manas accepted the invitation,
bringing with him Sïrghaq and Serek (and without killing the herald,
one can assume). The discrepancy helps to show how the narration of
Boqmurun's visit to Manas to get advice after Kökötöys death was an
innovation in Saghïmbay's telling.

The feasting ground, Boqmurun's itinerary, and timing (pp. 65–9)

The broad, well-watered valley of Qarqïra east of lake Issyk Kul today
lies mostly in Kazakhstan, with a portion in Kyrgyzstan, close to those

1.   *MWR*, p. 160.

two countries' borders with China. It was a major way-point on routes of migration and trade. The idea to locate the feasting ground at Qarqïra, on the border between the lands of Muslim Turkic nomads (and eventually the Russian Empire) to the west and Buddhist Mongol nomads (and eventually the Ch'ing Empire) to the east, reflects conditions as early as the mid-eighteenth century, when Qalmaq pastures were restricted within the borders of the Ch'ing Empire by the latter's destruction of the nomadic Junghar Empire. The grass of Qarqïra's excellent pastures famously grows to the height of a rider's stirrups by late summer. Saline springs put very pure salt within reach of anyone who can boil down the brine. It was contentions among nomads over the control of these key resources that caused the effective border to shift back and forth over the territory of Qarqïra. An annual fair brought nomads and traders together in the valley, and must have suggested to Kirghiz epic bards and audiences the scale and diversity of crowds that could gather there, and the possibilities of fights between Muslims and infidels. (By Saghïmbay's time in the early twentieth century, a shop flying an American flag at the Qarqïra fair was selling Singer sewing machines to nomads from across Asia.)

Saghïmbay continues a long tradition of siting Kökötöy's memorial feast at Qarqïra. Indeed, in this respect his version is more traditional than *MKNB* and *MKWR*, both of which feature different locations of the feast that their bards apparently offered to appeal to the foreign patrons of their epic performances. (The fact that Qarqïra was the traditional feasting ground is confirmed in another Kirghiz epic from the nineteenth century, *Joloy Khan*, which mentions Kökötöy's feast there in passing.) The choice by a khan of Tashken to hold a great memorial feast in distant Qarqïra clearly hinges on his political motivation to be near the border of Sino-Qalmaq territory so that he can welcome and lord it over those foreign heroes.

The itinerary that Saghïmbay's Boqmurun follows to bring his people and herds from Tashken to Qarqïra for the feast (pp. 68–9) is realistic in terms of intermediate stops (Tashken; Oluya-Ata, Chïmkent, and Sayram; Qozu-bashï and Qopo; Almatï; Eshik and Türgön; Chabdar; Üch Qarqïra). The realism of Kirghiz epic itineraries is also traditional. Itineraries were more than catalogues of places; they were poetically styled but subject to practical scrutiny by bards and audiences whose understanding of geography was profound. Even in *MKNB* and *MKWR*, with their non-traditional ending points, the itineraries that the bards constructed to get to those points are highly realistic, reflecting their extensive knowledge of the geography of the region. The bard of *MKWR* dealt realistically with the seasonal implications of Boqmurun's itinerary, stretching the migration out over a few months that would have been required to get a large number of people and grazing animals from the vicinity of Tashkent to the feasting ground on the border of China. For part of the way the route goes through passes and valleys at higher elevation, where the choicest grasses would have been found in summer. Saghïmbay too concerns himself with the availability of good grazing, noting mainly the length of stops in days, but not of the stages of movement between them. The total of thirty-eight days Saghïmbay mentioned as stops should be supplemented implicitly with another month at least for movement and for stops not fully accounted for, giving a realistic length of about two and a half months or more for the itinerary.

Saghïmbay is mostly consistent in his references to times of year at different points in the preparations for and conduct of the feast. After the burial, fifteen-year-old Boqmurun plans for the great memorial feast, "When two years have passed from this year – in the third year" (p. 56), but later Saghïmbay says, "Fully three years had passed and Boqmurun's promise had come up again" (p. 59), as the hero takes counsel on holding the feast. A short time later Boqmurun starts the migration at the beginning of autumn, which at the length reckoned above would have brought him to Qarqïra towards the end of the year. Upon arrival Boqmurun announces, "This year rounds out the third since my father's death" (p. 73), consistent with the first but not the second of the two previous statements. Then he sends Jash Aydar out to invite all the guests, a journey that takes nine months. It is best to accept that the guests all arrived as soon as those nine months had expired, as the feast started late that summer ("it was when the sweltering summer days had passed and autumn was coming on," p. 65).

Manas arrives one month after the first guests, and the poem ends about thirteen days later. During that time, while other sporting events and feasting are taking place, the horse race is run over eight days and one night, finishing the morning after. Saghïmbay is thus on fairly firm chronological footing when he remarks in passing near the finish of the horse race, "In the early autumn the nights are short." And later, Boqmurun is said to be nineteen years old. Only a reference to "the torrid dog days of summer" during the games clashes with the rest of the timing.

Saghïmbay's handling of the timing of the race – six days out and two days and a night back – is closer to realistic than the months-long courses in *MK*NB and *MK*WR (in the latter, after a start in the autumn, the race runs until the spring, see ll. 609–10). However, the actual distance planned out in Saghïmbay's version – Qarqïra to Türküstön on the Syr Darya – is an impossible fifteen hundred kilometers or so one way. See p. 257 above (note to p. 207).

Where the nineteenth-century versions of *MK* concerned themselves with the skillful timing of the migration to the feasting ground in the proper seasons, Saghïmbay broadened the time line to introduce a certain degree of consistency in chronology throughout the narrative.

The hospitality Manas receives at the feast (p. 102)

For his lodgings at the feast Manas is conducted into the luxurious white yurt of a maiden, Torum. This is strange. Manas's chief consort, his wedded wife Qanïkey, is found to be present at the feast later. It is in her tent, or in his own near hers, that Manas would be expected to spend his nights. The situation Saghïmbay depicts here comes at some cost to Qanïkey, but *MKWR* fleetingly attests that it was traditional. There, the gifts Boqmurun presents to Manas upon his arrival consist of a horse and a richly appareled maiden (ll. 479–84), yet Qanïkey appears later in that epic as well. These seemingly racy details in *MKWR* and *MKSO* appear to be hold-overs from an earlier period in the tradition when the different epics in the cycle were more distinct. At that stage, the separate poem about Manas's marriage to Qanïkey would have made no claims on the premises of any of the other epics as to whether they took place before or after the marriage, and nothing untoward would be implied in Manas's receiving a concubine at Kökötöy's memorial feast.

Presidency of the feast and horse race (pp. 100–101)

As discussed above in Fundamentals of the Plot, Boqmurun's and Manas's agendas as figures in the traditional structure of *MK* were at profound cross purposes. The unsolvable nature of this opposition is seen very well in the diverse and even contradictory ways in which the plots of the three *MK* epics handle the matter of who will preside over the feast, and specifically who will plan and direct the all-important horse race.

In *MKNB*, Kökötöy advises Baymïrza in his last testament to seek out Manas as the president of the great memorial feast (ll. 137–57). Boqmurun is raised as khan as soon as he has announced the masterful itinerary for the migration to the feast (ll. 373–81), and heroically sets out on a course to do on his own what his father had asked for Manas to do. In his invitations to the heroes, Boqmurun sends for Ay-qojo, asking him to preside over the feast; this seems to be a mere courtesy to the *khoja* (l. 1182). But when Boqmurun's steed

Maani-ker is demanded by an infidel hero (in *MKNB* it is Nezqara, not Qongurbay), Qoshoy fields the request in a way that implies that Manas, not Boqmurun, is in charge: "Indeed, Nez-kara, Infidel Khan and Little Prick, I shall go to Manas and ask him! I myself do not dispose of that horse. Yet if Manas should now say 'Give it him!' I shall bring it you. But if Manas denies you Maniker I shall not come and find you" (ll. 1466–73). Saghïmbay too makes more of Manas's position in this incident than Boqmurun would allow, having Manas announce, "As long as my brilliance shines like the sun, how can I give up my racer?" (*MKSO*, p. 120) when the racer does not belong to him.

Also in *MKNB*, Manas's high status at the feast becomes the subject of scurrilous talk that enrages Manas, when the infidels ask him, "Warrior Manas, Padishah, *sayin* Taji, Er Manas, as my lord Mejin at this feast *please* supervise and direct it, *do* preside over it in person! Now start the race!" and they ask for Ürbü to marshal the starters (ll. 1540–51). Once Manas has dispatched the impudent infidels with his whip, he presents the final plan of the race to Qoshoy: the horses will run six months outbound and six months back (ll. 1581–9). Boqmurun, however, directs the start of the race, mounting Jash Aydar on Maani-ker and assigning him to work as marshal behind the pack (ll. 1599–1627). It is also Boqmurun who posts prizes, announces events, and presents gifts of honor to the infidel heroes who are the losers in various sporting events. Thus Manas never openly assumes presidency of the feast or the race. Boqmurun's active role continues almost to the final act, where with undiminished khanly dignity he prevails upon Manas through speech and action to delay the start of hostilities over the stolen prize-herds until after his – Boqmurun's – feast is officially concluded (ll. 2578–608).

In *MKWR*, Boqmurun faces a nastier Manas. In pique at Boqmurun's invitation, which he perceives as insolent, Manas exhorts his Forty Companions, "*Let us profane his Memorial Feast!*" as he summons them to attend it with him (l. 399). But upon approaching, while still at some distance from the feasting ground, Manas takes the general commotion as a sign that a fight is under way between Muslims and infidels, and he flies into action to stop it (ll. 421–2). Soon after this, Manas assumes explicit presidency of the feast and the horse race. His friend Qoshoy and Ürbü contribute their counsels, Qoshoy's being to place Manas in charge. Manas, testy at Ürbü's inexpert advice, makes the final decision on the length of the course: starting in autumn and finishing in spring (ll. 520–615; in all three epics, Ürbü is present or mentioned in counsels on the planning of the race that enrage Manas and lead to his taking effective control of the proceedings). In *MKWR* Boqmurun still posts the prizes and calls the events as in *MKNB*, but that is all he does, and he silently disappears from the action. Yet in a very late scene, Joloy's wife Aq Sayqal relates a dream where she saw Joloy plundering gold and silver "in the presence of the Khan Lord Bok-murun," concluding, "I am afraid on that account. No good can come of it!" (ll. 1867–74). Boqmurun thus preserves his status in *MKWR* as well, if only by a reported inward vision.

In *MKSO*, Boqmurun's heroic plans and actions never include even his contemplated presidency over the feast or the race. There is never any doubt about who is supposed to dominate the action; Manas is the focus, starting with the prologue (pp. 3–6) and Kökötöy's testament ("the president of the feast will be none other than that child of the Kirghiz, Manas son of Bay Jaqïp," p. 24). Innovatively, Saghïmbay has Boqmurun travel to consult Manas on how to hold the funeral observances, and repeatedly refers to Manas as Boqmurun's choice as president. As soon as he arrives at the feast, Manas leads it, together with Qoshoy, though Manas is foremost (pp. 100–101).

A traditional epithet of Manas (p. 132)

Manas's old epithet "Sart of Samarqan," uttered here by Ürbü, may allude to Manas's different origin from the steppe heroes of the Noghay epic cycle. Though the Noghay heroes were Manas's allies in the Kirghiz epics from as early as the mid-nineteenth century, the Sarts were settled folk of towns and oases, ethnically distinct from and belittled by the steppe Turks. The epithet "Sart of Samarqan" for Manas occurs also in *MKNB* in a slightly more elaborate put-down implicating Anjïyan as well (ll. 259–64). In *MKWR*, Ürbü himself is identified as son of a Sart (l. 541).

Traditional and new sporting events (pp. 122–216)

The games played at the memorial feast in the three versions of the epic go in a traditional order. Each version features at least one event not found in the others: horse racing, the start and finish of which bracket the rest of the games (*MKNB*, ll. 1581–1627, 2273–457; *MKWR*, ll. 616–769, 1403–1553; *MKSO*, pp. 122–33, 207–16); foot racing (*MKWR*, ll. 920–73); shooting the ingot (*MKSO*, pp. 137–47); wrestling (*MKNB*, ll. 1628–1998; *MKWR*, ll. 994–1258; *MKSO*, pp. 149–79); jousting (*MKNB*, ll. 1999–2128; *MKWR*, ll. 1259–1341;

*MK*SO, pp. 187–201); untethering the camel (*MK*NB, ll. 2129–86; *MK*WR, ll. 1342–1402; *MK*SO, before the joust, pp. 181–4); a second wrestling bout (*MK*NB, ll. 2187–2272); wrestling on horseback (*MK*SO, pp. 203–204).

The wrestling breeches (pp. 161–71)

Anchored by the star turn of the beloved Muslim hero Qoshoy, enlivened with some of the most cinematic physical action in the poem, and fueled by an ironic premise, the wrestling bout between Qoshoy and Joloy is a high point in *MK*. The premise is that the giant Qoshoy, aged far past his sporting years, is still the Muslims' best hope for defeating the infidels' champion Joloy. Adding a twist to the set-up is the interlude of the search for a pair of wrestling breeches that will decently cover this old man's massive bulk while allowing him to move his legs around. In all three of our *MK* epics the stories of the wrestling match and the scenes with the breeches are basically similar. But Saghïmbay did more: he used the breeches passage to fore-shadow the transition from Manas to the next generation. Qanïkey, childless, makes the breeches, intending them for Qoshoy to wear so that with his blessing she can bear a son (*MK*SO, p. 166). The plan works, and Qoshoy predicts that she will bear Manas a son, the hero Semetey (pp. 170–71).

However, the scene with the breeches in *MK*SO has more narrative inconsistencies than thread. The main issues are in establishing Manas's knowledge of Qanïkey's having made the breeches and his knowledge of their qualities; and determining Manas's attitude toward Qanïkey – whether he praises or condemns her. To establish the mere fact of Manas's understanding that Qanïkey was responsible for the wondrous construction of the breeches, Saghïmbay takes several steps that double back on themselves.

In *MK*SO Manas is the first person to introduce the information that Qanïkey made a pair of breeches suitable for Qoshoy, and in doing so he praises her for it (p. 163). Manas's knowledge and praise are tradi-tional since the mid-nineteenth century. But later in the passage Manas seemingly shows no knowledge or interest, and has to be reminded and encouraged by Ajïbay and Chalïbay (pp. 167–8). The change occurs after Qoshoy has been unable to get the breeches over his legs in an ini-tial try-on. Chalïbay, on the point of despair when his avowals seem insufficient to sway Manas, recollects in a death-like trance (pp. 165–6) the relevant information about the breeches' origin (which was per-fectly well known in the nineteenth century, and to Manas just a moment ago here). It is also intimated with the help of the trance that heretofore Qanïkey supposedly kept the information secret (p. 166). Saghïmbay may have had to construct the trance-vision on the fly to reconfirm information that was introduced and then contradicted before (and the full knowledge of which would have caused Manas in particular to act very differently in this scene). Qanïkey, at least, knows everything throughout the passage. And in the end, Manas once again knows all about the breeches and approves of their maker, and knows about her wish to give birth to his heir (pp. 169–70). But in getting to this point we see Manas curse and threaten his wife.

For Manas to curse and threaten to kill Qanïkey (pp. 164–5) is an outrage, even for a hero from whom we have come to expect awful temper tantrums. From the perspective of narrative structure it is superfluous, and Manas's characterization hardly needed more grim features. Something about this seems not to have sat well with Saghïmbay. He has Qoshoy attempt to protect Qanïkey from Manas's ire before it happens: "He must not slash her on the right cheek" (p. 164), using a run of verses identical to those Qoshoy had just used to vilify Kökchö's wife (p. 162). Saghïmbay appears to have been comfortable with this narrative turn up to a point, but he may have crossed a line with the scribe or audience. In Manas's voice, he walks back the death threat almost as soon as it is uttered: "I won't kill Qanïkey, but my name is Manas the Bloodthirsty and I have an insatiable appetite for blood" (p. 165).

Other, minor enigmas rise to the disturbed surface of this stretch of oral narration. In Manas's state of "forgetfulness" he rebukes Ajïbay and Chalïbay for having oversold the breeches. In narrating this Saghïmbay neglects the fact that Manas had praised the breeches directly to Qoshoy. Thus when Manas tells Ajïbay and Chalïbay, "You two slaves have been the ones praising these pants from the very beginning. That was your fault!" (p. 165) the fact that his own words of praise anticipated theirs is ignored. By the time the passage in *MKso* draws to a close, Manas praises Qanïkey again to Qoshoy, telling him that she wants a child and that she made the breeches to attract his blessing (p. 170). The poet dutifully dealt with the resulting inconsistency in Qanïkey having made her husband a garment designed to fit another man, by airing the recollection that she far-sightedly measured both Manas and Qoshoy by eye, and made the breeches to fit them both (p. 166).

The reasons for all this are more difficult to accept than to understand. The pressures of oral composition and the complexity of Saghïmbay's ambitious new narrative design, familiar interpretive themes in these notes, are applicable here. But the quotation marks above ascribing "forgetfulness" to Manas in the epic point to a tragic situation in reality: Saghïmbay, as he narrated his *Kökötöy*, had begun to experience the bouts of memory loss that eventually overwhelmed him. In spite of this known context Saghïmbay should remain standing, not be laid down as a patient and deprived of his last property as an artist, responsibility. The bard was contending with the enormous burden of tradition while trying out new ways of lining up its parts to construct his epic super-plot; here he shuffled some steps in bearing the load.

Elsewhere I have described a recorded epic performance by "a good bard on a bad day";[1] this may be nearly all that need be said about Saghïmbay's narration of the scene with the wrestling breeches.

Sex games (pp. 181–4)

In the half-mistitled Part 13, "Oronghu Untethers the Camels; The Mangy Bald-Heads Fight," Saghïmbay blends two sexual spectacles. One, the real contest *töö chechken* 'untethering the camel', is so strange that it is best to start with the definition in Konstantin K. Iudakhin's *Kirghiz–Russian Dictionary*: "A bizarre entertainment of the feudal–tribal nobility: a naked woman, bending down, tried to untie with her teeth a camel tethered to a stake driven down low into the ground; the camel went to the woman who untied it." Everyday phrases like "to make someone untie the camel" (to intentionally embarrass) confirm that the sport for men was in getting a woman to trade public exposure of her nakedness for gain. Saghïmbay prefigures the game's occurrence here with mentions in Kökötöy's testament (*MKSO*, pp. 24, 29) and Boqmurun's counsel on planning for the feast (p. 62). The game takes place in both of the mid-nineteenth-century versions of the epic, with Oronghu the sole contestant (*MKNB*, ll. 2129–86; *MKWR*, ll. 1342–1402). The titillating spectacle of the camel-untethering game was not lost on the nineteenth-century bards, who showed the male heroes heaping crude sexual taunts on Oronghu, and more. But Oronghu has her say magnificently, in *MKNB* and *MKSO*, as Woman giving the male heroes their just deserts.

Saghïmbay eclipses the traditional camel-untethering game with another, simpler spectacle: watching a man and a woman have sexual intercourse beast-wise. Saghïmbay's graphic language for Oronghu's and Mardïkeleng's sex act incidentally provides clues to reconstruct similar but fleeting depictions in the earlier tradition, and thus to confirm that the entertainment was known in the mid-nineteenth century, at least in epic. In *MKWR*, when Oronghu is bending down to untie the camel, the hero Qoyluu-bay gets Manas's permission to go out and "share the winnings" (l. 1358). Here the sense of what is being done can be improved in light of Saghïmbay's explicit depiction of Mardïkeleng's contact with Oronghu from behind in *MKSO*. Hatto's translation of *MKWR*, ll. 1361–5 should read: "Koyluu-bay marched off and came up Oroŋgu from behind as she bent, he mounted her like a yearling bull," that is, a sexually mature bull in his second year. Thus *MKWR* shows how the all-fours posture required for a woman to untie the camel was seen by a man as an opportunity to take advantage of her sexually. His exploit forced her to share the prize with him, as if by an accepted rule. Mardïkeleng's initial intention in *MKSO*, "Let me see if I can just flick her," suggests that the man stood to win some lesser portion of the prize merely for the act of "counting coup" with his phallus on the woman's backside.[1]

Saghïmbay makes the sex act an official event, having both participants consent to it and to sharing the prize for it announced by the herald. Saghïmbay may have contrived the full event status of the public coupling on his own, at some expense to the traditional untethering of the camel. This is suggested by the facts that the passage contains differing accounts of the prize, and that Oronghu goes on to untether camels anyway, for which an event and prizes were never announced by the heralds. The wording of the section heading, "Oronghu Untethers the Camels" may signify that the scribe who added it in the heat of performance little suspected the narrative turn Saghïmbay was about to take into more explicit proceedings.

Infidels' counsels (pp. 207–10)

The lengthy, detailed depictions of parleys and wrangling among different Qalmaq and Qïtay leaders in the latter part of *MK* are new to the tradition with Saghïmbay's telling. The mid-nineteenth-century epics had hardly concerned themselves at all with goings-on among infidels that were not directly observed by Muslim heroes. This is in keeping with the straightforward concept of authorial point of view in

1. With the help of Saghïmbay's text, we can also see that Professor Hatto's translation of a brief passage in *MKNB* (ll. 1502–8) should read differently, with the heathen hero's and heroine's roles reversed as doer and done-to.

epic narration. Someone late in the tradition, likely Saghïmbay, was responsible for augmenting the narrative with generous views of heathen deliberations. This note considers new structural aspects of the parleys; the next one will look at the novel concepts Saghïmbay was able to bring into his epic narration by imagining the lives and thoughts of the infidels.

The augmentations look new because they mostly lack the traditionally formulated markers of speech, which included the name of the hero and his epithet or epithets before he speaks, and a conclusion like, "So said the hero." Such basic structures of heroic speeches, present in the parts of the epic that Saghïmbay inherited from mid-nineteenth-century bards, appear ornate in comparison with the infidels' parleys, where elliptical and telegraphic runs of statements have little or no attribution of a speaker or speakers. (Many of those markers have been reconstructed in the translation to improve the flow.)

When the infidels discuss what champion they are going to send out to face Manas in the joust (*MKso*, pp. 187–9), there are several dozen verses of narration where the attribution of who says what and even the issue of what is and is not direct or reported speech is difficult to sort out. In this passage (particularly beginning with the line, "When Surqan said this," p. 189), there are no discernible divisions between regular narration, quotations, and reported speech, and thus it is impossible to attribute discrete statements to individual speakers; the assembly is portrayed saying these things as a body, as if one speaker at a time, as depicted in the translation.

Saghïmbay may have thought up this parley to complement the earlier scene (p. 152–60) where the Muslims work through their inability to field a rival to Joloy in wrestling (which was traditional, as shown by the mid-nineteenth-century versions). The parley would compensate for the imputations of Muslim shortcomings and lack of heroic "depth" when it came to finding a wrestling champion, by showing the infidels' similar struggles to field their own champion in another major sporting event.

Saghïmbay wanted to innovate here, but the traditional narratives had given him few resources. In imagining the infidels' parleys, Saghïmbay began to construct a sub-plot with its own *dramatis personae* and their diverse backgrounds and motivations. That these figures were from the enemy side magnified the creative challenge. The Qalmaq and Qïtay heroes had received little background elaboration in the nineteenth century, so there were just a few terse epithets Saghïmbay could use to build some of them up as characters. Others, if Saghïmbay wished to depict a number of them, had to be contrived out of nothing. Eminently capable of coming up with new names for characters he invented, Saghïmbay shows the traditional side of his bardic art by the fact that these new characters are devoid of epithets and allusions to their doings outside this poem; there were none, so there could be none, for the fabulator Saghïmbay was also the traditional bard Saghïmbay.

Fly-on-the-wall narration of a scene taking place among characters who are not fully individualized by long tradition sounds less like an epic and more like a novel, a genre that Saghïmbay's modest literacy may have given him a chance to think about, if not read himself. The next note will examine the new and old views of ethnic and religious geopolitics that the Qalmaq and Qïtay heroes talked about in their counsels.

Opposed world-views and looking-glass enemies
(pp. 207–10)

In the previous note, the dearth of traditional epithets and even names of participants in the infidels' counsels suggested that Saghïmbay was working on his own with no precedents or resources from the tradition. Having expanded the stage for dramatic dialogue with the addition of the infidel counsels, Saghïmbay used them to explore what the infidels thought. He did so quite confidently and effectively, bringing into increasingly modern form the tradition of meditating on the dividing line between "us" and "them" that had engrossed mid-nineteenth-century bards and audiences before him.[1] The old epics voiced some infidels' remarks on the "Buruts" (the Kirghiz, in Sino-Qalmaq parlance), but Saghïmbay's characterizations of heathen thought are altogether more complex.

The most fully developed ideas that Saghïmbay's *MK* gives to the infidel heroes come from the mouths of Alooke (pp. 187–8) and Qongurbay (pp. 207–9), in speeches that incite their Qïtay and Qalmaq coalition-mates to act against the Buruts and the Muslims in general. The complaints are forceful and nuanced. Alooke's speech is especially complex from a structural standpoint, featuring his ruminations on what the Kirghiz in turn think about the infidels. In a twist, Saghïmbay reports the speech indirectly, summarizing what Alooke

1.   Besides *MK*, the mid nineteenth-century border epics are "Almambet, Er Kökchö and Ak-erkech; How Almambet Came to Manas" and "Köz-kaman," in *MWR*.

says: "how all those of 'contrary' religion had gone to Qïtay, [. . .] and how the wealth of those 'damned' people of Qalmaq origin should be broken up and how from the very beginning they all tried to 'create trouble'" (p. 187). Saghïmbay perceptively has Alooke call his own kind "people of the old religion" (p. 188) as if with a sense of seniority, for the religions of the Chinese and the Mongols are indeed older than Islam.

Ruefulness at the rise of this new religion and its great champions suffuses the Qïtay khans' speeches. For Qongurbay there is an elegiac feeling that the hour of the Kirghiz has come upon the world – that they are "acting as though they are independent and full of prowess" (p. 207) – and the infidels will pay a heavy price unless they act decisively to "nip them in the bud." It is all the more poignant for Qongurbay that this is a reversal of fortune, and a recent one. Qïtay used to be on top, but "The servant has grown clever." The Türks and Muslims are on the rise, and the Kirghiz will multiply and get the upper hand over Qïtay, and attack Tüp 'Ancestral' Beejin itself. When Qongurbay says, "The mountain-dwelling Kirghiz are becoming the equals of the Qïtay empire, and will one day surpass it; the Qïtays' kindled fire will one day be extinguished" (p. 208), he speaks with stark symbolism in the old idiom of Inner and Northern Asian peoples: the hearth fire of a family, clan, or race was held to be its life-energy and existence itself. The infidels' fortunes ride on their ability to combine all the forces assembled at the feast to make a massed attack on the Muslims.

It is remarkable enough that Saghïmbay imagined and gave empathetic voice to the concerns and strategic thinking of the infidels with respect to the Muslims. The poet then goes further, by depicting Qongurbay's position as but one side in a controversy involving strained bonds of loyalty between the Qïtays and the Qalmaqs. Ushang, a Qalmaq hero new to the tradition in Saghïmbay's telling, counters Qongurbay's speech; he mistrusts the ways the Qïtays have always used the Qalmaqs to their own ends and to the detriment of the Qalmaqs. But Ushang's thinking on Sino-Qalmaq politics is not completely transparent. It seems to be summed up in two sentences that are particularly difficult to decode on a syntactical level. My rendering, "The Qara Qïtay tribe must not be allowed to sit by with its pretense of fairness; in promoting a massacre of the Kirghiz, Qïtay has designs on both the Qara Kirghiz and the Qalmaq" (p. 209), supplies more meaning to Saghïmbay's lean lines than usual, but heeds the essential spirit of a supposed contention between the Qïtays and the Qalmaqs. It is telling that Saghïmbay's verses appear unsettled at this point where he was evidently innovating in a rather analytical vein.

Part of Ushang's reasoning in resisting Qongurbay's call for the Qalmaqs to unite with Qïtay is that the Qalmaqs and the Kirghiz are related deep down in their genealogies through Türk. Joloy Khan objects. He remains loyal to Qongurbay (his lower status than Qongurbay is new in Saghïmbay's telling), and rebuts Ushang's appeal to kinship with the Kirghiz: "How could I call them kindred?" (p. 209; see also p. 258). The Qalmaq heroes and heroines momentarily cannot decide which counsel to follow: "'If our first ancestor was Türk –' they puzzled, but could not for all their concentration figure out what to do" (p. 210). The majority side with Joloy and Qongurbay, as do a diversity of infidel peoples such as the Orus, Tarsa, Jööt, and Saqalat (broadly: Russians, East Syriac Christians, Jews, Slavs). But there is a costly falling-out between the two factions later on the battlefield; Saghïmbay comments, "because of that the Qalmaqs were divided and punished by God" (p. 210).

A broad thinker like Saghïmbay could use epic poetry to express thoughts on contemporary Eurasian geopolitics. On the one hand (in reality, in 1925) there were China and the Soviet Union, with Mongolia between: Inner and Outer Mongolia, in the talk of his times. On the other hand (in the epic) there are Qïtay and Kirghiz, with the Qalmaq between, and a set of terms (Chong 'Great' Beejin and Tüp 'Ancestral', 'Original', hence possibly 'Innermost' Beejin in MKSO; additionally, Chet Beejin 'Beejin-on-the-Marches' and Orto 'Middle' Beejin in other Manas poems by Saghïmbay) evoking exteriority and interiority from the point of view of China.

On the other side of the mirror, Muslims had their own worries over their standing in the world. As old Qoshoy faces the daunting challenge of defending the Muslims' honor against the infidel Joloy in wrestling, he harks back to better times that he has outlived: "If it were long ago when the Heathens and Muslims were equals on the broad face of the earth" (p. 160). This sentiment, unknown in the mid-nineteenth-century epics, is an allusion by Saghïmbay to the reduced state of Central Asian Muslims and perhaps of the Muslim world in general at the height of the western colonial era in the early twentieth century. Muslims and infidels are no longer equal, the latter having gained the upper hand.

This is not the first time that Saghïmbay has hinted at his knowledge of the wider world of his times, but it is the first time in *The Memorial Feast for Kökötöy Khan* that the hint comes through the words of a hero. Allusions to fairly recent events are very rare but not unknown in the mid-nineteenth-century tradition. Coincidentally, the most circumstantial of these are references to Qoshoy's supposed role in actual affairs in East Turkestan in the early nineteenth century (*MKNB*, ll. 535–50). The *Manas* stories in general and the epic memorial feast for Kökötöy in particular were explicitly set in long-ago times; Saghïmbay comments occasionally on how the feast predated and even inspired some present-day Kirghiz customs and traditions. Qoshoy, however, seems to have been one hero whom bards had grown comfortable treating in a subtly historical way in certain contexts.

Saghïmbay's version is the earliest witness, and perhaps the origin, of several major innovations in the *MK* tradition. Of all of these, the poet achieves the greatest success in his thoughtful imaginings of infidels' counsels and the counterpoints between Muslim and infidel world-views. It should not be surprising that Saghïmbay was the poet to achieve a new level of integration of the ethnic and religious geopolitics of his heroes and of the countries of Eurasia, since he had personally seen life in China as a refugee after the 1916 rebellion in Russian Turkestan.

Boqmurun's final act (pp. 227–33)

The cross purposes of the traditional figures of Boqmurun and Manas, which resulted in Boqmurun's role being curtailed in the early development of the epic, have come out in Fundamentals of the Plot above. Nevertheless, Saghïmbay saw the young hero through to his own little piece of the ending of *The Memorial Feast for Kökötöy Khan*. Giving Boqmurun a martial role in the revenge-raid after the horse race (pp. 222, 227–33) was not the last consideration that Saghïmbay showed to the hero. After the present poem, Saghïmbay concludes his superplot with his climactic epic called *The Great Campaign*, where he depicts Boqmurun taking part. In contrast, the bard's predecessors in the mid-nineteenth century had dropped Boqmurun out of sight before the end of *The Memorial Feast for Kökötöy Khan*, and did not have a separate *Great Campaign* poem in their repertoire, so far as we know.

Even though Manas and Qoshoy were effectively co-presidents in *MKSO*, Saghïmbay was sensitive to Boqmurun's lingering role as the organizer of the feast. It is Boqmurun who serves the lavish spread itself. At the finish of the horse race (having ignored Boqmurun through every one of the intervening sporting events, which shows that he had not even a vestigial role as president in Saghïmbay's day), the bard imagined an internally consistent and high-profile role for the young hero. Since as president Manas is tied down with tasks in wrapping up the feast, Saghïmbay has Boqmurun seize the opportunity to show his heroic ability, by setting out at the head of an army in pursuit of the enemies who have stolen the prize-herds.

Though he was attentive to the Boqmurun figure, Saghïmbay's reimagining shows rough spots. As Boqmurun spies Qongurbay taking the field opposite him, it is not clear why he says, "Riding Maani-ker I infiltrated their army last night and observed that Joloy has gone missing" (p. 228). No such incident was narrated. Saghïmbay may have been trying to suggest that Boqmurun would face off against Qongurbay because Joloy was not there to be his opponent, but the reasoning is obscure. The jousting bouts between Boqmurun and Qongurbay are awkwardly narrated, repeating not only passages from the earlier joust between Manas and Qongurbay, but also each other.

Four directors (p. 238)

The four heroes (none of them Manas) named at the end of the poem as the directors of the just-concluded feast – Khan Qoshoy of the Qataghan, Kökcho of the Qazaq, Töshtük son of Eleman, and Jamghïrchï of the Eshtek – have not been mentioned as such by Saghïmbay before. The four are all time-honored figures in steppe Turkic epic traditions with Noghay origins. Having brought Manas to a new, unprecedented peak of personal power in the climax of his poem *The Memorial Feast for Kökötöy Khan*, Saghïmbay seems to hark back to an earlier, decentralized era of the tradition upheld by old heroes like Qoshoy, Kökchö, Töshtük, and Jamghïrchï. Though Manas dominated this epic, Saghïmbay seems to say, the epic *tradition* is too vast and deeply rooted in time for even that great hero to control.

CONCLUSION

Feast guests may wrap up unfinished joints to bring home; readers may take away these three related conclusions: on oral composition, on the question of what *Manas* means and to whom, and on the nature of heroes.

Having come thus far through a terrain of tradition, of similarities and differences among three bards' oral realizations of fundamentally "the same" epic, the reader of this introduction will have gained by exercise some personal understanding of the workings of the bardic art and perhaps even thought of images or analogies to help visualize its subtleties. I would like to end by quoting Arthur Hatto's image of the peculiar enchantment of this art: "It is as though the bards held switches in their hands whose buds they could charm into leaves, side-shoots, blossoms or whole sprays, or let sleep, at will. No two performances by the same bard would be wholly alike, even as to the choice of buds to grow. The differences between a number of bards in this respect alone must be even greater."[1] Saghïmbay used this skill he learned from the older bards with unprecedented ambition, grafting his switches into a whole tree to support his *Manas* super-plot.

In Eurasia it is usual to speak of *Manas* as an *epos*, both an abstract textual totality in all its versions and a concrete national property to be possessed. Belief in a national *epos*, however, does not in itself give the believer the ability to see the nature of oral heroic epic poetry: the occupation of the three-sided partnerships of bards, patrons, and audiences joined in discrete performances over time. *Epos* is timeless; in reality a bard and his audience are historical actors. Saghïmbay's performed version of *Manas* from the 1920s has come to be accepted as an icon of the Kirghiz national *epos*. There are grounds to agree with this, but they are not where proponents of the national *epos* would desire to find themselves: there was no Kirghiz national *epos* before Saghïmbay's *Manas* made it possible to demonstrate its existence, and for historical reasons there could not have been one many years earlier than the Saghïmbay sessions.

The Kirghiz can exhibit not only a latter-day national *epos* carried on in performances today, but also some of the world's fullest, best preserved, and most richly contextualized records of an oral epic tradition. Thanks to the continuity provided by Saghïmbay and bards whose works were recorded before and after his, we can see a panorama of the evolution of an epic tradition in one culture, from its fully oral Heroic Period under the patronage of chiefly warriors, through a decadent, post-heroic Twilight Age, to a Classical Period inaugurated by the collaboration of an oral artist of genius and antiquarian bent with a vigorous new intellectual establishment capable of receiving the result.

Should not then the world's lovers of Homer and of the *Mahābhārata*, of *Beowulf* and of the *Chanson de Roland*, be beating a path to the Kirghiz epic tradition's door? If that happens, I believe that its unique panorama can reveal more than the history of an epic tradition: it can point to something deeply, disquietingly human about heroism, one of our oldest and most misunderstood ties between art and life.

1.   *MKNB*, p. 98.

A civilization can easily appreciate bloody heroics to the extent that an *Iliad* or a *Mahābhārata*, for instance, "contributed" to it on some accepted level. At the low point of vanity, we may even imagine that these heroics show us parts of "our," be it "Western," "Indian," or whatever, original assertion of collective self. An Achilles or a Duryodhana may seem more fathomable as heroes than a Manas or a Joloy, but that is because the former heroes have been to some extent domesticated, illuminated by political tricks of the light, and screened around by cultivation so old that the accumulated learning itself has affected the forms of the epics we read. People may find in heroic epic poetry a life more candid and forthright than the hypocrisies of our gentler age, or they may resist its many masks of naked power; the tempestuous public life of a self-motivated, strutting, ruthless leader can breed hero worship and contempt.

Saghïmbay sang *The Memorial Feast for Kökötöy Khan* just as the Kirghiz people were experiencing a loss of self-confidence in the face of world events they struggled to grasp. They had just experienced an avoidable humanitarian trauma, the deadly Flight of 1916, followed almost immediately by the revolutionary transition to Bolshevism in their homeland. Before those paroxysms, they had felt the slowly mounting miseries of colonization. They attempted to make sense of complex, unsolvable problems such as the expansion of empires (China, Russia), eddying bursts of peoples across religious and ethnic boundaries (invasion, holy war, refugees), and the question whether incomprehensibly vast individual wealth and unaccountably exclusive individual power can be reconciled with the need for a stable order. Like many before them and many since, they turned to stories that inspired confidence in heroes. May those who hear our stories look on us with empathy.

Glossary of Terms

Words marked with an asterisk are capitalized in the translation when they are used as titles or styles with names.

Allahu akbar "God is great" as an exclamation in Arabic.
almabash a type of firearm; the component words suggest a musket with an apple-wood stock.
alp a giant.

baatïr a hero.
bangzat a commander of five hundred men (Persian *pānṣad* five hundred).
Barayïz Islamic precepts of right living.
batman a unit of weight, in this text probably equal to about seven and a half kilograms.
bay a rich man.
bek a chief.
bidiya a donation from the chattels of the deceased for the atonement of his sins.
biy a chief.
buraq at a horse presented as a gift to the mullah who presides at a funeral.
buta a costly fabric.
buulum a costly fabric.

chong great, big.

datqa a high rank in the administration of the Khoqand Khanate in the nineteenth century (Persian *dādkhwāh*).
div a giant (the Kirghiz form of this originally Persian word, *döö*, appears in names).

dooron an Islamic ritual for the expiation of the sins of the deceased before burial, for which the officiating mullah received a fee.

*er a man of the better sort, a warrior.

ishan a Sufi holy man.

janaza the Islamic funeral prayer.
jang-jung a high-ranking Chinese military officer (*chiang-chun* 'military governor of a province').
jaysang a Qalmaq military officer.
jinn a supernatural being.

keperet a donation to the mullah for performing the ritual atonement of sins at a funeral.
ketelik an imaginary animal.
*khan a ruler.
khoja a member of an Islamic holy lineage (the Kirghiz form of this originally Persian word, *qojo*, appears in names).

namaz a prayer.
nar the hybrid from the mating of a dromedary (one-humped) male camel with a Bactrian (two-humped) female, a prized beast of burden larger, stronger, and hardier than either pure breed.

peri a supernatural being.

qadek a costly fabric.
qalday an officer in the Ch'ing army in Qalmaq territory, at a regimental rank approximately equal to captain (the rank appeared more exalted to Saghïmbay, who frequently calls Qongurbay, Khan of Qïtay, a *qalday*).
qarabayïr a breed of horse.
qazanat a breed of horse.
qibla the direction from any point toward the Kaaba in Mecca, facing which Muslims position themselves in prayer and corpses are laid to rest (for Central Asians, toward the west).
qutulas an imaginary animal.

sajide prostrations performed during prayer.
salootu namaz a prayer of consolation at a funeral.

shayinggi a type of leather made from the dehaired, untanned hides of horses or camels.

sungdung a high Chinese rank (the sense possibly from Chinese *tsung-tu* 'viceroy, governor-general', current in Ch'ing times; a closer-sounding term, *tsung-tung* 'president', was in use in the Republic of China after 1912).

tabït a bier.

tash a unit of length equal to about eight kilometers. As a measure of land, it may mean either a square *tash* or the land watered by one *tash* of irrigation canals.

tekbir glorification of God in prayer.

tïytay a Chinese provincial military commander under the Ch'ing dynasty.

tulpar the superior sort of steed for heroes, sometimes described as having wings.

ulama those possessing high levels of learning in Islam.

yuft durable Russian leather.

zerisabar a costly fabric.

Further Reading and Listening

No phonographic recordings of Saghïmbay's epic performances exist, but recordings of other bards can give an idea of what they sounded like. The oldest sound recording in the Kirghiz language is a short performance of the epic *Semetey* by the bard Kenje Qara from 1903 or 1904; my textual edition, musical transcription, and translation includes a sound disc of the wax-cylinder recording.[1] Starting in the 1950s, a Kirghiz epic bard a generation younger than Saghïmbay, Sayaqbay Qarala uulu (Saiakbai Karalaev), rose to fame through Soviet mass media; audio and film recordings of his *Manas* performances are widely available, including online.

The manuscript records of Saghïmbay's epic songs have been edited and published several times in Kirghiz. Publication of the complete scholarly edition was a post-Soviet project that experienced a long hiatus, coming to completion after nearly two decades; this is the edition referred to as *Mso a* in this book. The appearance of the *Kökötöy* volume and the completion of that series (2014) was anticipated by the publication in 2010 of a non-scholarly edition in one huge volume; this is the edition referred to as *Mso b*. There is also a good abridged edition of Saghïmbay's *Manas* containing a Russian translation.[2] Other works of interest are listed below.

Hatto, A. T., "Kirghiz (Mid-nineteenth Century)," in *Traditions of Heroic and Epic Poetry*, vol. 1, ed. A. T. Hatto (London: Modern Humanities Research Association, 1980), pp. 300–27. General overview of the older tradition.

1. *The Semetey of Kenje Kara: A Kirghiz Epic Performance on Phonograph*, ed. and trans. Daniel Prior (Wiesbaden: Otto Harrassowitz, 2006).
2. *Manas: A Kirghiz Heroic Epic*, 4 vols., ed. S. M. Musaev et al. (Moscow: Glavnaia redaktsiia Vostochnoi literatury, 1984–95), Kirghiz poetic text with edition and translation in Russian.

————(ed. and trans.), *The Manas of Wilhelm Radloff* (Wiesbaden: Otto Harrassowitz, 1990). M*WR* in this volume: re-edition of epics in Radloff, *Samples of the Folk Literature of the Northern Turkic Tribes*, vol. 5, with English translations and commentary.

————(ed. and trans.), *The Memorial Feast for Kökötöy-Khan (Kökötöydün ašı): A Kirghiz Epic Poem* (Oxford: Oxford University Press, 1977). M*KNB* in this volume: edited for the first time from a photocopy of the unique manuscript from the mid-nineteenth century, with English translation and commentary.

Howard, Keith, and Saparbek Kasmambetov, *Singing the Kyrgyz Manas: Saparbek Kasmambetov's Recitations of Epic Poetry* (Folkestone, Kent: Global Oriental, 2011). The creative life of a contemporary Kirghiz bard; includes audio samples.

Plumtree, James, "A Telling Tradition: Preliminary Comments on the Epic of Manas, 1856–2018," in *Medieval Stories and Storytelling: Multimedia and Multi-Temporal Perspectives*, ed. S. C. Thomson (Turnhout: Brepols, 2021), pp. 239–301. Historical analysis of the tradition with emphasis on relations between oral and written modes.

Prior, Daniel, "Bok Murun's Itinerary Ridden: Report on an Expedition through Kirghiz Epic Geography," *Central Asiatic Journal* 42, no. 2 (1998), pp. 238–82. Traces the heroic itinerary in M*KWR*, similar to the one in M*KSO*.

————, "Patron, Party, Patrimony: Notes on the Cultural History of the Kirghiz Epic Tradition" (Bloomington, Ind.: Indiana University, Research Institute for Inner Asian Studies, 2000). Intellectual and political uses of the *Manas* epics since the mid-nineteenth century.

————, "Sino-Mongolica in the Qırġız Epic Poem *Kökötöy's Memorial Feast* by Saġımbay Orozbaq uulu," in *Philology of the Grasslands: Essays in Mongolic, Turkic, and Tungusic Studies*, ed. Ákos Bertalan Apatóczky and Christopher P. Atwood (Leiden: Brill, 2018), pp. 230–57. Analyses of traditional and innovative elements in Saghïmbay's characterizations of the principal heathen foes.

————, "Sparks and Embers of the Kirghiz Epic Tradition," *Fabula* 51, no. 1–2 (2010), pp. 23–37. Characterizes Kirghiz heroic poetry in terms of plot structures and epic moments; traces the poems' transformation after the mid-nineteenth century.

Radloff, Wilhelm (ed. and trans.), *Samples of the Folk Literature of the Northern Turkic Tribes*, vol. 5, Dialect of the Qara-Kirghiz (St. Petersburg: Imperial Academy of Sciences, 1885), in Kirghiz, German, and Russian. Editions and German translations of nine

Kirghiz epic poems recorded in the field in the nineteenth century; preface influenced modern formulaic theory of oral poetry.

Reichl, Karl (ed. and trans.), *Edige: A Karakalpak Oral Epic as Performed by Jumabay Bazarov* (Helsinki: Academia Scientiarum Fennica, 2007). Edition, translation, and commentary of the work of a major twentieth-century bard in a related tradition, with multimedia samples.

——, *Turkic Oral Epic Poetry: Traditions, Forms, Poetic Structure* (New York: Garland, 1992). Survey of the histories and compositional techniques of numerous Turkic traditions, using perspectives from oral formulaic theory.

Simakov, G. N., *Social Functions of Kirghiz Folk Games at the End of the Nineteenth to the Beginning of the Twentieth Century* (Leningrad: Nauka, 1984), in Russian. Ethnographic descriptions and analyses of actual games depicted in *MK*.

Index

Entries in this index refer to personal, geographic, and ethnic names in the translated text only. A few ethnic and geographic names are also listed in more familiar modern forms as cross references. The personal titles Baatïr, Bay, Bek, Biy, Er, Khan, and others preceding or following names are defined in the Glossary of Terms and usually not indexed as parts of heroes' names. Names that occur also in the mid-nineteenth-century Kirghiz epics have their headwords set in small capitals; the spellings may differ from those used in Hatto's editions.[1]

The more than six hundred names of people, horses and other beasts, weapons, armor, places, and ethnic groups that Saghïmbay included in his telling of *The Memorial Feast for Kökötöy Khan* are testimony to three facets of the poet's gifts as an artist: his stewardship of the Kirghiz epic tradition, his learning and curiosity about the world, and his audacious ability to make things up. There is a different name for approximately every twenty verses in the poem; a great number of these names are found nowhere else in the tradition prior to Saghïmbay.

The poet's names for peoples stemmed from native knowledge only approximated by our own. Similarly, we must not assume that Saghïmbay's knowledge of the location, extent, or characteristics of a given place was the same as what we perceive through the lens of modern geography. That vision of the earth is most in line with Saghïmbay's near his home region of the central Tien Shan; the poet's divergences from modern knowledge tend to be greater the farther a place lies from this core area. Some places very distant from Saghïmbay's experience took on fantastic aspects. His imagining of the people of Itaalï 'Italy', for example, hints at how he could be both learned and wrong at the same time.

Aalï, the caliph Ali, by-name Shaymerden (Persian *Shāh-i Mardān* 'Ruler of Men'), a numinous personage in Islamic traditions: 176; Shaymerden,

1.   *MK*NB; *M*WR.